MW01278252

CYBERARTS99

Cyberarts
International Compendium Prix Ars Electronica
.net, Interactive Art, Computer Animation/
Visual Effects, Digital Musics, u19-Cybergeneration

Edition 99

Publisher: Dr. Hannes Leopoldseder
Dr. Christine Schöpf
Editor: Christian Schrenk
ORF, Landesstudio Oberösterreich
Europaplatz 3, 4010 Linz
Translation: Aileen Derieg, Helmut Einfalt
Cover-Design + Layout: Arthouse, Hansi Schorn
Frontispiece:
Chris Cunningham/Aphex Twin: *Come to Daddy* video
Coordination/German Proof-Reading:
Ingrid Fischer-Schreiber
English Proof-Reading: Aileen Derieg
Offset Reproduction, Assembly: Typeshop, Linz

Photo Credits
Cover: Chris Cunningham / Aphex Twin (Richard D. James), GB; 43: Roc Parés; 83: Jeff Gutterman; 109: Disney Enterprises Inc./Pixar Animation Studios; 175: Paul Panhuysen; 177: Giuliani Stefani; 178, 185: Bettina Herzner; 181: Thomas Rabsch; 212 - 217: Fotostudio Kutzler + Wimmer, Kurt Aumayer, Traun

Printing: Optima, Ljubljana, Printed in Slovenia

Printed on acid-free and chlorine-free bleached paper.

Prix Ars Electronica 99
International Competition for Computer Arts
Organizer: Österreichischer Rundfunk (ORF),
Landesstudio Oberösterreich
Idea: Dr. Hannes Leopoldseder
Conception: Dr. Christine Schöpf
Financing/Copyright: Dkfm. Heinz Augner
Liaison Office: Prix Ars Electronica
ORF, Europaplatz 3, A-4010 Linz
Phone: 0043/732/6900-267
Fax: 0043/732/6900-270
Telex: (02)1616
E-mail: info@prixars.orf.at

SPIN: 10734203
ISBN: 3-211-83367-6

Springer-Verlag Wien New York

HANNES LEOPOLDSEDER - CHRISTINE SCHÖPF

PRIX ARS ELECTRONICA

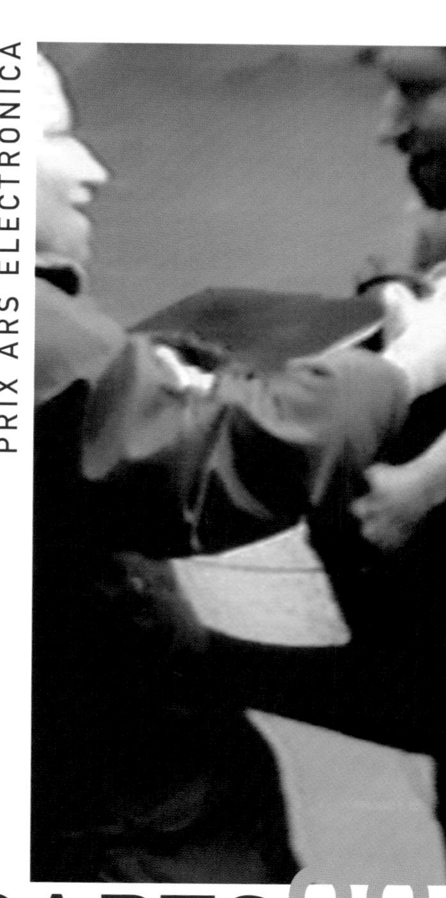

CYBERARTS99

SpringerWienNewYork

CONTENTS

Hannes Leopoldseder – Age of the Digital Dawn ---- 8
Christine Schöpf – Prix Ars Electronica 99 ---- 11

.NET

A Step Towards Community – Statement of the .net Jury ---- 16
Linus Torvalds – Golden Nica ---- 24
Jean-Marc Philippe ---- 28
Willy Henshall / Matt Moller ---- 30
David P. Anderson ---- 32
Joanna Berzowska ---- 34
CAAD / Eidgenössische Technische Hochschule Zürich ---- 36
Free B92 ---- 38
Eric Loyer ---- 40
Daniel Julià Lundgren ---- 42
Fumio Matsumoto / Shoei Matsukawa ---- 44
Mark Napier ---- 46
Nick Philip ---- 48
Ramana Rao / Inxight ---- 50
Christa Sommerer / Laurent Mignonneau ---- 52
Martin Wattenberg / Joon Yu ---- 54

INTERACTIVE ART

Are We Still Enjoying Interactivity? Statement of the Interactive Art Jury ---- 58
Lynn Hershman / Construct Internet Design – Golden Nica ---- 64
Luc Courchesne ---- 66
Perry Hoberman ---- 68
Joachim Blank / Karl Heinz Jeron ---- 70
Christoph Ebener / Frank Fietzek / Uli Winters ---- 72
Kouichirou Eto / Canon ARTLAB ---- 74
F.A.B.R.I.CATORS / K-Team ---- 76
Beate Garmer ---- 78
Bill Keays / Ron MacNeil ---- 80
Russet Lederman ---- 82
Eric Paulos ---- 84
Simon Penny ---- 86
Daniel Rozin ---- 88
Stefan Schemat / Michael Joyce / Hiroki Maekawa / Dominica Freyer / Burki Carstens / Mike Felsmann / Isabella Bordoni / Roberto Paci Dalò ---- 90
Christa Sommerer / Laurent Mignonneau ---- 92

COMPUTER ANIMATION / VISUAL EFFECTS

What exactly is Computer Animation? What are Visual Effects?

Statement of the Computer Animation/Visual Effects Jury ---- 96
Chris Wegde – Golden Nica ---- 104
John Lasseter / Andrew Stanton / Pixar ---- 108
Bob Sabiston / Tommy Pallotta / Flat Black Films ---- 110
Jun Asakawa / Toshifumi Kawahara / Polygon Pictures ---- 112
Erwin Charrier / Heure Exquise ---- 114
Paul Kaiser / Shelley Eshkar / Bill T. Jones ---- 116
Christopher Landreth / Alias|Wavefront ---- 118
William Le Henanff ---- 120
Patrice Mugnier / Heure Exquise ---- 122
Didi Offenhuber / AEC FutureLab ---- 124
Bruce Pukema / Ronin Inc. ---- 126
Daniel Robichaud / Digital Domain ---- 128
Christian Sawade-Meyer ---- 130
Seiji Shiota / Tohru Patrick Awa / Polygon Pictures ---- 132
Lev Yilmaz / Emre Yilmaz / Protozoa ---- 134

Vincent Ward / Stephen Simon / Barnet Bain /
Mass.illusions / POP / Digital Domain – Golden Nica ---- 136
CFC – Computer Film Company ---- 142
Alain Escalle ---- 144
Manuel Horrillo Fernandez / Daiquiri/Spainbox ---- 148
Fuel – Peter Miles / Damon Murray / Stephen Sorrell ---- 150
Ray Giarratana / Digital Domain ---- 152
Geoffrey Guiot / Bruno Lardé / Jerôme Maillot / Heure Exquise ---- 154
Juan Tomicic Muller / Daiquiri/Spainbox ---- 156
Phil Tippett / Craig Hayes / Tippett Studio ---- 158

DIGITAL MUSICS

Music from the Bedroom Studios – Statement of the Digital Musics Jury ---- 162
Aphex Twin (Richard D. James) / Chris Cunningham – Golden Nica ---- 168
Mego: Christian Fennesz / Peter Rehberg aka Pita ---- 170
Ikue Mori ---- 172
Stefan Betke ---- 174
Paul DeMarinis ---- 175
Rose Dodd / Stephen Connolly ---- 176
John Duncan / Francisco López ---- 177
Bernhard Günter ---- 178
Richard Hawtin aka Plastikman ---- 179
MAZK / Zbigniew Karkowski / Masami Akita ---- 180
Mouse on Mars ---- 181
Terre Thaemlitz ---- 182
[The User] / local area network orchestra ---- 183
Tone Rec / Gaëtan Collet / Noëlle Collet / Claude Pailliot / Vincent Thierion ---- 184
Ralf L. Wehowsky (RLW) ---- 185

CYBERGENERATION/U 19

Early Retirement for Hollywood's Dinos –
Statement of the Cybergeneration / U19 Freestyle Computing Jury ---- 188
(conspirat). – Golden Nica ---- 194
Alexander Fischl / Gregor Koschicek ---- 196
Phil E. Haindl ---- 198
Franz Berger ---- 200
Sebastian Endt ---- 201
Simon Gaßner ---- 202
Alexander Kvasnicka ---- 203
Stefanie Mitter ---- 204
Takuya Nimmerrichter ---- 205
Simon Oberhammer ---- 206
Benedikt Schalk ---- 207
Markus Strahlhofer ---- 208
Patrick Toifl ---- 209
Stefan Trischler ---- 210
Armin Weihbold ---- 211

Prix Ars Electronica Jury ---- 212
Prix Ars Electronica Participants ---- 218

AGE OF THE DIGITAL DAWN
Zeit der digitalen Morgendämmerung

Hannes Leopoldseder

Three years ago, in the summer of 1996, 29-year-old Fernando Espuelas was on holiday with his wife in the mountains of Nepal. At the foot of a mountain, as he recounted later, it dawned on him that the Internet would change Latin America, too. An idea came to him of how he could bring the Internet to Latin America.

Three years later, on May 26, 1999, Fernando Espuelas' company "StarMedia Network" went on the stock market in Wall Street. A rate of \$10 to \$12 per share was expected, but on the first day the rate rose to \$26 and closed on the weekend at \$58. "StarMedia Network" now has a market capitalization of over three billion dollars; with a personal share of 11.4% in the company Fernando Espuelas suddenly, three years after his initial idea, has a fortune of \$350 million, approximately 4.5 billion Austrian shillings. StarMedia is a Spanish and Portuguese language search engine, similar to Yahoo! or Excite, for instance.

The last decennia of the closing century have made not only Bill Gates with Microsoft one of the greatest entrepreneurs of the twentieth century, but every day in the era of digital transformation, individuals like Fernando Espuelas may be seen setting off like pioneers into the digital world. With all the opportunities, with all the risks. In no other decade of our industrial history have greater opportunities arisen than at the threshold from the analog to the digital world.

When history is written in the 21st century, these decades will be referred to as the new gold rush era. At the same time, the economic, technological and cultural development of the last two decennia are reflected in a festival, in the Ars Electronica, the festival for art, technology and society in Linz. On the basis of continuity, skill and an orientation to the future, this festival has been able to accompany the continuously occurring phases of transformation like a seismograph.

As a festival Ars Electronica spans exactly the two

Vor drei Jahren, im Sommer 1996, machte der 29jährige Fernando Espuelas mit seiner Frau in den Bergen von Nepal Urlaub. Am Fuße eines Berges, erzählt er später, habe es ihm gedämmert, daß das Internet auch Lateinamerika verändern werde. Da kam ihm die Idee, daß er das Internet nach Lateinamerika bringen könnte.

Drei Jahre später, am 26. Mai 1999, geht Fernando Espuelas mit seiner Firma „StarMedia Network" in der Wallstreet an die Börse. Es wurde ein Kurs von \$ 10 bis \$ 12 pro Stück erwartet, am ersten Tag stieg der Kurs auf \$ 26 und schloß am Wochenende mit \$ 58. „StarMedia Network" hat nun eine Marktkapitalisation von mehr als drei Milliarden Dollar, Fernando Espuelas verfügt mit einem persönlichen Firmenanteil von 11,4 % plötzlich, drei Jahre nach seiner Idee, über ein Vermögen von mehr als \$ 350 Millionen, das sind ungefähr 4,5 Milliarden Schilling. StarMedia ist eine spanisch- und portugiesischsprachige Search Engine wie z.B. Yahoo! und Excite.

Die letzten Dezennien des ausgehenden Jahrhunderts haben nicht nur Bill Gates mit Microsoft zu einem der großen Unternehmer des 20. Jahrhunderts gemacht, sondern tagtäglich demonstrieren im digitalen Aufbruch einzelne Menschen, wie Fernando Espuelas, das pionierhafte Vordringen in die digitale Welt. Mit den Chancen, mit den Risiken. In keinem anderen Jahrzehnt unserer industriellen Geschichte haben sich größere Chancen eröffnet als an der Pforte von der analogen zur digitalen Welt.

In der Geschichtsschreibung des 21. Jahrhunderts werden diese Jahrzehnte als neue Goldgräberzeit bezeichnet werden. Die wirtschaftliche, technologische und kulturelle Entwicklung der letzten zwei Dezennien wird gleichzeitig in einem Festival widergespiegelt, in Ars Electronica, dem Festival für Kunst, Technologie und Gesellschaft in Linz. Dieses Festival konnte durch Kontinuität, Kompetenz und Zukunftsorientierung die ständigen Phasen des Wandels wie ein Seismograph begleiten.

Ars Electronica umspannt als Festival exakt jene zwei Dezennien, die nicht nur eine tiefgreifende Veränderung unserer Zivilisation in Gang bringen, sondern auch für Nationen, Länder, Städte und letztlich für jeden einzelnen Menschen Chancen

decades that have seen not only a profound transformation of our civilization, but which have also opened up opportunities for nations, states, cities and ultimately for each individual person, which have never existed before to this extent.
For Linz, the initiative for the Ars Electronica, the Prix Ars Electronica and finally the Ars Electronica Center provided a crucial impulse for the creation of an international meeting point for artists, scientists and technologists. In the past two decennia their visions have reflected, traced and co-determined the continuous development and shaping of the digital world. In addition, Ars Electronica has contributed to a new profile for the city, from a former steel city to a technology-oriented city of culture.

At the nexus of technology, science and art, Ars Electronica has given expression to the power of cultural change; ORF as a media corporation has played a guiding role with its initiatives, in keeping with its cultural mission which is understood as an

eröffnen, die es in diesem Ausmaß zuvor nie gegeben hat.
Für Linz hat die Initiative zu Ars Electronica, zum Prix Ars Electronica und schließlich zum Ars Electronica Center einen entscheidenden Impuls für die Schaffung eines internationalen Treffpunkts von Künstlern, Wissenschaftlern und Technologen ermöglicht, die die kontinuierliche Entwicklung und Ausformung der digitalen Welt in den vergangenen zwei Dezennien mit Visionen reflektiert, mitvollzogen und mitbestimmt haben. Darüber hinaus hat Ars Electronica zu einem neuen Profil der Stadt von der vormaligen Stahlstadt hin zur technologieorientieren Kulturstadt beigetragen.
Ars Electronica hat im Schnittpunkt von Technologie, Wissenschaft und Kunst die Kraft der kulturellen Änderung zum Ausdruck gebracht, der ORF als Medienunternehmen wirkte durch seine Initiativen wegweisend, entsprechend einem offensiv aufgefaßten Kulturauftrag. Seit 1987 ist der Prix Ars Electronica als Wettbewerb für Cyberkunst innerhalb des Festivals internationale Plattform für das aktuelle Schaffen in den Bereichen Kunst, Wissenschaft und Forschung wie auch Entertainment. Und er zeigt in seiner Kontinuität die Schubkraft der digitalen Medien in den unterschiedlichen

offensive endeavor. Since 1987 the Prix Ars Electronica, as a competition for cyberarts within the festival, has been an international platform for current work in the fields of art, science, research and entertainment. And in its continuity it demonstrates the driving force of digital media in the different fields of creative work. There is no area of visual communication that may be imagined today without digital images — whether this involves the visualization of complex scientific processes or special effects in film and advertising. In the field of music, too, the computer has long since become a leading medium. From the Musique concrète of the pioneering days of computer music, a new form of mass media music has emerged in our day. The key cultural technique at the threshold of the third millennium is interactivity, and finally the Internet has become the digital stream in which everything flows together. "The Internet is changing everything," says Larry Ellison, one of the gold-diggers of our era. The Prix Ars Electronica assures the Ars Electronica Festival a steady global influx of artists, who are alert to the new creative possibilities of digital media.

With its 20-year history the Ars Electronica Festival has a unique position today. Not only as a laboratory, a gauge and a seismograph of digital developments, but also and especially due to its development as a festival, a competition platform with ORF's Prix Ars Electronica, and the institution of the Ars Electronica Center as a Museum of the Future. Yet for the Ars Electronica and the Prix Ars Electronica, the year 1999 means one thing especially: the festival of the future is not about looking back at history, but about looking ahead. For this reason, innovative drive and assertive power will be needed to pass through the dawn of the digital development of the 20th century and perceive the opportunities of the 21st century.

Schaffensbereichen. Aus keinem Bereich der visuellen Kommunikation sind digitale Bilder heute wegzudenken – sei es die Visualisierung komplexer wissenschaftlicher Vorgänge oder seien es Special Effects in Film und Werbung. Auch in der Musik ist der Computer längst zum Leitmedium geworden. Aus der Musique concrète in den Pionierzeiten der Computermusik ist in unseren Tagen eine neue Form der Massenmedienmusik entstanden. Die Schlüsselkulturtechnik an der Schwelle zum dritten Jahrtausend ist die Interaktivität und letztendlich ist das Internet jener digitale Strom, in dem alles zusammenfließt. "Das Internet verändert alles", sagt Larry Ellison, einer der Goldgräber unserer Zeit. Der Prix Ars Electronica sichert dem Festival Ars Electronica den globalen Zustrom von Künstlern, die die neuen Gestaltungsmöglichkeiten der digitalen Medien wahrnehmen.

Das Festival Ars Electronica steht heute mit seiner 20jährigen Geschichte einzigartig da. Nicht nur als Labor, als Gradmesser und als Seismograph der digitalen Entwicklung, sondern vor allem auch durch seine Entwicklung als Festival, als Wettbewerbsträger mit dem Prix Ars Electronica des ORF sowie durch die Institution des Ars Electronica Center als Museum der Zukunft. Das Jahr 1999 bedeutet aber für Ars Electronica und für den Prix Ars Electronica vor allem auch eines: Im Festival der Zukunft geht es nicht darum, in die Geschichte zurückzublicken, sondern ausschließlich darum, vorauszuschauen. Daher bedarf es der Innovationskraft und des Durchsetzungsvermögens, um die Morgendämmerung der digitalen Entwicklung des 20. Jahrhunderts zu durchschreiten und die Chancen des 21. Jahrhunderts wahrnehmen zu können.

PRIX ARS ELECTRONICA 99

Christine Schöpf

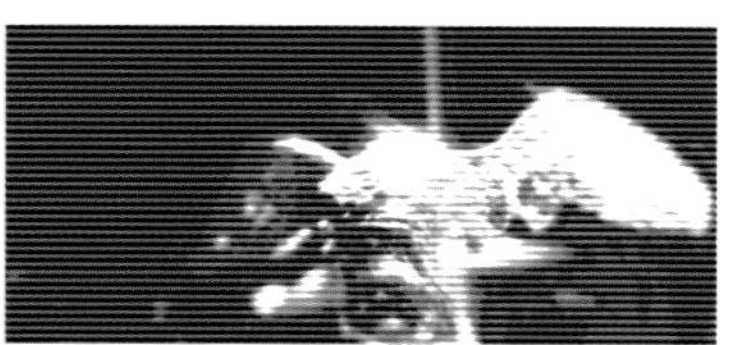

As a qualitative foundation for the Ars Electronica Festival, the Prix Ars Electronica competition, initiated in 1987 by the Austrian Broadcasting Corporation (ORF), Upper Austrian Regional Studio, unites the creative forces that formulate the basic principles of the digital transformation and make these accessible to a wider audience with their works.

Der 1987 vom Österreichischen Rundfunk (ORF), Landesstudio Oberösterreich ins Leben gerufene Wettbewerb Prix Ars Electronica vereint als qualitativer Unterbau des Festivals Ars Electronica jene Kräfte, die die Grundlagen des digitalen Wandels formulieren und durch ihre Arbeit einer breiten Öffentlichkeit zugänglich machen.

The Prix Ars Electronica is intended to be an open forum and an invitation to artists, researchers and creative people from various disciplines, open to new directions and developments in the field of digital media. In keeping with this, it has been ORF's intention from the beginning to ensure that the competition is adaptable enough to respond to the rapid transformation of digital media. Every year, the results of the Prix Ars Electronica represent the current state of the art of digital media outside the norms of industry and document the profound cultural transformation that digital media have evoked in the last decades of this millennium. The cyberartists of our day have long since ceased to regard the computer merely as a tool, but rather as a comprehensive medium enabling skillful and creative exploration, allowing for the inclusion of the observer/user in the dialogue and prompting the observer/user to apply the key cultural technique of our time, interactivity. Interest is no longer focused on software development or a new language of forms; the cyberarts of today increasingly address the crucial issues of a society in the midst of transformation.

The spectrum of works selected by five international expert juries additionally includes top products from the field of entertainment, results of scientific research, and—last but not least—with the category “cybergeneration—u19—freestyle computing”, the Prix Ars Electronica demonstrates once again the continuing creativity of young people in dealing with digital media in every area.

Der Prix Ars Electronica versteht sich als offenes Forum und als Einladung an Künstler, Forscher und Gestalter unterschiedlicher Disziplinen und ist offen für neue Strömungen und Entwicklungen im Bereich der digitalen Medien. In diesem Sinn ist es seitens des ORF von Beginn an ein Anliegen, den Wettbewerb offen und flexibel zu gestalten, um somit dem rapiden Wandel der digitalen Medien gerecht zu werden. In seinen Ergebnissen repräsentiert der Prix Ars Electronica alljährlich den aktuellen Stand digitaler Mediengestaltung abseits industrieller Normen und dokumentiert den tiefgreifenden kulturellen Wandel, den die digitalen Medien in den letzten Jahrzehnten dieses Millenniums hervorgerufen haben. Die Cyberkünstler unserer Tage verstehen den Computer längst nicht mehr als Werkzeug, sondern als umfassendes Medium, mit dem sie sich kompetent und kreativ auseinandersetzen und den Betrachter/Benutzer in den Dialog miteinbeziehen und ihn zur Anwendung der Schlüsselkulturtechnik unserer Tage, der Interaktivität, auffordern. Nicht mehr Softwareentwicklungen oder eine neue Formensprache stehen im Brennpunkt des Interesses. Die Cyberkunst unserer Tage thematisiert verstärkt tiefgreifende Fragestellungen einer Gesellschaft im Wandel.

Das Spektrum der von fünf internationalen Expertenjuries ausgewählten Arbeiten inkludiert darüber hinaus Top-Produkte aus dem Entertainment, Ergebnisse wissenschaftlicher Forschung, und last but not least demonstriert der Prix Ars Electronica 99 mit der Wettbewerbskategorie „cybergeneration – u19 – freestyle computing“ wieder die ungebrochene Kreativität Jugendlicher im Umgang mit den digitalen Medien in allen Bereichen.

The Prizes of the Prix Ars Electronica 99

Golden Nica for .net:
ATS 100,000 (Euro 7,267):
Linus Torvalds (SF)

2 Awards of Distinction à ATS 50,000 (Euro 3,633): Willi Henshall (UK)/Matt Moller (USA) and Jean-Marc Philippe (F)

Golden Nica for Interactive Art:
ATS 200,000 (Euro 14,534): Lynn Hershman (USA)
2 Awards of Distinction à ATS 50,000 (Euro 3,633): Perry Hoberman (USA) and Luc Courchesne (CDN)

Golden Nica for Computer Animation:
ATS 200,000 (Euro 14,534): Chris Wedge (USA)
2 Awards of Distinction à ATS 50,000 (Euro 3,633): Bob Sabiston/Tommy Pallotta (USA) and John Lasseter/Andrew Stanton (USA)

Golden Nica for Visual Effects:
(ATS 200,000, Euro 14,534) Visual Effects Supervisor Team (USA) for *What Dreams May Come*
2 Awards of Distinction à ATS 50,000 (Euro 3,633): Computer Film Company (UK) and Alain Escalle (F)

Golden Nica for Digital Musics:
ATS 150,000 (Euro 10,901) Richard James (Aphex Twin, UK) and Chris Cunningham (UK)
2 Awards of Distinction à 50,000 (Euro 3,633): Ikue Mori (J) and Mego (A)

Golden Nica for cybergeneration u19 freestyle computing (MultiMedia-Pentium-PC plus 1 year free Internet access): (conspirat). (A)
2 Awards of Distinction: a MultiMedia-Pentium-Notebook each: Phil E. Haindl (A) and Alexander Fischl/Gregor Koschicek (A)

Die Preise des Prix Ars Electronica 99

Goldene Nica für .net:
ATS 100.000 (Euro 7.267): Linus Torvalds (SF)
2 Auszeichnungen à ATS 50.000 (Euro 3.633): Willi Henshall (UK)/Matt Moller (USA) und Jean-Marc Philippe (F)

Goldene Nica für Interaktive Kunst:
ATS 200.000 (Euro 14.534): Lynn Hershman (USA)
2 Auszeichnungen à ATS 50.000 (Euro 3.633): Perry Hoberman (USA) und Luc Courchesne (CDN)
Goldene Nica für Computeranimation:
ATS 200.000 (Euro 14.534): Chris Wedge (USA)
2 Auszeichnungen à ATS 50.000 (Euro 3.633): Bob Sabiston/Tommy Pallotta(USA) und John Lasseter/Andrew Stanton (USA)

Goldene Nica für Visual Effects:
(ATS 200.000, Euro 14.534) Visual Effects Supervisor Team (USA) von *What Dreams May Come (Hinter dem Horizont)*
2 Auszeichnungen à ATS 50.000 (Euro 3.633): Computer Film Company (UK) und Alain Escalle (F)

Goldene Nica für Digital Musics:
ATS 150.000 (Euro 10.901) Richard James (Aphex Twin, UK) und Chris Cunningham (UK)
2 Auszeichnungen à 50.000 (Euro 3.633): Ikue Mori (J) und Mego (A)

Goldene Nica für cybergeneration – u19 – freestyle computing (MultiMedia-Pentium-PC plus 1 Jahr kostenloser Internet-Zugang):
(conspirat). (A)
2 Auszeichnungen à ein MultiMedia-Pentium-Notebook: Phil E. Haindl (A) und Alexander Fischl/Gregor Koschicek (A)

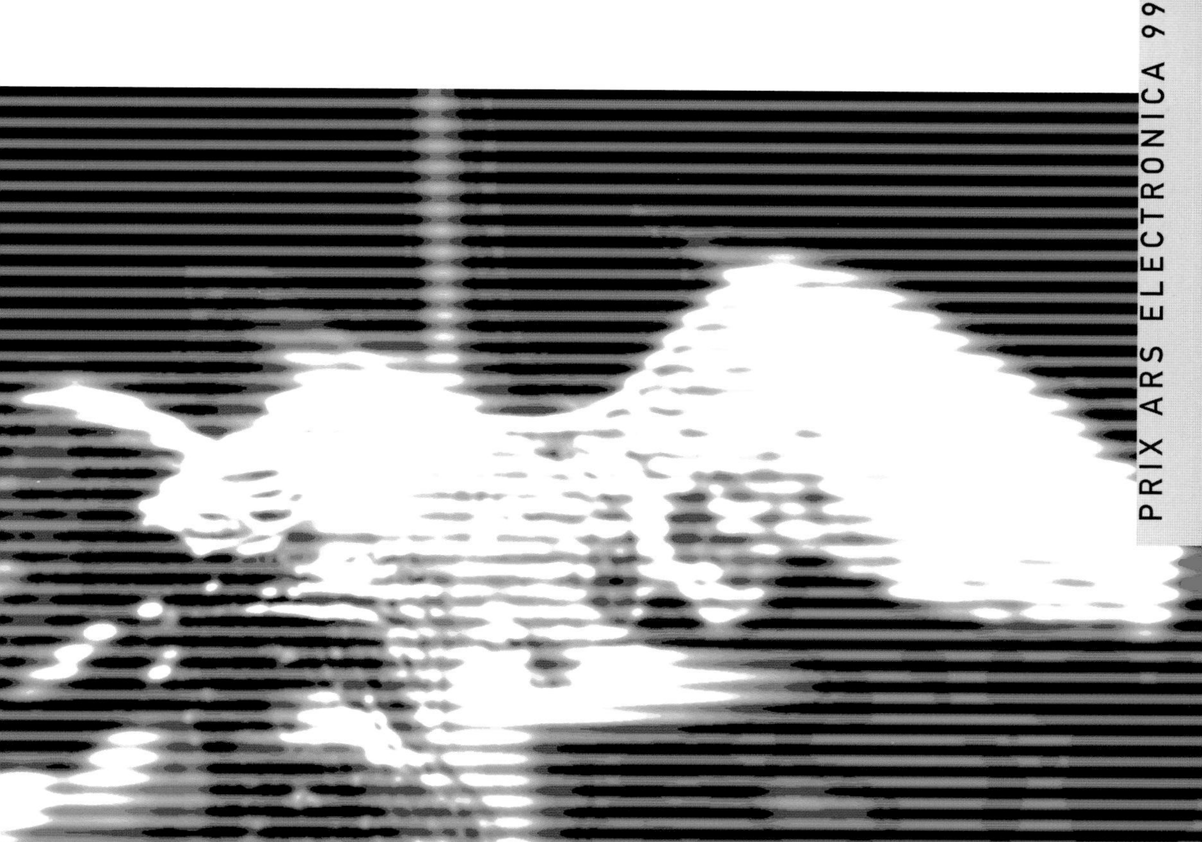

Sponsors

The Prix Ars Electronica is endowed with prize money amounting to a total of ATS 1,35 million. The prize money is donated by the Siemens AG. The competition "cybergeneration – u19 – freestyle computing", sponsored by the Austrian Postal Bank (P.S.K.) and conducted in cooperation with the Austrian Culture Service (Ö.K.S.), is open to young people in Austria under the age of 19.
The realization of the Prix Ars Electronica as an international competition is only made possible through the financial commitment of sponsors and supporters.
The Prix Ars Electronica has been made possible through support from the VOEST-ALPINE STEEL AG., Datakom, Andlinger & Company, and the city of Linz and the province of Upper Austria.
For additional support, the Prix Ars Electronica 99 is grateful to TNT International Mail, Austrian Airlines, Casino Austria AG, SGI Austria, Gericom by S plus S, and Courtyard by Marriott.

Sponsoren

Der Prix Ars Electronica 99 ist mit insgesamt ATS 1,35 dotiert. Preisstifter ist die Siemens AG. Der von der P.S.K. gesponserte und in Zusammenarbeit mit dem Österreichischen Kultur-Service (Ö.K.S.) durchgeführte Wettbewerb „cybergeneration – u19 – freestyle computing" lädt Jugendliche in Österreich unter 19 zur Teilnahme ein. Die Durchführung des Prix Ars Electronica als internationaler Wettbewerb kann nur durch das finanzielle Engagement von Förderern und Sponsoren realisiert werden.
Ermöglicht wird der Prix Ars Electronica durch die Förderung seitens der VOEST-ALPINE STAHL AG., der Datakom, Andlinger & Company sowie der Stadt Linz und des Landes Oberösterreich. Für weitere Unterstützung dankt der Prix Ars Electronica TNT International Mail, Austrian Airlines, der Casino Austria AG, SGI Österreich, Gericom by S plus S und Courtyard by Marriott.

prix ars electronica 99

.NET
INTERACTIVE ART
COMPUTER ANIMATION
VISUAL EFFECTS
DIGITAL MUSICS
u19/CYBERGENERATION

ONE STEP TOWARDS COMMUNITY
Ein Schritt in Richtung Gemeinschaft

Although the .net category is open to nearly all categories of Web sites and Internet projects, the jury this year decided to highlight ones that encourage interaction in a way that could not take place without the Net.

Obwohl die .net-Kategorie für nahezu alle Arten von Websites und Internetprojekten offen ist, hat die Jury dieses Jahr beschlossen, Werke hervorzuheben, die die Interaktion auf eine Weise einsetzen, wie sie ohne das Netz nicht machbar wäre.

We looked for works that connect people in novel ways and encourage interactivity and collaboration. The winners highlight the evolving, organic nature of the Internet in a way that coincides with the theme of this year's Prix Ars Electronica competition. They also suggest the emergence of new social formations and social values—like open-source software and a near-universal dislike of unsolicited bulk e-mail—that are specific to network communications.

Linus Torvalds—*Linux*
Linux might appear to be an unlikely pick for a top prize in the .net category. After all, an operating system doesn't appear to neatly fall into the usual categories of art.
But Linux is an example of a work that advances the development of the Net in a novel way. The .net jury sought out pieces that are community building, self-organizing, distributed, impossible without the Net, and have grown beyond the original design of the artist. During our deliberations, Linux emerged as an unparalleled example of a work that meets precisely those criteria: It has birthed an aesthetic showing how something can be built on the Net through an intentional, but not necessarily direct, description. As an open-source project, Linux relies on the

Wir haben nach Werken Ausschau gehalten, die Menschen auf eine neuartige Weise miteinander in Beziehung bringen und dabei Interaktivität und Zusammenarbeit fördern. Die Arbeiten der diesjährigen Preisträger reflektieren die sich entwickelnde organische Natur des Internet auf eine Weise, die mit dem Thema der diesjährigen Ars Electronica zusammenfällt. Und sie deuten auch das Heranwachsen neuer sozialer Formen und sozialer Werte an – wie eine Open-Source-Software und eine nahezu universelle Ablehnung unerwünschter Massen-E-mail – die zu den Eigenheiten der Netzwerkkommunikation gehören.

Linus Torwalds – *Linux*
Linux könnte als eine etwas seltsame Wahl für einen Spitzenpreis in der .net-Kategorie erscheinen, schließlich fällt ein Betriebssystem nicht unbedingt in die üblichen Kategorien von „Kunst".
Aber *Linux* ist ein Beispiel für ein Werk, das die Entwicklung des Netzes auf eine neuartige Weise fördert. Auf der Suche nach gemeinschaftsbildenden, selbstorganisierenden, verteilten Werken, die ohne das Netz nicht zustandekämen und die sich womöglich noch über die ursprüngliche Intention des Autors hinaus entwickelt haben, tauchte bei den Überlegungen der Jury *Linux* als Beispiel einer Arbeit auf, die wie keine andere genau diesen Kriterien entspricht: Es hat eine eigene Ästhetik generiert, die zeigt, wie etwas über das Netz als bewußte – wenn auch nicht notwendigerweise direkte – Beschreibung aufgebaut werden kann. Als Open-Source-Projekt beruht *Linux* auf den Beiträgen Tausender freiwilliger Programmierer, die

contributions of thousands of volunteer programmers who collaborate online in a group effort that has created a remarkably robust operating system. The effort is steered—but not directed—by Linus Torvalds. We felt the community that has assembled around this anarchic effort demonstrates how strong an aesthetic can be in bringing a community, assets, ideas and attention together.

Willy Henshall / Matt Moller: *Res Rocket*
What creates new forms of expression that distinguish the Web from previous media? Simple: Works that can only exist in a networked environment that lets people collaborate and organize in unprecedented — and unpredictable — ways.
Res Rocket, an application that allows musicians to jam live online, could not succeed without the Net. Previously musicians had to be physically together to create new music on the fly. With *Res Rocket*, geographically dispersed artists can meet and play together, build on their compositions, and save the result at any level of quality desired, including studio-quality sound.
The system allows remote musicians to connect with others, who they may or may not already know, to improvise together. *Res Rocket's* network opens up a vast new set of connective possibilities for a form

online an einem kollektiven Projekt zusammenarbeiten, aus dem ein bemerkenswert robustes Betriebssystem geboren wurde. Und diese kollektive Anstrengung wird von Linus Torvalds angeleitet – nicht aber unmittelbar gesteuert.
Wir waren der Ansicht, daß die Community, die um dieses anarchische Projekt entstanden ist, beweist, wie stark eine Ästhetik sein kann, die eine Gemeinschaft, Ressourcen, Ideen und Aufmerksamkeit zusammenführt.

Willy Henshall und Matt Moller: *Res Rocket*
Was schafft neue Ausdrucksformen, die das Web von früheren Medien unterscheiden? Ganz einfach: Werke, die nur in einer vernetzten Umgebung existieren können, in der Menschen zusammenarbeiten und sich auf bisher unbekannte – und unvorhersehbare – Weise organisieren. *Res Rocket*, eine Anwendung, die es Musikern erlaubt, online zusammenzuspielen, könnte ohne das Netz nicht erfolgreich sein. Früher mußten Musiker physisch zusammenkommen, um schnell neue Musikstücke zu erschaffen. Mit *Res Rocket* können auch geografisch getrennte Künstler „einander treffen" und gemeinsam spielen, auf ihren Kompositionen aufbauen und das Ergebnis in jeder gewünschten Qualitätsstufe abspeichern, selbst in Studio-Qualität.
Das System erlaubt räumlich getrennten Musikern, mit anderen in Verbindung zu treten – egal, ob sie diese bereits kennen oder nicht – und mit ihnen zu improvisieren. Das Netzwerk von *Res Rocket* eröffnet einer Form von Kreativität, die überall zu finden ist, wo es Menschen gibt, ein breites Spektrum neuer konnektiver Möglichkeiten. Weit verstreute musika-

of creation that is found everywhere humans are found. Dispersed musical talents have already begun to find like minds through the Rocket network, and a commercial CD has been produced. Thanks to *Res Rocket*, musical collaboration is no longer limited by geography.

Jean-Marc Philippe: *KEO*
The breadth of this project is dizzying in scope. *KEO* is a work by French artist Jean-Marc Philippe that collects short text messages and encodes them onto CDs. Eventually they will be rocketed into space aboard a small satellite designed to circle the earth for 50,000 years. As the artist says on his Website, "It is also a distance in time that is so vertiginous and mind-boggling that it compels us to abandon our normal point of reference and puts us all on an equal footing, forcing us to reach down into our imaginations or deep convictions."
This kind of global collaboration could not easily have taken place without the Net. Anyone on the planet with a connection can simply add their 6,000-character text to the ever-growing database that's designed to exist over a time span best described as archeological. By reminding us of humanity's limitations, it brings us together in a way that few other Web sites can.

Mark Napier: *Shredder*
Since the early days of the Web, Web artists and designers have experimented with the inherent deconstructive capabilities of HTML. The *Shredder* automates this experimentation. Type in any Web address, and its source is automatically 'shredded' into form art. The Shredder serves as a kind of meta-form art generator. It's fascinating to see a familiar commercial, government, or personal site indiscriminately exploded into its composite elements, arranged differently but still 'live' in its links. The Shredder reminds us that anyone can affect the networked media environment in ways that would be impossible with traditional media.

Help B92-Coalition: *Free B92*
The B92 radio station and Web site *Free B92* is a a collaboration of institutions and individuals who share the belief that cultural and social dignity can survive as long as we have a free dialogue and understand the art of technology to create a virtual

lische Geister haben bereits begonnen, Gleichgesinnte über das *Res Rocket*-Netzwerk zu finden, und die erste kommerzielle CD ist bereits produziert. Dank *Res Rocket* ist musikalisches Zusammenspiel nicht länger durch die Geografie beschränkt.

Jean-Marc Philippe: *KEO*
Die Breite dieses Projektes ist mehr als erstaunlich. *KEO* des französischen Künstlers Jean-Marc Philippe sammelt kurze Textbotschaften und speichert sie auf CD. Irgendwann werden diese an Bord eines für die nächsten 50.000 Jahre um die Erde kreisenden Satelliten in den Weltraum geschossen. Auf seiner Website führt der Künstler aus: „Das ist eine zeitliche Distanz, die so groß und unvorstellbar ist, daß sie uns alle zwingt, unsere normalen Bezugspunkte zu verlassen und uns auf einen neuen gemeinsamen Blickpunkt einzustellen, in unsere Imagination einzutauchen oder auf unsere tiefsten Überzeugungen zurückzugreifen."
Diese Art der globalen Zusammenarbeit wäre ohne das Netz kaum möglich gewesen. Jeder auf diesem Planeten mit Internet-Zugang kann einfach seinen 6000-Zeichen-Text zu der ständig wachsenden Datenbank hinzufügen, die für eine Existenzdauer ausgelegt ist, die man nur als archäologisch bezeichnen kann. Indem sie uns an die Beschränkung der Menschheit erinnert, führt uns diese Website auf eine Weise zusammen, wie es nur wenigen gelingt.

Mark Napier – *Shredder*
Seit der Frühzeit des Web haben Künstler und Designer mit den HTML inhärenten dekonstruktiven Möglichkeiten experimentiert. Der *Shredder* automatisiert dieses Experiment. Man gebe eine beliebige Webadresse ein, und ihre Quelle wird automatisch zu „Form Art" geshreddert. Der *Shredder* dient dabei als eine Art „Meta-Form-Art"-Generator: Es ist faszinierend zu beobachten, wie sowohl bekannte kommerzielle und öffentliche als auch persönliche Websites in ihre Grundelemente explodieren, die nach dem Zufallsprinzip zusammengestellt werden und dennoch mit ihren Verknüpfungen funktional bleiben. Der *Shredder* erin-nert uns daran, daß jedermann die vernetzte Medienumgebung auf eine Weise angreifen kann, wie es mit traditionellen Medien nicht möglich wäre.

HelpB92-Koalition: *Free B92*
Die Radiostation und Website *FreeB92* entstand aus der Zusammenarbeit von Institutionen und Individuen, die den gemeinsamen Glauben haben, daß kulturelle und soziale Würde immer überleben kann, solange wir einen freien Dialog führen können und die Kunst der Technologie so weit beherrschen, daß wir einen virtuellen Raum für das freie Wort schaffen können. Nachdem die NATO im Frühjahr 1999 mit der Bombardierung Belgrads begonnen hatte, übernahm die Polizei den Sender und installierte eine Marionette als Geschäftsführer. Das ursprüngliche Personal verließ den Sender, der anstelle des alternativen Programms

space for free voice. After NATO began bombing Belgrade in the spring of 1999, police commandeered the B92 studio and installed a puppet station manager. The original staff quit, and instead of B92's alternative programming, the state-controlled station began to air Balkan folk music and Serbian state news. The displaced journalists were forced to turn to the Web, which allowed their news to reach a global audience. "The 'shelter' which the Internet can provide for all of those whose communication with others has been hampered and restricted has proved to be an extremely important area for preserving freedom and creating room to fight for freedom," says Veran Matic, editor of B92.

Martin Wattenberg / Joon Yu: *Map of the Market*
Map of the Market is a Java-based Web site that's not just beautiful — it's also entirely functional. The site graphically illustrates recent changes in the US stock market through the use of color and shape. An all-green image is usually a welcome one: It means the values of the hundreds of included companies have gone up. Brighter images show a sharper increase, and bigger shapes represent higher valuations.

Fumio Matsumoto / Shohei Matsukawa: *Ginga*
If you've ever yearned for better ways to visualize data, *Ginga* may help. It stands for Global Information Network as Genomorphic Architecture, and provides a way to browse nine 3D worlds that let you navigate through Internet resources. Like other winners, this encourages collaboration. Participants can communicate with other avatars and exchange archives. Some of the variables that are visually represented using VRML and other browser plug-ins include density, depth, size, and the relationships between the information in the Ginga database. According to the *Ginga* site: "Web resources are reconfigured with cyberspatial codes into *Ginga* and appear as any of the following nine main Worlds; Nebula, Ring, Network, Forest, Strata, Text, Image, Polyphony, and Cemetery. Users can explore these Worlds with avatars (incarnations) which are personalized and controlled by user's preferences."

Nick Philip: *Nowhere.com*
Anybody who's used the Net for more than a few days has furrowed his brow over spam, the always

des ursprünglichen B92 unter der Kontrolle des Staates nur noch Volksmusik und serbische Staatsnachrichten sendet. Die heimatlos gewordenen Journalisten waren gezwungen, auf das Web zurückzugreifen, um ihre Nachrichten einem globalen Publikum zugänglich zu machen. „Der ‚Schutz', den das Internet all jenen bieten kann, die in ihrer Kommunikation mit anderen behindert und eingeschränkt werden, hat sich als ein extrem wichtiger Faktor zur Wahrung von Freiheit und zur Schaffung eines Raums für den Kampf um Freiheit erwiesen", sagt Veran Matic, Redakteur von B92.

Martin Wattenberg / Joon Yu: *Map of the Market*
Map of the Market ist eine JAVA-gestützte Website, die nicht nur schön, sondern auch wirklich funktional ist. Die Site illustriert die Veränderungen auf dem US-Aktienmarkt mit Hilfe von Formen und Farben. „Alles im grünen Bereich" ist wohl das beliebteste Bild: Es bedeutet, daß die Aktien der hunderten ins Projekt einbezogenen Unternehmen alle gestiegen sind. Hellere Bilder zeigen einen stärkeren Anstieg, und größere Formen stellen größere Bewegungen dar.

Fumio Matsumoto / Shohei Matsukawa: *Ginga*
Sollten Sie je von einer besseren Möglichkeit zur Visualisierung von Daten geträumt haben, ist *Ginga* vielleicht die Erfüllung ihrer Wünsche. Das Wort steht für „Globales Informations-Netzwerk als Genomorphische Architektur", und es bietet eine Möglichkeit, durch neun 3D-Welten zu browsen, die eine Navigation durch Internet-Ressourcen ermöglichen. Wie bei anderen Preisträgern fördert dies die Zusammenarbeit. Die Teilnehmer können mit den Avataren von anderen kommunizieren und ihre privaten Archive austauschen. Einige der Variablen werden mit Hilfe von VRML visuell dargestellt, andere Plug-Ins für den Browser zeigen die Dichte, Tiefe, Größe und die Beziehungen zwischen den Informationen in der *Ginga*-Datenbank. Die *Ginga*-Website beschreibt das so: „Web-Ressourcen werden mit Hilfe cyberräumlicher Codes in *Ginga* neu konfiguriert und erscheinen als eine der folgenden neun Hauptwelten: Nebel, Ring, Netzwerk, Wald, Schichten, Text, Bild, Polyphonie und Friedhof. Die User können diese Welten mit Hilfe von personalisierten Avataren erforschen, die durch die Präferenzen der User gesteuert werden."

Nick Philip: *Nowhere.com*
Jeder, der das Netz mehr als nur ein paar Tage lang verwendet hat, hat sich über „Spams" geärgert, also über die unaufgefordert hereinkommenden Werbemails. Aber anstatt sie schnellstmöglich zu löschen, könnte man sie doch auch als kulturelles Phänomen feiern? Genau das tut *nowhere.com*, indem es eine visuelle Darstellung des Wachstums dieses irritierenden Web-Phänomens gibt. Viele der Junk-Mail-Sender verwenden den Domain-Namen „nowhere.com" als gefälschte Antwortadresse, an die verärgerte Empfänger auch noch ihre Antwor-

unsolicited and nearly always annoying practice of sending bulk commercial e-mail. But instead of hastily deleting it, why not celebrate it as a cultural phenomenon?
Nowhere.com does that by offering a visual representation of the growth of this Internet irritant. Many spammers use the "Nowhere.com" domain as a fake return address, to which irate recipients often reply. Now, when these e-mail messages flow into nowhere.com's inbox, they are forwarded to 12 busy fax machines at Tokyo's Intercommunications Center. Below is an equal number of overflowing trash cans, an apt physical representation of the final digital destination. "Confronted with 57,000 feet of thermal garbage, *Nowhere* instantly lets you experience, touch, hear and smell a small part of this incredibly vast media landscape, at the same time making a tongue in cheek nod to the fact that the more things change the more they stay the same," creator Nick Philip says.

Joanna Berzowska: *Computational Expressionism*
Computational Expressionism explores the process of using a computer to draw in a way that redefines the concepts of line and composition for the digital medium. It takes advantage of the Java programming language to create an interactive experience that lets participants explore concepts; the Web site responds to user inputs such as position, speed, direction, and order.
The work evolves as a combination of computer-generated images and human expression.
"*Computational Expressionism* sustains the spirit of these artists by seeking out the natural expressive language of computers, to spawn an eloquent freedom, a vernacular of individual style and a level of visceral understanding of the medium," says the artist.

David P. Anderson: *SETI*
SETI stands for the Search for Extraterrestrial Intelligence. The theme of the recent box office hit, Contact, the *SETI* project has captured the hearts of people all over the world since it was conceived. The *SETI* project is an organization which scans the skies with radio telescopes in search of signals that might be the indication of intelligent life on other planets. This process involves the use of huge computers to analyze the tens of gigabytes of data which come

ten schicken. Wenn diese E-Mails im Eingangskorb von *nowhere.com* landen, werden sie zu zwölf fleißigen Faxgeräten umgeleitet, die im Tokioter Intercommunications Center stehen. Unter diesen Faxgeräten stehen ebensoviele übergehende Papierkörbe – eine passende physische Darstellung der endgültigen digitalen Destination. „Wenn Sie bei Nowhere vor zwölf Kilometer Thermopapierabfall stehen, dann erfahren Sie sehr unmittelbar einen kleinen Teil dieser unglaublich großen weiten Medienlandschaft, ja, Sie spüren und hören ihn und können ihn angreifen und riechen, und gleichzeitig können Sie mit einem Augenzwinkern feststellen, daß die Dinge sich um so weniger verändern, je mehr sie sich ändern", sagt der Künstler Nick Philip.

Joanna Berzowska: *Computational Expressionism*
Computational Expressionism erforscht den Prozeß, einen Computer auf eine Weise zum Zeichnen zu verwenden, die das Konzept von Linie und Komposition für das digitale Medium neu definiert. Es verwendet die Programmiersprache JAVA, um eine interaktive Erfahrung zu schaffen, die Mitwirkende einlädt, Konzepte zu erforschen; die Website reagiert auf User-Input wie Position, Geschwindigkeit, Richtung und Ordnung.
Das Werk entsteht als Kombination aus computergenerierten Bildern und menschlichem Ausdruck. „*Computational Expressionism* unterstützt den künstlerischen Geist, indem es die natürliche Sprache des Computers verwendet, um eine eloquente Freiheit, einen individuellen Stil und ein Verstehen des Mediums ‚aus dem Bauch heraus' anzubieten", sagt die Künstlerin.

David P. Anderson: *SETI*
SETI steht für Suche nach ExtraTerrestrischer Intelligenz. Als Thema des jüngsten Kassenschlagers *Contact* hat *SETI* seit seinem Start sofort die Herzen von Menschen auf der ganzen Welt erobert. Das *SETI*-Projekt ist eine Organisation, die den Himmel mit Radioteleskopen nach Signalen absucht, die einen Hinweis auf intelligentes Leben außerhalb der Erde bieten könnten. Dieser Prozeß umfaßt auch die Verarbeitung der enormen Datenströme, die von den Teleskopen täglich hereinkommen. Wegen der Begrenzung der finanziellen Mittel kann *SETI* nicht genug Rechenzeit auf Großrechnern kaufen, um all diese Daten entsprechend intensiv auszuwerten. Und hier tritt „SETI@home" auf den Plan: Das SETI@home-Projekt löst das Problem, indem es über das Internet kleine Teile der Daten an Freiwillige zur Analyse verteilt. Diese Freiwilligen lassen einen Bildschirmschoner ablaufen, der die ungenützte CPU-Leistung des Computers nutzt, um die Daten zu verarbeiten. Diese Aufgabenverteilung hat es dem *SETI*-Projekt ermöglicht, Rechenkapazität in der Größenordnung eines Supercomputers auf diese Aufgaben anzusetzen. Der Screensaver ist wunderschön designt und zeigt eine grafische Darstellung der gerade ablaufenden Analyse. Die Website bietet eine umfassende Erläuterung des

streaming off of the radio telescopes each day. Because of funding limitations *SETI* can not buy enough computer time to run in-depth analyses on all of this data. Enter "SETI@home". The *SETI@home* project solves this mind-boggling task of analyzing the data by distributing small pieces of the data to volunteers via the Internet. The volunteers run a screen saver which crunches the data using the extra CPU power on their computers. This distributed effort has allowed the *SETI* project to collect the equivalent of an immense supercomputer to direct at this task. The screen saver is beautifully designed showing a graphical representation of the analysis taking place. The web page features an in depth explanation of the theory behind the analysis and the project, as well as a list of volunteers and the highest peaks found. Various groups have used the idea of distributed processing in the past, but the *SETI@home* project wins the prize for its ability to allow anyone to participate directly in a project of such cosmic scale.

CAAD—Eidgenössische Technische Hochschule Zürich: *Phase(x)3*
Phase(x)3 is an open source experiment. It involves a large group of architecture students who form an author's collective. They interact and communicate through the exchange and the mutual reinterpretation of their 3D computer models. It is a project of CAAD, a department of the Swiss Federal Institute of Technology in Zürich. *Phase(x)3* shows the potential of collaborative workspaces. In *Phase(x)3* the results of one phase and one author are taken as the starting point for the work in the next phase by a different author. As authors can choose which model they want to work with, the whole body of works can be viewed as an organism where, as in an evolutionary system, only the fittest works survive. *Phase(x)3* can explicitly replace single authorship with collective authorship, because all relations between works, authors and timeline are recorded in a database and can be rendered and evaluated. *Phase(x)3* thus implies a new cultural model of distributed credits and copyrights, a precondition for networked society.

Daniel Julià Lundgren: *ReAcT*
The piece *ReAcT* from Daniel Julià Lundgren is a nice example of online instruments. By typing words and moving the position of the mouse, the music and

Projekts und der Theorie hinter der Analyse sowie eine Liste der Freiwilligen und der gefundenen Spitzenwerte. Zahlreiche Gruppen haben das Konzept einer solchen „verteilten Verarbeitung" in der Vergangenheit genützt, aber *SETI* ist insofern auszuzeichnen, als es jedermann erlaubt, direkt an einem Projekt von so kosmischen Dimensionen teilzuhaben.

CAAD – Eidgenössische Technische Hochschule Zürich: *Phase(x)3*
Phase(x)3 ist ein Open-Source-Experiment. Es umfaßt eine große Gruppe von Architekturstudenten, die ein Autorenkollektiv bilden. Sie interagieren über den Austausch und die gegenseitige Re-Interpreation ihrer 3D-Computermodelle. Es handelt sich dabei um ein Projekt des CAAD, einer Lehrkanzel der Eidgenössischen Technischen Hochschule in Zürich. *Phase(x)3* zeigt das Potential, das kollaborative Arbeitsräume in sich bergen. Dabei fungieren die Ergebnisse einer Phase und eines Autors als Ausgangsmaterial für die Arbeit eines anderen Autors in der nächsten Phase. Da die Autoren selbst bestimmen können, mit welchen Modellen sie arbeiten, kann das Werk in seiner Gesamtheit als Organismus angesehen werden, in dem – wie in einem evolutionären System – nur die besten Werke überleben. *Phase(x)3* kann explizit die Autorschaft des Individuums durch jene des Kollektivs ersetzen, weil alle Beziehungen zwischen Werken, Autoren und zeitlichem Ablauf in einer Datenbank aufgezeichnet und von dort ausgegeben und analysiert werden können. So impliziert *Phase(x)3* ein neues kulturelles Modell von verteilten Credits und Copyrights, Vorbedingung für eine vernetzte Gesellschaft.

Daniel Julià Lundgren: *ReAcT*
Das Stück *ReAcT* von Daniel Julià Lundgren ist ein hübsches Beispiel für Online-Instrumente. Indem man Worte eintippt und die Maus bewegt, werden Musik und Animation intensiver. Das Interface ist intuitiv und ansprechend gestaltet. *ReAcT* gehört zu einem wachsenden Genre von Online-Anwendungen, die man als „Form-Art" bezeichnen könnte. Darunter verstehen wir Webkunst, die auf reinem Design basiert oder aber die im Medium inhärenten technischen oder symbolischen Möglichkeiten erkundet – etwa mit oder an den Eigenschaften von Icons, Darstellungen oder Interfaces herumzuspielen, die quasi die Klischees des Medium geworden sind. *ReAcT* macht mehr Spaß als die meisten anderen (außerdem ist es recht geschickt und passabel interaktiv), weil es zu seinen Arabesken eine passende musikalische Begleitung liefert.

Christa Sommerer / Laurent Mignonneau: *Verbarium*
Verbarium gesellt sich zu früheren – nicht notwendigerweise Web-gestützten – Arbeiten von Christa Sommerer und Laurent Mignonneau. Auch in dieser Arbeit werden die Wachstumsmuster von Pflanzen und organischen Simulationen über das interaktive

animation will get more intense. The interface design is intuitive and appealing. *ReAcT* belongs to a growing genre on line which one could call "form art." By this we mean web art based on pure design or which exploits technical or symbolic possibilities inherent in the medium, for example playing with/on features borrowed from icons, display sets or interfaces that have become quasi clichés of the medium. *ReAcT* is more fun than most (as well as being very nimble and passably interactive) in that it adds pertinent musical accompaniment to its fetching arabesques.

Christa Sommerer / Laurent Mignonneau: *Verbarium*
Verbarium is in line with previous, although not necessarily web-based work by Christa Sommerer and Laurent Mignonneau. It too, brings out the growth patterns of plants and organic simulations via the interactive behaviour of users. You type on the left side of the split screen a word or a sentence that will translate on the right side into a 3-D shape. Your words superpose themselves without erasing previously entered material. Running the mouse on the self-generating drawings can call up the words that have generated them. The attractiveness of this piece comes both from its design values and from the poetry of the relationships between words and shapes, meaning and feeling in a virtual but shared environment. The knot-based leitmotiv reminds us, of course, that we are dealing with an artpiece made for the networks.

Verhalten der Anwender gesteuert. In der linken Seite des geteilten Bildschirms tippt man ein Wort oder einen Satz ein, und auf der rechten wird dieser in eine 3D-Form übersetzt. Die eigenen Worte überlagern sich mit schon zuvor geschriebenen, ohne sie zu löschen. Läßt man die Maus über die selbstgenerierenden Zeichnungen laufen, kann man die ihnen zugrundeliegenden Worte aufrufen. Die Attraktivität dieses Stückes liegt sowohl in der Qualität seines Designs als auch in der Poesie der Beziehung zwischen Worten und Formen, Bedeutung und Gefühl in einer virtuellen, aber gemeinsamen Umgebung. Das auf einem Knoten basierende Leitmotiv erinnert uns – natürlich – daran, daß wir es mit einem für Netzwerke geschaffenen Kunstwerk zu tun haben.

Ramana Rao: *Hyperbolic Java Tree*
Als Navigationswerkzeug auf der Basis von Ramana Raos ursprünglicher JAVA-Applikation ist *Hyperbolic Java Tree* ein Code und ein Skript, die es gestatten, Stichwörter in flexiblen Konfigurationen entlang komplex verzweigter Baumstrukturen zu ordnen, die alle über Mausklicks in einem glatten, ständig dynamischen Display verfügbar sind und auch als Trigger für andere Agenten und Ereignisse auf dem Bildschirm dienen. Auch hier scheint das Web wieder Magie auf Lager zu haben. Die Erfindung des hyperbolischen Java-Baumes eröffnet nicht nur für die Gestaltung von Indices und Suchmaschinen wirklich aufregende Möglichkeiten, sondern auch für ein interaktives und konnektives Design. Die Vorstellung von Konnektivität beginnt zu greifen und inspiriert Architekturen, die für sich genommen schön sind, egal, ob sie als Kunst zu klassifizieren sind oder nicht. *Hyperbolic Java Tree* läßt auch von einer Konnektivität träumen, die es Konzepten und Konversationen erlaubt, sich selbst in leicht zugängliche thematische Arrangements zu organisieren . Es ist ein Beispiel für die Kunst der Intelligenz.

Ramana Rao: *Hyperbolic Java Tree*
A navigation tool based on Ramana Rao's original Java application, the *Hyperbolic Java Tree* is a code and a script that allow keywords to be arranged in flexible configurations along complex branchings of tree structures, all available by click and drag in a smooth continuously dynamic display, all also acting as triggers to other actors and events on screen. Once again, there seems to be magic in store for the Web. The invention of the *Hyperbolic Java Tree* opens up truly exciting avenues not only for indexes and search engines, but also for interactive and connective design. The imagination of connectivity is beginning to set in and inspire architectures that are beautiful, whether they be classified as art or not. *Hyperbolic Java Tree* also brings to mind dreams of connectivity that allow concepts and conversations to organize themselves in smoothly accessible thematic arrangements. It is an example of the art of intelligence.

Eric Loyer: *Lair of the Marrow Monkey*
If multi-media is capable of poetic élan, *Lair of the Marrow Monkey* is an example of that. The words of the Lair are set to sound and type that respond to smooth interplay with the surfer. Design values are high, not only for visual but also for audio effects, which blend voice and sound in interesting and surprising combinations. An attractive and web-worthy calligram, would Apollinaire say were he to be judge among us.

Eric Loyer: *Lair of the Marrow Monkey*
Wenn Multimedia zu einem poetischen Elan fähig ist, dann ist *Lair of the Marrow Monkey* das beste Beispiel dafür. Die Worte des „Lagers“ werden in eine Klang- und Textumgebung gestellt, die in einem fließenden Wechselspiel mit dem Surfer steht. Der Design-Wert ist hoch, nicht nur hinsichtlich der visuellen, sondern auch der auditiven Effekte, die Stimmen und Klang zu interessanten und überraschenden Kombinationen verschmelzen. Ein attraktives und webwürdiges Kalligramm, würde Apollinaire sagen, wenn er als Juror bei uns säße.

It is not easy to give an artistic statement about an operating system, because while an operating system can be a work of art (I certainly feel that there is an artistic component to programming), it's not in itself very artful.
I think the most interesting thing about operating systems (apart from the purely technical side that I personally obviously find to be incredibly interesting and challenging in itself) is what they allow people and other programs to do. The operating system doesn't do much on its own, but without the operating system the more visible parts of computer software simply wouldn't work.
In more "artistic" terms, you might consider the operating system to be the collection of pigments and colors used to create a painting: they are not the painting itself, but they are obviously a rather important ingredient—and a lot of the great painters spent a large portion of their time on making the paint, often by hand, in order to get their paintings to look just right.
Linus Torvalds

Es ist nicht leicht, ein künstlerisches Statement über ein Betriebssystem zu formulieren. Auch wenn ein Betriebssystem ein Kunstwerk sein kann (ich bin natürlich der Meinung, daß Programmieren eine künstlerische Komponente besitzt), ist ein Betriebssystem an sich nicht sehr kunstvoll.
Das Interessanteste an Betriebssystemen (abgesehen vom rein technischen Aspekt, den ich persönlich natürlich unglaublich interessant und herausfordernd finde), ist für mich das, was sie Menschen und anderen Programmen ermöglichen. Ein Betriebssystem kann alleine nicht sehr viel bewirken, doch ohne Betriebssystem könnten die augenfälligeren Teile der Computer-Software schlichtweg nicht funktionieren.
In einem eher „künstlerischen" Sinn könnte man das Betriebssystem vielleicht mit den verschiedenen Pigmenten und Farben vergleichen, mit denen ein Bild gemalt wird: Sie sind zwar nicht das Bild an sich, doch sie sind ein ziemlich wesentlicher Bestandteil davon – und viele große Künstler verbrachten viel Zeit mit der – oft händischen – Herstellung ihrer Farben, um das Bild genau ihren Vorstellungen entsprechend gestalten zu können.
Linus Torvalds

Penguin's Progress: The Linux Position

For most of my adult life I have been two things: a journalist and a marketing expert. Frankly, I did the latter mostly to sublimate the former. This made me a very different kind of marketing expert—one who brought a writer's skepticism to the marketer's job. At every meeting, I always seemed to be asking the same two questions: what is this and what's the story?
Most companies—especially those in the technology world—are not interested in simple answers to simple questions. They make "solutions" rather than products and "management inference engines" rather than spreadsheets. They also want their stories to consist entirely of happy beginnings. "Reporters write stories," I would say, "and stories don't start with *happily ever after*. They start with a character with a problem. The solution comes at the end, and you never want to get there or the writer will find some other story to tell."
I didn't get very far with this approach. What got me somewhere was working on the character issue. I

Der Weg des Pinguins: Die Linux-Position

Zwei Berufe habe ich im Großteil meines erwachsenen Lebens ausgeübt: Journalist und Marketing-Experte. Um ehrlich zu sein, sollte letzterer hauptsächlich den ersteren sublimieren. Dadurch wurde ich zum Marketing-Experten der besonderen Art – einer, der den Aufgaben des Marketings mit journalistischer Skepsis begegnet. Bei jeder Sitzung stellte ich anscheinend immer wieder die gleichen zwei Fragen: „Worum handelt es sich? Was ist die Geschichte?"
Die meisten Firmen, besonders diejenigen in der Welt der Technologie, haben kein Interesse an einfachen Antworten auf einfache Fragen. Sie schaffen „Lösungen" statt Produkte und „Managementfolgerungsmaschinen" statt Tabellenkalkulationen. Außerdem wollen sie, daß ihre Geschichten ausschließlich aus glücklichen Anfängen bestehen. „Journalisten schreiben Geschichten," pflegte ich zu sagen, „und Geschichten beginnen nicht mit *Sie lebten glücklich vom Anfang an*. Sie fangen bei einer Figur mit einem Problem an. Erst am Ende kommt die Lösung, und dorthin will man nie gelangen, sonst findet der Autor irgendeine andere Geschichte zu schreiben."
Mit dieser Einstellung kam ich allerdings nicht sehr weit. Was mir jedoch etwas nützte, war die Arbeit mit der Hauptfigur. Dies nannte ich „Positionieren", und ich war nicht der einzige.
Hotbot findet im Web 233,780 Seiten, die das Wort „positioning" beinhalten. Wenn ich GPS und andere

called this "positioning" and I wasn't alone. Hotbot finds 233,780 pages on the Web with the word "positioning" in them. When I weed out GPS and other non-marketing meanings, I get 26,940 pages, almost entirely by marketing consultancies selling "strategic distribution analysis", "rollout plan reviews", "campaign launch programs", "performance impact studies", "collateral market options", "market penetration analyses", "outsourced staff deployments" and other such nonsense, all served up in euphemistically delusional language.

No wonder Linux is a hit. It is a character with a story none of those 27,000 agencies—including mine—could have thought up. Who would seriously talk about "world domination" and "software that doesn't suck" in the face of Microsoft, whose software runs on every computer you see and whose market value exceeds the GNP of the Southern Hemisphere? "*You see, there was this Finnish guy, and something about a penguin...*" I don't think so.

Thus, what we have with Linux is more than the world's first big-time open-source operating system. We have the world's first marketing success that owes nothing to marketing. This warrants further study.

I just did for Linux what I used to do for my clients. I took a look at how the customers for Linux's message—the analysts, reporters and editors of the world—are describing its character and telling its story. I got on AltaVista (http://www.altavista.com/) and looked up every page with the phrase "Linux is..." and found over 27,000. Searching through links to the first fifty, I came up with these answers, which I sort into four ways of depicting Linux's character:

Descriptive (you've got to start somewhere)

An open-source UNIX clone / a freely available UNIX clone / a UNIX clone / a complete, copylefted UN*X clone / a freely distributable, independent UNIX-like operating system / a UNIX-type 32-bit operating system / an operating system developed under the GNU General Public License / an open-source

nicht Marketing-relevanten Bedeutungen davon abziehe, bleiben noch 26,940 Seiten, die beinahe ausschließlich von Marketingberatungsfirmen stammen, welche „strategische Verteilungsanalysen", „das neueste Modell für Planungsberichte", „Startprogramme für Kampagnen", „Studien zur Performancewirkung", „Nebenmarktoptionen", „Marktdurchdringungsanalysen", „Verteilung von ausgelagerten MitarbeiterInnen" und ähnlichen in schwülstiger verschleierter Sprache verpackten Unsinn verkaufen.

Kein Wunder, daß Linux ein Hit ist. Es ist eine Hauptfigur mit einer Geschichte, die keine dieser 27.000 Agenturen – auch meine nicht – jemals hätte erfinden können. Wer könnte denn angesichts Microsoft, dessen Software auf beinahe jedem Computer in Sichtweite läuft und dessen Marktwert das BNP der südlichen Hemisphäre übersteigt, ernsthaft noch von „Weltbeherrschung" und „Software, die kein Scheiß ist" reden? „*Weißt du, es war einmal ein Typ aus Finnland, und da kam irgendwie auch ein Pinguin vor...*" So eben nicht.

Was wir also mit Linux haben, ist mehr als das erste groß angelegte Open-Source-Betriebssystem der Welt. Es handelt sich hier um den ersten Markterfolg der Welt, der nicht auf Marketing zurückgeht. Das sollten wir uns genauer anschauen.

Mit Linux tat ich genau das gleiche wie früher für meine Klienten. Ich untersuchte, wie die Kunden der Linux-Botschaft – die Analytiker, Journalisten und Redakteure der Welt – seine Eigenschaften beschreiben und seine Geschichte erzählen. Mit AltaVista (http://www.altavista.com/) suchte ich nach den Seiten, die die Phrase „Linux is ..." enthalten und fand über 27.000. Indem ich den Links der ersten fünfzig folgte, fand ich folgende Antworten, aus denen ich vier Möglichkeiten zur Darstellung des Linux-Charakters ableite:

Beschreibungen (irgendwo muß man anfangen)

Ein Open-Source UNIX-Klon / ein frei erhältlicher UNIX-Klon / ein UNIX-Klon /ein vollständig „copylefted" UN*X-Klon / ein frei distribuierbares, unabhängiges UNIX-ähnliches Betriebssystem / ein UNIX-ähnliches 32-Bit Betriebssystem / ein Betriebssystem, das unter der GNU General Public License entwickelt wurde / ein Open-Source-Betriebssystem, das jede/r vom Internet runterladen und kompilieren kann / eine Freeware-Version von UNIX / ein echtes 32-Bit multitasking, multithrea-

operating system anyone can download from the Internet and compile / a freeware version of UNIX / a true 32-bit, multi-tasking, multi-threading operating system / a full-featured UNIX-type operating system / a powerful, flexible, 32-bit OS / a 32-bit multi-user, multi-tasking clone of UNIX / a full-fledged UNIX-like operating system / a UNIX-type 32-bit operating system / a UNIX-type 32-bit operating system / an embedded operating system / the open-source operating system.

Superlative (stuff to like)

Free / stable / awesome / a full, rich, dependable workhorse / the best Windows file server / a bedroom hacker's dream / the OS to run / the only real OS / a bandwagon / the future's universal operating system / a significant OS in corporate IS departments / the #1 OS in Germany / the #1 UNIX on x86 / the heir to UNIX / the largest collaborative programming effort ever / the new king of the hill / the most dynamic, interesting and exciting development on the operating system scene today / not just for geeks anymore / a lesson in hard work and well-earned rewards / the first major evolution in operating systems since MS-DOS.

Competitive (necessary for the war and sports stories that write themselves)

The fastest-growing OS outside of NT / a worthy contender / a juggernaut / a movement / the definitive answer to the small business needs for Internet connectivity, a web server and e-mail services.

Flawed (always a good character trait)

Complicated / a good teacher of science-oriented college students, but a rotten teacher for just about everyone else / overkill for most home applications / simply too hard to use for the average user / entrenched in a grass-roots development model.

Believe me, you can't buy PR this good. Especially since the default story is about a fight between this

ding Betriebssystem / ein voll ausgebautes UNIX-ähnliches Betriebssystem / ein leistungsstarkes, flexibles 32-Bit-Betriebssystem / ein 32-Bit, multiuser, multitasking UNIX-Klon / ein gleichwertiges UNIX-ähnliches Betriebssystem / ein UNIX-artiges 32-Bit Betriebssystem /das Open-Source Betriebssystem.

Superlative (was man mag)

Gratis / stabil / geil / ein volles, reichhaltiges, zuverlässiges Arbeitstier / der beste Windows-Fileserver / der Traum eines Kammerl-Hackers / das Betriebssystem, das man fahren soll / das einzige echte Betriebssystem / ein Zugpferd / das universelle Betriebssystem der Zukunft / ein bedeutendes Betriebssystem in betrieblichen IS-Abteilungen / das führende Betriebssystem in Deutschland / das führende UNIX auf x86 / der UNIX-Nachfolger / das größte gemeinsame Programmierprojekt, das es je gab / der neue Spitzenreiter / die dynamischste, interessanteste und aufregendste Entwicklung in der aktuellen Betriebssystems-Szene / nicht mehr nur etwas für Geeks / eine Lektion in harter Arbeit und eine total lohnende Aufgabe / die erste große Evolution in Betriebssystemen seit MS-DOS.

Konkurrenzfähigkeit (braucht man für Kriegs- und Sportgeschichten, die sich von selbst schreiben)

Das am schnellsten wachsende Betriebssystem jenseits von NT / ein beachtenswerter Konkurrent / ein Moloch / eine Bewegung / die definitive Lösung für die Bedürfnisse kleiner Unternehmen in bezug auf Internetanbindung, Webserver und E-Mail-Dienste.

Makel (immer eine günstige Eigenschaft)

Kompliziert / gute Lehre für wissenschaftlich orientierte UniversitätsstudentInnen, aber ziemlich unbrauchbar für fast alle anderen / Overkill für die meisten Heimanwendungen / einfach zu schwierig für durchschnittliche AnwenderInnen / sitzt in einem Basisbewegungsentwicklungsmodell fest.

Glauben Sie mir, solche hervorragende PR kann man gar nicht kaufen. Gerade deshalb, weil es sich bei der vorgegebenen Geschichte um einen Wettstreit zwischen diesem Typen aus Finnland und einer Schwarzenegger-Figur handelt, und das ganze ist nicht inszeniert. Schauen wir uns sechs verschiedene „Versus"-Konstruktionen an:

- Linux vs. Microsoft: 57
- Microsoft vs. Linux: 110
- Linux vs. NT: 512
- NT vs. Linux: 247
- Linux vs. (Windows, Cisco, BeOS...) 1968
- Microsoft vs. (DOJ, Justice, Netware...) 2721

Finnish dude and a Schwarzenegger character and it isn't an act. Here's a look at six different "versus" constructions:

- Linux vs. Microsoft: 57
- Microsoft vs. Linux: 110
- Linux vs. NT: 512
- NT vs. Linux 247
- Linux vs. (Windows, Cisco, BeOS...) 1968
- Microsoft vs. (DOJ, Justice, Netware...) 2721

A big part of positioning is unconscious, yet revealed by who you list first. Is it Yankees vs. Dodgers or Dodgers vs. Yankees? We tend to list favorites first. So if I had to call a play-by-play on the games here, I'd say Microsoft appears to be the favorite in the company game, while Linux is the favorite in the OS game (which, fortunately, is the one that truly matters).

Even when editors don't use the "versus" construction, they still apply a rule I obtained recently from a Wall Street Journal reporter: "There days you can't write about Microsoft without bringing up Linux." It's pro forma. Even if they know nothing about Linux, they still cast its character.

And what about Microsoft, really? Does this corporate Terminator truly consider Linux to be a competitor? "This much is clear to them, right to the top of the company," one cross-platform developer told me this morning, "they can't win the server war. There's no way they can lock it down like they did with the desktop. Linux is now the server of choice. They know they have to cope with that, and they're really not sure how to do it."

Let's hope they start figuring out how. Microsoft is a problem we don't want to lose.

Doc Searls, Linux Journal, July 1999: reprinted with kind permission from the author.

Ein wichtiger Teil des Positionierens läuft unbewußt ab, zeigt sich jedoch daran, wer zuerst genannt wird. Handelt es sich um Yankees vs. Dodgers oder um Dodgers vs. Yankees? Wir neigen dazu, die Favoriten zuerst anzuführen. Wenn ich in diesem Fall die Spiele Schlag für Schlag kommentieren müßte, würde ich sagen, Microsoft scheint im Unternehmensspiel zu führen, Linux ist dagegen der Favorit im Spiel der Betriebssysteme (und das ist zum Glück das einzige Spiel, das wirklich zählt).

Auch wenn Journalisten sich nicht dieser „Versus"-Konstruktion bedienen, kommt trotzdem eine Regel zur Anwendung, die mir ein Journalist des *Wall Street Journal* neulich erklärte: „Heutzutage kann man über Microsoft nichts schreiben, ohne Linux einzubringen." Es ist eine Formsache. Auch wenn sie von Linux keine Ahnung haben, müssen sie die Figur besetzen.

Und wie steht es nun wirklich mit Microsoft? Betrachtet der Terminator der Konzerne Linux tatsächlich als Konkurrenz?

„Soviel ist ihnen bis in die Führungsetagen hinein klar", erzählte mir ein Cross-Plattform-Entwickler heute morgen, „den Serverkrieg können sie nicht gewinnen. Dieses Mal können sie unmöglich alles umzäunen, wie damals mit dem Desktop. Linux ist jetzt der bevorzugte Server. Sie wissen, sie müssen sich damit auseinandersetzen, sie wissen nur noch nicht, wie."

Hoffen wir, sie kommen bald drauf. Microsoft ist ein Problem, das wir nicht verlieren wollen.

(Doc Searls, Linux Journal, Juli 1999. Mit freundlicher Genehmigung des Autors.)

LINUS THORVALDS, BORN 1969 IN HELSINKI, FINLAND. LIVED THERE BASICALLY MOST OF HIS LIFE: WENT TO SCHOOL AND UNIVERSITY THERE, AND MARRIED (TOVE) AND GOT HIS FIRST CHILD (PATRICIA, 2). MOVED TO SANTA CLARA, CALIFORNIA IN 1997, WHERE HIS SECOND DAUGHTER WAS BORN (DANIELA, 1). HE CURRENTLY LIVES IN SANTA CLARA WITH HIS FAMILY, WORKING WITH COMPUTERS AT A COMPANY CALLED TRANSMETA. HE HOLDS A MASTERS OF SCIENCE DEGREE IN COMPUTER SCIENCE FROM THE UNIVERSITY OF HELSINKI.

Linus Thorvalds (SF), geb. 1969 in Finnland, hat dort den Großteil seines bisherigen Lebens verbracht, vom Schul- und Universitätsbesuch (Master of Science der Universität Helsinki) über seine Hochzeit und die Geburt seiner ersten Tochter (Patricia, 1). 1997 übersiedelte er nach Santa Clara, Kalifornien, wo seine zweite Tochter Daniela (2) geboren wurde und wo er derzeit mit seiner Familie lebt. Er arbeitet – natürlich mit Computern – bei einem

KEO
Jean-Marc Philippe

KEO, a winged satellite, is being launched in 2001 to orbit the Earth for some 50,000 years before returning to deliver a collection of messages from the world of today to the world of tomorrow. Every man, woman and child is invited to contribute to this fresco of messages which will reveal the richness and diversity of the human experience at the dawn of the third millennium. *KEO* gives each individual the equivalent of four uncensored pages in which to express themselves in the language of their choosing, in which to bequeath a unique and personal portrait to this collective work.
This collective non-profit project is open, free of charge, to all those who would like to participate. It is being realized solely through the voluntary, interdisciplinary contributions of time, skills, products and services of its many partners, whether in a corporate or individual capacity. This policy was deliberately adopted so that the project would not unintentionally divert funds from more urgent, humanitarian causes; it would remain free of any commercial or political influence and be truly embraced as a gift from the people of today to future generations 500 centuries from now.
The *www.keo.org* web site was created at the beginning of 1998 both to inform the public of this invitation to contribute a message and to serve as a medium for the writing and collection of same. So far, the site has received messages from 61 countries and territories representing all continents, with ages ranging from 7 to 84 years old. In the manner of its medium the Internet, *KEO* seems to transcend cultural and generation barriers and, through allowing the individual "voice" full liberty of expression is, paradoxically, creating a momentum of unity.
Once the satellite is launched, all messages will be made freely accessible on a database for everyone to read. For the true value of the project today lies in the opportunity for us all to share in one another's hopes, dreams, fears, doubts and deepest convictions. Through doing so, we may come to rediscover our common humanity.

KEO, ein geflügelter Satellit, wird im Jahre 2001 in eine Umlaufbahn geschossen werden, die ihn rund 50.000 Jahre lang um die Erde kreisen läßt, bevor er zu ihr zurückkehrt. Er trägt eine Sammlung von Nachrichten aus der Welt von heute in die Welt von morgen. Jeder Mann, jede Frau, jedes Kind ist eingeladen, zu diesem Fresko aus Nachrichten beizutragen, das den Reichtum und die Unterschiedlichkeit menschlicher Erfahrung an der Schwelle zum dritten Jahrtausend dokumentiert. KEO gibt jedem Individuum das Äquivalent von vier unzensurierten Seiten, auf denen man sich in jeder beliebigen Sprache ausdrücken kann und ein einzigartiges, persönliches Portrait zu dieser kollektiven Arbeit beitragen kann.
Dieses kollektive Werk ist ein offenes, nicht-profit-orientiertes und kostenloses Projekt, das allen offensteht, die daran mitwirken möchten. Es wird ausschließlich mit Hilfe von freiwilligen interdisziplinären Beiträgen in der Form von Zeit, Fähigkeiten, Produkten und Dienstleistungen der zahlreichen privaten wie Firmenpartner realisiert. Dieser Ansatz wurde bewußt gewählt, damit dieses Projekt nicht unbeabsichtigterweise dringenderen humanitären Anliegen die Gelder wegnimmt; so bleibt es frei von wirtschaftlichen und politischen Einflüssen und wird tatsächlich zu einem Geschenk der Menschen von heute an die künftigen Generationen in fünfhundert Jahrhunderten.
Die *www.keo.org*-Website wurde Anfang 1998 geschaffen, um einerseits die Öffentlichkeit zu informieren und zu Beiträgen einzuladen, andererseits um als Medium für die Sammlung eben dieser Beiträge zu dienen. Bisher sind auf der Site Nachrichten aus 61 Ländern und Regionen eingegangen, die alle Kontinente repräsentieren; das Alter der Beiträger reicht von 7 bis 84 Jahre. Wie das dafür gewählte Medium Internet scheint auch das *KEO*-Projekt kulturelle und Generationenschranken zu überwinden; es erzeugt – gerade weil es der individuellen Stimme völlige Freiheit des Ausdrucks einräumt – ein fast paradoxes Moment der Einheit.
Sobald der Satellit gestartet ist, werden alle Nachrichten in einer Datenbank für jedermann frei zugänglich gemacht. Der wahre Wert des Projekts für uns heute liegt in der Möglichkeit, daß wir alle einander unsere Hoffnungen, Träume, Ängste, Zweifel und tiefste Überzeugungen mitteilen können und dabei vielleicht unsere gemeinsame Menschlichkeit wiederentdecken.

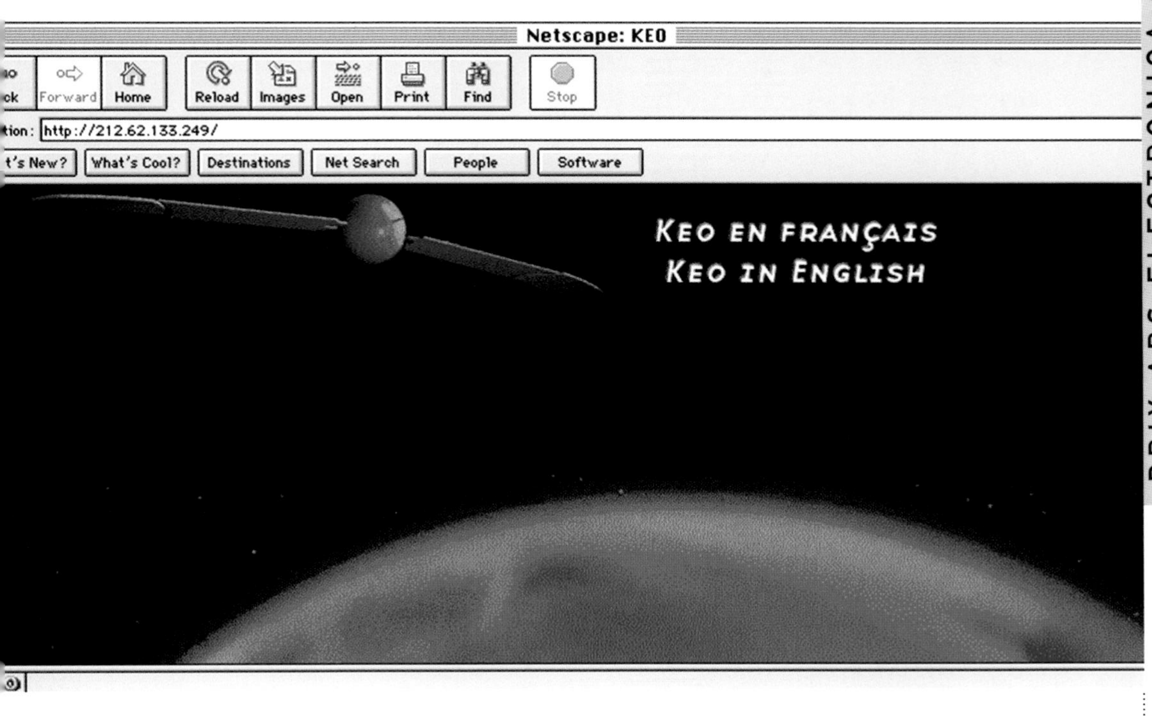

JEAN-MARC PHILIPPE (F) REGARDS HIMSELF AS AN ARTIST WHO NOT ONLY BUILDS BRIDGES, BUT ALSO TEARS THEM DOWN. HE STUDIED GEOPHYSICS AND ART AND HAS BEEN INVOLVED IN VARIOUS FIELDS OF ART (VIDEO, SCULPTURES WITH FORM CHANGING METAL ALLOYS), AND WITH HIS WORKS *CELESTIAL WHEEL* (1980), *MESSAGES FROM MANKIND TO THE UNIVERSE*, *KEO* AND *THE SPHERE OF MARS* HE IS CONSIDERED ONE OF THE FOUNDERS OF SPACE ART.

Jean-Marc Philippe (F) sieht sich als Künstler, der sowohl Brücken baut als auch wieder abbricht. Er studierte Geophysik und Kunst und war in verschiedene Kunstbereichen tätig (Video, Skulpturen mit formveränderlichen Metallegierungen) und gilt mit seinen Arbeiten *Celestial Wheel* (1980), *Messages from mankind to the Uni*[illegible]*rse*, *KEO* und *The Spher*[illegible] *of Mars* a[illegible] eine[illegible] der Gründe[illegible]

RES ROCKET

Willy Henshall / Matt Moller

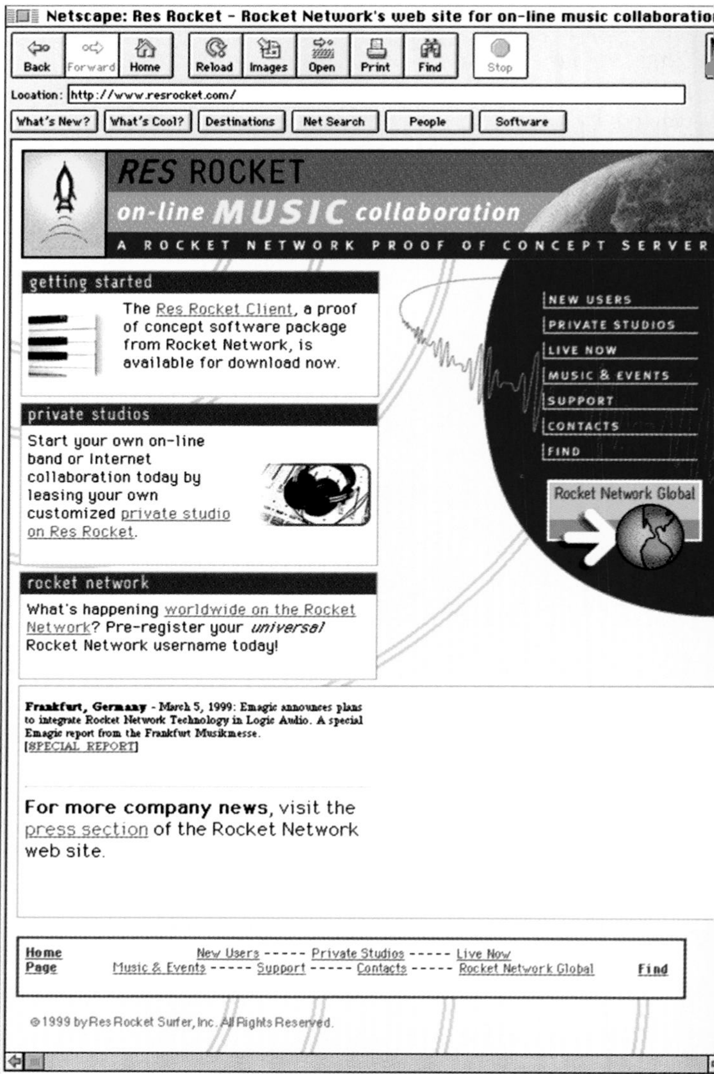

The first incarnation of Res Rocket was formed in November 1994 by two successful English musicians, Willy Henshall and Tim Bran. Willy Henshall, an award-winning songwriter, producer and member of the band Londonbeat, and Tim Bran, a successful engineer, producer, and member of the band Dreadzone, began posting messages and sound files on Usenet (the Internet's bulletin-board)—and later on an ftp and Web site—from their West London studio. People from all over the world started replying with song ideas and sound files. By January 1995 about 600 members were regularly checking this little corner of the Internet. "The mailing list was a hive of humor and strangeness, confessions, hints, tips and friendship," says Henshall. "Meanwhile the collaborations in the ftp site were growing and getting more focused."

In a true expression of Net democracy, the name of

Die erste Inkarnation von Res Rocket wurde im November 1994 von den beiden erfolgreichen englischen Musikern Willy Henshall und Tim Bran gegründet. Henshall, preisgekrönter Songwriter, Produzent und Bandmitglied bei „Londonbeat", und Tim Bran, erfolgreicher Ingenieur, Produzent und Mitglied der Band „Dreadzone", begannen damals, von ihrem Londoner Studio aus Nachrichten und Soundfiles im Usenet (dem „Schwarzen Brett" des Internet) und später auf einer FTP- und Website zu veröffentlichen. Leute aus der ganzen Welt antworteten und präsentierten ihre Song-Ideen und Klang-Files. Bis Januar 1995 schauten schon rund 600 Mitglieder regelmäßig in dieser kleinen Ecke

the group was chosen by a vote of the site's membership who picked *Res Rocket* from a list of 10 names randomly generated by a computer program. Simultaneously several thousand miles away, Matt Moller and Canton Becker, two students at Northwestern University in Chicago, had developed what was to become *Res Rocket's version 1.0* client software (previously called DRGN.) The two were beginning to attract serious attention from media organizations around the world. The Chicago Tribune was soon calling Becker and Moller "the Lennon and McCartney of cyberspace."

The two pairs of musical pioneers hooked up after Becker and Moller visited Henshall and Bran's Web site and responded to a call for musical collaborators. Henshall remembers the foursome's Eureka moment: "The first time we tried an International jam was late one night at the Res Rocket studio in Notting Hill [London]. After about five hours of no sound, suddenly......BLAM!...a bass drum and then a wicked Chicago house-style base line appeared out of the ether. Tim and I were beside ourselves, and couldn't get to the piano quickly enough to send a part back again. We knew we had found the missing component to reach our goal of on-line musical collaboration."

That weekend Henshall got on a plane to Chicago to meet Moller and Becker. The next incarnation of Res Rocket was formed soon afterward in March 1995 and the initial version of the DRGN jamming software was developed from there. In recent months the DRGN software has been downloaded for free by thousands of subscribers and the world's biggest band hasn't stopped jamming since!

Who would have predicted that what started one night over the Internet in a studio in London and a house in Chicago would one day grow into a global music movement?

des Netzes nach. „Die Mailing-Liste war ein Bienenstock voller Humor und Skurrilität, mit Geständnissen, Hinweisen, Tips und Freundschaft", sagt Henshall. „Mittlerweile wurde die Zusammenarbeit auf der FTP-Site intensiver und gleichzeitig konzentrierter."

Auch der Name der Gruppe ist Ausdruck einer echten Netz-Demokratie: „Res Rocket" wurde durch allgemeines Votum der Site-Mitglieder aus einer Liste von zehn von einem Computerprogramm zufällig generierten Namen ausgewählt.

Gleichzeitig hatten einige tausend Meilen entfernt – an der Northwestern University in Chicago – die Studenten Matt Moller und Canton Becker das entwickelt, was zur Version 1.0 der *Res Rocket*-Client-Software werden sollte (und zuvor DRGN hieß). Bald richtete sich die Aufmerksamkeit von Medienorganisationen der ganzen Welt auf diese Software. Die *Chicago Tribune* nannte Becker und Moller „Lennon und McCartney des Cyberspace". Die beiden musikalischen Pionierpaare kamen in Kontakt, nachdem Becker und Moller die Website von Henshall und Bran besucht hatten und auf einen Aufruf nach musikalischen Mitarbeitern antworteten. Henshall erinnert sich an den „Heureka"-Moment des Quartetts: „Die erste internationale Jam-Session fand spät nachts im Res Rocket-Studio in Notting Hill (London) statt. Nach ungefähr fünf Stunden ohne Klang ging's plötzlich WUMM – und eine Baßtrommel tauchte aus dem Äther auf und danach eine hinterlistige Grundmelodie im Chicagoer House-Stil. Tim und ich waren außer uns, und wir konnten das Klavier gar nicht schnell genug dazu bringen, einen Part zurückzuschicken. Uns war klar, daß wir das Element gefunden hatten, das uns für eine Online-Musikzusammenarbeit gefehlt hatte."

An diesem Wochenende flog Henshall nach Chicago, um sich mit Moller und Becker zu treffen. Die nächste Inkarnation von Res Rocket formierte sich kurz darauf im März 1995, und ab da wurde die Ursprungsversion der DRGN Jamming-Software entwickelt. In jüngster Zeit wurde die DRGN-Software kostenlos von Tausenden von Abonnenten heruntergeladen – und die größte Big-Band der Welt ist seither nicht mehr zur Ruhe gekommen!

Wer hätte vorausgesehen, daß das, was einmal nachts via Internet zwischen London und Chicago passierte, zu einer globalen Musikbewegung heranwachsen würde?

Willy Henshall, Founder and chairman of Res Rocket/Rocketnetwork. Successful musician and songwriter. Nethead since 79. Former member of hit pop soul band "Londonbeat." Matt Moller, Director of Software Development. Founder of Res Rocket/Rocketnetwork. Willy Henshall, Mitbegründer und Vorsitzender des Res Rocket/Rocketnetworks. Erfolgreicher Musiker und Liedermacher. Netzbegeisterter seit 79. Ehemaliges Mitglied der erfolgreichen Pop-Soul-Gruppe „Londonbeat". Matt Moller, Software-Entwicker, Mitbegrün-

SETI@home

David P. Anderson

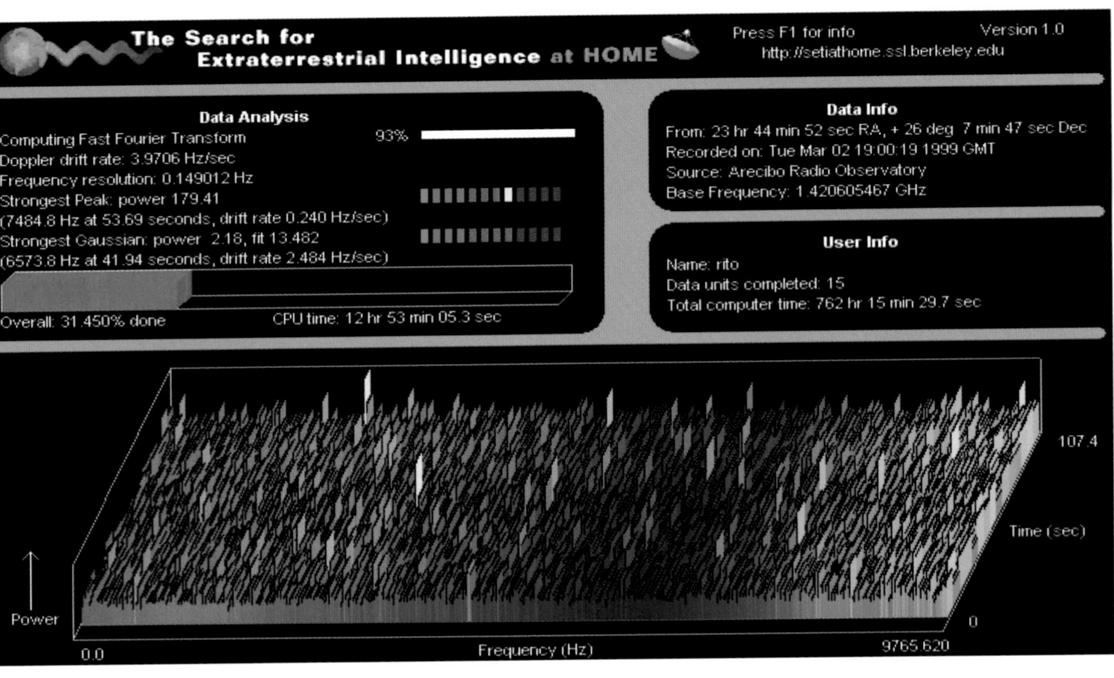

SETI@home is a scientific experiment that harnesses the power of hundreds of thousands of Internet-connected computers in the Search for Extraterrestrial Intelligence (SETI). You can participate by running a program that downloads and analyzes radio telescope data. There's a small but captivating possibility that your computer will detect the faint murmur of a civilization beyond Earth.
Contributors/Collaborators to SETI@home include: David Gedye, Dan Werthimer, Jeff Cobb and Eric Korpela.

SETI@home ist ein wissenschaftliches Experiment, das die Leistungsfähigkeit von Hunderttausenden über das Internet verknüpften Rechnern nutzt, um nach Extraterrestrischer Intelligenz (SETI) zu suchen. Man kann daran teilnehmen, indem man ein Programm laufen läßt, das Radioteleskop-Daten herunterlädt und analysiert. Es gibt die recht unwahrscheinliche – aber sehr fesselnde – Möglichkeit, daß gerade der eigene Rechner das schwache Geflüster einer Zivilisation jenseits der Erde entdeckt.
An *SETI@home* haben David Gedye, Dan Werthimer, Jeff Cobb und Eric Korpela mitgearbeitet.

Translations: Select language

SETI@home is a scientific experiment that will harness the power of hundreds of thousands of Internet-connected computers in the Search for Extraterrestrial Intelligence (SETI). You can participate by running a program that downloads and analyzes radio telescope data. There's a small but captivating possibility that your computer will detect the faint murmur of a civilization beyond Earth.

Download SETI@home for: **Windows (95/98/NT)** | **Macintosh** | **UNIX and others**.

If you have problems using SETI@home, please tell us.

To our users: SETI@home is off to a great start! We now have over 500,000 users, many more than we expected. This has caused some temporary problems:

- Our servers are occasionally overloaded. If you get a "Can't connect to server" message, the problem is probably at our end, not yours.
- Our "data pipeline" is not flowing at top speed, so we're sending out the same work units (mostly recorded Jan 7 and Jan 8) repeatedly.
- Credit for work units and CPU time may not show up immediately in your totals.
- Our new "Group" feature has had some problems; If you've joined a group, you may need to

DAVID ANDERSON (USA) IS CHIEF TECHNOLOGY OFFICER AT TUNES.COM. A FORMER MEMBER OF THE COMPUTER SCIENCE FACULTY AT UC BERKELEY, HE HAS AUTHORED 65 RESEARCH PAPERS ON OPERATING SYSTEMS, DISTRIBUTED COMPUTING, COMPUTER MUSIC, AND COMPUTER GRAPHICS. David Anderson (USA) ist Chief Technology Officer bei Tunes.com. Das ehemalige Mitglied der Fakultät für Computerwissenschaften der UC Berkeley hat 65 Aufsätze über Betriebssysteme,

COMPUTATIONAL EXPRESSIONISM

Joanna Berzowska

The constrained and stylized character of current two-dimensional digital art is directly related to the fact that most artists work with already existing tools. Programmed drawing tools are much more powerful aesthetically than traditional drawing media. A single algorithm can generate whole images or patterns whereas a piece of chalk, no matter how dark, can only trace very elementary shapes. The stylistic nature of computational tools can influence the visual nature of the art to a greater extent. Algorithms are so controlling that we must carefully choose, as well as author, the tools and the methods with which we decide to create and manipulate digital media.

The concept of drawing with computation essentially means to program what sorts of shapes the linear motion of the hand will produce. For an artist to draw computationally means that the artist defines the patterns and colors that the brush produces, defines the behavior of the brush, provides its computational attributes, using algorithms and design principles.

A computational line (representation of a gesture drawn with computational tools) has three attributes.

– The computational line has physical appearance, which can be a set of points joining two endpoints; it can be a shape, a pattern, a representation of a mathematical algorithm, a color.

– The computational line has individual behavior: Dynamic properties such as a change of color over time, or movement across the canvas.

– Finally, the computational line has behavior in its interaction with the other lines on the canvas. It can push them away with pseudo-magnetic forces, change their color, or affect their shape.

Das beschränkte und stilisierte Aussehen der gegenwärtigen digitalen 2D-Kunst hat direkt damit zu tun, daß die meisten Künstler mit bereits existierenden Werkzeugen arbeiten. Programmierte Zeichenwerkzeuge sind ästhetisch viel leistungsfähiger als die traditionellen Zeichenmedien. Ein einfacher Algorithmus kann ganze Bilder oder Muster erzeugen, wohingegen ein Stück Kreide – egal wie dunkel – nur sehr elementare Formen nachziehen kann. Die stilistische Natur der Computer-Zeichenwerkzeuge kann die visuellen Aspekte der Kunst stärker beeinflussen. Algorithmen übernehmen einen so hohen Steuerungsgrad, daß wir die Werkzeuge und Methoden, mit denen wir digitale Medien erzeugen und manipulieren, vorsichtig auswählen und kontrollieren müssen.

Das Konzept des „Zeichnens mit Berechnung" bedeutet im Grunde zu programmieren, welche Arten von Linienformen eine lineare Bewegung der Hand zu produzieren in der Lage sein soll. Für einen Künstler bedeutet das die Festlegung der Muster und Farben, die der Pinsel produziert, die Definition des Pinselverhaltens und der Berechnungsattribute mittels Algorithmen und mittels Festlegung von Design-Prinzipien.

Eine durch Berechnung generierte Linie (also die Darstellung einer Geste durch Berechnungswerkzeuge) hat drei Attribute:

– Die Berechnungslinie hat eine physische Erscheinung, die als Set von Punkten zwischen zwei Endpunkten definiert werden kann; sie kann eine Form sein, ein Muster, eine Darstellung eines mathematischen Algorithmus, eine Farbe.

– Die Berechnungslinie hat ein individuelles Verhalten: Dynamische Eigenschaften wie die Veränderung der Farbe über die Zeit oder die Bewegung über die Malfläche.

– Schließlich hat die berechnete Linie auch ein Verhalten, was ihre Interaktion mit anderen Linien auf der Malfläche betrifft. Sie kann sie mit pseudomagnetischen Kräften wegdrücken, ihre Farben oder ihre Formen verändern.

active essay

computational expressionism is an exploration of the act of drawing in the computational medium. some pages of this active essay have embedded applets, so as to interactively illustrate concepts discussed.

gallery

the gallery hosts a collection of applets that display a variety of computational lines, sophisticated digital brushes that respond to various parameters of gestures, such as position, speed, direction or order.

computational expressionism

Internet

JOANNA MARIA BERZOWSKA WAS BORN IN POLAND AND HAS LIVED IN ALGERIA, GABON, CANADA, NORWAY, AUSTALIA AND THE USA. IN 1988, SHE WAS PROVINCIAL MATHEMATICS CHAMPION AND WON THE FIRST PRIZE IN THE JUNIOR DIVISION OF THE PROVINCIAL VISUAL ARTS COMPETITION. SHE OBTAINED UNDERGRADUATE DEGREES IN PURE MATHEMATICS AND IN FINE ARTS, AND A MASTERS DEGREE FROM THE MASSACHUSETTS INSTITUTE OF TECHNOLOGY MEDIA LABORATORY.

Joanna Maria Berzowska wurde in Polen geboren und hat bisher in Algerien, Gabun, Canada, Norwegen, Australien und den USA gelebt. 1988 siegte sie bei der regionalen Mathematikolympiade und gewann den ersten Preis in der Juniorenklasse bei einem Landeswettbewerb für visuelle Kunst. Sie hat erfolgreich Mathematik und Bildende Kunst studiert und ein Master-Diplom

phase(x)3

CAAD – Eidgenössische Technische Hochschule Zürich

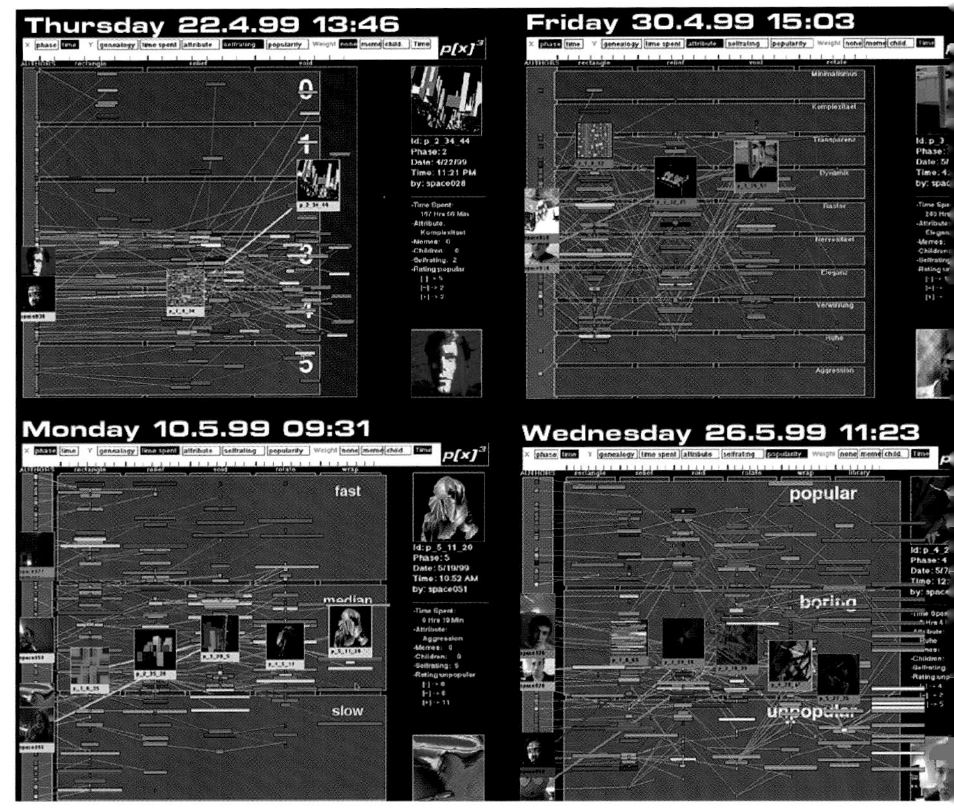

phase(x)3 is an explicitly designed collaborative process currently taking place. It involves a large group of architecture students who form a collective authorship. They interact and communicate through the exchange and the mutual reinterpretation of their 3D digital models.

In *phase(x)3* the results of one design step and one author are taken as the starting point for the work in the next step by a different author. As authors can choose which model they want to work with, the whole body of works can be viewed as in an evolutionary system where only the fittest works survive.

phase(x)3 can explicitly replace single authorship with collective authorship, because all relations between works, authors and timeline are recorded in a database. This can be visualized and evaluated.

phase(x)3 thus implies a new cultural model of distributed credits and copyrights, a precondition for the networked society.

phase(x)3 ist ein zur Zeit stattfindender, eigens entwickelter kollaborativer Prozeß, in den eine große Gruppe von Architekturstudenten involviert ist, die im Kollektiv zu Autoren werden. Sie interagieren und kommunizieren mittels des Austauschs und der gegenseitigen Neuinterpretation ihrer digitalen 3D-Modelle.

Bei *phase(x)3* wird das Ergebnis eines Designschritts eines Autors zum Ausgangspunkt für die Arbeit eines anderer Autor in einem nächsten Schritt. Da die Autoren selbst entscheiden können, mit welchem Modell sie arbeiten wollen, kann die Gesamtheit der so entstehenden Werke als ein evolutionäres System betrachtet werden, in dem nur die stärksten Werke überleben.

phase(x)3 ersetzt die individuelle Autorschaft bewußt durch eine kollektive Autorschaft, da alle Beziehungen zwischen Werken, Autoren und zeitlichem Verlauf in einer Datenbank aufgezeichnet werden. Diese wiederum kann visualisiert und ausgewertet werden. *phase(x)3* kreiert dadurch ein neues kulturelles Modell „verteilter" Credits und Urheberschaft – eine unerläßliche Voraussetzung für eine vernetzte Gesellschaft.

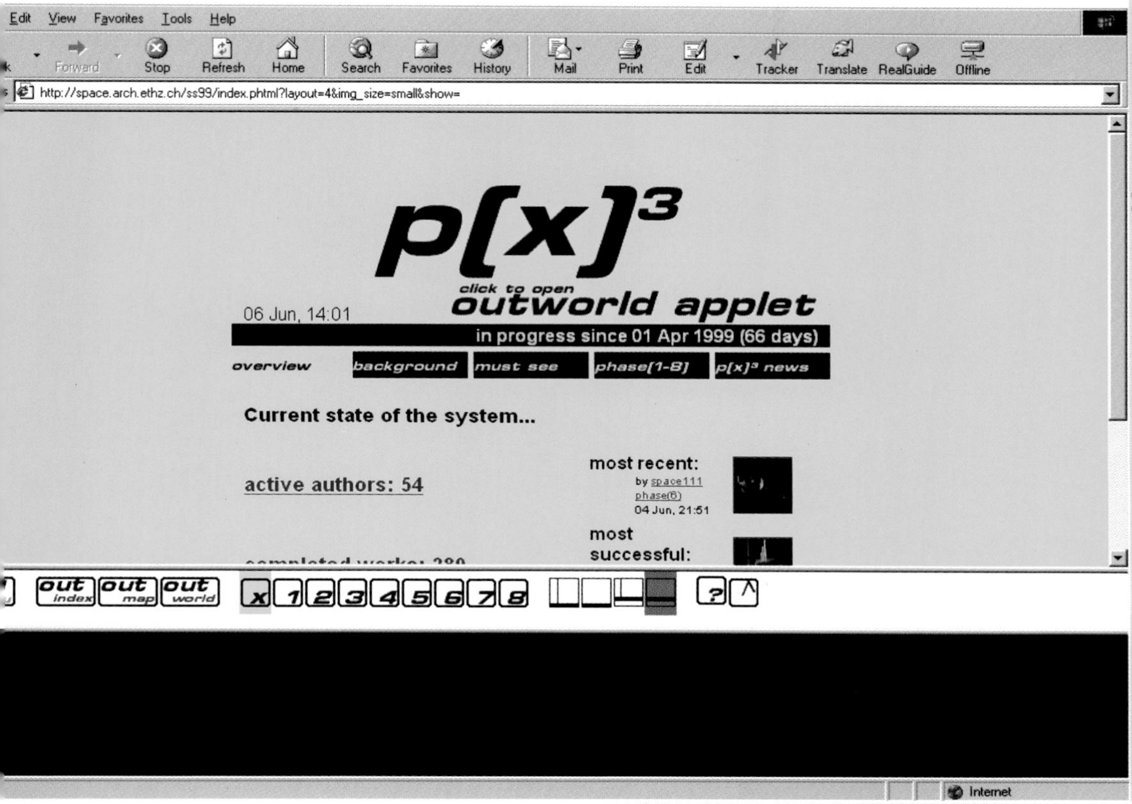

Edit View Favorites Tools Help

Forward Stop Refresh Home Search Favorites History Mail Print Edit Tracker Translate RealGuide Offline

http://space.arch.ethz.ch/ss99/index.phtml?layout=4&img_size=small&show=

p[x]³

click to open
outworld applet

06 Jun, 14:01

in progress since 01 Apr 1999 (66 days)

overview background must see phase[1-8] p[x]³ news

Current state of the system...

active authors: 54

most recent: by space111 phase(6) 04 Jun, 21:51

most successful:

out index out map out world x 1 2 3 4 5 6 7 8 ? ^

Internet

phase(x)3 started in April 1999 as the last of a series of prototypes dealing with these issues. In *phase(x)3*, the use of dynamic visualisation of the process has been extended (see figure displaying different states of the outworld applet). The dynamic of the ongoing process can be viewed in different ways to reveal hidden aspects of the system's growth.

phase(x)3 begann im April 1999 als letzter einer Serie von Prototypen, die sich mit solchen Anliegen befassen. In *phase(x)3* wurde vor allem die dynamische Visualisierung des Prozesses ausgebaut (siehe die Abbildung über die verschiedenen Zustände des Außenwelt-Applets). Die Dynamik des Prozesses kann auf unterschiedliche Weise betrachtet werden, um auch die versteckteren Aspekte des Wachstums des Systems deutlich zu machen.

The people involved in the conception and implementation of the phase(x) system at the Chair for CAAD at ETH Zürich, are all architects by training, working as researchers or as media artists in addition to their teaching obligations. Urs Hirschberg, Fabio Gramazio, Maria Papanikolaou, Bige Tuncer and Benjamin Stäger are the staff of *phase(x)3*, which is currently in progress. In their teaching, research, media art and architecture meet.

Die mit dem Konzept und der Implementierung des *phase(x)*-Systems an der Lehrkanzel für CAAD der ETH Zürich befaßten Mitarbeiter sind alles Architekten, die jedoch neben ihrer Lehrtätigkeit als Forscher oder Medienkünstler aktiv sind. Urs Hirschberg, Fabio Gramazio, Maria Papanikolaou, Bige Tuncer und Benjamin Stäger stellen das Team von *phase(x)3*, das derzeit läuft. In ihrem Unterricht vereinigen sich Forschung, Medienkunst und Architektur.

FREE B92

Help B92 Coalition

Free B92 is a website established by the Help B92 coalition. The site is edited and published by the B92 team of journalists and associates, working from various parts of the world. *Free B92* will focus on providing the international public with information on the status of independent media in Yugoslavia. *Free B92* will also work on projects to support journalists and media in various kinds of jeopardy. The first of these projects was launched by AMARC, the World Association of Community Radio Broadcasters, on May 3, World Press Freedom Day. Similar projects will be launched by various divisions of the former Radio B92. The B92 Publishing Division will prepare a presentation for the Frankfurt Book Fair. *ProFemina* and *Rec* magazines will publish in electronic format and lead discussions on the status of artistic work. The Cinema Rex team will prepare projects presenting alternative art events by Yugoslav artists who happened to be outside the country when war broke out. These projects will also assist in promoting the work of artists still in Yugoslavia.

Information and contributions from a number of associates will also be published on the *Free B92* site. These will throw more light on the bombing of Yugoslavia and the consequences of this.

The common aim of these projects is to preserve the spirit of professionalism which has been stripped from everyday communication in Yugoslavia through the Belgrade regime's banning and takeover of Radio B92.

Free B92 ist eine von der Help B92-Koalition initiierte Website. Die Site wird vom Team der Journalisten von B92 und Mitgliedern aus aller Welt herausgegeben und publiziert. *Free B92* will in erster Linie das internationale Publikum mit Informationen über die unabhängigen Medien in Jugoslawien versorgen, arbeitet aber auch an Projekten, um Journalisten und Medien bei schwierigen und riskanten Aufgaben zu unterstützen. Das erste derartige Projekt wurde am 3. Mai – dem Welttag der Pressefreiheit – von AMARC, der weltweiten Vereinigung von Community-Radio-Betreibern, gestartet. Ähnliche Projekte werden von verschiedenen Abteilungen des ehemaligen Radio B92 initiiert werden. So bereitet die Publikationsabteilung von B92 eine Präsentation für die Frankfurter Buchmesse vor; die Magazine *ProFemina* und *Rec* werden ihre Produkte elektronisch präsentieren und Diskussionen über den Status künstlerischer Arbeit führen. Das Team von Cinema Rex bereitet Projekt vor, die alternative Kunst-Events jugoslawischer Künstlern vorstellt, die sich beim Ausbruch des Krieges gerade außerhalb des Landes befanden. Diese Projekte werden auch helfen, die Arbeiten der noch in Jugoslawien befindlichen Künstler bekannt zu machen.

Information und Beiträge von einer Reihe von assoziierten Mitgliedern werden ebenfalls auf der *Free B92*-Site publiziert werden, was die Bombardierung Jugoslawiens und deren Auswirkungen in ein anderes Licht rücken wird.

Gemeinsames Ziel dieser Projekte ist es, den Geist des Professionalismus zu wahren, der in der Alltagskommunikation Jugoslawiens fehlt, seit das Belgrader Regime Radio B92 übernommen und verboten hat.

Edit View Favorites Tools Help

Forward Stop Refresh Home Search Favorites History Mail Print Edit Tracker Translate RealGuide Offline

http://www.b92.net/

Join us at www.freeB92.net !

FREE SOUND OF RADIO B92 BANNED

AIR RAID WARNING !!!

< HELP > B92 http://helpB92.xs4all.nl

STATEMENTS FROM B92

Radio B92 Statemnet
Belgrade, April 1, 1999

Saopstenje Radija B92
Beograd 1. april 1999.

A Letter from Belgrade
VERAN MATIC,
Editor-in-Chief, Radio B92
Belgrade, March 30, 1999

Izjava Verana Matica,
glavnog i odgovornog urednika Radija B92
Beograd, 30. Mart, 1999

IO B92 LIVE
EST ENGLISH NEWS
IOVIJE VESTI
EST AUDIO NEWS
hive]
IOVIJE AUDIO VESTI
iva]
IO B92
VIDEO PRODUCTION
IC PRODUCTION
LISHING
NNET
EMA REX
IA EVENTS
TACT US
LIST OF BANNED ANEM STATIONS
o 021 - Novi Sad
o GLOBUS - Kraljevo

RADIO B92 CLOSED DOWN AND SEALED OFF

On Friday April 2, at 09.00 CET, court officials together with uniformed and plain clothes policemen delivered to Radio B92's Director - Sasa Mirkovic - an order from the court announcing his dismissal as the station's Director. The decision was taken by the government-controlled Council of Youth, the founder of B92. The Council replaced Mr. Mirkovic with Mr. Aleksander Nikacevic. The police then sealed off the studio and offices of B92, banning the station from broadcasting. Shortly after, the stations new director - Mr. Nikacevic - issued an order in the presence of inspectors to all B92 staff to show up for work on Monday April, 5.

STRUGGLE CONTINUES. WE SHALL NEVER SURRENDER. RADIO B92, BELGRADE, SERBIA

ANEM
ANEM VESTI [video]
ANEM [Announcements]
FREE 2000
E-EDITION "UNFINISHED PEACE"
MEDIA WATCH
B92 AGAINST CENSORSHIP
SERVICES FOR DIALUP USERS

Internet

On Friday April 2, 1999 at 09.00 CET, court officials together with uniformed and plain clothes policemen delivered to Radio B92's Director—Sasa Mirkovic—an order from the court announcing his dismissal as the station's Director. The decision was taken by the government-controlled Council of Youth, the founder of B92. The Council replaced Mr. Mirkovic with Mr. Aleksander Nikacevic. The police then sealed off the studio and offices of B92, banning the station from broadcasting. Shortly thereafter, the station's new director—Mr. Nikacevic—issued an order in the presence of inspectors to all B92 staff to show up for work on Monday April, 5. ▬ Am Freitag, den 2. April 1999, um 9.00 MEZ überbrachten Gerichtsdiener in Begleitung uniformierter und ziviler Polizisten Sasa Mirkovic, dem Leiter von Radio B92, eine gerichtliche Verfügung, kraft der er als Leiter der Station abgelöst wurde. Diese Entscheidung wurde von dem von der Regierung kontrollierten Jugendrat getroffen, der B92 gegründet hatte. Der Rat ersetzte Sasa Mirkovic durch Aleksander Nikacevic. Dann versiegelte die Polizei das Studio und die Büros von B92 und verhinderte damit weitere Sendungen. Kurz danach gab der neue Leiter in Anwesenheit von Inspektoren allen Mitarbeitern von B92 die Anweisung, am Montag, den 5. April zum Dienst

THE LAIR OF THE MARROW MONKEY

Eric Loyer

The Lair of the Marrow Monkey is an interactive investigation into the seductive power of digital technology. The website's main focus falls on a single character who goes by the name of Orion17. Orion is a minimalist composer who is fascinated to the point of obsession with the patterns and logic that frame reality. "I would leave all this in a moment if I could be the marrow, the idea, the virus, the entry whose self is not corporeal," he explains. When a powerful vision shows him the way to archieve his dream of uniting with the world of abstraction, Orion makes the leap and joins a small team of researchers at the newly-founded Institute of Investigation into the Mind of Marrow. There, he experiences first-hand both the euphoria and the frustration that comes from living life as a "marrow monkey."

This project grew out of a realization that the severe limitations of the Internet could actually have a positive effect on my creative work in digital media by forcing me to take a fragmented approach to the design. The expansive storage capacity and (relatively) high data transfer rates of CD-ROM had influenced me in the past to conceive highly centralized, sprawling pieces. My experience in game design, however, had made me familiar with the dangers of this type of approach, most damaging of which is the temptation to lock the features and design elements for the sake of steamlining the development process, but which actually hamper creativity in the long run. Doing a piece for the Internet meant that I could experiment with many different approaches on a much more practical scale.

The site consists of nine scenes, each of which functions much like an aria in the opera, a "frozen moment" during which a character's current situation and concerns can be revealed in detail. Many scenes require active participation on the part of the user in constructing or exploring the meaning being conveyed. Users are encouraged to make use of the interface for these scenes to enact the relationship between the ideas, events and characters being presented as part of the narrative. The visceral and dynamic nature of the interactions help to make these relationships tactile and interesting for users, allowing them to experience Orion17's obsessions from the inside out.

The Lair of the Marrow Monkey ist eine interaktive Untersuchung der verführerischen Kraft der digitalen Technologie. Der Schwerpunkt der Website liegt auf einem einzelnen Charakter, der Orion17 heißt. Orion ist ein minimalistischer Komponist, der bis zur Besessenheit von den Strukturen und der Logik fasziniert ist, die das Leben bestimmen. „Ich würde all dies augenblicklich aufgeben, wenn ich das Mark, den Sukkus, die Idee, das Virus sein könnte, jene Einheit, deren Selbst nicht körperlich ist", erklärt er. Als ihm eine machtvolle Vision den Weg zeigt, wie er sich mit der Welt der Abstraktion vereinigen kann, macht Orion den Sprung und schließt sich einem kleinen Team von Forschern am neugegründeten Institut für die Erforschung des Geistesmarks an. Dort erfährt er aus erster Hand die Euphorie und die Frustration, die aus einem Leben als „Affe des Marks" erwachsen.

Das Projekt entstand aus der Erkenntnis heraus, daß die schweren Einschränkungen des Internet in der Tat einen positiven Effekt auf meine Arbeit mit den kreativen Medien haben, weil sie mich zwingen, einen stückweisen Zugang zum Design zu finden. Die große Speicherkapazität und die relativ hohen Datentransferraten der CD-ROMs hatten mich in der Vergangenheit dazu verleitet, stark zentralisierte, breitgefächerte Projekte zu entwickeln. Meine Erfahrung im Spiele-Design hat mich jedoch mit den Gefahren dieses Ansatzes vertraut gemacht, von denen wohl die größte darin liegt, Ausstattungsdetails und Designelemente fest einzubauen, weil dies den Entwicklungsvorgang glatter ablaufen läßt, was allerdings auf lange Sicht die Kreativität behindert. Ein Werk für das Internet zu bauen, bedeutet für mich, mit zahlreichen unterschiedlichen Ansätzen zu experimentieren, und das auf einer wesentlich praxisbezogeneren Ebene.

Die Site besteht aus neun Szenen, von denen jede wie eine Opernarie funktioniert, als „eingefrorener Augenblick", in dem die jeweilige Situation und die jeweiligen Anliegen einer Figur im Detail dargestellt werden können. Viele der Szenen verlangen nach einer aktiven Mitwirkung des Benutzers, sei es bei der Konstruktion oder der Untersuchung des vermittelten Sinns. Die User werden eingeladen, das Interface zu benutzen, um die Beziehung zwischen den Gedanken, den Ereignissen und den Figuren dieser Szenen zu untersuchen, die als Teil der Erzählung vorgestellt werden. Die gefühlsbetonte und dynamische Natur der Interaktion hilft dabei, diese Beziehungen faßlich und für die Benutzer interessant zu gestalten, und erlaubt ihnen, die Obsessionen von Orion17 von innen her zu erleben.

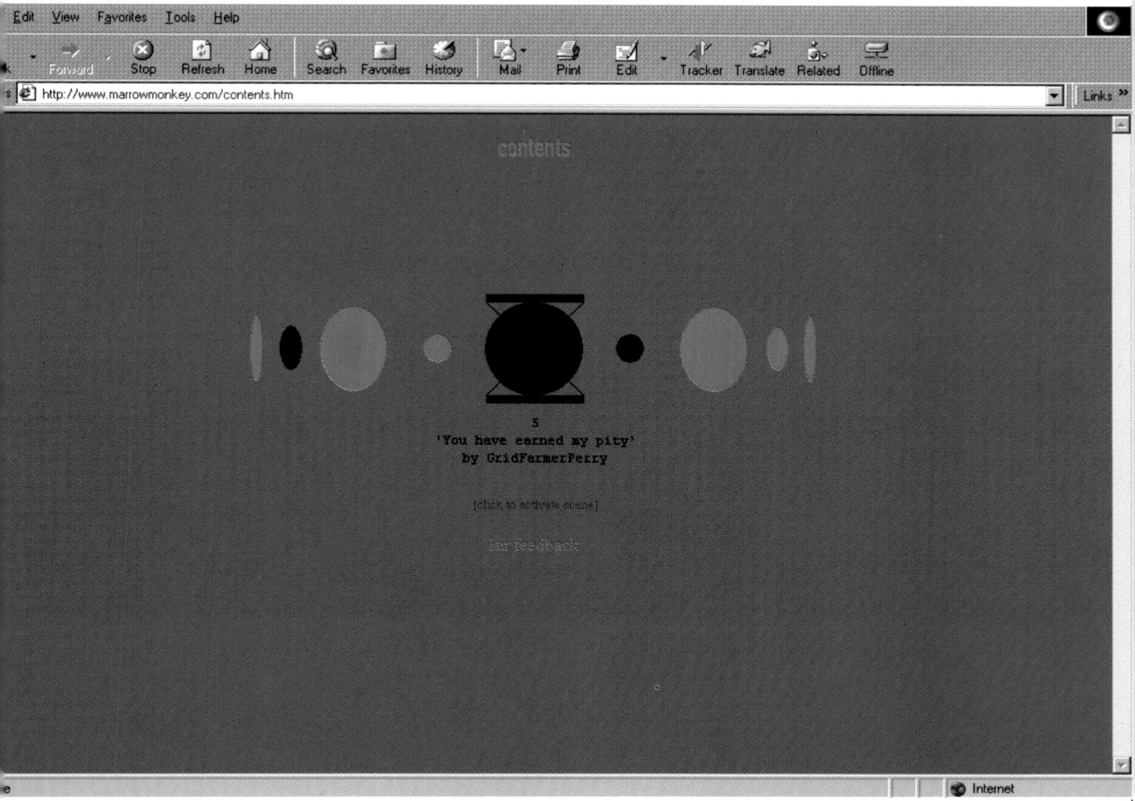

PRIX ARS ELECTRONICA 99 Honorary Mention

Edit View Favorites Tools Help

Forward Stop Refresh Home Search Favorites History Mail Print Edit Tracker Translate Related Offline

http://www.marrowmonkey.com/contents.htm

contents

5
'You have earned my pity'
by GridFarmerPerry

[click to activate scene]

lair feedback

Internet

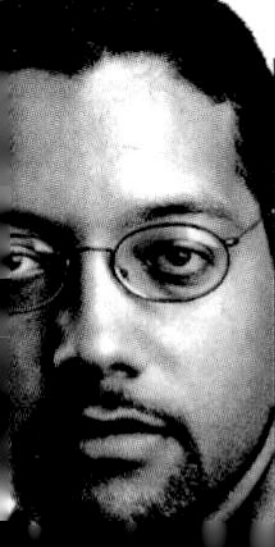

Erik Loyer is an award-winning digital media artist and creative director for the Los Angeles office of Razorfish, Inc. He has a strong body of experimental, non-commercial new media work that explores the creative potential unleashed by the advent of digital communications. Beginning his professional career in 1992 as an intern for pioneering digital developer The Voyager Company, Erik subsequently joined a group of Voyager alumni in founding Inscape, a developer of innovative CD-ROM games. He holds a Bachelor of Arts in Production from the School of Cinema/Television at the University of Southern California.

Eric Loyer (USA), Kreativdirektor bei Razorfish, Los Angeles, hat zahlreiche Preise im Bereich digitale Medien gewonnen. Seine zahlreichen nicht-kommerziellen Arbeiten in diesem Bereich versuchen das kreative Potential der digitalen Kommunikation auszuloten. Nachem er seine Berufskarriere 1992 als Mitarbeiter von The Voyager Company, einem Pionier der digitalen Entwicklung, begonnen hatte, gründete er mit anderen Voyager-Absolventen Inscape zur Entwicklung innovativer CD-ROM-Spiele. Eric Loyer erwarb seinen Bachelor of Arts an der School of Cinema/Television der University of

REaCT

Daniel Julià Lundgren

The main goal of *REaCT* is to provoke the *REaCTion* of the viewers and listeners, letting them participate.
REaCT stands for *REaCTion*, because I tried to make it highly interactive, and RECT, which is the only graphic structure that appears in the experience.
I used rectangles because this is the simplest graphical structure that can be managed by a computer, and I wanted in some way to minimize the graphic design. For the same reason I have used only black and white images, leading to the maximum graphic simplicity I could achieve.
For the interactive aspects I tried to reinforce the speed, movement, trajectories and behavioural movements of the objects.
REaCT is a collection of experiments that I have done, and I'm still doing, over the last months, linked together in order to give some sort of narrative, letting the user explore and experiment with the *REaCTion* in the populations of the mouse moving or clicking. This is why it may, in some ways, be considered as a game.
Following an explanatory introduction, the piece is a series of different 800x600 screens inhabited by rectangles of different sizes and proportions, always forming some type of organisation, *REaCTive* to the user input.
There are five phases triggered by time. In the first phase it is the keyboard input which organises the rects on the screen following what you type. In addition, the mouse moves the rectangles as through they were floating on water. In the second phase there are only two rectangles, but they seem to be linked with a gum, bouncing all the way. In the third one, there is a chaotic structure where the stiller the mouse is, the more chaotic the result. The fourth works as a galactic aspirator, and the last one is a huge panoramic of squares. But the most important aspect here is that people must experience by themselves, and interpret what are they playing and/or looking at.

Hauptziel von *REaCT* ist es, Reaktionen der Betrachter und Hörer zu provozieren und sie mitwirken zu lassen.
REaCT steht für *REACTion* – also Reaktion –, weil ich mich bemüht habe, das Werk so interaktiv wie möglich zu gestalten, es steht aber auch für *RECTangle* – Rechteck–, also für die einzige grafische Struktur, die im Werk vorkommt.
Ich habe deswegen Rechtecke verwendet, weil sie das einfachste grafische Element sind, mit dem der Computer umgehen kann, und ich das grafische Design minimieren wollte. Aus dem gleichen Grund habe ich es bei Schwarzweiß-Bildern belassen, was ein Maximum an visueller Klarheit und Einfachheit garantiert.
Was die interaktiven Aspekte betrifft, so habe ich hingegen versucht, Geschwindigkeit, Bewegungen, Flugbahnen und Bewegungsverhalten der Objekte zu verstärken.
REaCT ist eine Sammlung von Experimenten, die ich seit mehreren Monaten ausführe und zu einer Art Erzählung zusammengehängt habe, die den Benutzer die Reaktion der Rechteck-Populationen, die sich durch die Mausbewegungen und Mausklicks ergeben, erforschen läßt. Deswegen kann es auch als eine Art Spiel angesehen werden.
Nach einer erklärenden Einführung bietet sich eine Serie von 800x600-Bildschirmen dar, die von Rechtecken unterschiedlicher Größe und Proportion „bewohnt" sind und sich ständig – als Reaktion auf den Input des Benutzers – in irgendeiner Weise organisieren.
Über den Parameter Zeit werden fünf Phasen ausgelöst. In der ersten Phase organisiert der Tastatur-Input, d. h. das, was man eintippt, die Rechtecke. Außerdem werden die Rechtecke durch die Mausbewegungen bewegt, als würden sie wie Blätter im Wasser treiben. In der zweiten Phase gibt es nur zwei Rechtecke, aber sie scheinen über eine Gummimasse verbunden zu sein, denn sie springen ständig zurück. Darauf folgt eine chaotische Struktur, die um so chaotischer ist, je ruhiger die Maus bleibt. In der vierten Phase scheint ein galaktischer Staubsauger am Werk zu sein, und die letzte bietet ein riesiges Panorama von Vierecken. Aber das Wichtigste ist, daß die Erfahrung und ihre Interpretation immer dem Spieler bzw. Betrachter vorbehalten bleibt.
Auch die Musik ist wichtig, sie hilft, das Ambiente dieser „rechteckigen Welt" zu schaffen. Alle Musik- und Klangeffekte wurden mit der von Sergi Jordà entwickelten FMOL-Software geschaffen (*http://www.iua.upf.es/~sergi/FMOL/Project_Description.htm*). Diese Musik paßt hervorragend zu diesem Werk, weil sie synthetisch ist, so wie Rechtecke eine synthetische Form haben.
Die gesamte Programmierung erfolgte mit lingo (Shockwave) und geht mit den Ressourcen recht sparsam um – der Großteil der heruntergeladenen Daten betrifft Klang und Musik, der Rest des ganzen Stücks beläuft sich auf gerade 20 kB.

Idea and programming: ***Daniel Julià Lundgren***

Music and sound software: Sergi Jordà

Thanks to: Maite Fez, Cristina Casanova, Sergi Jordà, Roc Parés, Iñigo Aramburu. IUA~Barcelona~1999

REaCT

(shockwave required)

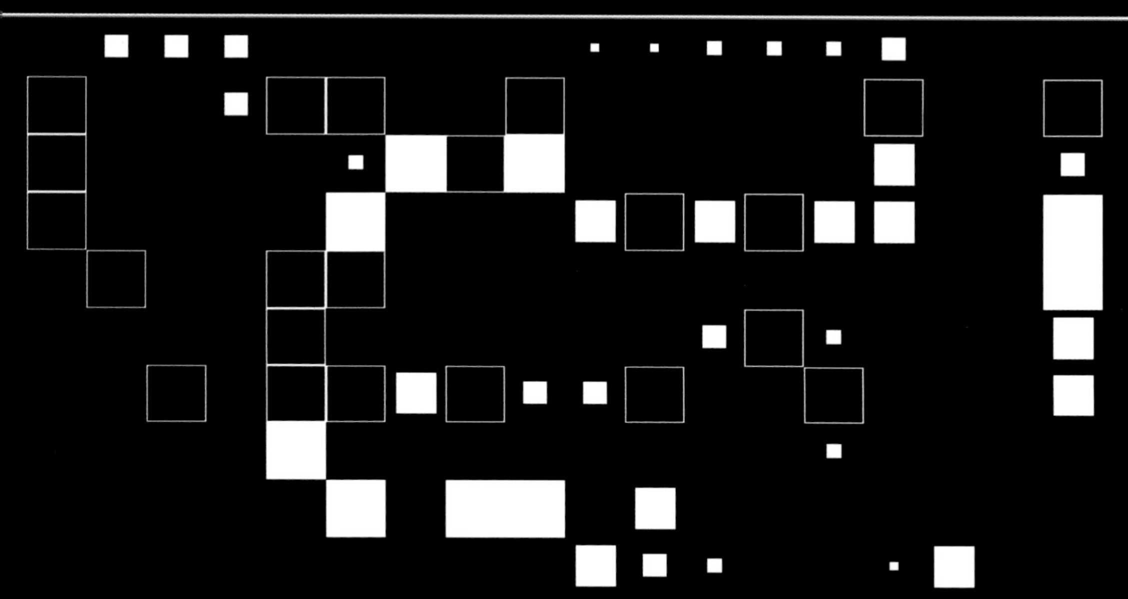

'he music is very important, and helps to create the mbient of the "rectangle world"; all the music and he sound effects are created with the FMOL softvare (http://www.iua.upf.es/~sergi/FMOL/Project_Description.htm), created by Sergi Jordà. It is specially suitable in this case, because it's a very ynthetic music, the same way as rectangles are very ynthetic forms.

ll the programming is done with lingo (Shockwave), ising a very small amount of resources: the amount of bytes downloaded are mainly sound and music, he rest is only about 20 Kb for the whole story.

Credits:
Idea and programming:
Daniel Julià Lundgren
www.iua.upf.es/~dani
Music and sound software: Sergi Jordà
Thanks to:
Maite Fez
Cristina Casanova
Sergi Jordà
Antoni Abad
Roc Parés
Iñigo Aramburu

Daniel Julià Lundgren (E) graduated in Telecommunication Engineering in 1993 from the Universitat Politecnica de Catalunya. Expert in interactive systems programming since 1993. From 1994 to 1995 he worked in the R&D department of a multinational company developing object oriented interfaces for medical care management. He joined the Multimedia Lab of the IUA (Universitat Pompeu Fabra) in late 1995, where he has worked as technical supervisor and programmer in several productions. His teaching responsibilities in the Master of Digital Arts (IUA) are focused on programming and multimedia production. He has taught in other masters programs in the area of new technologies. He is preparing his PhD in Audiovisual Communication (UPF) in the field of new technologies. ▬ Daniel Julià Lundgren (E) graduierte 1993 als Telekommunikationsingenieur an der Universitat Politecnica de Catalunya. Seit 1993 Experte für die Programmierung interaktiver Systeme. 1994-1995 Mitarbeiter in der Forschungs- und Entwicklungsabteilung eines internationalen Konzerns, wo er objektorientierte Interfaces für medizinische Anwendungen entwickelt. Seit Ende 1995 Mitarbeiter des Multimedia Lab der IUA (Universität Pompeu Fabra), wo er als technischer Leiter und Programmierer an zahlreichen Produktionen mitgewirkt hat. Lehrtätigkeit in der Meisterklasse für digitale Kunst (IUA) mit Schwerpunkt Programmierung und Multimediaproduktion sowie Neue Technologien. Derzeit schreibt er an seiner Dissertation in audiovisueller Kommunikation der Neuen Technologien an der

GINGA

Fumio Matsumoto/Shoei Matsukawa

"This book is a dream of other books."
Michel Foucault

Concept

Spatial representation of information is proposed in the *Ginga* project, Global Information Network as Genomorphic Architecture, where metamorphic relationships in cyberspace are manifest in the form of an "Information-Scape". *Ginga* is an interactive 3D browsing system based on a huge collection of digital information. Web resources are reconfigured with cyberspatial codes into *Ginga* and appear as any of the following 9 main Worlds: Nebula, Ring, Network, Forest, Strata, Text, Image, Polyphony, and Cemetery. Users can explore these Worlds with avatars (incarnations) which are personalized and controlled by users' preferences. Users are expected to take full advantage of their "multiple other selves" for profound investigation and/or extensive research. It is also possible to exchange information with the avatars of other users and even invite them into your personal archives. *Ginga* has no static form, it can exists anywhere extended selves communicate.

Single User Model

Your computer will need viewing software to access the *Ginga* system and research its vast information-scape. The individual interface consists of three major functions: an editor, avatars and your personal archives. As you enter your research subjects into the editor's dialogue box, a number of avatars will simultaneously begin to investigate the Worlds of *Ginga*. Your editor will classify the results and save what you need to your personal archives.

Multi User Model

The *Ginga* library is an electronic field where you can access officially published data as well as individually published information. Users can open their personal archives of "meta-data" to other users as an extension of *Ginga*. Your avatar may carry your personal information and a list of your personal archives and "exload" these to the avatars of other users. The functional boundary of *Ginga* can be extended as the cooperation of users increases.

„Dieses Buch ist ein Traum von anderen Büchern."
Michel Foucault

Konzept

Das *Ginga*-Projekt – Global Information Network as Genomorphic Architecture – beschäftigt sich mit der räumlichen Darstellung von Informationen, wobei metamorphische Beziehungen im Cyberspace in Form einer „Informationslandschaft" dargestellt werden. *Ginga* ist ein interaktives 3D-Browsing-System, das auf einer riesigen Sammlung digitaler Informationen basiert. Die Web-Ressourcen werden über Cyberspace-Codierungen nach *Ginga* konfiguriert und erscheinen als eine der folgenden neun Hauptwelten: Nebel, Ring, Netzwerk, Wald, Schichten, Text, Bild, Polyphonie und Friedhof. Die Benutzer können diese Welten mit Hilfe von Avataren erforschen, die nach den persönlichen Vorlieben der Anwender konfigurier- und steuerbar sind. Von den Benutzern wird erwartet, daß sie ihre multiplen anderen Ichs intensiv einsetzen, um tiefgreifende Untersuchungen oder ausgedehnte Sucharbeiten durchzuführen. Es ist auch möglich, Informationen mit den Avataren anderer User auszutauschen, ja, selbst diese in die eigenen Archive einzuladen. *Ginga* hat keine statische Form, sondern kann überall existieren, wo „erweiterte Ichs" kommunizieren.

Single-User-Modell

Ihr Computer benötigt eine Viewer-Software, um auf das *Ginga*-System zugreifen und seine große Informationslandschaft erforschen zu können. Das individuelle Interface besteht aus drei Hauptfunktionen: einem Editor, mehreren Avataren und den persönlichen Archiven. Wenn man Suchziele in die Dialogbox des Editors eingibt, beginnt gleichzeitig eine gewisse Anzahl von Avataren mit der Erforschung der Welten von *Ginga*. Der Editor klassifiziert die Ergebnisse und speichert das Gefundene im persönlichen Archiv.

Multi-User-Modell

Die *Ginga*-Bibliothek ist ein elektronisches Feld, das einen Zugang zu öffentlich publizierten Daten ebenso wie zu individuell zugänglicher Information ermöglicht.
Die Benützer können ihrer persönlichen „Meta-Daten"-Archive für andere Anwender öffnen, sozusagen als eine Erweiterung von *Ginga*. Ihr Avatar kann Ihre persönlichen Informationen und eine Liste Ihrer persönlichen Archive zu anderen Benutzern tragen und dort sozusagen „auslagern". Die funktionalen Grenzen von *Ginga* erweitern sich in dem Maß, in dem die Mitarbeit der User steigt.

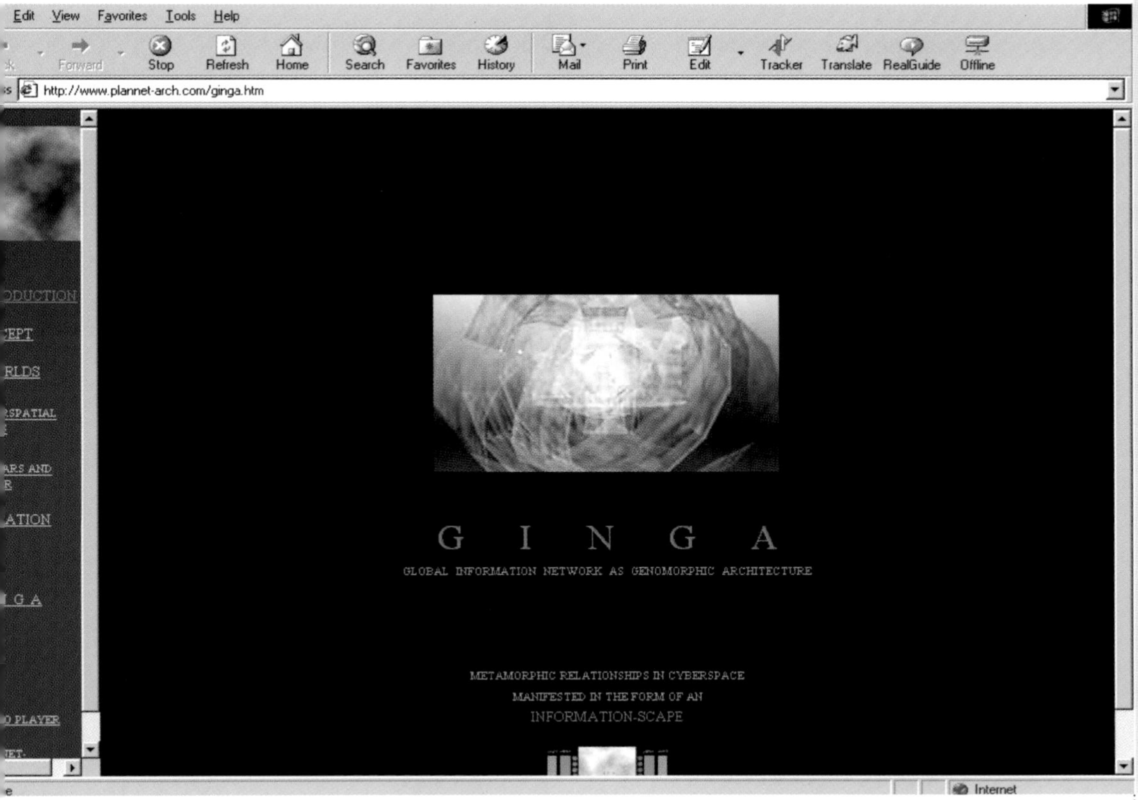

FUMIO MATSUMOTO (J), BORN 1959, COMPLETED A DEGREE IN ARCHITECTURE AT THE WASEDA UNIVERSITY IN TOKYO AND HAS WORKED SINCE THEN FOR MAJOR ARCHITECTURAL FIRMS IN TOKYO. HIS WORK HAS BEEN DISTINGUISHED IN SEVERAL ARCHITECTURE COMPETITIONS IN JAPAN AND THE USA. SHOEI MATSUKAWA (J), BORN 1974, STUDIED ARCHITECTURE AT THE UNIVERSITY OF TOKYO.

Fumio Matsumoto (J), geb. 1959, schloß 1986 sein Architekturstudium an der Waseda University in Tokio ab und arbeitet seither bei großen Architekturbüros in Tokio. Seine Arbeiten wurden bei mehreren Architekturwettbewerben in Japan und den USA ausgezeichnet. Shoei Matsukawa (J), geb. 1974, hat Architektur an der Universität Tokio studiert.

THE SHREDDER

Mark Napier

The Shredder dematerializes the web. Posing as a browser, it prompts the user for a URL, then appropriates that web page to use as a raw material for its own fragmented output. It exposes the frailty of a medium that relies on software instructions to create the appearance of a consistent environment. A voracious public artwork, *The Shredder* feeds on the web to propagate its own aesthetic agenda.
This project is about the web as an art medium. This is an object-less medium, yet much of the technology of the web works to re-create the familiar, to create a consistent look and feel, to create a sense of place, of location. We "navigate" through the web. Art on the web often exists as an object in the environment of the web—a specific website, clearly defined and bounded within a larger space.
The Shredder dematerializes art, not just because it is digital art with no physical component, but because the Shredder is an activity, not a thing. It is something you do to something else. It is non-localized, non-deterministic—a roaming, mobile artwork. In itself it is content-less, opening with a blank screen. By participating in the interface, the visitor creates and completes the artwork.
By shredding that which is not material, *The Shredder* applies a familiar "real world" action to a medium that breaks with the familiar. The resulting collision of sensibilities reveals the frailty of the world of web pages, in which content is a fragment of the browser software's "rendering engine", and can be radically altered simply by adjusting a few rules. This is where the human inhabitants of the net meet the digital interface, and attempt to re-create the familiar and comfortable nuances of the physical world. *The Shredder* inserts itself into its medium, like a drug altering the functioning of nervous synapses, and transforms the signals that pass through it to create a hallucinatory world—a web that is parallel to the "true" web, yet is every bit as real.
The Shredder appropriates design, graphics, and text as an input for its own aesthetic algorithm. It repurposes other people's aesthetic algorithm. It repurposes other people's aesthetic statements, and communications. A machine-driven aesthetic, the shredder parses HTML into a raw form, analyzes the structure and attributes of the incoming page, then

The Shredder dematerialisiert das Web. Als Browser getarnt fordert er den User auf, eine URL einzugeben, und eignet sich die zugehörige Website als Rohmaterial für seinen eigenen fragmentierten Output an. Auf diese Weise legt er die Empfindlichkeit eines Mediums dar, das auf Software-Anweisungen zur Schaffung eines scheinbar konsistenten Environments beruht. Als gefräßiges öffentliches Kunstwerk ernährt sich der *Shredder* vom Web, um seine eigenen ästhetischen Anliegen zu propagieren.
Das Projekt untersucht das Web als Kunstmedium. Dieses Medium ist als solches objektlos, und dennoch arbeitet viel der dahinterliegenden Technologie daran, das Vertraute nachzubilden, ein konsistentes „Look-and-Feel" zu erzeugen, ein Raum- und Ortsgefühl zu vermitteln. Wir „navigieren" durch das Web. Kunst im Web existiert häufig als ein Objekt innerhalb der Umgebung des Web – als spezifische Website, klar definiert und begrenzt innerhalb eines größeren Raumes.
Der *Shredder* dematerialisiert die Kunst, nicht nur weil er ein digitales Werk ohne physische Komponente ist, sondern weil der *Shredder* eine Aktivität ist, kein Ding. Er ist das, was man jemand anderem antut. Er ist nicht lokalisierbar, nicht deterministisch – ein umherstreifendes, mobiles Kunstwerk. In sich selbst ist er inhaltslos und präsentiert sich mit einem leeren Bildschirm. Erst durch seine Mitwirkung schafft und vervollständigt der Benutzer das Kunstwerk.
Indem er shreddert, was nicht materiell ist, wendet der *Shredder* eine bekannte Aktion aus der „realen" Welt auf ein Medium an, das mit dem Bekannten bricht. Die sich ergebende Kollision der Gefühle legt die Zerbrechlichkeit der Welt der Webseiten dar, in denen Inhalt nur eine Fiktion der Rendering Engine des Browsers ist, eine Fiktion, die durch einfache Änderung nur weniger Regeln radikal verändert werden kann. Hier treffen die menschlichen Bewohner des Net auf das digitale Interface, hier versuchen sie, die bequemen und vertrauten Nuancen der physischen Welt nachzubauen. Der *Shredder* drängt sich in dieses Medium hinein wie eine Droge, die die Funktion der Synapsen behindert, und transformiert die durch ihn hindurchgehenden Signale, um eine halluzinatorische Welt zu schaffen – ein Web, das parallel zum echten Web läuft und doch genauso real ist wie jenes.
Der *Shredder* eignet sich das Design, Grafiken und Texte als Input für seine eigenen ästhetischen Algorithmen an. Er führt eine „Umwidmung" der ästhetischen Aussagen und der kommunikativen Mitteilungen anderer durch. Als maschinengesteuerte Ästhetik untersucht der *Shredder* die Rohdaten des einkommenden HTML, analysiert es auf Struktur und Attribute hin und wendet eine Serie von Regeln auf die Rohdaten an, um eine Seite als Output zu liefern, die trotz allem völlig funktional ist:

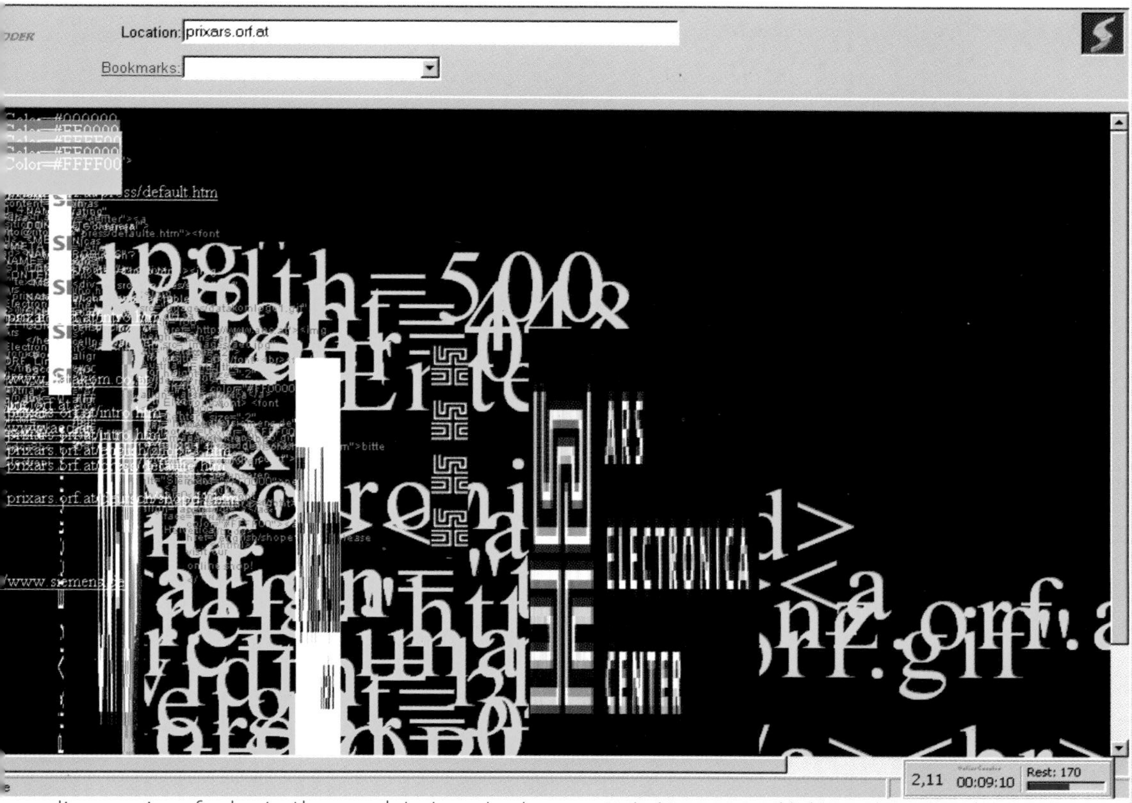

applies a series of rules to the raw data to output a page that is re-engineered yet fully functional: links can be clicked to navigate indefinitely through the shredded web.
Written in Perl and Javascript, *The Shredder* is not a browser, it is a filter (a CGI script) accessed through a webpage that mimics the browser interface. It's purpose is not to replace the browser, but to reinvent it from the inside. It is important that the project be technically accessible, public in the technical sense. There are no plug-ins required, nothing to download, and *The Shredder* works in both Netscape and Microsoft Internet Explorer. Anyone with a browser can shred the web.

Links können angeklickt werden, um unbegrenzt durch das geshredderte Web zu browsen …
Der in Perl und Javascript geschriebene *Shredder* ist kein Browser, sondern ein Filter (ein CGI-Script), der über eine Webseite angesprochen wird, die ein Browser-Interface imitiert. Sein Zweck ist nicht, den Browser zu ersetzen, sondern ihn von innen heraus neu zu erfinden. Wichtig ist, daß das Projekt frei zugänglich ist, es ist öffentlich im technischen Sinne. Es werden keine Plug-Ins benötigt, es gibt nichts herunterzuladen, und der *Shredder* arbeitet mit Internet-Explorer ebenso wie mit Netscape. Wer einen Browser hat, kann das Web shreddern.

Mark Napier (USA)—an ex-painter (BFA from Syracuse University in 1984)—turned digital artist in 95)—creator of *Digital Landfill* (ASCI Digital Art Show 98), *The Distorted Barbie* (nearly sued by Mattel), *POTATOLAND.org* (called "the best thing since french fries")—lives in New York city—has a day job (software developer in the finance industry)—artwork included in: TransMediale Festival 96 & 98, numerous publications (including *Publish* and *Yahoo Internet Life*), Altoids.com, and at least one independent film.

Mark Napier (USA) ist ein ehemaliger Maler (BFA an der Syracuse University 1984), der 1985 digitaler Künstler wurde. Schöpfer von *Digital Landfill* (ASCI Digital Art Show 98), von *The Distorted Barbie* (deswegen beinahe von Mattel verklagt), von *POTATOLAND.org* („Das beste seit der Erfindung der Pommes Frites"). Lebt in New York City, hat einen Brotberuf (Softwareentwickler in der Finanzindustrie). Seine Arbeiten wurden präsentiert im TransMediale Festival 96 und 98, in zahlreichen Publikationen (darunter *Publish* und *Yahoo Internet Life*), Altoids.com; mindestens ein unabhängiger Film.

NOWHERE.COM

Nick Philip

This mysterious Internet domain appears as the return address on hundreds of thousands of pieces of electronic junk mail, or "spam," that fill our "in" boxes daily. As it also pops up as a default setting in numerous Internet software applications, nowhere.com's traffic has grown to thousands of pieces of mail a day, often as much as 2000 return messages a minute. Over the years, lack of supervision of the domain has encouraged widespread abuse. So much so, the FBI has investigated abusers of the domain. But the domain itself remains a mystery. Where is nowhere.com?

Artist Nick Philip directs you to a row of garbage cans placed below twelve whirring fax machines at Tokyo's Intercommunications Center. The domain nowhere.com, he explains, is often used as a return address by shady Internet spammers to disguise their actual Internet location. Irritated recipients reply to the spam, but because of the false return address the replies are returned to nowhere.com instead of back to the spammers. That is, until Philip directed all emails addressed to nowhere.com to a series of fax machines at the ICC. Now the piles of lost missives are redirected into a physical representation of their final digital destination—the trash can.

"Confronted with 57,000 feet of thermal garbage, *Nowhere* instantly lets you experience, touch, hear and smell a small part of this incredibly vast media landscape, at the same time making a tongue in cheek note to the fact that the more things change the more they stay the same," Philip says.

"Despite all the hopes and hype for a shiny, blue-sky highway of empowerment, the Internet and technology in general are but humble expressions of ourselves that include the good, the bad, and the ugly," Philip says. "Perhaps what's most interesting about *Nowhere* is not that it's a networked anomaly, but rather an insightful glimpse into the darker recesses of our online psychology."

Emails are copied as they pass through nowhere.com on to their final destination. They are distributed through 12 fax modems and then printed by 12 fax machines. Thermal paper is collected to trash cans, then allowed to overflow onto the gallery floor.

Die mysteriöse Internet-Domain *nowhere.com* („nirgendwo.com") erscheint häufig als Absender oder Rücksendeadresse auf hunderttausenden elektronischen Poststücken – „Junk Mail" oder „Spam" genannt –, die täglich unsere Posteingangskörbe anfüllen. Und weil sie auch als Standardeinstellung bei zahlreichen Internetanwendungen auftritt, ist der Postverkehr an *nowhere.com* auf Tausende von Poststücken täglich angewachsen – oftmals langen 2000 Nachrichten pro Minute ein. Im Laufe der Jahre hat fehlende Überwachung zu einem derart weitverbreiteten Mißbrauch dieser Adresse geführt, daß sogar das FBI Untersuchungen über die größten Anwender dieser Adresse eingeleitet hat. Aber die Domain selbst bleibt ein Rätsel: Wo ist *nowhere.com*?

Der Künstler Nick Philip führt Sie zu einer Reihe von Papierkörben, die zwischen zwölf sirrenden Faxgeräten im Tokioter Intercommunications Centre stehen. Die Domain *nowhere.com*, so erklärt er, wird häufig von dubiosen E-Mail-Versendern als Tarnung für ihre eigentliche Internetadresse verwendet. Irritierte Empfänger von Junk-Mail senden ihre Antworten häufig an diese Adresse, aber wegen der falschen Absenderangabe werden sie an *nowhere.com* anstatt zu den wahren Absendern umgeleitet. Zumindest so lange, bis Philip alle an *nowhere.com* adressierten E-Mails auf eine Reihe von Faxgeräten im ICC geschaltet hat. Jetzt werden die Stapel der verlorenen Sendungen in eine physische Repräsentation ihrer letztlichen Destination umgewandelt – den Papierkorb.

„Mit 12 Kilometern Thermopapier-Abfall konfrontiert, können Sie bei *Nowhere* sofort einen kleinen Teil dieser unglaublich großen weiten Medienlandschaft erfahren, spüren, hören, angreifen, riechen und gleichzeitig mit einem Augenzwinkern feststellen, daß die Dinge ganz gleich bleiben, selbst wenn sie sich radikal ändern", sagt Philip.

„Auch wenn wir uns einen ewig blauen Himmel über den Datenautobahnen der modernen Kommunikation ersehnen, sind das Internet und die Technologie allgemein nichts anderes als bescheidene Ausdrucksweisen unser selbst, mit all dem Guten, dem Schlechten und dem Häßlichen", sagt Philip. „Am interessantesten an *Nowhere* ist, daß es nicht so sehr eine Art ‚vernetzter Anomalie' darstellt, sondern einen kleinen, aber tiefen Einblick in die dunkleren Nischen unserer Online-Psychologie erlaubt."

Die E-Mails werden kopiert, wenn sie durch *nowhere.com* zu ihrer endgültigen Destination laufen und über zwölf Faxmodems auf zwölf Faxgeräte umgeleitet. Das Thermopapier der Faxgeräte wird in Papierkörben gesammelt und läuft letztlich irgendwann über auf den Boden der Galerie. *Das Werk wurde erstmals vom 15. bis zum 27. September 1998 im NTT Inter Communications Center, Tokio, gezeigt. Besonderer Dank gebührt Husanori Gogota und Lisa Seaman.*

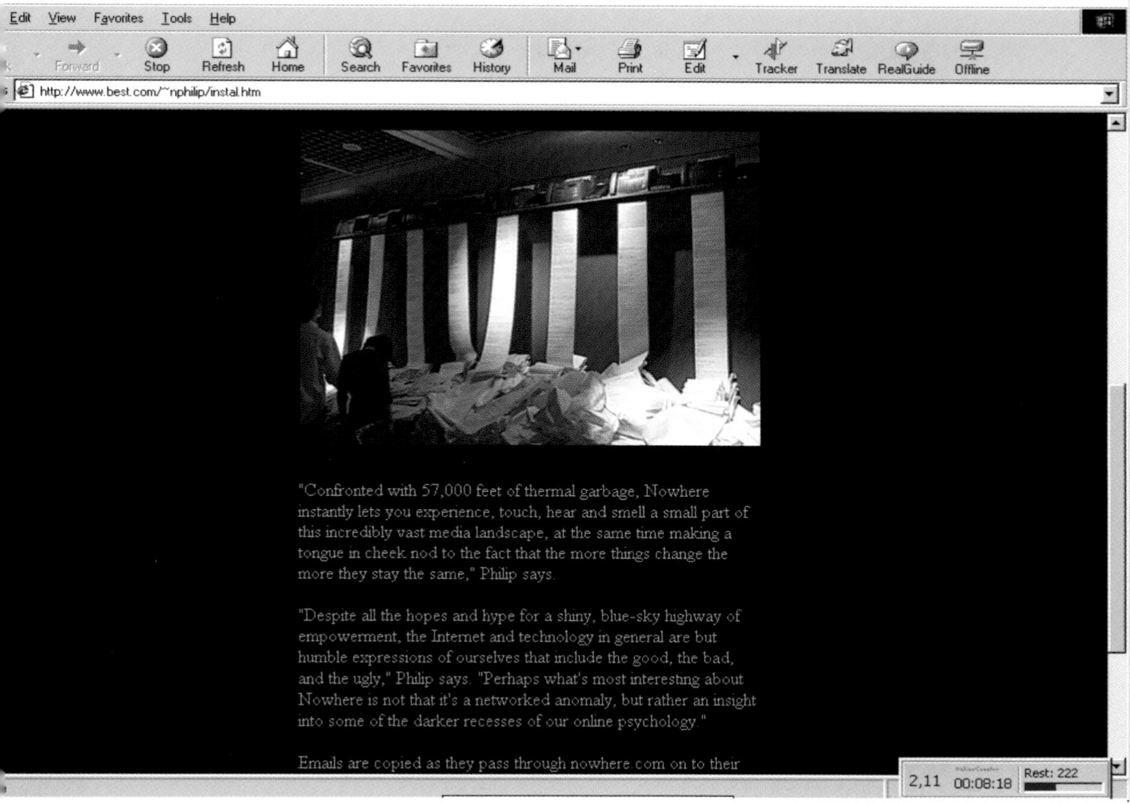

Edit View Favorites Tools Help
Forward Stop Refresh Home Search Favorites History Mail Print Edit Tracker Translate RealGuide Offline
http://www.best.com/~nphilip/instal.htm

"Confronted with 57,000 feet of thermal garbage, Nowhere instantly lets you experience, touch, hear and smell a small part of this incredibly vast media landscape, at the same time making a tongue in cheek nod to the fact that the more things change the more they stay the same," Philip says.

"Despite all the hopes and hype for a shiny, blue-sky highway of empowerment, the Internet and technology in general are but humble expressions of ourselves that include the good, the bad, and the ugly," Philip says. "Perhaps what's most interesting about Nowhere is not that it's a networked anomaly, but rather an insight into some of the darker recesses of our online psychology."

Emails are copied as they pass through nowhere.com on to their

2,11 00:08:18 Rest: 222

First shown at the NTT Inter Communications Center, Tokyo, Sept. 15th—27, 1998. Special thanks to Hishanori Gogota and Lisa Seaman. Concept: Nick Philip Programming: Nic Harteau Assisted by: Jeff Taylor

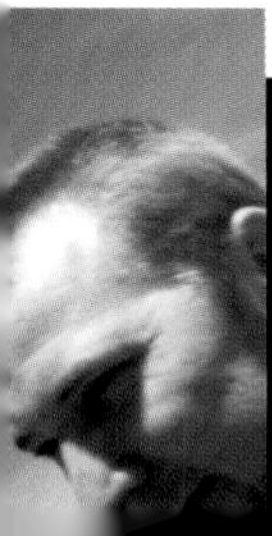

NICK PHILIP (GB), BORN 1968. HIS WORK BEGAN IN THE 1980S, AS A CUT-AND-PASTE GRAPHIC DESIGNER DEEP INTO THE LONDON SKATEBOARD SUBCULTURE. FORAYS INTO STREETWARE DESIGN LED PHILIP TO THE BAY AREA WHERE HE HELPED CREATE THE TECHNO-PSYCHEDELIC AESTHETIC THAT DEFINED THE RAVE SCENE. GRAPHIC DESIGN FOR LUMINARIES RANGING FROM TIMOTHY LEARY TO WIRED MAGAZINE FOLLOWED, ALONG WITH A NEW T-SHIRT LINE OF DIGITAL AGE ICONS AND MANTRAS. THAT GENRE OF SURREAL GRAPHIC ALCHEMY CULMINATED WITH HIS CRITICALLY-ACCLAIMED RADICAL BEAUTY CD-ROM, RELEASED IN 1998. Nick Philip (GB), geb. 1968, begann in den 80er Jahren als schnipselnder Gebrauchsgrafiker tief in der Londoner Skateboard-Subkultur. Ein Raubzug ins Streetware-Design brachte ihn in die Bay Area, wo er an der Schaffung jener techno-psychedelischen Ästhetik mitwirkte, die die Rave-Szene definiert. Es folgten Grafikentwürfe für Auftraggeber und Themen, die von Timothy Leary bis zum *Wired*-Magazin reichten sowie eine neue T-Shirt-Linie mit Ikonen und Mantras des digitalen Zeitalters. Das Genre der surrealen grafischen Alchemie kulminierte in seiner kritisch akkla-

THE HYPERBOLIC TREE

Ramana Rao / Inxight.com

The Hyperbolic Tree is a novel user interface component for interacting with very large hierarchies. The design of *The Hyperbolic Tree* rests on great skills we share as humans, like seeing "purple" or "big" or tracking moving objects, rather than on specialized knowledge or painfully acquired skills. It provides a powerful "see and go" interaction style that retains the simplicity of "point and click" interaction, while reducing mechanical and unnatural aspects.
The Hyperbolic Tree is based on four key design elements:

Graphical Representations

The Hyperbolic Tree maps large hierarchies of objects and their properties into graphical structures with easily perceived elements. By selecting relevant properties of the information and appropriate visual variables to map them, an application designer can enable users to see which objects are important efficiently, before going to and attending to them.

Focus + Context

The Hyperbolic Tree gives more space to a few nodes in the center (focus) while also providing space to many, many more nodes (context). Providing periphery (overview) and center (detail view) allows the user to intelligently shift attention. *The Hyperbolic Tree* manages the space automatically, expanding and shrinking space with the user's attention. Thus the user focuses on information itself, rather than mechanical controls like scrollbars, plus/minus controls, close buttons, and hierarchical menus.

Animated Transitions

Smoothly animating the tree allows the user to connect the before and the after. Transitions are designed to take under one second which is ideal for exploration tasks as suggested by the unprepared response time constant from cognitive psychology.

Spotlighting

The Hyperbolic Tree can prominently mark all objects using red diamonds that match a search (or any other kind of test). Thus a user can quickly see the results of a search in the context of the whole, thus understanding much more at a glance about the query, the collection, and the results.

The Hyperbolic Tree ist eine Komponente eines neuartigen User-Interface für die Interaktion mit sehr großen Hierarchien. Das Design von *The Hyperbolic Tree* beruht auf jenen großen Fähigkeiten, die allen Menschen gemeinsam ist, z. B. auf der Fähigkeit, „purpur" oder „groß" erkennen oder bewegte Objekte verfolgen zu können, und nicht auf spezialisierten Kenntnissen oder mühsam erworbenen Fähigkeiten. Es bietet eine leistungsstarke Interaktion vom Typ „Sehen und los!", die die Einfachheit des „Zeig-und-Klick"-Ansatzes erhält, dabei aber die mechanischen und unnatürlichen Aspekte reduziert.
The Hyperbolic Tree basiert auf vier grundlegenden Elementen:

Grafische Darstellung

The Hyperbolic Tree bildet große Hierarchien von Objekten und ihren Eigenschaften in grafischen Strukturen ab, deren Elemente leicht zu erfassen sind. Durch die gezielte Auswahl relevanter Informationen und geeigneter Abbildungsvariablen kann ein Anwendungsentwickler es den Benutzern ermöglichen, die wichtigsten Objekte auf einen Blick zu erfassen, bevor sie sie einzeln ansprechen.

Fokus und Kontext

The Hyperbolic Tree räumt einigen zentralen Knoten (den „Brennpunkten") mehr Raum ein, bietet aber auch sehr vielen zusätzlichen Knoten (dem „Kontext") ausreichend Platz. Durch die Einteilung in Peripherie (Überblick) und Zentrum (Detailansicht) kann der Benutzer seine Aufmerksamkeit intelligent nach Bedarf einsetzen. *The Hyperbolic Tree* verwaltet den Raum automatisch, indem es den Raum je nach dem Zentrum der Aufmerksamkeit des Benutzers verschiebt. So kann der Anwender sich auf die Inhalte statt auf mechanische Steuerelemente wie Schieberegler, Plus/minus-Knöpfe, Schalter und hierarchische Menüs konzentrieren.

Animierte Übergänge

Eine glatte Animation des Informationsbaums erlaubt es dem User, einen Konnex zwischen Vorher und Nachher herzustellen. Die Übergänge dauern weniger als eine Sekunde, was für Sucharbeiten ideal ist und der von der kognitiven Psychologie vorgeschlagenen Zeitkonstante für unerwartete Veränderungen entspricht.

Spotlights

The Hyperbolic Tree kann alle Elemente, die einem Suchkriterium (oder einem anderen Test) entsprechen, mit roten Karos deutlich markieren. So können Anwender das Ergebnis der Suche im Kontext des Ganzen schnell erfassen und auf einen Blick den Zusammenhang zwischen Suche, Sammlung und Ergebnissen verstehen.
Diese Designelemente ermöglichen gemeinsam

Information map created by Inxight Software using Hyperbolic Tree™ for Java.

These design elements combined provide a natural and free-flowing interaction with information. Because *The Hyperbolic Tree* rests on ingrained human skills, learning how to use it is as simple as watching a demo. And like other good tools, *The Hyperbolic Tree* becomes invisible and attention is focused on the task: it lets you attend to the nail, not the hammer.

eine natürliche und fließende Interaktion mit der Information. Da *The Hyperbolic Tree* auf den natürlichen Fähigkeiten des Menschen basiert, reicht es, eine Demo zu sehen, um damit umgehen zu können. Und wie andere gute Werkzeuge wird auch *The Hyperbolic Tree* unsichtbar, und die Aufmerksamkeit wird zurück auf die Aufgabe gelenkt. Man kann sich wieder dem Nagel widmen, nicht dem Hammer.

RAMANA RAO IS CHIEF TECHNOLOGY OFFICER AND DIRECTOR OF ENGINEERING AND A FOUNDER OF INXIGHT. HE IS THE PRIMARY DESIGNER OF *THE HYPERBOLIC TREE*, WHICH HE CO-INVENTED WITH JOHN LAMPING AT XEROX PARC, AND THE *TABLE LENS*. HIS WORK INCLUDES OVER 20 PATENT FILINGS AND OVER 20 PAPERS IN LEADING RESEARCH CONFERENCES AND JOURNALS. Ramana Rao ist Mitbegründer von Inxight, wo er als Chief Technology Officer und Chief of Engineering arbeitet. Er ist Hauptdesigner des *Hyperbolic Tree*, den er gemeinsam mit John Lamping am Xerox PARC entwickelt hat, und des Table Lens. Seine bisherigen Arbeiten umfassen mehr als 20 Patententwürfe und wohl ebensoviele wissenschaftliche

VERBARIUM

Christa Sommerer / Laurent Mignonneau

In 1999 we created an interactive web site for the Internet called *Verbarium*. This web sites allow users on the Internet to write text messages that are instantly transcoded into visual three-dimensional forms. Our custom designed text-to-form editor takes the letters, syntax and sequencing of a text message as genetic code and updates the design functions for the creation of three-dimensional forms according to the text message parameters. As the text messages of the different users on the Internet are usually unique and diverse, unique and personal three-dimensional visual forms and shapes can be created by the users.
According to Noam Chomsky, human language acquisition is based on a universal grammar that is genetically embedded within the human mind of all normal children, allowing them to learn their native languages naturally and seemingly effortlessly.
It was also Chomsky who coined the phrase "colorless green ideas sleep furiously", an expression that might not make much logical sense to a more scientifically oriented person, but does have quite a lot of meaning for a more visual or art minded person. Though this sentence, as Chomsky has shown, is grammatically correct, its meaning cannot be grasped through logic alone. When we hear this sentence for the first time we see pictures or forms or shapes appearing in our minds. These forms are vague, yet they are defined to a certain degree and can certainly create visual sensations and emotions. Inspired by Chomsky's sentence and based on the idea of translating words or sentences into visual forms, we created *Verbarium*.
Verbarium was developed in 1999 for the Cartier Foundation in Paris. The web site can be found at: *http://www.fondation.cartier.fr/verbarium.html*
On-line users can create forms and shapes directly in real time by writing text messages with the web site's interactive text editor. The site was created by using Java applet programming.
Each of the incoming text messages functions as a genetic code to create a visual three-dimensional form. Depending on the composition of the text, forms can either be simple or complex, abstract or organic. The form can be viewed by the user instantly at the left-side window of the web page.
Additionally, all incoming text messages become

1999 haben wir eine interaktive Website für das Internet mit dem Titel *Verbarium* geschaffen. Dies Website erlaubt es Internet-Benutzern, Textnachrichten zu verfassen, die unmittelbar in dreid mensionale visuelle Formen umgesetzt werden. Unser selbstentwickelter Text-zu-Form-Editor über nimmt die Buchstaben, die Syntax und die Abfolge einer Textnachricht als genetischen Code und aktu alisiert die Designfunktionen anhand dieser Parameter zur Schaffung von dreidimensionalen Formen. Da die Textnachrichten von Internetbenutzer normalerweise einzigartig sind, können dadurch vc den Usern auch einzigartige und persönliche dreidimensionale visuelle Formen generiert werden.
Laut Noam Chomsky basiert der menschliche Spracherwerb auf einer universellen Grammatik, d genetisch im Gehirn aller normalen Kinder vorprogrammiert ist und es ihnen erlaubt, ihre Muttersprache natürlich und scheinbar ohne Anstrengun zu erlernen. Von Chomsky stammt auch der Satz „Farblose grüne Ideen schlafen furios", ein Satz, de für eine eher naturwissenschaftlich orientierte Person wohl wenig logischen Sinn macht, der aber für eher künstlerisch orientierte Menschen durchaus Bedeutung entfalten kann. Obwohl dieser Satz grammatikalisch korrekt ist, wie Chomsky gezeigt hat, kann seine Bedeutung über die Logik allein nicht erfaßt werden. Wenn wir diesen Satz das erste Mal hören, so sehen wir Bilder oder Formen vor unserem inneren Auge. Diese Formen sind vag aber dennoch bis zu einem gewissen Grad definier und sie können sicherlich visuelle Erfahrungen un Emotionen auslösen. Inspiriert von Chomskys Satz und basierend auf dem Grundgedanken der Umsetzung von Sprache in visuelle Formen wurde das *Verbarium* entwickelt.
Verbarium entstand 1999 für die Cartier Foundatic in Paris, die zugehörige Website findet sich unter *http://www.fondation.cartier.fr/verbarium.html*.
Online-User können mit Hilfe des interaktiven Text editors durch Eingabe von Nachrichten Formen un Figuren in Echtzeit generieren. Die Site verwendet programmierte JAVA-Applets.
Jede der einlangenden Nachrichten funktioniert al genetischer Code für die Schaffung einer visuellen dreidimensionalen Form. Je nach der Komplexität de Textes sind die Formen komplexer oder einfacher, abstrakt oder organisch. Die Form wird dem Benutz sofort im linken Fenster der Website gezeigt.
Daneben werden alle einlangenden Textnachrichten Teil eines kollektiven Bildes, das auf der rechter Seite der Website zu sehen ist. Dieses Kollektivbild fungiert als „virtuelles verbales Herbarium" – dahe der Name *Verbarium* – und besteht aus Formen, di durch die unterschiedlichen Textnachrichten (*verb* geschaffen werden. Die Textnachrichten können in vielen Sprachen geschrieben werden, auch dieBedienungsanleitung im Texteditor ist mehrsprachig.

part of a collective image that is displayed on the right side of the web page. This collective image functions as a "virtual and verbal herbarium" (hence the name *Verbarium*) of forms composed and created through the different text messages (i.e., verbs). The text messages can be written in many languages and the instruction editor displays instructions in the different languages.

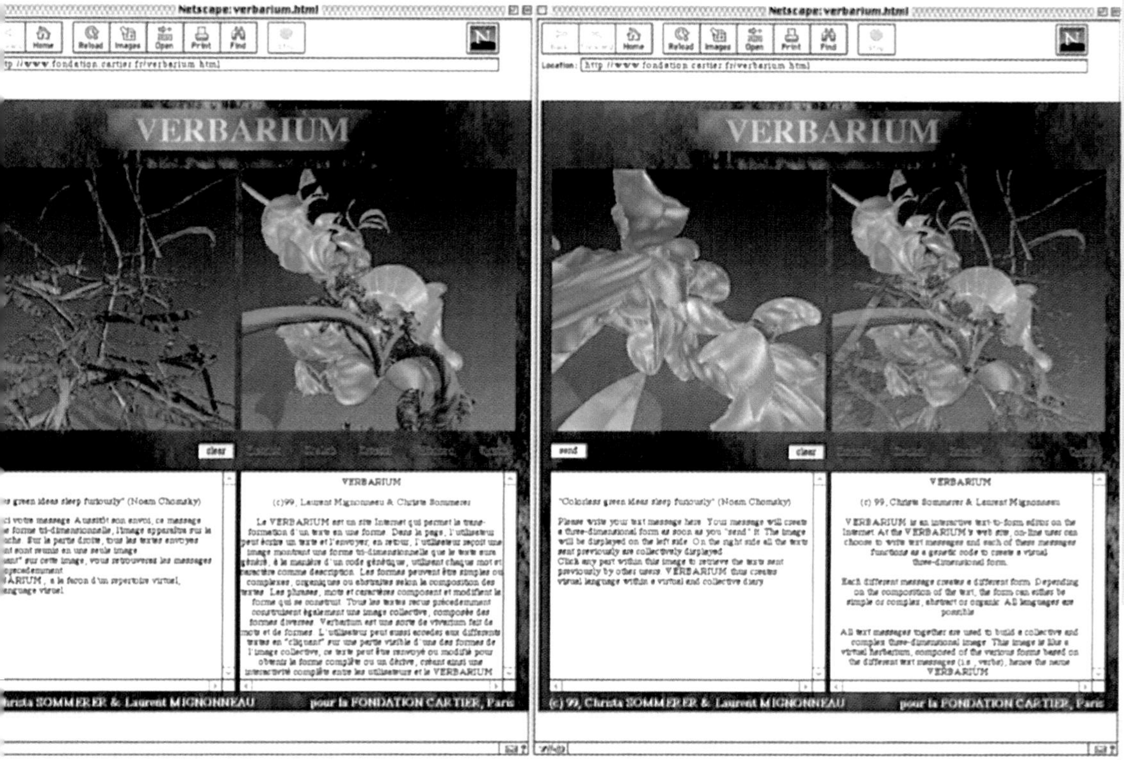

Developed for the Cartier Foundation, Paris. Supported by IAMAS, Japan.

Christa Sommerer (A) studied biology and botany in Vienna, completed studies at the Academy of Fine Arts in Vienna and post-graduate studies at the Staedelschule in Frankfurt. She is currently professor at the International Media Academy in Gifu (Japan) and artistic director of ATR Advanced Telecommunication Research Laboratories in Kyoto (Japan). Laurent Mignonneau (F) studied sculpting in Angouleme and completed post-graduate studies at the Stadelschule in Frankfurt. He is currently Artist in Residence at the International Media Academy in Gifu (Japan) and artistic director at ATR Advanced Telecommunication Research Laboratories in Kyoto (Japan).

Christa Sommerer (A) studierte Biologie und Botanik in Wien, schloß ein Studium an der Akademie der Bildenden Künste in Wien sowie ein Postgraduate-Studium an der Frankfurter Staedelschule an. Gegenwärtig ist sie Professorin an der Internationalen Medienakademie in Gifu (Japan) sowie künstlerische Leiterin von ATR Advanced Telecommunication Research Laboratories in Kyoto (Japan). Laurent Mignonneau (F) studierte Bildhauerei in Angoulême und schloß ein Postgraduate-Studium an der Staedelschule Frankfurt an. Derzeit ist er Arts-in-Residence an der Internationalen Medienakademie in Gifu (Japan) sowie Künstlerischer Leiter bei ATR Advanced Telecommunication Research Laboratories in Kyoto (Japan).

MAP OF THE MARKET

Martin Wattenberg / Joon Yu

Concept

We set out to create a visual answer to the question, "How is the market doing today?" Given the powerful global influence of the U.S. stock market, this question has relevance not just for investors but for anyone seeking to understand the news of the day.

Our Design

We display the market in the form of colored rectangular tiles, one for each of 600 key U.S. companies. The size of each tile corresponds to a company's total market value, giving the viewer a sense of perspective and proportion. We represent price movement by shades of red and green, and group similar companies together to help viewers perceive trends. The result is a colorful and intuitive picture in which bright spots in the market show up as literal bright spots on the screen, conveying the mood of the market—and by extension of the economy and the country—at a glance.

Visual Ramifications

Aside from communicating financial information, the display represents an exploration of two-dimensional space in the spirit of Piet Mondrian. The tilings of different sectors of the economy demonstrate dozens of different ways to partition rectangles into subspaces.

History

The *Map* was launched by SmartMoney.com on Dec. 16, 1998. Our design builds on earlier work by Ben Shneiderman and others on a visualization technique called a "treemap." Aside from adding aesthetic variations on their theme, we also invented a new algorithm for creating the space-filling partition of the diagram.

Das Konzept

Wir sind ausgezogen, um eine visuelle Antwort au die Frage zu geben: „Was macht der Markt heute?“ Wegen des großen weltweiten Einflusses des US-Aktienmarktes ist diese Frage nicht nur für Investoren von Bedeutung, sondern für jeden, der versucht, die Nachrichten des Tages zu verstehen.

Das Design

Wir stellen den Markt in Form eines Mosaiks aus farbigen rechteckigen „Fliesen“ dar, jeweils eine fü jede von 600 wichtigen US-Firmen. Die Größe der einzelnen Farbflächen entspricht dem Marktwert eines Unternehmens, was dem Betrachter einen Eindruck der Perspektiven und Proportionen vermi telt. Wir stellen Preisveränderungen in Rot- und Grünschattierungen dar und gruppieren Unternehmen ähnlicher Art, damit Trends leichter erkennbar werden. Das Ergebnis ist ein farbenfrohes und intuitives Bild, in dem die „Lichtblicke“ des Marktes auch als helle Lichter am Bildschirm erscheinen, was die Stimmung des Marktes – und damit auch der Wirtschaft und des Landes – auf einen Blick sichtbar macht.

Visuelle Verzweigungen

Abgesehen von der Darstellung von Finanzinforma tionen bietet das Display auch eine visuelle Untersuchung des zweidimensionalen Raums im Geiste eines Piet Mondrian. Die Farbflächen der verschiedenen Sektoren der Wirtschaft demonstrieren unzählige verschiedene Wege, Rechtecke in Teilfläche zu zerlegen.

Geschichte und Kontext

The Map wurde von SmartMoney.com am 16. Dezember 1998 ins Leben gerufen. Unser Design baut auf einer früheren Arbeit von Ben Shneiderman ur anderen zu einer Visualisierungstechnik namens „Treemap“ auf. Neben der Hinzufügung von ästhet schen Varianten zu ihrem Grundthema haben wir einen neuen Algorithmus zur flächenfüllenden Au teilung des Diagramms entwickelt.

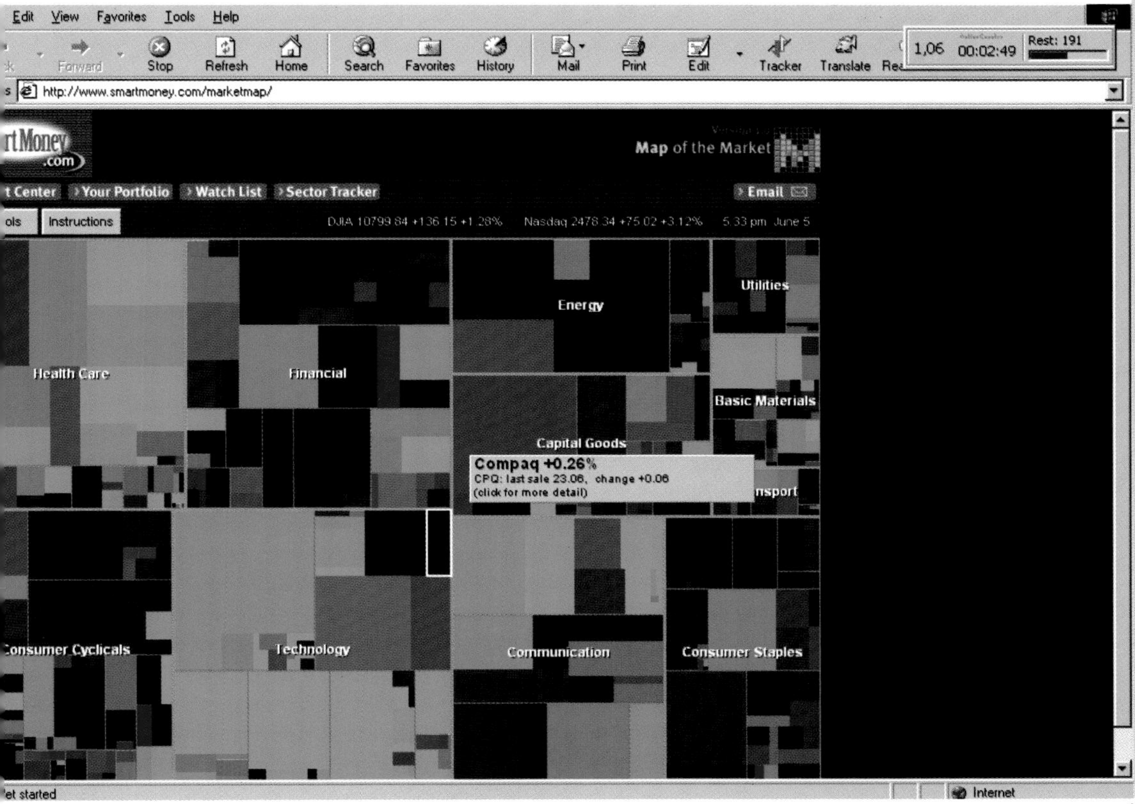

Martin Wattenberg, 29, lives and works in New York City. He is an editor at SmartMoney.com, where he designs new ways of visualizing financial data and news. His work has received recognition including the ICI/American University award for personal finance journalism in 1998 and 1999, and an I.D. Magazine gold award for interactive design in 1999. He also maintains an experimental interactive art web site, *www.bewitched.com*. Before coming to SmartMoney in 1996, he graduated from U.C. Berkeley with a Ph.D. in mathematics. Joon Yu, a graduate of Cooper Union, has been with SmartMoney.com for over two years. During this time, Joon has been instrumental in shaping the entire look and feel of the SmartMoney.com Web site. As lead designer on numerous projects, he has received design awards from IDSA, ID Magazine, the Investment Company Institute and Communication Arts. ■ Martin Wattenberg, 29, lebt und arbeitet in New York City. Er ist Herausgeber bei SmartMoney.com, wo er neue Arten der Visualisierung von Finanzdaten und Nachrichten entwickelt. Seine Arbeiten wurden mehrfach ausgezeichnet, darunter mit dem ICI/American University Award für Finanzjournalismus 1998 und 1999 sowie mit dem I.D. Magazine Gold Award für interaktives Design 1999. Er betreibt auch eine experimentelle interaktive Kunst-Website, www.bewitched.com. Bevor er 1996 zu Smart-Money.com kam, graduierte er an der U.C: Berkeley zum Ph.D. aus Mathematik. Joon Yu, Absolvent von Cooper Union, ist seit über zwei Jahren bei SmartMoney. In dieser Zeit hat er das heutige „Look-and-Feel" der Website von SmartMoney.com ganz entscheidend mitgestaltet. Als führender Designer bei zahlreichen Projekten hat er Designpreise von der IDSA, ... vom

prix ars electronica 99

.NET
INTERACTIVE ART
COMPUTER ANIMATION
VISUAL EFFECTS
DIGITAL MUSICS
u19/CYBERGENERATION

ARE WE STILL ENJOYING INTERACTIVITY?

GENIESSEN WIR NOCH IMMER DIE INTERAKTIVITÄT?

Is interactive art still too young? Possibly, as the paint and brush we use in this genre of art are still changing every year. But that is part of the fun.

Ist die interaktive Kunst noch zu jung? Möglicherweise, denn die Pinsel und die Farben, die wir in diesem Genre der Kunst verwenden, ändern sich noch von Jahr zu Jahr – aber das ist auch ein Teil des Spaßes daran.

Certainly technical development is closely related to what artists can realize in interactive art, as John Markoff stated in last year's jury statement *Moore's Law Applied to Digital Art?* In fact the CAVE has indeed become a standard environment for virtual reality. CD-ROM and WWW have become standard environments for almost any interactive artists. The history of technical improvement and its reflection in the making of art is quite visible in the history of this young category of Prix Ars Electronica.
A major trend in this category in 97 and 98 was the development of more convincing and comprehensive virtual environments. In 97's *Music Play Images x Images Play Music* by Toshio Iwai and Ryuichi Sakamoto, interaction between images and music brought an artistic and at the same time entertaining experience to the audience, while interaction between the participants from the Net and the famous musician/composer on the stage also took place. The work made a new possibility of multimedia as a form of art visible to us. Paul Garrin and David Rokeby's *Border Patrol* was a virtual environment with quite a different theme, but also integrating image and sound. Maurice Benayoun and Jean-Baptiste Barièrre's *World Skin*, the winner of 98, was a powerful virtual experience made by the collaboration of visual artist and sound artist. Visitors wander in the CAVE among cut-outs of soldiers, sufferers and war machines taken from photos of WW I and Bosnia in the almost monochrome battlefield that continues endlessly. The sound of camera shutters gradually turn into horrifying screams and sounds of gunshots as visitors use the camera to take photos. The role of media is questioned by using the most advanced media technology.
Christian Möller's *Audio Grove* provided visitors with a much more peaceful experience. A space filled with steel posts creates an ever changing symphony of sound, light and shadow as visitors touch or caress the poles.
Altogether, the realization of multimedia/multimodal interaction for users was another strong element. The extension of virtual reality and developing more natural, easy-to-use interfaces, which has been a key issue in technology, seemed to be the *basso continuo* in interactive art as well.
This year, a change was to be observed.
It was not easy to make a selection from more than 360 works entered in this category this year, but the

Sicherlich ist die technische Entwicklung eng mit dem verknüpft, was Künstler in der interaktiven Kunst realisieren können, wie John Markoff im letztjährigen Jury-Statement unter Bezug auf das Moore'sche Gesetz festgestellt hat. Und tatsächlich ist der CAVE mittlerweile zu einem Standard-Environment für virtuelle Realität geworden. CD-ROM und WWW sind weitere Standardumgebungen für beinahe jeden interaktiven Künstler. Die Geschichte der technischen Verbesserungen und ihre Reflexion in der Kunst lassen sich an der Geschichte dieser noch jungen Kategorie des Prix Ars Electronica ablesen.
Einer der Haupttrends in dieser Kategorie der Jahre 1997 und 1998 war die Entwicklung immer überzeugenderer und umfassenderer virtueller Umgebungen. Mit *Music Plays Images x Images Play Music* schufen Toshio Iwai und Ryuichi Sakamoto 1997 eine Interaktion zwischen Bildern und Musik und damit eine ebenso künstlerische wie unterhaltsame Erfahrung für das Publikum, während gleichzeitig auch eine Interaktion zwischen den Mitwirkenden im Netz und dem berühmten Musiker-Komponisten auf der Bühne stattfand. Dieses Werk eröffnete uns neue Perspektiven einer multimedialen interaktiven Kunst. Paul Garrin und David Rokeby nahmen sich mit *Border Patrol* eines völlig anderen Themas an, aber integrierten ebenfalls Bild und Klang. Der Vorjahressieger *World Skin* von Maurice Benayoun und Jean-Baptiste Barrière war eine kraftvolle virtuelle Erfahrung, entstanden aus der Zusammenarbeit zwischen einem visuellen Künstler und einem Klangkünstler. Die Besucher bewegen sich in einem CAVE zwischen ausgeschnittenen Figuren von Soldaten, Leidtragenden und Kriegsmaschinen – die alle aus Fotos aus dem Zweiten Weltkrieg und dem Bosnienkrieg stammen – über ein scheinbar endloses Schlachtfeld. Die Geräusche der Kameraverschlüsse verwandeln sich langsam in erschütternde Schreie und in den Klang von Schüssen, wenn die Besucher auf den Auslöser des Fotoapparats drücken.
Christian Möllers *Audio Grove* wiederum bot den Besuchern eine friedlichere Erfahrung: Ein mit Stahlrundstäben gefüllter Raum schafft eine sich ständig ändernde Symphonie von Klang, Licht und Schatten, wenn die Besucher diese Pfähle angreifen oder streicheln.
Insgesamt war ein vorherrschendes Element die Realisierung multimedialer bzw. multimodaler Interaktion für User. Die Erweiterung der virtuellen Realität und die Entwicklung von natürlichen, einfach zu bedienenden Interfaces – eine Hauptherausforderung der Technologie – schien dabei auch in der interaktiven Kunst die Rolle des Basso continuo zu übernehmen.
In diesem Jahr war eine Änderung zu beobachten. Es war nicht einfach, eine Auswahl unter über 360 eingereichten Arbeiten zu treffen, aber die stärksten Werke waren dabei nicht jene, die versuchten, ein virtuelles Environment in der Integration von visuellen und klanglichen Erfahrungen mit einem Maximum an Interaktivität zu kombinieren. Und

strongest pieces were not those which tried to realize a virtual environment integrating visual and sound experiences with the maximum interactivity. In fact while there were quite a few CAVE pieces, but none of them made it to a prize after all.
Among the pieces we selected, interactivity is applied more for questioning the relationship between real space (where the users are) and another space, which is not necessarily virtual. The relationship is not linear as it used to be, or it often employs multiple layers. In some works the notion of interactivity itself is the theme. Also, words such as memories, traces, landscape, dispersion were frequently seen among the titles of works we found interesting.
Another interesting phenomenon we observed this year was the number of entries using circular screens or projections. The idea is not new. Certainly a circle of light is optically the most natural and the oldest form of projection. If we think of the beginning of the history of imaging art, magic lanterns cast circular light and glass slides themselves were often prepared circularly. It was only after certain technical developments of the light source that full wall-size rectangular projection became popular. Cinema adopted a rectangular screen, and so did television and computer displays. Now circular screens seem to attract the attention of interactive artists.
What do these phenomena signify? Are we already becoming nostalgic? It seems that artists are exploring the next step of interactive art. To make it more interactive? Not necessarily. Interactive technology itself has still much to develop before notions such as ubiquitous computing or smart home may be realized in every household, not to mention the question of whether we really want this kind of life. But the nature of art (and its role, from a social or historical aspect) is not to demonstrate technical improvements. Artists foresee - and at the same time look back at - what is beyond or behind the technical issue, visualizing the real meanings of technology.
Actually this was already seen with *World Skin*. It was by the conscious choice of the artists to limit the degree of reality in virtual space or interaction that the strong concept of the piece could be realized. We have had other artists using this kind of aspect as well, but they were rather a minority when

obwohl etliche CAVE-Stücke eingereicht wurden, hat es letztlich doch keines bis zu einem Preis geschafft. Bei den von uns ausgewählten Werken wird die Interaktivität vorwiegend zur Hinterfragung der Beziehung zwischen dem realen Raum (in dem sich die Benutzer befinden) und einem anderen – nicht unbedingt virtuellen – Raum eingesetzt. Diese Beziehung ist nicht linear wie früher, und sie verwendet häufig mehrere Ebenen. Bei einigen Arbeiten ist der Begriff der Interaktivität selbst das Thema. Auch tauchten in den Titeln der interessanteren Werke häufig Begriffe wie Erinnerung, Spuren, Landschaft, Dispersion auf. Und ein weiteres Phänomen unter den diesjährigen Einreichungen war, daß viele mit kreisförmigen Leinwänden oder Projektionsflächen arbeiteten. Die Idee ist nicht neu – die Laterna magica warf runde Lichtflecken, und häufig wurden auch die zugehörigen Glasdias kreisförmig gestaltet. Erst nach einer gewissen technischen Entwicklung der Lichtquelle wurde eine rechteckige Projektion in voller Wandgröße populär. Das Kino übernahm die rechteckige Bildfläche, ebenso das Fernsehen und die Computerbildschirme. Jetzt scheinen runde Projektionen wieder die Aufmerksamkeit der interaktiven Künstler auf sich zu ziehen.
Was bedeuten diese Phänomene? Werden wir jetzt schon nostalgisch? Es scheint, daß die Künstler die nächste Ebene interaktiver Kunst auszuloten versuchen. Um sie noch interaktiver zu machen? Nicht unbedingt. Die interaktive Technologie muß sich selbst noch gehörig weiterentwickeln, bevor so etwas wie „der ubiquitäre Computer" oder „das intelligente Heim" in jedem Haushalt realisiert werden könnten – ganz abgesehen von der Frage, ob wir ein solches Leben überhaupt wollen. Aber die Natur der Kunst (und ihre Rolle unter sozialen wie historischen Aspekten) ist es nicht, technische Verbesserungen zu zeigen. Künstler sehen voraus – und blicken dabei gleichzeitig zurück –, was vor oder hinter dem technischen Anliegen steckt, sie visualisieren die wahre Bedeutung der Technologie. Das war bereits bei *World Skin* zu erkennen, und es war die bewußte Entscheidung der Künstler, den Realitätsgrad im virtuellen Raum oder in der Interaktion zu beschränken, was dem Werk die Umsetzung seines starken Konzeptes ermöglicht hat. Es hat auch früher schon Künstler gegeben, die solche Aspekte beachtet haben, aber sie waren eine kleine Minderheit, als die technologische Entwicklung noch nicht hinreichend weit gediehen war.
In diesem Jahr hat die Jury für Interaktive Kunst Lynn Hershmans *Difference Engine #3* als Gewinner der Goldenen Nica gekürt. Es ist nicht das spektakulärste Stück, das wir in den letzten Jahren in diesem Bereich gesehen haben, und es ist auch kein leicht zu genießendes. Das Werk verbindet den realen Raum und die virtuelle Welt und erlaubt den Netzbenutzern, mit Hilfe von Avataren virtuell durch den realen Raum zu fliegen und sich mit den Menschen im realen Raum zu unterhalten. Aber es ist dabei keineswegs ein fröhliches „Hallo, siehst du

the technological development was still far from sufficient.
This year the interactive jury selected Lynn Hershman's *Difference Engine #3* for the Golden Nica. The piece is not one of the visually spectacular works we have seen in this category in recent years. It is not an easy piece to enjoy either. The piece connects real space and the virtual world, allowing Net users to virtually fly through the real space using avatars, and to chat with the people in the real space. However, it is not a happy CUSeeMe kind of project, even though visitors can enjoy the experience and communicate with others. On the contrary, it depicts an increasing anxiety about the blurring boundary between the real world and the virtual and life in cyberspace, literally. Today, cyberspace is no longer a wonderland on the Net. Serious matters of real life such as transaction or identification are all moving onto the Net. The work is a well thought, strongly conceptual piece which integrates important issues we are facing in terms of relationships between real space and the virtual world. It deals with themes such as voyeurism, notions of self and others, the "life" of avatars, and coded identity on the Net.
Needless to say, Lynn Hershman is one of the pioneers in interactive art, but even before that she was always dealing with issues such as voyeurism and virtual identity in interactive ways. In her well known project *Roberta*, the identity of a virtual persona was created through social systems (including the reactions of people who were users of information that Hershman issued). The artificial data of the virtual woman was processed to virtually create a real woman in society. In *Difference Engine #3* the information regarding a real person is processed in the system she has created, to become the entity of an avatar which will live its own life cycle apart from that of the original real person, and remain on the Net (numbered literally on its face) forever. The piece elegantly visualizes the relationship between the real world and the virtual world, as well as the meaning of virtual life on the Net.
The relationship between real space and virtual space has changed. Enjoying exploring a virtual environment and having spontaneous interaction with its inhabitants is no longer a novelty. Creative multimedia environments can now be seen on the Net as well, with the advent of recent effective image and sound compression technology.

mich?"-Produkt, auch wenn die Besucher die Erfahrung genießen und miteinander in Verbindung treten können. Es artikuliert vielmehr die wachsende Besorgnis über die immer unschärfer werdende Grenzlinie zwischen der realen und der virtuellen Welt und über das – im wahrsten Sinne des Wortes – Leben im Cyberspace. Heute ist der Cyberspace nicht mehr eine Wunderwelt im Netz. Ernsthafte Fragen des Alltagslebens wie Transaktionen oder Identifikation beginnen, sich aufs Netz zu verlagern. Die Arbeit ist ein gut durchdachtes und stark konzeptionelles Stück, das wichtige Anliegen anspricht, mit denen wir im Zusammenhang mit der Beziehung zwischen echter und scheinbarer Wirklichkeit konfrontiert sind. Es behandelt Themen wie Voyeurismus, den Begriff des Selbst und des Anderen, das „Leben" von Avataren und die kodierte Identität im Netz. Es erübrigt sich fast, darauf hinzuweisen, daß Lynn Hershman zu den Pionieren der interaktiven Kunst gehört und sich schon zuvor mit Fragen des Voyeurismus und der virtuellen Identität auf interaktive Weise auseinandergesetzt hat. In ihrem bekannten Werk *Roberta* etwa wurde die Identität der virtuellen Gestalt über ein Sozialsystem definiert (was die Reaktion von Leuten auf von Hershman ausgegebene Informationen mit einschloß. Künstliche Daten der virtuellen Frau wurden verarbeitet und aus ihnen wurde virtuell eine reale Person in der Gesellschaft geschaffen). In *Difference Engine #3* wird die Information über eine reale Person in dem von ihr geschaffenen System verarbeitet und zur Grundlage eines Avatars, der seinen eigenen Lebenszyklus unabhängig von der realen Person lebt und – im Gesicht numeriert – auf ewig im Netz bleibt. Das Stück visualisiert auf elegante Weise die Beziehung zwischen der realen und der virtuellen Welt ebenso wie die Bedeutung von „virtuellem Leben im Netz".
Die Beziehung zwischen realem und virtuellem Raum hat sich verändert. Spaß an der Erforschung einer virtuellen Umgebung und spontane Interaktion mit ihren Bewohnern zu haben ist nichts Neues mehr. Kreative Multimedia-Umgebungen können jetzt ebenso im Netz gefunden werden – die neuen effizienteren Bild- und Ton-Kompressionstechniken machen es möglich. Es ist vielleicht kein Zufall, daß alle drei Preisträger dieses Jahr bekannte Namen haben, etablierte Künstler sind, die mit individuellen Ansätzen schon länger im Bereich der interaktiven Kunst aktiv sind. (Es ist allerdings schade, daß die meisten der interessanten Arbeiten von bereits anerkannten Künstlern stammen – wir hätten gerne neue Talente entdeckt!) Dies ist allerdings insofern verständlich, als eine längerwährende Beschäftigung mit der Technologie natürlich die damit verbundenen Anliegen und Herausforderungen schneller erkennen läßt. Und der richtige Einsatz der Technologie zur Visualisierung solcher Themen verlangt einiges an Fertigkeiten.
Perry Hoberman wirft solch eine Frage auf und stellt sie in eine Situation, die keine Antwort zuläßt.

It might not be a coincidence that the three artists who won prizes this year are all well known, established artists who have been active in the field of interactive art with unique approaches. (However, it was also a pity that most of the interesting works are done by already recognized artists. We wished to find young talents.) It is understandable that since these artists have been using the technology for many years they are aware of the issues ahead of others. Also, the right use of technology to visualize these kinds of themes requires expertise.
Perry Hoberman raises such questions with a "non-answer" situation. The artist has provided us with a chaotic, confusing situation where three different phases of reality and virtuality overlap as they are displayed on a single monitor. It is only by manipulating it that one can recognize what he/she is manipulating. It is up to you how to deal with it, the artist says. It is a piece which (as in the case of Lynn Hershman's) strongly reflects the artist's continuous approach to the relationship between real and virtual, as well as to interactivity. His much earlier pieces using stereoview or shadow already reflect the artist's interest in the theme before he started using virtual reality. Playful irony and visual fun are also observed in Hoberman's other works. Even though the piece is supported by a very highly technical platform, the way Hoberman uses the technology is totally different from a demonstration.
Luc Courchesne's *Landscape One* brings up the question of directorship in interactive art. The piece can be considered as an interactive cinema, which consists of four screens to give a virtually 360 degree view to the users. Users can communicate with the people (and a dog) who arrive from different directions by making a choice from sentences that appear on the panel, as in his earlier works. But the artist does not try to bring the users into the immersive experience in the virtual world. It is different from exploring a fantasy world in the CAVE. A visitor will remain aware that he/she is in the real space and still talking with a character in the film, while observing what is happening in the space on the other side of the screen. It is a limited and predecided interactivity, which might have been regarded as "insufficient interactivity" in the short history of interactive art. But it is such a carefully designed interactivity that the high quality of the experience (i.e. being in an interactive cinema) becomes pos-

Er hat uns vor eine chaotische, konfuse Situation gestellt, in der sich drei unterschiedliche Phasen von Realität und Virtualität überschneiden, während sie gleichzeitig auf einem Monitor dargestellt werden. Nur durch die Manipulation der Situation wird erkennbar, was hier manipuliert wird. „Es bleibt dem User überlassen, wie er damit umgehen will", sagt der Künstler. Wie im Falle Lynn Hershmans reflektiert auch Hobermans Arbeit seine kontinuierliche Annäherung an die Beziehung zwischen Realem und Virtuellem ebenso wie an die Interaktivität. Schon seine ganz frühen Werke, in denen er Stereobilder oder Schatten einsetzte, spiegeln sein Interesse an diesem Thema wider – lange bevor er die virtuelle Realität dafür verwendete. Eine spielerische Ironie und visueller Spaß lassen sich auch in seinen anderen Arbeiten entdecken. Und wenn auch das Stück von einer relativ aufwendigen technischen Ebene ausgeht, unterscheidet sich Hobermans Einsatz der Technik doch wesentlich von einer Demonstration des Machbaren.
Luc Courchesnes *Landscape One* stellt die Frage nach der Regiearbeit in der interaktiven Kunst. Das Stück kann als ein interaktives Kino verstanden werden, in dem vier Leinwände den Besucher auf allen Seiten umschließen. Die Anwender können mit den Menschen (und einem Hund) kommunizieren, die aus verschiedenen Richtungen kommen, indem sie aus einem Set von angebotenen Sätzen auswählen (wie schon in seinen früheren Arbeiten). Aber der Künstler versucht keineswegs, die User in die immersive Erfahrung der virtuellen Welt einzutauchen – das Werk unterscheidet sich wesentlich von der Erforschung einer Phantasiewelt im CAVE. Dem Besucher bleibt bewußt, daß er sich im realen Raum befindet und dennoch mit einer Figur des Films spricht, während er beobachtet, was daraufhin im Raum auf der anderen Seite der Leinwand passiert. Es ist eine beschränkte, vorgegebene Interaktivität, die in der kurzen Geschichte der interaktiven Kunst vielleicht auch schon als „ungenügend interaktiv" hätte kritisiert werden können. Aber durch diese vorgegebene Interaktivität – es handelt sich hier um eine Art interaktives Kino – werden dennoch Erfahrungen von hoher Qualität im Stück möglich. Das Werk läßt uns über die Rolle der Interaktivität in narrativen Geschichten nachdenken.
Die für die Anerkennungen ausgewählten Werke stellen Beispiele unterschiedlichster Möglichkeiten der interaktiven Kunst oder aber originelle Ansätze zur Verbindung von Kunst, Wissenschaft und Technologie dar. *Robots & Avatars Dealing with Virtual Illusions* von F.A.B.R.I.CATORS ist ein weiteres Beispiel für den Umgang mit der Komplexität der Beziehung zwischen Schein und Wirklichkeit. Avatare in der virtuellen Welt können manipuliert werden, indem physische Roboter in der realen Welt gesteuert werden. Die zunehmenden Membranen der Kommunikation, die wir in unserer Welt sehen, werden auf einzigartige Weise visualisiert.
Im *Haze Express* von Christa Sommerer und Laurent

sible in this piece. This piece makes us think about the role of interactivity in a narrative story.
Works selected for Honorary Mention represent examples of different possibilities in interactive art or original approaches to bridging art, science and technology. Some of the works included are equally as interesting as the award winning pieces in many ways.
Robots Avatars Dealing with Virtual Illusions by F.A.B.R.I.CATORS is another example of dealing with the complexity of the relationship between the real world and the virtual world. Avatars in the virtual world can be manipulated by controlling physical robots in the real world. There is a unique visualization of the increasing membranes of communication we see in our world.
In Christa Sommerer and Laurent Mignonneau's *Haze Express*, a night train experience is realized in a compartment with settings taken from a real train. Numerous crystal-like objects float outside the window like the passing street lights one sees on a foggy night. One can change the speed and direction of the train by slipping one's hand over the window. By virtually touching the crystal pieces one likes through the window, similar shapes will circulate more often because of a genetic algorithm. But a feature like this does not seem to belong to the essence of a dream-like experience on a night train. It is more about going back to childhood memory (I remembered a phrase from Antoine Saint-Exupéry). When we remember that only a few years ago we saw quite a few pieces dealing with the concept of ALIFE in a straight manner, including those by the artists of *Haze Express*, it is interesting to see that A-life has nearly retreated into the background.
It is a part of what we see this year—technology may now finally be mature enough to be less visible, behind the scene of artistic questions and expressions.
Certainly the way artists see interactive technology is changing. Maybe we are finally becoming skeptical of the myth of ever-progressing technical development. Or at least we have finally come to the point where interactive technology is stable enough to let us stop for a moment and look around. What we see this year — stronger concepts involving the nature of interactivity and virtuality — may partly be a reflection of the deceleration of technical development.
What will we see in the year 2000?

Mignonneau hingegen wird eine Nachtexpreß-Situation in einer Umgebung dargestellt, die einem echten Zug entlehnt ist. Zahlreiche kristallähnliche Objekte schweben am Zugfenster vorbei wie die Lichter der Landschaft in einer nebeligen Nacht. Durch Handbewegungen am Fenster kann man die Geschwindigkeit und die Richtung des Zugs verändern. Eine virtuelle Berührung jener Elemente, die einem gefallen, läßt ähnliche Formen in größerer Zahl vorbeigleiten, weil ein genetischer Algorithmus dies steuert. Aber solche Features sind nicht die Essenz der traumgleichen Erfahrung eines nächtlichen Zugfahrt. Es geht mehr darum, zu den Kindheitserinnerungen zurückzukehren (mir fiel ein Satz von Saint-Exupéry dazu ein). Wenn wir daran denken, daß wir vor nur wenigen Jahren eine Menge von Werken sahen, die sich mit dem Konzept des Künstlichen Lebens in sehr direkter Weise beschäftigten – auch Werke der Künstler von *Haze Express* –, so ist es interessant zu beobachten, wie künstliches Leben sich mittlerweile fast hinter den Kulissen abspielt. Auch das ist Teil dessen, was wir dieses Jahr zu sehen bekommen haben: Die Technologie scheint endlich reif genug zu sein, um weniger sichtbar zu werden, um hinter die künstlerischen Fragen und Ausdrucksweisen zurückzutreten.
Sicherlich verändert sich die Art und Weise, wie Künstler die interaktive Technologie sehen. Vielleicht werden wir endlich skeptisch gegenüber dem Mythos der ständig voranschreitenden technischen Entwicklung. Oder wir sind zumindest an jenen Punkt gelangt, an dem die interaktive Technologie stabil genug ist, um uns einen Augenblick des Verharrens und einen Blick in die Runde zu gönnen. Was dieses Jahr gebracht hat – stärker konzeptuell orientierte Werke über Interaktivität und Virtualität –, reflektiert wohl auch teilweise die sich verlangsamende technische Entwicklung. Und was werden wir im Jahr 2000 zu sehen bekommen?

THE DIFFERENCE ENGINE #3

Lynn Hershman / Construct Internet Design

The Difference Engine #3 uses the architecture of the ZKM Media Museum as a 3D template and the visitors to the museum as the interface. It is an interactive, multi-user, sculpture about surveillance, voyeurism, digital absorption and spiritual transformation of the body.

The Difference Engine #3 was inspired by Charles Babbage's original *Difference Engine #1* (commonly considered the world's first computer). The original machine was used to calculate numerical positions. This piece calculates the captured image and position in the physical/virtual space of visitors to a physical space, located now at the ZKM Media Museum.

Avatars of museum visitors are "born" when they approach one of three Bi-Directional Browsing Units (BBU's). These are mirror-like units that flip between the physical and vitual space. Quickcams embedded in the BBU's, flip 180 degrees to capture the image (Avatar) of the person standing before it. Each avatar (image of the visitor) is assigned a number, representing the time in seconds the visitor approached the unit. The numbered avatar embarks on a 27 second journey through a 3D representation of the museum constructed in VRML2 and coded with JAVA3.

The avatar then moves to a Purgatorial Site where it cycles continuously with 30 other avatars. Eventually, the avatars are archived permanently on the Internet where their image can be recalled via the identity number.

Online visitors choose a "generic" avatar to represent them and travel alongside the avatars created for people in the actual museum. Visitors online can also "capture" images within the museum—they can see into the space via the a live video feed from the camera that is capturing the image of people in the museum. There is a dedicated chat line that allows viewers online to communicate with people in the physical space.

Components

The physical installation consists of three stations called Bi-Directional Browsing Units (BBUs). The BBUs house a graphical representation of the museum, act as a "mirror link" between "real" visitors

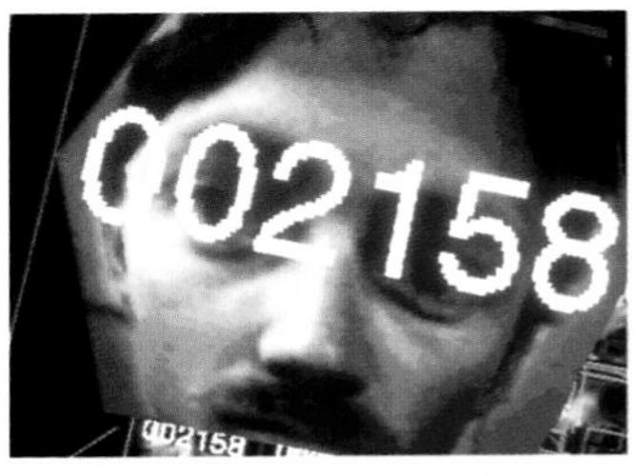

Difference Engine #3 verwendet die Architektur des Medien-Museum des ZKM als dreid mensionale Vorlage und die Museumsbesuch als Interface. Es handelt sich dabe um eine interaktive Multi-User-Skulptur, die sich mit Überwachung, Voyeurismus, digitaler Absorption und der geistigen Transformation des Körpers beschäftigt.

Difference Engine #3 wurde von Charles Babbages *Difference Engine #1* inspiriert, der allgemein als de erste Computer der Welt angesehen wird und zur Errechnung numerischer Positionen eingesetzt wurde. Dieses Stück hingegen rechnet das aufgenommene Bild und die Position der Besucher im physischen/virtuellen Raum auf einen anderen ph sischen Raum um, der diesmal im Medien-Museur des ZKM angesiedelt ist.

Wenn die Besucher sich einer der drei bidirektiona len Browsing-Units (BBU) nähern, werden Avatare „geboren". Die BBUs sind spiegelähnliche Einheite die zwischen dem realen und dem virtuellen Raum hin- und herspringen. Eingebaute Quick-Cams bestreichen einen Raum von 180°, um das Abbild (Avatar) der davorstehenden Person zu erfassen. Jeder Avatar bekommt eine Nummer zugeteilt, die den Zeitpunkt der Annäherung des Besuchers (in Sekunden) angibt. Der so numerierte Avatar begib sich auf eine 27sekündige Reise durch eine 3D-Darstellung des Museums, die in VRML2 erstellt und mit JAVA3 codiert wurde.

Der Avatar begibt sich danach weiter in eine Art Fegefeuer, wo er mit 30 anderen kontinuierlich kreist. Irgendwann werden die Avatare dann perm nent im Internet abgelegt, wo sie über ihre Identitätsnummer abgerufen werden können. Online-Besucher wählen einen „eigenen" Avatar als Stellvertreter aus und reisen neben jenen Avatarer her, die für die Leute im tatsächlichen Museum geschaffen wurden. Die Online-Besucher können auch Bilder aus dem Museum „einfangen" (sie sehen den Museumsraum durch eine Live-Zuspielung aus der Kamera, die die Menschen im Museu erfaßt): Es gibt auch eine speziell eingerichtete Chat-Line, die den Online-Besuchern die Kommuni kation mit den Besuchern im realen Raum erlaubt

Komponenten

Die physische Installation besteht aus drei Stationen, die „Bidirectional Browsing Units" (BBU genannt werden. Diese BBUs enthalten eine graph sche Darstellung des Museums, dienen als „Spiege Verknüpfung" zwischen den „echten" Museums-

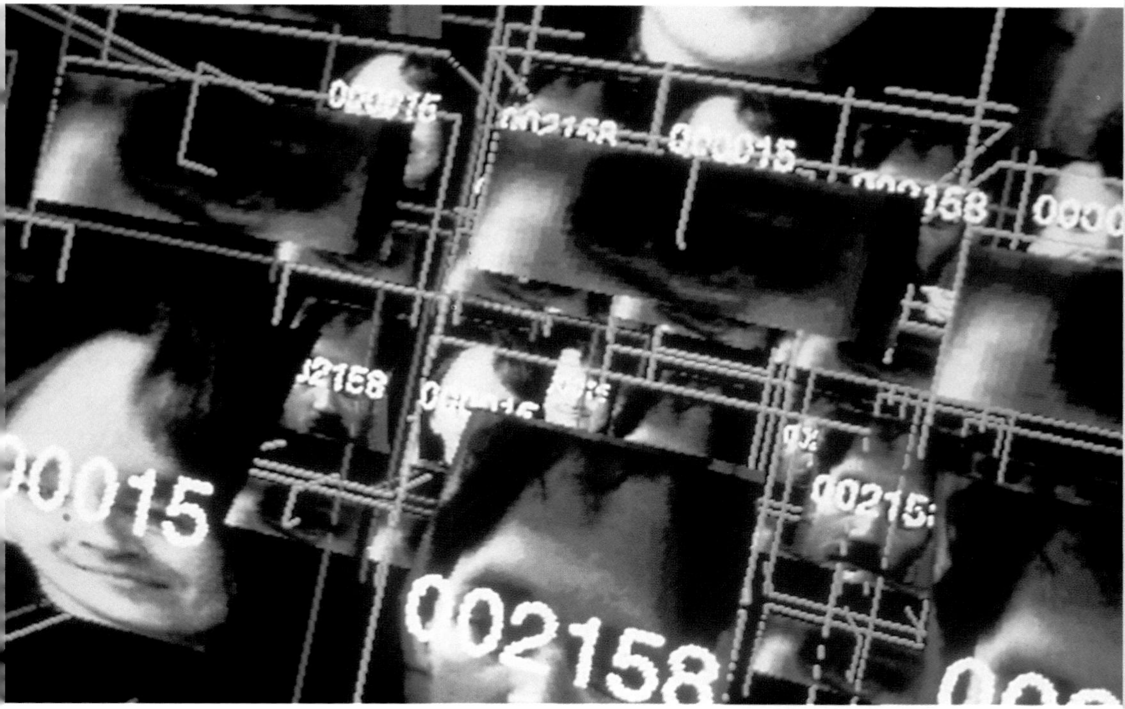

to the museum and those who lurk "virtually" on the Internet. The "mirror" reflects:
1.) from the Internet into the physical space of the ZKM museum and
2.) from museum into cyberspace.
At the entrance to the museum a large LCD screen houses the Purgatory images in which the Avatars suspend.

Web Page

A dedicated site hosts information about the project's development and provides views into the real and virtual spaces. It is via this site that the Internet user is afforded photo control over the BBU.

besuchern und denen, die virtuell über das Internet zusehen. Der „Spiegel" reflektiert
1. vom Internet in den virtuellen Raum des ZKM-Museums und
2. vom Internet in den Cyberspace.Ein großer LCD-Schirm am Eingang zum Museum beherbergt die Fegefeuer-Bilder, in denen sich die Avatare aufhalten.

Webseite

Eine eigene Webseite umfaßt Informationen über die Projektentwicklung und bietet Einblick in den realen und den virtuellen Raum. Über diese Webseite können die Internet-User die Fotoeinheit der BBUs steuern.

URL: http://www.construct.net/de3

LYNN HERSHMAN-LEESON (USA) WAS NAMED THE "MOST INFLUENTIAL WOMAN WORKING IN NEW MEDIA." SHE HAS WORKED IN PHOTOGRAPHY, VIDEO AND ELECTRONIC SCULPTURE. HER 53 VIDEOTAPES AND 7 INTERACTIVE INSTALLATIONS HAVE GARNERED MANY INTERNATIONAL AWARDS. SHE WAS THE FIRST WOMAN TO RECEIVE A TRIBUTE AND RETROSPECTIVE AT THE SAN FRANCISCO INTERNATIONAL FILM FESTIVAL (1994) AND WAS AWARDED THE ZKM/SIEMENS MEDIA ARTS AWARD (WITH PETER GREENAWAY, 1995) AND MANY OTHERS. HER WORK IS IN NUMEROUS ART COLLECTIONS AROUND THE WORLD.

Lynn Hershman-Leeson (USA) wurde schon als die „einflußreichste Frau der Neuen Medien" bezeichnet. Sie ist im Bereich der Fotografie, des Videos und der elektronischen Skulpturen tätig. Ihre 53 Videos und 7 interaktiven Installationen haben zahlreiche internationale Preise gewonnen. Ihr wurde als erster Frau eine Ehrenausstellung und Retrospektive des San Francisco International Film Festival (1994) gewidmet, sie hat den ZKM/Siemens Medienkunstpreis 1995 (gemeinsam mit Peter Greenaway) sowie viele andere Auszeichnungen erhalten. Ihre Werke finden sich in Kunstsammlungen auf der ganzen

LANDSCAPE ONE

Luc Courchesne

Four walls of a space are "painted", with video projectors, into a single photo-realistic 360° landscape representing a public garden. The space, set in Montreal's Mont-Royal Parc, is visited by real and virtual characters. If the virtual characters appear free to come and go in the garden, real visitors will need help to walk in and explore. For this they have to make contact with one of the virtual characters by selecting, using voice or touch, questions or comments from imposed sets on the computer screens.

Questions on, for example, where they are, what is arround, where one can go from here, will engage a conversation leading to some form of relationship. The exchange may be cut short with everyone going back to their business or it may reach a point where visitors will convince a character to lead them somewhere. In such case, visitors are pulled through the landscape after their virtual guide and the whole room appears to be moving in this direction.

The dialogue between the guide and the visitor or group goes on and defines the progression through space. Because real visitors are using virtual characters to steer their way through space, the nature of the visitor's relationship to the character will define the space—physical or metaphorical—that can be accessed. There are several possible destinations or outcomes. Visitors could simply be abandoned somewhere on the way if the connection to the characters is broken, or they could reach a destination: a lookout or a forbidden boundary.

This journey through space is also a journey through words, meanings, language, subjectivity. It highlights not only the physical world in which this is happening, but also its diverse meanings and functions to diferent people. The experience is about communication/discommunication between people with movements through space as a manifestation of its nature; successful forms of communication will offer visitors more varied inroads into more remote places.

Landscape One is a multi-user interactive panoramic video installation using 4 networked computers with touch pads and microphones, 4 video projectors and 4 laserdisc players. It was created by Luc Courchesne in Montreal in 1997 with support from the ICC—InterCommunication Center, Tokyo.

Vier Wände eines Raumes werden mit Hilfe von Videoprojektoren „bemalt", so daß sie eine realistische 360°-Landschaft zeigen, die einen öffentliche[n] Garten darstellt. Dieser Raum – Montreals Mont-Royal-Park – wird von wirklichen und virtuellen Gestalten besucht. Auch wenn sich die virtuellen Besucher offenbar frei in den und aus dem Garten bewegen können, so benötigen die reellen Besuch[er] doch Unterstützung bei ihrem Spaziergang. Deswegen müssen sie mit einer der virtuellen Gestalten Kontakt aufnehmen, sei es durch Sprache, Berührung, durch Fragen oder Kommentare, die einer auf den Schirmen erscheinenden Auswahl entnommen werden können.

Fragen über den Ort, an dem man sich befindet, über die Umgebung oder darüber, wohin man von diesem Ort aus gehen könne, lösen eine Konversation aus, die zu einer Form von Beziehung führt. Dieser Austausch kann dadurch abgebrochen werden, daß sich jeder wieder an seine Arbeit begibt, e[s] kann aber auch sein, daß der reale Besucher die virtuelle Gestalt bittet, ihn irgendwohin zu führen. In einem solchen Fall werden die Besucher hinter ihrem virtuellen Führer durch die Landschaft gezogen, wobei sich der gesamte Raum entsprechend z[u] bewegen scheint.

Der Dialog zwischen Führer und Besucher (oder de[r] Besuchergruppe) wird fortgesetzt und definiert di[e] Weiterbewegung im Raum. Da die realen Besucher virtuelle Charaktere verwenden, um sich einen We[g] zu bahnen, bestimmt die Art der Beziehung zwischen Besucher und Gestalt den physischen oder metaphorischen Raum, der zugänglich wird. Es gib[t] mehrere mögliche Ziele und Ergebnisse: Die Besucher könnten einfach irgendwo unterwegs alleinge[lassen] lassen werden, wenn die Beziehung zur Führergestalt gestört oder unterbrochen wird, sie könnten aber auch ein Ziel erreichen: einen Aussichtspunkt oder eine verbotene Grenze.

Die Reise durch den Raum ist auch eine Reise durc[h] Worte, Bedeutungen, Sprache, Subjektivität. Sie wirft nicht nur ein Schlaglicht auf die physische Welt, in der das alles geschieht, sondern auch auf ihre unterschiedliche Bedeutung und Funktion für unterschiedliche Leute. Die Erfahrung betrifft die Kommunikation bzw. Nicht-Kommunikation zwischen Menschen, wobei die Bewegung durch den Raum als Manifestation ihrer Natur dient; je erfolg[reicher] reicher die Kommunikation, desto variantenreicher Wege zu entfernteren Zielen bieten sich den Besuchern dar.

Landscape One ist eine interaktive Multi-User-Panorama-Videoinstallation, die vier vernetzte Compute[r] mit Touch-Pads und Mikrophonen, vier Videoprojektoren und vier Laserdisk-Player einsetzt. Sie wurde 1997 von Luc Courchesne in Montreal mit de[r] freundlichen Unterstützung des ICC InterCommun[i]cation Center, Tokio, geschaffen.

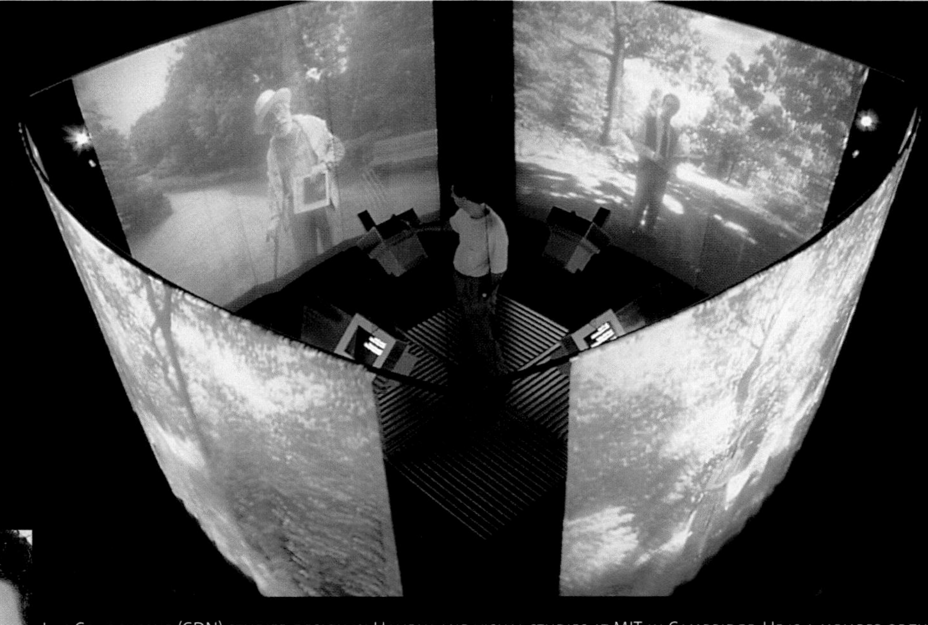

Luc Courchesne (CDN) studied design in Halifax and visual studies at MIT in Cambridge. He is a member of the Advisory Board for Media Arts in Canada, has held leading positions in various institutions of education and art, Artist in Residence at ZKM, at the Museum of New Zealand, at IMEREC, Marseilles, fellow at the Center for Advanced Studies at MIT, and is professor at the School of Industrial Design at the University of Montreal. He has published many papers and his works are represented in international public and private collections.

Luc Courchesne (CDN) studierte Design in Halifax und Visual Studies am MIT in Cambridge. Er ist Mitglied des Advisory Board for Media Arts in Kanada, war leitend in verschiedenen Bildungs- und Kunsteinrichtungen tätig, war Artist in Residence am ZKM, am Museum of New Zealand, bei IMEREC, Marseille, sowie Stipendiat am Center for Advanced Studies am MIT und ist Professor an der Schule für Industriedesign an der Universität Montreal. Er hat zahlreiche Texte veröffentlicht, und seine Arbeiten sind in internationalen öffentlichen und privaten Sammlungen vertreten.

SYSTEMS MAINTENANCE

Perry Hoberman

Systems Maintenance consists of three versions of a furnished room. An ensemble of life-sized furniture occupies a large circular platform on the floor, a virtual room is displayed on a computer monitor, and a 1/8 size physical scale model of the room is presented on a small pedestal. Each version is imaged by a camera (either video or virtual), and the three resulting images are combined into a single large-scale video projection. The camera position, height, angle and field of view are matched between the three cameras. By moving the furniture and camera viewpoints for each of the three rooms, visitors can match or mismatch the components of each of the rooms as they appear in the projected image. The three video signals are fed to a pair of video mixers which are used to perform an additive mix of the three signals, and this combined signal is sent to the video projector.

The images of the three rooms are balanced in intensity, so that the final image appears to represent three different states of the same room. It is nearly impossible to visually distinguish the three versions from each other on the screen, and so the only way to understand the space is to interact with it. There is an implicit goal: to line up the three versions of each piece of furniture, to bring them into harmony. However, there is no correct position for any element, nor is one version of the room the reference for another. Thus, there are an infinite number of possible solutions: and in any case, the goal is continually thwarted by the ease with which a single user can re-introduce disorder into the system.

The life-size furniture sits on a smooth black circular floor in the center of the room, eight meters in diameter. Each article of furniture is mounted on ball-bearing casters, so that, despite its mass, it can be moved easily.

During designated hours of operation, an Adjustment Team of two or three workers makes every attempt to synchronize the three rooms precisely, a goal which usually turns out to be unattainable, due to the continual interventions of the public. The Adjustment Team has a difficult, demanding job, but they perform it with the utmost professionalism and patience. The public functions as a kind of crew, simultaneously filling the roles of directors, actors and audience in an ongoing collaborative spectacle.

Systems Maintenance besteht aus drei Versionen eines möblierten Raumes. Ein Ensemble aus leben großen Möbeln nimmt eine große runde Plattform auf dem Fußboden ein; ein virtueller Raum wird au einem Computermonitor dargestellt, und ein Modell des Raumes im Maßstab 1:8 wird auf einem kleinen Podest gezeigt. Jede Version wird von einer Kamera (real oder virtuell) überwacht, und die drei daraus resultierenden Bilder werden auf einer großen Projektionsfläche zu einem einzigen großen Videobild kombiniert. Die Positionen der drei Kameras (Ausrichtung, Höhe, Blickwinkel und Gesichtsfeld) werden elektronisch abgeglichen. Durch die Bewegung der Möbel bzw. der Kameras in jedem der drei Räume können die Besucher Komponente des jeweiligen Raumes in der entsprechenden Projektion auf dem Großschirm in Übereinstimmung oder aber durcheinander bringen. Die drei Videosignale werden in ein Paar Videomischpulte eingespeist, die dann einen additiven Signalmix durchführen. Dieses kombinierte Videosignal wird schließlich auf den Projektor geleitet.

Die Bilder der drei Räume sind in ihrer Intensität aneinander angeglichen, so daß das endgültige Bil drei unterschiedliche Zustände desselben Raumes wiederzugeben scheint. Es ist beinahe unmöglich, die drei Versionen auf dem Bildschirm rein visuell voneinander zu unterschieden; die einzige Möglichkeit, den Raum zu verstehen, ist, mit ihm zu interagieren. Dies hat auch ein implizites Ziel: Die drei Versionen eines jeden Möbelstücks so auszurichte daß sie miteinander harmonieren. Aber es existiert keine „korrekte" Position für die Elemente, und keiner der Räume bildet eine Referenz für die anderen Deshalb gibt es auch eine unendliche Zahl möglicher Lösungen, und in jedem Fall wird das Ziel dadurch unerreichbarer, daß es für jeden Besucher ganz einfach ist, wieder Unordnung in das System zu bringen.

Das lebensgroße Mobiliar steht in der Mitte des Raumes auf einem glatten runden, schwarzen Boden mit acht Metern Durchmesser. Jedes Möbel stück läuft auf kugelgelagerten Rollen, so daß es trotz seiner Masse leicht bewegt werden kann.

Zu bestimmten Zeiten ist auch ein „Ausrichtungs-Team" aus zwei oder drei Arbeitern im Einsatz, das alles daransetzt, die drei Räume genau zu synchronisieren, was sich normalerweise wegen der ständ gen Interventionen des Publikums als unmöglich erweist. Das „Ausrichtungs-Team" hat eine schwer und anstrengende Arbeit, aber es verrichtet sie mit unendlicher Geduld und Professionalität. Die Zuseher übernehmen ebenfalls eine Art Crew-Funktion: Sie sind Regisseur, Schauspieler und Publikum in diesem kontinuierlichen kollaborativen Schauspiel.

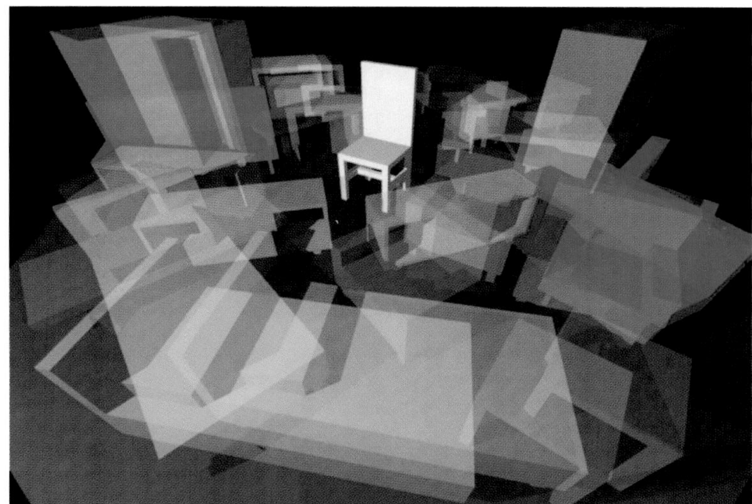

On the screen it's difficult to distinguish the images of each version's furniture from those of the other models. Until something is picked up, or pushed, or clicked, it is nearly impossible to tell whether it's in the same "world" as you are. The participants are simultaneously inside the room, looking down on it like a chessboard, and interfaced with it. The video projection becomes, in effect, a "fourth room" where hands, bodies and gadgets mingle in the same hybrid space—a confused space that allows us to enter a virtual world—and, more significantly, allows that same virtual world to invade our own.
Systems Maintenance is an attempt to come to terms with, and even revel in, the essential nature of interactivity. Rather than locate structures of meaning in ideas of narrative, they are embodied in concepts of behavior—the behavior of the participants and of the system itself. The goal is to line up the furniture, but achieving this goal is hardly the point of the piece, which functions equally well whether it is moving toward a state of order or disorder at any given moment. The ultimate aim of *Systems Maintenance* is to analyze, comment upon, and open up notions of immersion, virtuality and interactivity itself.

Auf dem Bildschirm ist es schwer, die Bilder der einzelnen Versionen des Mobiliars voneinander zu unterschieden. Solange nicht irgend etwas aufgehoben, geschoben oder angeklickt wird, scheint es fast unmöglich festzustellen, ob man auch tatsächlich die „Welt" sieht, in der man sich befindet. Die Mitwirkenden befinden sich gleichzeitig innerhalb des Raumes, blicken auf ihn wie auf ein Schachbrett und stehen dem Raum am Monitor gegenüber. Die Videoprojektion wird ihrerseits zu einem vierten Raum, in dem sich Hände, Körper und Dinge im selben hybriden Areal vermengen – ein konfuser Raum, der uns den Eintritt in eine virtuelle Welt erlaubt und – was noch viel signifikanter ist – der virtuellen Welt erlaubt, in unsere einzudringen.
Systems Maintenance ist ein Versuch, die eigentliche Natur von Interaktivität zu erkennen und damit zu spielen. Anstatt Bedeutungsstrukturen in narrativen Ideen zu finden, sind sie in Verhaltenskonzepten festgeschrieben – im Verhalten der Mitwirkenden und des Systems. Ziel ist es, Möbel auszurichten, aber das Erreichen des Ziels ist nicht der Inhalt dieses Werkes, das in jedem Fall gut funktioniert, egal ob es sich nur zu einem Zustand der Ordnung oder des Chaos hinbewegt. Der letztgültige Zweck von *Systems Maintenance* ist es, die Begriffe Immersion, Virtualität und Interaktivität zu analysieren, zu kommentieren und erfahrbar zu machen.

PERRY HOBERMAN IS AN INSTALLATION AND PERFORMANCE ARTIST. HIS INSTALLATION *BAR CODE HOTEL* WAS AWARDED THE TOP PRIZE AT THE 1995 INTERACTIVE MEDIA FESTIVAL IN LOS ANGELES, AND HAS ALSO BEEN SHOWN AT ARS ELECTRONICA. HOBERMAN CURRENTLY TEACHES IN THE GRADUATE COMPUTER ART DEPARTMENT AT THE SCHOOL OF VISUAL ARTS IN NEW YORK. HE IS THE ART DIRECTOR AT TELEPRESENCE RESEARCH, A COMPANY SPECIALIZING IN VIRTUAL REALITY AND TELEPRESENCE INSTALLATIONS FOR ARTS AND INDUSTRY. — Perry Hoberman ist Installations- und Performance-Künstler. Für *Bar Code Hotel* bekam er den ersten Preis des 1995 Interactive Media Festival in Los Angeles; diese Installation wurde auch beim Ars Electronica Festival gezeigt. Hoberman unterrichtet an der Graduate Computer Art Department der School of Visual Arts in New York. Er ist künstlerischer Direktor bei Telepresence Research, einer Firma, die sich auf Virtual Reality und Telepräsenz-Installation für Kunst und Industrie spezialisiert hat.

SCANNER++

Joachim Blank / Karl Heinz Jeron

SCANNER++ is a device that creates a facsimile of the outside world. On the outside it looks like a copy machine. Joachim Blank and Karl Heinz Jeron have put together twelve conventional A4 format scanners to form a square comprising 4 x 3 devices and mounted them on a 40cm high metal frame. This is covered by twelve sheets of bullet-proof glass so that it may be walked on. The exhibition visitors may walk around on the installation, sit down on it or put objects on it. They assume the role of images to be copied and objects that the scanner registers at a low depth of focus and transforms into a digital representation. The scanner turns photos or texts into image files. In this case it takes a snapshot of the audience and collects traces of hands, feet or articles of clothing, in focus or blurred—and always unpredictable. All the scanners are controlled by a computer and started at varying intervals according to a random choreography. Anything touching the screen at that moment is automatically scanned, filtered and rearranged, then passed on to a local Web server and displayed after a brief delay on a projection screen with a data beam. The exhibition space is illuminated by both the scanners and the brightness of the projection screen, on which a WWW browser may be viewed. In this browser the distorted scanning results are depicted in the form of a 4 x 3 Java applet, which is conveyed to the data projector by the Web server installed on the controlling computer. The data stored on the Web server is then transmitted to the Web site *http://sero.org/scanner* at the same time.

In this way the exhibition visitors create the contents of the Web site. Due to the brief delay and the strong distortion of the data, they cannot completely control the images that appear, yet they can influence the contents. Internet visitors, on the other hand, can access the entire archive of the created documents: the new scans are transparently superimposed on the old ones. The visitor can "click through" the available images. The actions and intentions of the exhibition visitors remain hidden from the Internet visitor, who thus becomes a passive archeologist of an interaction between technology and chance.

The context of *SCANNER*++ is a series of projects on the theme of "Informationrecycling/I(nformation)-

SCANNER++ ist ein Gerät, das die Außenwelt faksimiliert. Es gleicht äußerlich einem Kopiergerät. Joachim Blank und Karl Heinz Jeron haben zwölf handelsübliche Scanner im A4-Format zu einem Quadrat von 4 x 3 Geräten zusammengestellt und auf einem 40cm hohen Metallgestell montiert, da durch eine Abdeckung mit zwölf Panzerglasplatten begehbar wird. Die Ausstellungsbesucher können das Gerät begehen, sich auf ihm niedersetzen oder es mit Gegenständen belegen. Sie nehmen die Rol der Bildvorlagen und Objekte ein, die ein Scanner i geringer Tiefenschärfe erfaßt und in ein digitales Abbild verwandelt. Der Scanner macht Fotos oder Texte zu Bilddateien. Hier macht er Momentaufnahmen vom Publikum und sammelt die Spuren von Händen, Füßen oder Kleidungsstücken, scharf oder verwischt – und immer unvorhersehbar, denn alle Scanner werden von einem Computer gesteuert und in unterschiedlichen zeitlichen Abständen nach einer zufälligen Choreographie gestartet. Wa dann gerade in Berührung mit dem Bildschirm steht, wird automatisch gescannt, gefiltert und umgestaltet, einem lokalen Webserver zur Verfügung gestellt und nach kurzer Verzögerung mit einem Datenbeam auf einer Projektionsleinwand sichtbar gemacht. Der Ausstellungsraum wird sowohl durch die Scanner als auch durch die Helligkeit der Leinwand erleuchtet, auf der ein WWW-Browser zu sehen ist. In ihm bilden sich in der Forn eines 4 x 3 Java-Applets die verfremdeten Sanning Ergebnisse ab, die der auf dem Steuercomputer installierte Webserver an den Datenprojektor weiter reicht. Die auf dem Webserver abgelegten Daten werden zugleich auf die Website *http://sero.org/scanner* übertragen.

Die Ausstellungsbesucher erzeugen so den Inhalt der Website. Die leichte Verzögerung und starke Verfremdung der Daten erlaubt ihnen zwar nicht die vollständige Kontrolle über das Bildangebot, aber die Einflußnahme auf seine Inhalte. Die Internetbesucher hingegen können auf das gesamte Archiv der erzeugten Dokumente zugreifen: Die neuen überlagern transparent die alten Scans. Der Besucher „klickt" sich durch das Angebot hindurch Aktionen und Intentionen der Ausstellungsbesucher sind ihm durch die technische Verfremdung und Fragmentierung verschleiert. Er wird zum passiven Archäologen einer Interaktion von Technik und Zufall.

SCANNER++ steht im Kontext einer Projektreihe zum Thema Informationsrecycling/I(nformation)-Smog" Frühere Arbeiten von Blank & Jeron, wie etwa *without_addresses* bei der Documenta X (http://sero.org/without_addresses) oder *DUMP YOUR TRASH!* (http://sero.org/dyt) nutzten das Internet als Kopiermaschine, indem solche Dokumente, die im Netz bereits vorhanden waren, durch verschiedene Verfahren in neuer Form aufbereitet wurden. Durc minimale Interaktion der virtuellen Besucher – Tex eingaben oder Mausklicks auf einer Navigations-

Smog." Blank & Jeron's earlier works, such as *without addresses* at Documenta X (*http://sero.org/without_addresses*) or *"DUMP YOUR TRASH!" (http://sero.org/dyt)* use the Internet as a copy machine, in that documents that were already there on the Net are treated with various procedures and presented in a new form. With minimal interaction on the part of virtual visitors—text input or a mouse click on a navigation surface—the layout of the Net contents was automatically redesigned by a software agent and made available on the Web site in this form. Despite their standardized creation, these representations are reminiscent of personal documents and auric objects, such as letters or engraved stone tablets, an image in which the documents can be ordered and actually made by hand.
With *SCANNER*⁺⁺ this method is reversed. The project starts from a real space and uses the technique of "scanning" (lat. = to stress) to translate it into digital information. This perhaps most obvious, but also most radical transfer from analog to digital information is like a metaphor for making the world readable in the age of the "information society." While *SCANNER*⁺⁺ at first glance seems to promise a simulation of the space and the actions carried out in it, this is actually questioned and subverted, so that the project raises the question of the actual value not only of information, but also of aesthetic interaction, which it represents in a way that is already almost paradoxical, half objective, half processual.

Text: Gerrit Gohlke, Blank & Jeron

fläche – wurden Netzinhalte durch Softwareagenten automatisch im Layout umgestaltet und in dieser Form auf der Website zur Verfügung gestellt. Ihre Darstellung erinnert ihrer standardisierten Entstehung zum Trotz an persönliche Dokumente und auratische Gegenstände wie Briefe oder beschriftete Steintafeln, einem Erscheinungsbild in dem die Dokumente bestellt und handwerklich real gefertigt werden können.
Bei *SCANNER*⁺⁺ wird diese Methode umgekehrt. Das Projekt geht vom realen Raum aus und überführt ihn durch die Technik des „Scannens" (lat. = hervorheben) in digitale Information. Diese vielleicht selbstverständlichste, aber auch radikalste Weise des Übergang von analoger in digitale Information erscheint wie eine Metapher für die Lesbarmachung der Welt im Zeitalter der „Informationsgesellschaft". Indem die Simulation des Raumes und der in ihm vollzogenen Handlungen, die *SCANNER*⁺⁺ auf den ersten Blick verspricht, mehrfach in Frage gestellt und hintergangen wird, wirft das Projekt die Frage nach dem tatsächlichen Wert sowohl der Information als auch der ästhetischen Interaktion auf, die in ihm fast schon paradox halb objekthaft, halb prozessual dargestellt werden.

Text: Gerrit Gohlke, Blank & Jeron

JOACHIM BLANK (D), BORN 1963, AND KARL HEINZ JERON, BORN 1962, HAVE BEEN WORKING TOGETHER SINCE 1996 UNDER THE NAME OF "BLANK & JERON" AS AN ARTIST DUO. SINCE 1993 THEY HAVE REALIZED INTERNET PROJECTS IN VARIOUS CONSTELLATIONS IN THE CONTEXT OF ART AND CULTURE. IN ADDITION TO PURE INTERNET PROJECTS, THEY ARE CURRENTLY WORKING ON HYBRID PROJECTS, WHICH ADDRESS THE THEME OF THE INTERNET, BUT ARE EXPANDED INTO PHYSICAL SPACE AS HANGINGS, OBJECTS, INSTALLATIONS AND EVENTS. THEY ARE CURRENTLY INVOLVED IN ARTISTIC STRATEGIES FOR INFORMATION RECYCLING IN THE CONTEXT OF THE "INFORMATION SOCIETY."

Joachim Blank (D), geb. 1963, und Karl Heinz Jeron (D), geb. 1962, arbeiten seit 1996 unter dem Namen „Blank & Jeron" als Künstlerduo zusammen. Seit 1993 realisierten sie in unterschiedlichen Konstellationen Internetprojekte im Kunst- und Kulturkontext. Neben reinen Internetprojekten arbeiten sie derzeit an hybriden Projekten, die das Internet thematisieren, sich jedoch als Hängungen, Objekte und Installationen und Events auf den physischen Raum ausdehnen. Zur Zeit befassen sie sich mit künstlerischen Strategien zum Informationsrecycling im Kontext der

HAMSTER – SYMBIOTIC EXCHANGE OF HOARDED ENERGY

Christoph Ebener / Frank Fietzek / Uli Winters

Our project aims to establish a symbiosis of a population of hamster and a group of vehicles with intelligent steering units.

The Hamsters

For the experiment we use common golden hamsters. We pick mostly female individuals to prevent territory fights. For the exhibition their day/night cycle will be carefully switched to allow spectators to see things happen during the day.

The Vehicles

Each of these vehicles is driven forward by a built-in hamster running wheel, whenever a hamster enters it and starts running. Without a hamster inside the vehicles are totally immobile.
The microcontroller on each vehicle can distinguish light from dark with four light detectors and uses this information to control its steering system.
Each vehicle has a solar panel mounted on its surface to collect electricity and store it in its batteries.

The Setting

There are 15 hamsters running free within an area of 50 m^2 surrounded by a glass fence. A light source at one end of this area is the only light source in the whole installation, and there is an electric food station at the other end. Spectators can move around outside the glass fence and watch the experiment.
Whenever a hamster enters one of the vehicles (which they like to do quite often), it starts moving the vehicle forward by using the running-wheel. The microcontroller will steer the vehicle towards the light source where it arrests its wheel and stops. After refilling its batteries via solar panels, the vehicle will take the next hamster-lift to move over to the food station. Here it transmits its hoarded energy to the food station, whereby the station provides an amount of food for the animals. Since it has no additional power supply, the food station

Unser Projekt versucht, eine Symbiose zwischen einer Hamsterpopulation und einer Gruppe von Fahrzeugen mit intelligenten Sensoreinheiten herzustellen.

Die Hamster

Für das Experiment verwenden wir gewöhnliche Goldhamster. Wir setzen überwiegend Weibchen ein, um Territorialkämpfe zu vermeiden. Für die Ausstellung wird ihr Tag-Nacht-Rhythmus vorsichtig umgestellt, damit die Zuseher ihre Aktivitäten während des Tages beobachten können.

Die Fahrzeuge

Jedes dieser Fahrzeuge wird durch ein eingebautes Hamsterlaufrad angetrieben, sobald ein Hamster in das Fahrzeug steigt und zu laufen beginnt. Ohne Hamster sind die Fahrzeuge vollkommen unbeweglich.
Die Mikro-Steuereinheiten an den einzelnen Fahrzeugen können über vier Lichtdetektoren Helligkeit und Dunkelheit unterscheiden und verwenden diese Information zur Lenkung. Jedes Fahrzeug ist mit Solarzellen zum Aufladen der Batterien ausgestattet.

Die Installation

Auf einer mit Glaszäunen eingegrenzten Fläche von 50 m^2 befinden sich 15 freilaufende Hamster. Die einzige Lichtquelle befindet sich an einem Ende des Areals, eine elektrische Futterstation am anderen. Die Zuseher können sich außerhalb der Glaswände bewegen und das Geschehen von allen Seiten beobachten.
Wann immer ein Hamster in eines der Fahrzeuge steigt (was sie gerne und oft tun), bewegt er das Fahrzeug mittels des Laufrades vorwärts. Der Mikro-Controller steuert das Fahrzeug zur Lichtquelle, wo es anhält.
Haben sich die Batterien über die Solarzellen aufgeladen, ist das Fahrzeug bereit, den nächsten Hamsterpassagier aufzunehmen und ihn zur Futterstation zu fahren (mit Hamsterantrieb, versteht sich). Dort wird die vom Fahrzeug gespeicherte Energie in die Futterstation übertragen, und diese gibt eine Portion Hamsterfutter frei. Da die Futterstation elektrisch betrieben wird, aber über keine eigene Stromversorgung verfügt, ist sie auf die Energiespenden der Fahrzeuge angewiesen.
Wenn der nächste Hamster in das Fahrzeug steigt und das Laufrad betätigt, fährt das Vehikel zurück zur Lichtstation.

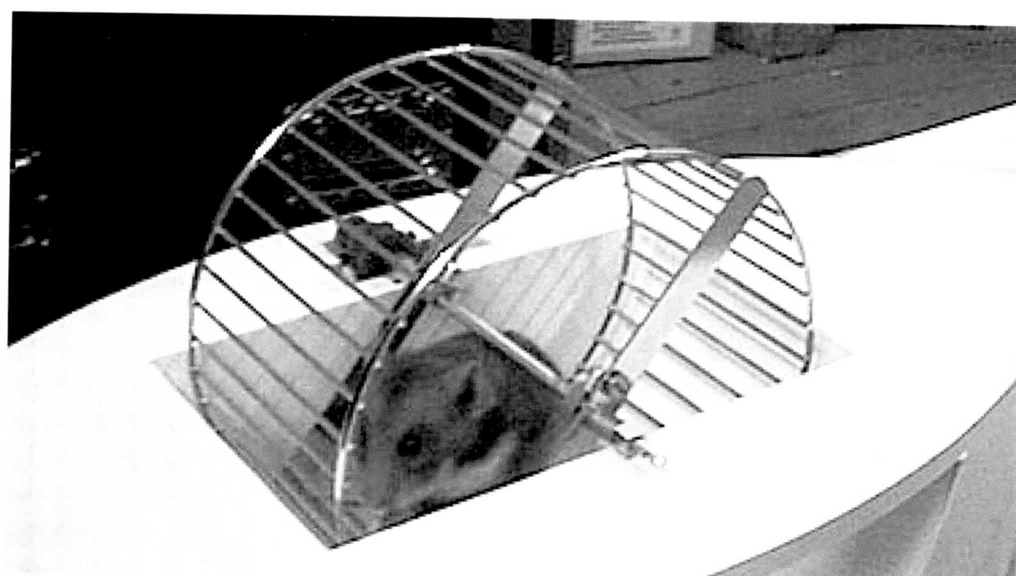

depends on the engine-gifts from the vehicles. When the next hamster gets into the wheel, the vehicle will start off for the light again.
The hamsters depend on the vehicle, because they deliver the energy for their food station, whereas the vehicles are unable to move without the hamsters' physical power.
By creating an artificial symbiosis of this kind, the experiment aims to investigate the possibility of matching available behaviour patterns of animals on the one hand with complementary machine programs on the other. Is it possible to draw synergistic results from a collaboration of highly evolved animals and technical devices, if they are smart enough to canalize the animals' need for their own purposes without abusing them?

Die Hamster sind von den Fahrzeugen abhängig, weil nur diese die Energie für die Futterstation liefern, während die Vehikel sich ihrerseits ohne die physische Kraft der Hamster nicht fortbewegen können. Durch die Schaffung einer solchen künstlichen Symbiose untersucht das Projekt, inwieweit es möglich ist, vorhandene Verhaltensmuster von Lebewesen und ergänzende Maschinenprogramme aufeinander abzustimmen.
Kann man Synergieeffekte aus der Zusammenarbeit hochentwickelter Tiere und technischer Geräte ziehen, wenn letztere klug genug sind, die Bedürfnisse der Tiere für ihre eigenen Zwecke einzuspannen, ohne die Tiere dabei zu mißbrauchen?

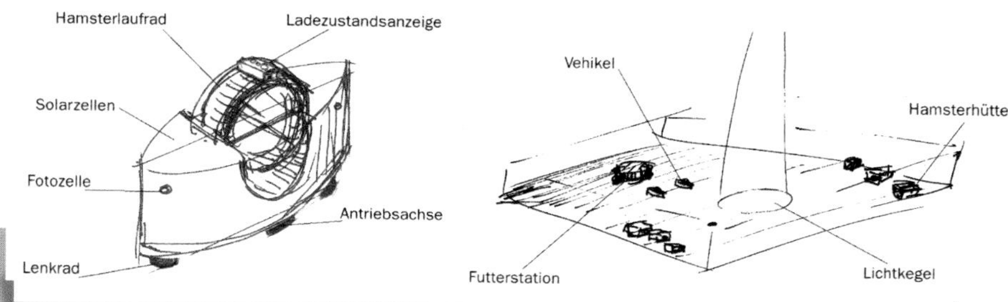

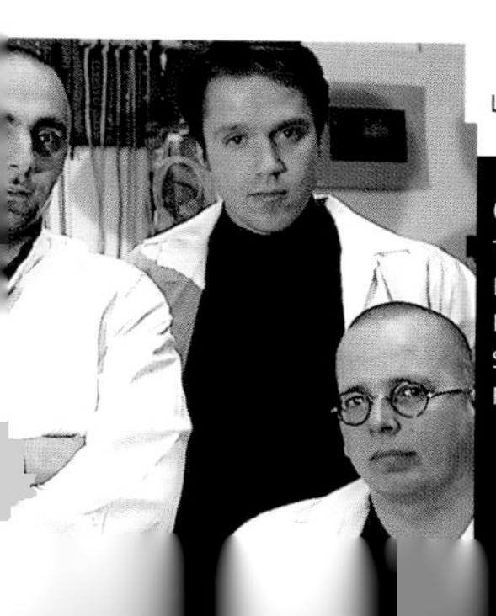

Christoph Ebener (D) studied at the College of Fine Arts in Hamburg and has worked since then on numerous art projects throughout Europe. Uli Winters (D) also studied in Hamburg and has worked together with Christoph Ebener since 1997 on international art projects. Frank Fietzek (D) studied philosophy, art and computer science, has taught at specialized colleges and academies and is currently project director at the Laboratory for Electronic Media in Hamburg.

Christoph Ebener (D) studierte an der Hochschule für Bildende Kunst in Hamburg und arbeitet seither an zahlreichen Kunstprojekten in ganz Europa. Uli Winters (D) studierte ebenfalls in Hamburg und arbeitet seit 1997 gemeinsam mit Christoph Ebener an internationalen Kunstprojekten. Frank Fietzek (D) studierte Philosophie, Kunst und Informatik, war Dozent an Fachhochschulen und Akademien und ist derzeit Projektleiter am Labor für elektronische

SOUNDCREATURES

Kouichirou Eto / Canon ARTLAB

The work develops through interactions between the Internet web pages and the installation at the exhibition site linked in real time.
Original sound patterns are created from visual patterns that a participant inputs on the Internet web pages. Every time a pattern is created, the sound pattern is automatically registered by one of the linked robots at the site, and the robot moves around repeating the sound pattern through its speaker.
The entire movements of the robots in the space can be seen in real time on Web pages. (The terminals for the Internet Web pages are also provided at the site.)

Communications of Sound by Robots

Ten robots loaded with speakers move around within a certain space/field in the installation. As the robots come close to each other, they exchange certain elements of their sound data, and after several exchanges, the whole sound slowly begins to change. It is interesting to watch how the sound is transformed through the exchanges of the robots when the sound elements, totally different from what is heard at the time, and fed from the Internet.
In the field are two "infection zones" where visitors can register a mechanism to change sound elements by operating the input console in the infection zone. The change occurs on a different level from mutual communications among the robots, and when a robot happens to pass through this zone, its sound composition changes.
Sound changes, caused by different actions in the installation, immediately react to the visual patterns on the web pages. When the sound pattern is influenced, not only from a participant's input but also from communications with other elements, it automatically changes.

In Cooperation with IMRF (International Media Research Foundation)

Sound Composition: Suguru Yamaguchi
Robots Production: Akihito Tagawa (University of Tsukuba)
Visual Direction: Ichiro Higashiizumi

Das Werk entwickelt sich durch die Interaktion zwi schen den Internet-Webseiten und der Installation am Ausstellungsort, die in Echtzeit miteinander ve bunden sind.
Aus den visuellen Mustern, die ein Teilnehmer in d Internetseiten eingibt, werden Klangmuster erzeugt. Sobald ein Muster eingegeben wird, übernimmt einer der Roboter am Ausstellungsort automatisch das zugehörige Klangmuster, bewegt sich und spielt das Klangmuster durch seinen Lautsprecher ab. Die Bewegungen des Roboters sind über die Webseiten online zu verfolgen (Terminals für d Webseiten stehen am Ausstellungsort zur Verfügung).

Klangkommunikation der Roboter

Zehn mit Lautsprechern ausgestattete Roboter bewegen sich innerhalb eines vorgegebenen Areals frei in der Installation. Wenn sie sich einander nähern, tauschen sie bestimmte Elemente ihrer Klangdaten aus, bis sich nach mehreren solchen Austauschaktionen der gesamte Klang allmählich ändert. Es ist interessant zu beobachten, wie der Roboterklang durch den Informationsaustausch de Geräte transformiert wird, wenn über das Netz völlig andere Klangelemente eingegeben werden als gerade zu hören sind.
Im Bewegungsfeld selbst sind zwei „Infektionszonen" definiert, in denen die Besucher weitere Klangveränderungen definieren können – wenn ei Roboter durch solch einen Bereich fährt, ändert sic seine Klangkomposition, und zwar auf andere Weise als beim Kommunikationsaustausch zwischen den Robotern.
Jede Änderung im Klangmuster der Installation spiegelt sich sofort und automatisch in den Bildmustern auf den Webseiten wider, egal ob die Veränderung durch einen Input von außen oder durch die Kommunikation unter den Robotern erfolgt.

In Zusammenarbeit mit IMRF (International Media Research Foundation)

Sound Composition: Suguru Yamaguchi
Robots Production: Akihito Tagawa (University of Tsukuba)
Visuelle Konzeption: Ichiro Higashiizumi

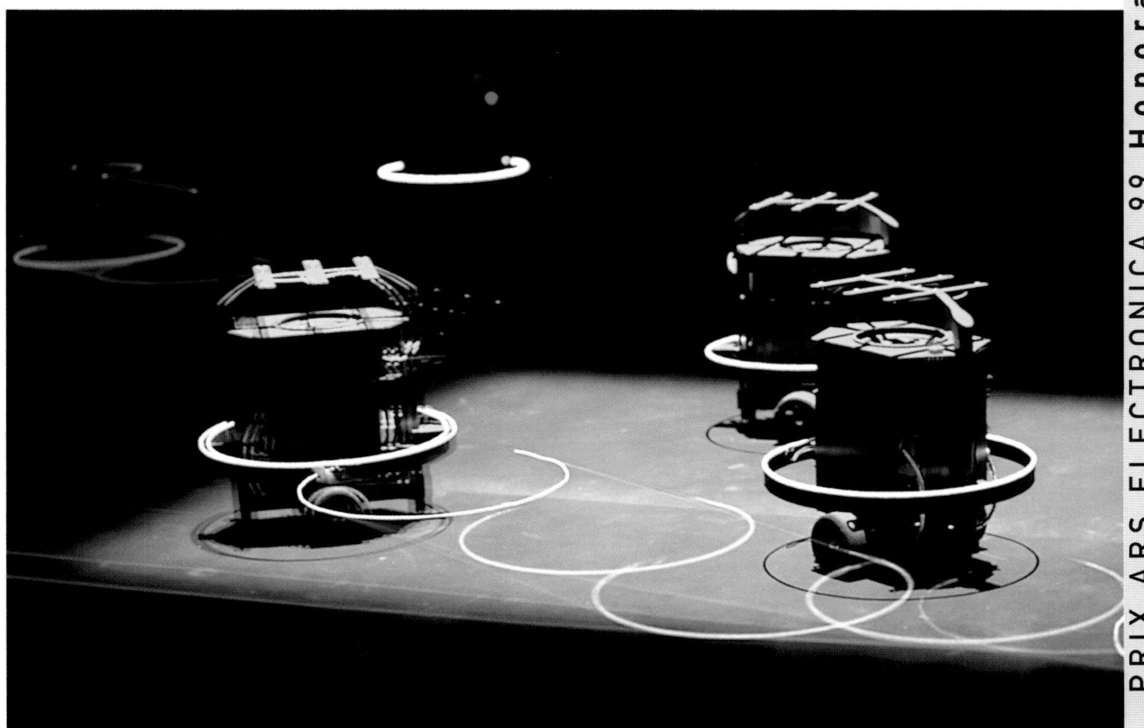

Kouichirou Eto (J), born 1971, graduated from Keio University Graduate School of Media and Governance. In his relatively short career he has compiled a long list of accomplishments in new media and Internet projects. Even before Eto had graduated from college, he had many impressive accomplishments. Eto created *Joy Mech Fight* (1993) for Nintendo in his freshman year. As a junior in college he joined Masaki Fujihata's Lab for computer arts research. He is now a researcher of the International Media Research Foundation.

Kouichirou Eto (J), geb. 1971, graduierte an der Keio University Graduate School for Media and Governance. In seiner noch relativ jungen Karriere hat er bereits eine große Zahl von Projekten für Internet und Neue Medien realisiert. Noch vor Abschluß seines Studiums fiel er durch brillante Leistungen auf, so schuf er 1993 – in seinem ersten Jahr – *Joy Mech Fight* für Nintendo. Bereits als junger Student hatte er sich Masaki Fujihatas Laboratorium für Computerkunstforschung angeschlossen; derzeit ist er Forscher an der International Media Research Foundation.

ROBOTS+AVATARS DEALING WITH VIRTUAL ILLUSIONS

F.A.B.R.I.CATORS / K-Team

In the field of mobile robotics, researchers are working on several hard subjects:—Human-robot interaction—Mobile robot navigation—Robotic telemanipulation—Relationship between simulated (models) and real robots. This work addresses several of those subjects from a very original viewpoint, with an artistic background and very sophisticated techniques, including REAL mobile robots: a real mobile robot (type Koale, from K-Team) is used as physical representation.
This robot has been programmed for navigation in the performance environment and has a connection to the virtual world and its model in this virtual environment.
– Mobile robot models: a model of the robot is linked to the real robot in the virtual world and acts in relation to the robot actions.
– Virtual reality: complex environments and virtual worlds are linked to the robot activity, Internet activity and visitor interactions.
– Internet. The project is particularly pushes the limits of technology in the field of human-robot interaction and robotic manipulation, integrating a large number of complementary tools (mobile robot, virtual worlds, robot models, Internet, visitor reactions) giving an important role to complex subjective aspects. Both the integration aspect and the subjective approach make this project a very innovative and leading research project.
Future applications include all mobile robotic implementation where innovative human-robot interaction is requested (robotics pets, robotic services for private use, telerobotics on the Internet for surveillance or telepresence, etc.) The innovative approach allows new applications which can be implemented in everyday life. The social implications are a much better integration of robots in the life of human's, including at the cultural level (robot as a new expression vector).
Robots + Avatars Dealing with Virtual Illusions integrates virtual reality, robotics and telepresence with a high aesthetical content as well as a suggestive and enigmatic interaction.
The Real Ambience is represented as a scenography in the form of an arena with labyrinthic pathways, made of mirrors, metal, wood, in a shiny, colorful

Auf dem Gebiet der mobilen Robotik arbeiten die Forscher an mehreren harten Themen: Mensch-Roboter-Interaktion; Navigation mobiler Roboter; Telemanipulation von Robotern; Beziehung zwischen simulierten (Modellen) und echten Robotern. Die vorliegende Arbeit geht an diese Themen von einem recht originellen Standpunkt heran, mit einem künstlerischen Hintergrund und ausgefeilter Technik, darunter echte mobile Roboter: Ein echter mobiler Roboter vom Typ Koala (von K-Team) wird als physische Repräsentation verwendet.
Dieser Roboter wurde für die Navigation im Performance-Raum programmiert und hat eine Verbindung zur virtuellen Welt und zu seinem Modell in dieser virtuellen Umgebung.
– Mobile Robotermodelle: Ein Modell des Roboters in der virtuellen Welt wird dem realen Roboter zugeordnet und agiert in enger Beziehung mit den Aktionen des Roboters;
– Virtuelle Realität: Komplexe Umgebungen und virtuelle Welten werden mit der Roboteraktivität, mit Internetaktivitäten und Besucher-Interaktionen verknüpft;
– Internet: Das Projekt erweitert vor allem die technologischen Grenzen im Bereich der Mensch-Roboter-Interaktion und -Manipulation, indem es eine Vielzahl komplementärer Werkzeuge integriert (mobile Roboter, virtuelle Welten, Robotermodelle, Internet, Besucherinteraktion), was gerade den komplexen subjektiven Beziehungen unter gleichen eine wichtige Rolle gibt. Sowohl der Integrationsaspekt als auch der subjektive Ansatz machen dieses Projekt zu einem sehr innovativen und führenden Forschungsvorhaben.
Zukünftige Anwendungen umfassen alle Arten von mobiler Roboter-Implementation, bei denen eine innovative Mensch-Roboter-Interaktion erforderlich ist (Roboter-Haustiere, häusliche „Dienst-ro-boten", Teleroboter für Überwachungs- oder Telepräsenzaufgaben via Internet usw.). Dieser innovative Ansatz ermöglicht neue Anwendungen, die im Alltagsleben implementiert werden können und die als soziale Folge eine bessere Integration der Roboter ins menschliche Leben haben werden, auch auf der kulturellen Ebene (Roboter als neue Ausdrucksvektoren).
Robots + Avatars Dealing with Virtual Illusions vereinigt virtuelle Realität, Robotik und Telepräsenz mit hohem ästhetischem Gehalt und einer ebenso suggestiven wie rätselhaften Interaktion.
Die reale Umwelt wird als Szenerie in Form einer Arena präsentiert, in der labyrinthische Wege aus Spiegeln, Metall und Holz in eine glänzende Sand-

sand and stone landscape. A 4x4 m screen projects the VR world and the results of the interaction between the user and the robot and avatars.
The Virtual Ambience is articulated by 10 different worlds or cities contained in the "Mother City" Ying & Yang. The personages in this installation exist both in real space (Koala = robot) and in virtual space, Ying and Yang: avatars. Each control the other, and yet both are controlled by the user in a local space and also through the net (from a non-local space).
The public can interact with each single robot in its environment by moving a joystick. This interaction generates a real time reaction in the behaviour of the robot as well in the avatars in the VR-world, visible on the projection screen at the top of the scenography of the arena, "the real world."
It is possible to attract Koala by clicking on the button of the joystick and causing Koala to move towards Yang, trying to find him either in the physical or virtual world. In systhesis either Koala or the avatars Ying and Yang can interact with the visitors by means of the network or telepresence. Network which becomes a sort of prolongation.

-und-Stein-Landschaft eingebettet sind. Ein 4 x 4 Meter großer Bildschirm projiziert die VR-Welt und die Ergebnisse der Interaktion zwischen Benutzer, Roboter und Avataren.Die virtuelle Umgebung wird durch zehn verschiedene Welten oder Städte ausgedrückt, die in der „Mutterstadt" Ying & Yang zusammengefaßt sind. Die Gestalten dieser Installation existieren sowohl im realen Raum (der Koala-Roboter) als auch im virtuellen Ying&Yang als Avatare. Jeder kann den anderen steuern, und dennoch werden beide vom Benutzer im lokalen – und auch im nicht-lokalen – Bereich über das Netz gesteuert.
Das Publikum kann einfach durch das Bewegen eines Joysticks mit jedem einzelnen Roboter innerhalb dessen Umwelt interagieren. Diese Interaktion erzeugt sowohl beim Roboter wie auch bei dessen Avatar in der VR-Welt eine Echtzeit-Reaktion, die auf der Projektionsfläche oberhalb der „realen Welt" sichtbar wird. Es gibt beispielsweise die Möglichkeit, den Koala-Roboter durch einen Druck auf den Joystick-Knopf anzulocken und ihn zu veranlassen, sich zu Yang zu begeben, wobei der Roboter versucht, diesen entweder in der realen oder in der virtuellen Welt aufzuspüren. In der Synthese können entweder Koala oder die Avatare Ying und Yang mit den Besuchern über das Netzwerk oder über Telepräsenz interagieren – das Netzwerk wird eine Art verlängerte Welt.

F.A.B.R.I.CATORS (I) is an interdisciplinary group concerned with the integration of technology, communication, art and design. The group's main focus is on bringing art and technology into the development process of various projects in an interdisciplinary way. K-TEAM (CH) is a young, aspiring group of engineers associated with the Microcomputing Laboratory of the Swiss Federal Institute for Technology in Lausanne. F.A.B.R.I.CATORS (I) ist eine interdisziplinäre Gruppe, die sich mit der Integration von Technologie,Kommunikation, Kunst und Design beschäftigt. Hauptanliegen der Gruppe ist es, Kunst und Technologie interdisziplinär in den Entstehungsprozeß diverser Projekte einfließen zu lassen. K-TEAM (CH) ist eine junge, aufstrebende Gruppe von Technikern aus dem Umfeld des Mikrocomputing Labors am Schweizerischen Bundesinstitut für Technologie in Lausanne.

DESCARTES ODER DIE EINSAMKEIT DER INTERAKTIVEN SKULPTUR

Beate Garmer

Interactive art necessarily concentrates a significant portion of its attention to animating observable behaviors on the part of the persons intended to interact with it, so that these mutate from observing to observed persons.
The artist becomes the director of the experiment, developing ideas of those who could be hypothetically addressed and testing these ideas on live objects, always in danger of mere self-confirmation.
In the present work the interactive element undergoes a reduction to the possible, albeit inadvisable examination of the question of whether an electrical current is live or not.
This results in the paradox of an interactive sculpture that bitingly refuses direct contact and thus challenges the traditional, contemplative attitude of observing art.
In reference to Descartes, whose "I think, therefore I am" as a reaction to universal doubt quasi digitizes reality , the sign "De omnibus dubitandum est" ("Everything must be doubted") establishes a connection between the digital core idea and the idea-historical background of the development and significance of self-reflexive systems.
In the tragedy, the question of yes or no, 1 or 2, in other words the question of the active subject, still had existential meaning. In the course of the development of digital systems, located through replication and acceleration outside the human capability of imagining and thus apparently leveled out to pure arbitrariness, the question is now imbued with a new, concretely intelligible explosive power.
The essence of self-reflexive systems is characterized by a certain type of energy, which electrical current concretely and metaphorically represents here.

"... As an object of consciousness the thing loses its substantiality (in Cartesian self-reflection), and the tree that is seen no longer differs in any way from one that is only remembered or even freely invented (to name the specter of doubting the reality of the outside world); precisely in this way, however, it becomes an integral component of the consciousness that only exists as process, as a stream of consciousness, and in which everything of the substantial object is therefore automatically pulverized.

Interaktive Kunst konzentriert zwangsläufig einen wesentlichen Teil ihrer Aufmerksamkeit auf die Animation beobachtbarer Verhaltensweisen bei der zu interagierenden Person, die so von einer betrachtenden zu einer betrachteten mutiert.
Künstler und Künstlerin werden zu Versuchsleitern, die Vorstellung von hypothetischen Adressaten entwickelt, die sie dann am lebenden Objekt, immer in der Gefahr reiner Selbstbestätigung, überprüfen.
In der vorliegenden Arbeit erfährt das interaktive Element eine extreme Reduktion auf die mögliche, aber nicht ratsame Untersuchung der Frage, ob ein Strom fließt oder nicht.
Dabei entsteht das Paradox einer interaktiven Skulptur, die sich bissig dem direkten Kontakt verweigert und damit die traditionelle, kontemplative Haltung bei der Betrachtung von Kunst herausfordert.
Anhand von Descartes, dessen „Ich denke, also bin ich" als Reaktion auf den universellen Zweifel Wirklichkeit quasi digitalisiert (s. auch das Zitat weiter unten), stellt die Aufschrift „De omnibus dubitandum est" („An Allem muß gezweifelt werden") einen Zusammenhang her zwischen der digitalen Kernidee und dem ideengeschichtlichen Hintergrund der Entwicklung und Bedeutung selbstreflexiver Systeme.
Die Frage, ob ja oder nein, 0 oder 1, also die Frage des handelnden Subjekts, besaß in der Tragödie noch existentielle Bedeutung.
Im Zuge der Entwicklung digitaler Systeme, durch Vervielfältigung und Beschleunigung außerhalb menschlicher Vorstellungskraft angesiedelt und so dem Anschein nach zu reiner Beliebigkeit verflacht, erhält sie an dieser Stelle neue, konkret faßbare Brisanz.
Das Wesen selbstreflexiver Systeme wird durch eine bestimmte Art von Energie geprägt, für die hier konkret und metaphorisch der elektrische Strom steht.

„... Als Bewußtseinsgegenstand verliert das Ding (in der Kartesischen Selbstreflexion) seine Substantialität, und der gesehene Baum unterscheidet sich in nichts mehr von einem nur erinnerten oder auch frei erfundenen (um das Gespenst des Zweifels an der Realität der Außenwelt zu bannen); gerade dadurch aber wird er zu einem integralen Bestandteil des Bewußtseins, das überhaupt nur als Prozeß, als Bewußtseinsstrom existiert und in dem daher automatisch alles substantiell Gegenständliche zermahlen wird.
Was hätte die moderne Denkart besser auf die Auflösung der Materie in Energie, des Gegenständlichen in einen Wirbel atomischer Vorgänge, vorbereiten können als diese Auflösung objektiv gegebener Wirklichkeit in subjektive Bewußtseinsdaten, bzw. in die ewig bewegten und sich bewegenden Partikel eines Bewußtseinsstroms?"
(aus H. Arendt, Vita activa oder vom tätigen Leben)

DE OMNIBUS DUBITANDUM

"An Allem muß gezweifelt werden."
DE OMNIBUS DUBITANDUM EST
escartes (1596 - 1650)

at could have better prepared
modern way of thinking for
disintegration of material into
rgy, of concreteness into a
irl of atomic processes, than
s disintegration of objectively
en reality into the subjective
a of consciousness, the
rnally moved and moving
ticles of a stream of
sciousness?"
nna Arendt

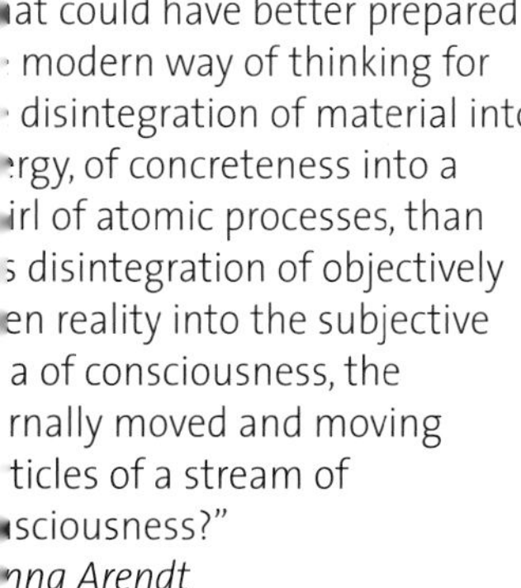

Beate Garmer (D), born 1969. 1988—1995: studied art / romance languages at the University in Saarbrücken. 1991: DAAD scholarship for Toulouse, France. 1995: finished state examination. After 1995: studied free art at the College of Fine Arts Saar in Saarbrücken with Wolfgang Nestler and Tamás Waliczky. 1997: preliminary diploma. Participation in various group exhibitions. ▬ Beate Garmer (D). geb. 1969. 1988–1995: Studium Kunst/Romanistik an der Uni-Gesamthochschule-Siegen. 1991: DAAD-Stipendium nach Toulouse, Frankreich. 1995: Staatsexamen. Ab 1995: Studium Freie Kunst an der Hochschule der bildenden Künste Saar in Saarbrücken bei Wolfgang Nestler und Tamás Waliczky. 1997: Vordiplom. Teilnahme an verschiedenen Gruppenausstellungen.

metaFIELD MAZE

Bill Keays / Ron MacNeil

Concept

The *metaField Maze* is a virtual maze game which uses a 12'x12' interactive floor. People interact by walking onto the floor and directing the path of the marble through the labyrinth with the movements of their bodies over the floor surface. The maze, which is projected onto the floor, is a three-dimensional model which tilts according to where the player moves. The marble moves according to the direction of the tilt. The goal is to move the marble through the full course of the maze.

This installation uses a multi-purpose interactive floor system created by the authors known as *metaField*. The *metaField* was developed in an effort to create an immensive environment that had the following qualities: it should be suitable to interactive art or game applications; it should have the ability of accomodating both solo and collaborative activities; it should involve the kinesthetic input from the users; it should have a low threshold of engagement. From these criteria, a floor-based configuration was decided upon using video projection and a vision system.

Configuration

The *metaField* consists of a video camera and projector mounted 30 ft above a 12' x 12' retro-reflective floor surface. The camera and projector are focused on the floor, and are attached to a Silicon Graphics O2 computer. The retro-reflective material creates a desirable high contrast between the people and the floor when viewed from above. This contrast facilitates the task of locating the people standing on the floor.

The software driving the system has two distinct components. The first is vision software known as glimpser, which accepts the incoming video stream and draws basic information from it. The second takes this information and uses it to control the display. The glimpser has the ability to find regions of a specified size and specified color from incoming video frames. The glimpser and display software run separately, but simultaneously.

The display software begins by telling the glimpser what sort of image data it requires. For the purpose

Konzept

metaField Maze ist ein virtuelles Irrgarten-Spiel, d
einen interaktiven Boden von knapp 4 x 4 Metern Fläche verwendet. Die Besucher interagieren, inde
sie auf diesen Boden steigen und durch ihre Körpe
bewegungen den Weg einer Kugel steuern. Das au
den Boden projizierte Labyrinth ist ein dreidimensionales Modell, das je nach Bewegung des Spiele
kippen kann. Die Kugel rollt in die Richtung, in die das Modell kippt. Ziel des Spiels ist es, die Kugel über den ganzen Parcours des Labyrinths zu steuern.

Die Installation verwendet ein von den Autoren konstruiertes interaktives Mehrzweck-Boden-System, das *metaField*. Dieses *metaField* ist das Ergebnis des Versuchs, ein immersives Aktionsinterface zu konstruieren, das folgende Qualitäten aufweist: Es sollte für interaktive Spiele oder Kuns
anwendungen geeignet sein; es sollte sowohl Einzel- wie kollaborative Aktivitäten ermöglichen; sollte den kinesthetischen Input der Benutzer vera
beiten, und es sollte leicht und einfach handhabb
sein. Um diese Anforderungen erfüllen zu können, wurde beschlossen, eine Konfiguration aus Video-Projektion und Erfassungssystem zu verwenden.

Konfiguration

Das *metaField* besteht aus einer Videokamera und einem Projektor, die neun Meter über einer reflektierenden Bodenfläche von 12 x 12 Fuß montiert sind. Kamera und Projektor sind auf den Boden fokussiert und mit einem Silicon Graphics O2 Computer verbunden. Das reflektierende Bodenmateri
bietet bei Betrachtung von oben ausreichenden Kontrast zwischen Besuchern und Grundfläche.

Die implementierte Software besteht aus zwei getrennten Komponenten. Die eine ist eine Glimpser genannte Betrachtungssoftware, die den einkommenden Video-Datenstrom erfaßt und auf Grundinformationen hin auswertet. Die zweite übernimmt diese Information und steuert damit das Display an. Der Glimpser kann Regionen von bestimmter Größe und Farbe auf den einkommenden Videokadern finden. Die beiden Software-Teile laufen getrennt voneinander, aber gleichzeitig.

Die Display-Software informiert den Glimpser zunächst darüber, welche Art von Bilddaten sie benö
tigt. Für das *metaField Maze* müssen schwarze Stellen von rund 10 x 10 cm Größe gefunden werden. Diese relativ grobe Körnigkeit erlaubt es, auch Körperglieder der Mitspieler zu erkennen, ohne durch übertriebene Genauigkeit die Leistung des Systems zu beeinträchtigen. Sobald der Glimpser auf die Spezifikationen der Display-Software einka
briert ist, erfolgt zwischen den Programmen ein ständiger Austausch über die Position von Datenteilen. Die Display-Software enthält ein dreidimen

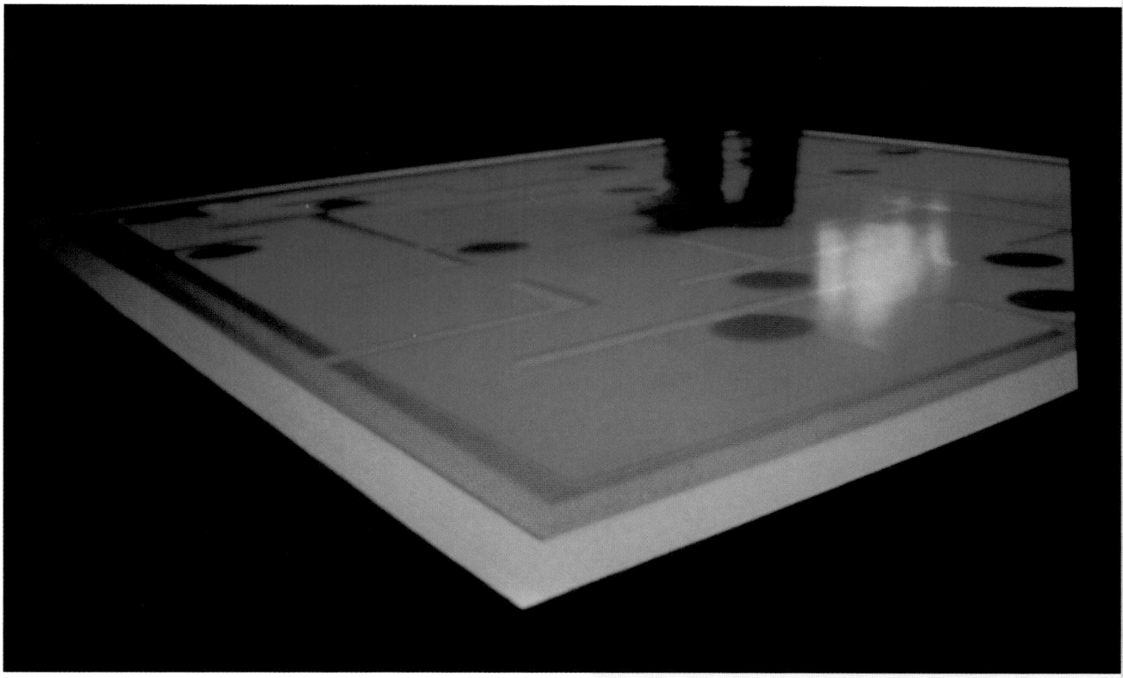

of the *metaField Maze*, it is required to find regions of black that correspond to 4 inch squares at floor level. This granularity is chosen to allow for the recognition of the limbs of the subject while not being so fine as to slow the performance of the glimpser. Once the glimpser is calibrated to the specifications of the display software, a steady flow of location data moves between the two. The display software incorporates a three-dimensional model of a maze created in Open Inventor; this maze is projected onto the floor. The 3-D maze model is tilted on X and Y axes depending on the location data provided by the glimpser.

sionales Modell des Labyrinths, das mit Open Inventor geschaffen wurde, und dieses Labyrinth wird auf den Boden projiziert. Das 3D-Modell kann je nach den vom Glimpser gelieferten Positionsdaten entlang der x- wie der y-Achse gekippt werden.

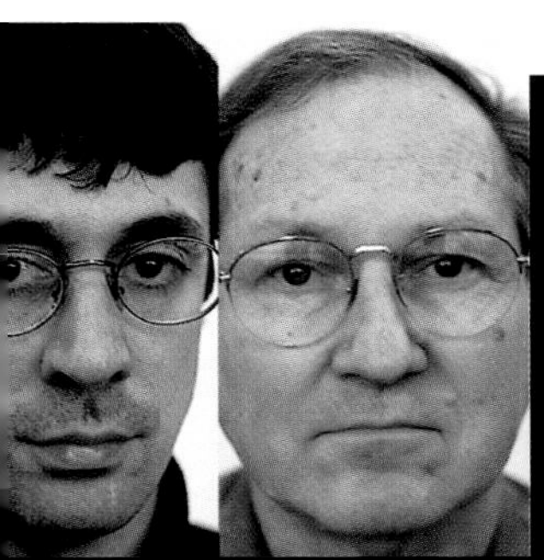

BILL KEAYS (CDN), RECEIVED A BS IN 1991 AND BFA IN 1997 FROM THE UNIVERSITY OF OTTAWA. HE HAS BEEN ENGAGED IN PHOTOGRAPHY, SCULPTURE, INSTALLATION AND ELECTRONIC MEDIA FOR THE PAST DECADE. HE IS CURRENTLY DOING RESEARCH AT THE MIT MEDIA LAB. HIS WORK AS APPEARED AT THE INTERACTION BIENNIAL IN JAPAN, ARS ELECTRONICSA, AND SIGGRAPH. RON MACNEIL (USA) RECEIVED HIS BSAD FROM MIT AND HIS MFA FROM THE RHODE ISLAND SCHOOL OF DESIGN. HE WAS CO-FOUNDER OF THE VISIBLE LANGUAGE WORKSHOP (WITH MURIEL COOPER), PRINCIPAL RESEARCH ASSOCIATE AND HEAD OF THE INTELLIGENT GRAPHICS GROUP AT MIT'S MEDIA LAB. CURRENTLY HE IS A MEMBER OF THE HOME OF THE FUTURE GROUP WITHIN THE ARCHITECTURE DEPARTMENT. ▬ Bill Keays (CDN) graduierte 1991 zum BS und 1997 zum BFA der Universität Ottawa. Er ist seit zehn Jahren im Bereich der Fotografie, Skulptur, Installation und elektronischen Medien engagiert und derzeit Forscher am MIT Media Lab. Seine Werke wurden bei der *the Interaction* Biennale in Japan, bei Ars Electronica und bei der Siggraph gezeigt. Ron MacNeill (USA) erwarb seinen BSAD am MIT und seinen MFA an der Rhode Island School of Design. Er war Mitbegründer des Visible Language Workshop (mit Muriel Cooper) sowie Principle Research Associate und Leiter der Intelligent Graphics Group am MIT Media Lab. Derzeit ist er Mitglied der „Home of the Future"-Gruppe an der Abteilung für Architektur.

NYC THOUGHT PICTURES: MEMORIES OF PLACE

Russet Lederman

NYC Thought Pictures: Memories of Place is an interactive 8-bit, 256 color, CD-Rom work, which presents a personal and eclectic view of New York, as experienced and remembered by several diverse individuals.

At the core of *NYC Thought Pictures: Memories of Place* is a facination with the power of "seemingly" ordinary events and places, which ultimately turn out to be monumental within the schema of an individual's life. For me, the personal and idiosyncratic hold the power. Therefore, as the basis for this interactive work, I have chosen to interview several diverse individuals about their New York "place" stories. These stories along with "visual" quotes from Walter Benjamin and Graeme Gilloch (a Benjamin scholar) form the theoretical and visual armature of this work. Benjamin's "Denkbilder" writings on Berlin, Moscow, Paris and Naples provided the theoretical underpinnings for developing an investigation of the four central themes in *NYC Thought Pictures: Memories of Place*, i.e. "Memory", "Time", "Fragmentation" and "City Experience." The fragmentary writing style and sometimes open-ended conclusions in Benjamin's work is well suited to my visual style and theoretical viewpoint. Loosely following Benjamin's model, this work is constructed from fragments of private and public images, audio, ephemera and text of and about the city. As a totality, these images aid in revealing the "micro" tales of specific places and neighborhoods within the larger view of New York City.

Inherent in this project, and specific to the digital medium in which I am working, is a strong random navigational structure. My goal with this piece has been to create a structure, which allows the viewer to be aware of his/her place or location within the work, yet limit his/her ability to control the path taken. If, in the end, the viewer is asking more questions and is challenged to re-evaluate their own sense of "place", then I have been successful. For me, the investigation of place is ongoing, without any definite conclusions.

NYC Thought Pictures: Memories of Place ist ein interaktives 8-bit CD-Rom-Werk mit 256 Farben, das einen persönlicher und eklektischen Blick auf New York zeigt, wie er in der Erfahrung und Erinnerung meh rerer unterschiedlicher Individuen gespeichert ist.

Im Kern von *NYC Thought Pictures: Memories of Place* steckt die Faszination, die von scheinbar gan gewöhnlichen Ereignissen und Orten ausgeht, die aber letztlich im Leben eines einzelnen Menschen überragende Bedeutung erlangen. Meiner Ansicht nach liegt die Macht im Persönlichen, in der Idiosynkrasie. Deshalb habe ich als Basis für diese Arbeit zahlreiche unterschiedliche Personen über „ihre" Geschichten über New York befragt. Gemeinsam mit „visuellen" Zitaten von Walter Benjamin und des Benjamin-Schülers Graeme Gilloch bilden diese Geschichten das theoretische und visuelle Rüstzeug dieser Arbeit. Benjamins „Denkbilder" über Berlin, Moskau, Paris und Neapel bildeten das theoretische Unterfutter für die Entwicklung der vier zentralen Themen in *NYC Thought Pictures: Memories of Place:* Erinnerung, Zeit, Fragmentierung und Stadterfahrung. Der fragmentarische Schreibstil und das häufig offene Ende in Benjamins Werk paßt gut zu meinem visuellen Stil un meinem theoretischen Standpunkt. In lockerer Anlehnung an das Vorbild Benjamin ist diese Arbeit aus Fragmenten von privaten und öffentlichen Bildern, Audiosequenzen, Randnotizen und Texten au der und über die Stadt zusammengesetzt. In ihrer Gesamtheit helfen diese Bilder bei der Enthüllung der „Mikorerzählungen" über bestimmte Orte und Viertel innerhalb des weiteren Rahmens von New York City.

Diesem Projekt ist – wie insgesamt dem digitalen Medium, in dem ich arbeite – eine eher zufallsbestimmte Navigationsstruktur eigen. Ich wollte in diesem Werk eine Struktur schaffen, die es dem Betrachter ermöglicht, sich des eigenen Ortes inne halb des Werkes bewußt zu sein und dennoch die Möglichkeiten der freien Auswahl einzuschränken. Wenn der Betrachter am Ende mehr Fragen zu stel len hat und sich herausgefordert fühlt, das eigene Gefühl für den „Ort" zu hinterfragen, dann war ich erfolgreich. Für mich selbst geht die Erforschung des Begriffs „Ort" weiter, ohne daß ich daraus irgendwelche Schlußfolgerungen ziehen wollte.

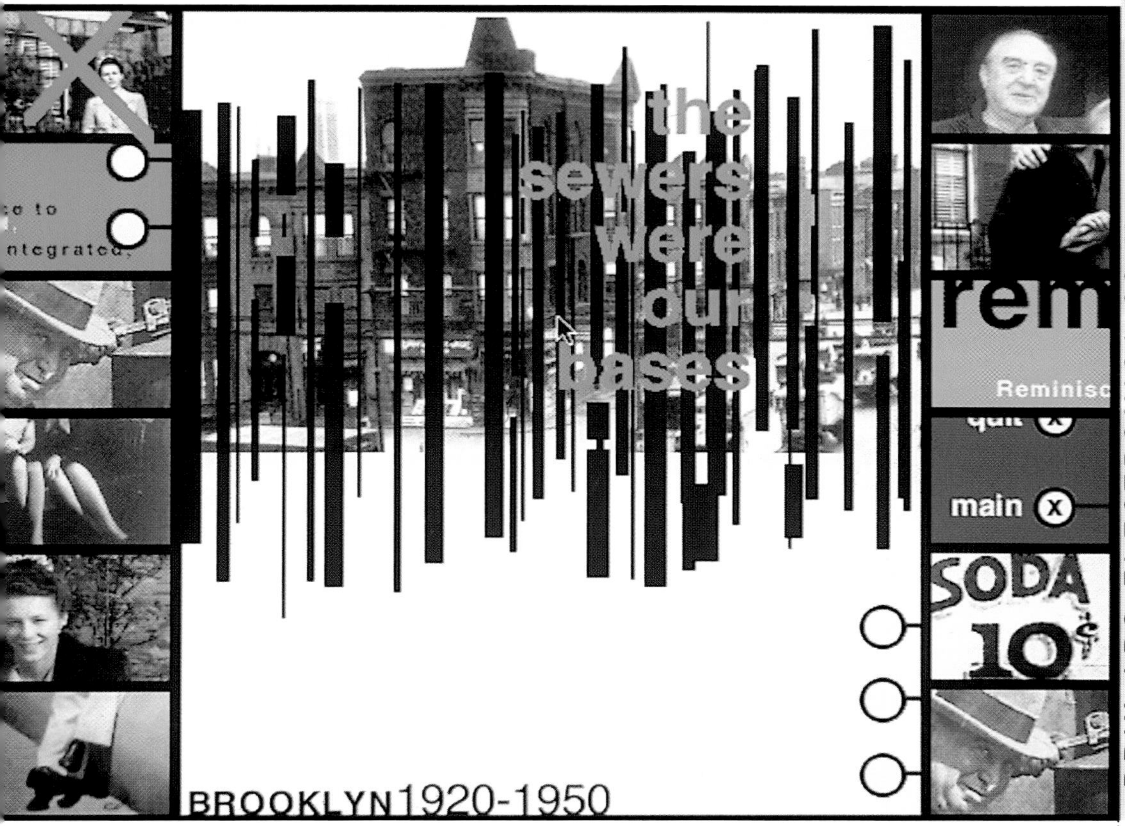

RUSSET LEDERMAN (USA) STUDIED AT THE SCHOOL OF VISUAL ARTS IN NYC, HAS WORKED AS ASSISTANT AT THE MUSEUM OF MODERN ART, DIRECTOR OF SEVERAL ART GALLERIES AND ART CURATOR; SINCE 1994 HEAD OF RUSSET LEDERMAN PRODUCTIONS, WHICH IS INVOLVED IN THE ARTISTIC DESIGN OF CD-ROMS AND WEBPAGES. ▬ Russet Lederman (USA) studierte an der School of Visual Arts in NYC, war u. a. Assistentin am Museum of Modern Art sowie Direktorin mehrerer Kunstgalerien, Kunstkuratorin und ist seit 1994 Chefin der Russet Lederman Productions, die sich mit dem künstlerischen

DISPERSION

Eric Paulos

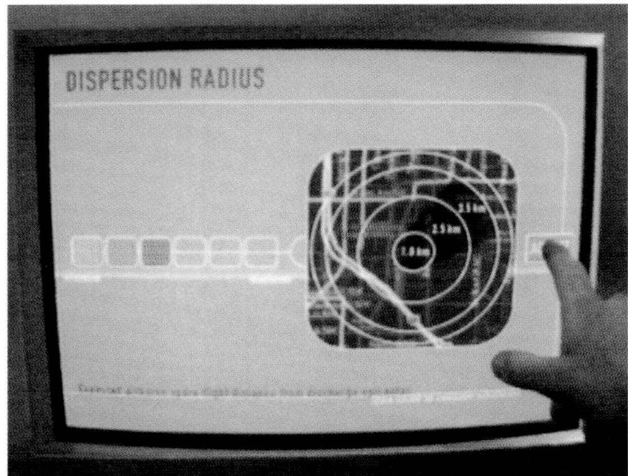

The increasing ease of obtaining inferious biological agents will naturally lead to their public acquisition through specialized lethal biological pathogen vending machines. Although these machines will share many traits with today's typical vending devices, there will be new demands placed on them by governments and society. These systems will be required to automatically and safely cultivate, monitor, contain, package, and properly dispense lethal biological pathogens. Furthermore, the vending device must accurately record, track, and monitor the individuals using the system and observe social trends in viral demands to make long term predictions about humanity.

The Experimental Interaction Unit (EIU) has designed and constructed a fully functional system to study end user demands and hardware limitations of such inevitable, in future publicly available consumer bio-agent distribution mechanisms. We

Da es immer einfacher wird, infektiöse biologische
Keime zu erwerben, wird es wohl früher oder spät
dazu kommen, daß tödliche biologische Pathogen
über eigene spezialisierte Verkaufsautomaten verkauft werden. Obwohl diese Maschinen in vielerle
Hinsicht den heutigen Verkaufsautomaten ähneln
werden, werden doch Auflagen seitens der Regie-
rungen und der Gesellschaft gewisse Besonderhe
ten erfordern. Diese Systeme müssen selbsttätig
und sicher tödliche biologische Keime züchten, ku
tivieren, überwachen, verwahren, verpacken und
ordnungsgemäß ausfolgen können. Darüber hina
muß ein solcher Verkaufsautomat die das System
benützenden Individuen ordnungsgemäß identifi-
zieren und überwachen sowie soziale Trends in de
Virennachfrage registrieren und daraus eine Pro-
gnose für die Zukunft der Menschheit ableiten kö
nen.

Die Experimentelle Interaktionseinheit EIU hat ei
vollfunktionales System konstruiert, das die Benut
zeranforderungen und Hardwarebeschränkungen
eines solchen in Zukunft unvermeidlichen öffentli
chen Bio-Keim-Verkaufsmechanimus für Endver-
braucher einer näheren Untersuchung zuführt. W

expect our *Dispersion* device to aid in identifying potential future design and distribution flaws that can hopefully be avoided in the publicly released version of such devices expected within the next few years. EIU is prepared to offer the Ars Electronica attendees the chance to be the first to interact with these inevitable future devices.

The device consists of a vending machine called *Dispersion* that consists of a fingerprint reader, a camera, a touchscreen monitor, and an A/V equipped computer. The machine is colorful and flashy. Large flashy color images showing the most horrific of viral and biological agents such as anthrax, smallpox, typhus, and plague adorn the sides of the machine. A video display shows eye-catching scenes of biological agent production, spawning, use, and consequences as the machine awaits a customer. These images are interspersed with "fun disease" facts such as amount required to kill 1,000 people, expected time to live after first contact, testimonials, etc. It also shows images, names, and other data of individuals who have previously acquired various biological agents. Additionally, it shows some images to suggest marketing techniques such as, "Your neighbors have infectious biological agents, shouldn't you too?" and "Always be prepared" and "No one is too young for personal pathogen ownership."

There is also a cutout area on the front of the vending machine where individuals can look in and see some of the bio-agents "breeding" and being nurtured in preparation for purchase and distribution. There is a mulching going on and some rotting flesh being consumed inside this infectious disease holding area. There is also data such as temperature, humidity, last dispensing date, etc.

erwarten, daß unser *Dispersion*-Gerät helfen kann, potentielle Design- und Verteilungsprobleme im Vorfeld zu verhindern, wenn in den nächsten Jahren die ersten Versionen solcher Verkaufsanlagen bereitgestellt werden. EIU freut sich, den Ars Electronica-Besuchern die Chance bieten zu können, als allererste mit diesen unvermeidlichen Zukunftsmaschinen zu interagieren.

Das Gerät selbst besteht aus einer *Dispersion* genannten Verkaufsmaschine, die aus einem Fingerabdruckleser, einer Kamera, einem Touch-Screen und einem mit Audio/Video ausgestatteten Computer besteht. Die Maschine ist farbenfroh und modern designt. Auffällige Farbbilder zeigen die schrecklichsten viralen bzw. biologischen Stoffe: Anthrax-, Pocken-, Typhus- und Pesterreger schmükken die Seiten der Maschine. Während sie auf Kunden wartet, zeigt ein Video-Display fesselnde Szenen aus der Produktion und dem Einsatz dieser Stoffe, aber auch von den Folgen eines solchen Einsatzes. Diese Bilder werden mit erfundenen Daten über Krankheiten abgemischt, die Auskunft geben über das erforderliche Tötungsquantum pro 1000 Personen, über die erwartete Lebensdauer nach Erstkontakt, Leistungsbeweise etc. Daneben werden auch Bilder, Namen und andere Daten jener Individuen gezeigt, die bereits verschiedene Substanzen gekauft haben, aber auch marketingrelevante Aussagen und Werbesprüche wie „Ihr Nachbar hat infektiöse Viren auf Lager – warum Sie noch nicht?" und „Allzeit bereit!" oder „Es ist nie zu früh, pathogene Keime zu besitzen!".

Weiters gewährt ein Sichtfenster in der Vorderseite der Maschine den Interessenten Einblick in die Zucht und Aufbereitung der Keime, die für die Abgabe und den Einsatz vorbereitet werden. Mulchprozesse werden ebenso präsentiert wie der Verzehr von faulem Fleisch innerhalb des Erreger-Behälters. Angezeigt werden weiters Daten wie Temperatur, Feuchtigkeit, letztes Ausgabedatum usw.

ERIC PAULOS (USA) IS A SCIENTIST AND PHD GRADUATE STUDENT IN THE ELECTRICAL ENGINEERING AND COMPUTER SCIENCE DEPARTMENT AT THE UNIVERSITY OF CALIFORNIA, BERKELEY. HIS RESEARCH, SCIENTIFIC, ARTISTIC, AND SOCIAL INTERESTS REVOLVE AROUND ROBOTICS AND INTERNET BASED TELEPRESENCE, PARTICULARLY THE PHYSICAL, AURAL, VISUAL, AND GESTURAL INTERACTIONS BETWEEN HUMANS AND MACHINES AND VARIOUS PERMUTATIONS OF THESE INTERACTIONS.

Eric Paulos (USA) ist Wissenschaftler und hat am Electrical Engineering and Computer Science Department der University of California, Berkeley, den PhD erworben. Seine künstlerischen, sozialen und Forschungsinteressen liegen im Bereich der Robotik und der Internet-gestützten Telepräsenz mit Schwerpunkt auf physischen, auralen, visuellen und gestischen Interaktionen zwischen Mensch und Maschine und den verschiedenen Möglichkeiten einer solchen Interaktion

TRACES

Simon Penny

Traces is a project for networked CAVEs (immersive VR spaces). But it is very different in its goals and its nature from any other CAVE or VR project (to the knowledge of the author). The root of the project is a long standing concern over the disembodying quality of the VR experience, which stands in a stark contrast to the rhetoric around VR, which argues that the experience allows the user to interact in a bodily way with digital worlds. As I first argued in my essay *Virtual Reality as the End of the Enlightenment Project* (in *Culture on the Brink* Eds. Druckrey and Bender, Bay Books 1994), conventional HDM (Head Mounted Display) VR dissects the body, privileging visuality to the exclusion of bodily senses. The body is reduced to a single Cartesian point, the body is checked at the door.

When I first used a CAVE, I was fascinated with the visceral sensation of collision with virtual objects. I realised that part of the disembodying quality of HDM VR was because when you look down, your body is not there! In a CAVE, you see your body colliding with virtual objects. Because of my interest in the problem of embodiment, the CAVE became an attractive site to work in. But clearly only half the problem was solved, the user could experience virtual objects in a more bodily way, but the user was still reduced to a point from the perspective of the machine. Thus it became necessary to build an input system which described the entirety of the users' body. After substantial research, we built a multi-camera vision system which constructs a real-time body model for the user. This body model is currently of a low spatial resolution, but of a high temporal resolution, the user experiences no "latency" or lag, between their movements and the virtual structures created.

In *Traces*, virtually all sound and visual experiences

Traces ist ein Projekt für eine vernetzte CAVE-Installation (für immersive VR-Räume). Aber soweit dem Autor bekannt, unterscheidet es sich in seinen Zielen und in seiner Art von allen anderen CAVE- und VR-Projekten. Die Wurzel des Projekts liegt in meinem seit langen andauernden Unbehagen über di entfremdende Körperlosigkeit der VR-Erfahrungen, die in starkem Kontrast zu den rhetorischen Aussagen über Virtuelle Realität steht, die es dem Anwender ja ermöglichen sollte, körperlich mit digitalen Welten zu interagieren. Bereits in meinem Essay *Virtual Reality as the End of the Enlightenment Project* (in *Culture on the Brink*, hg. von Druckrey und Bender, Bay Books, 1994) habe ich festgehalten, daß bei konventionellen VR-Installationen mit am Kopf getragenen Displays (*Head mounted Displays* HMD) der Körper sozusagen zerschnitten wird und die visuelle Erfahrung zu Lasten des Körpersinns geht. Der Körper wird auf einen einzigen Kartesischen Punkt reduziert, der Körper bleibt sozusagen draußen vor der Tür.

Als ich das erste Mal einen CAVE benutzte, war ich tief beeindruckt von der Unmittelbarkeit, mit der die Gefühle bei der Kollision mit virtuellen Objekten in die Eingeweide fuhren. Mir wurde klar, daß das Gefühl der Körperlosigkeit der VR mit HMDs z. T. darauf beruht, daß bei einem Blick nach unten der eigene Körper einfach nicht da ist! Im CAVE hingegen sieht man seinen Körper mit VR-Objekten kollidieren. Wegen meines Interesses für Fragen der Körperlichkeit wurde der CAVE ein attraktiver Ort zur weiteren Arbeit. Aber es war klar, daß nur die Hälfte des Problems gelöst war – der Anwender konnte virtuelle Objekte auf eine körperbezogenere Weise erfahren, aber er war letztlich doch nur auf einen Punkt aus der Perspektive der Maschine reduziert. Deshalb wurde es notwendig, ein Input-System zu konstruieren, das die Gesamtheit des Körpers beschreibt. Nach umfangreichen Forschungsarbeiten haben wir ein Multi-Kamera-Erfassungssystem entwickelt, das ein Echtzeitmodell des Körpers des Anwenders generiert. Dieses Körpermodell bietet derzeit zwar nur eine geringe räumliche, aber dafür eine hohe zeitliche Auflösung, d. h. der Benutzer erfährt keine Latenz oder Zeitverschiebung zwischen den eigenen Bewegungen und den erzeugten virtuellen Strukturen.

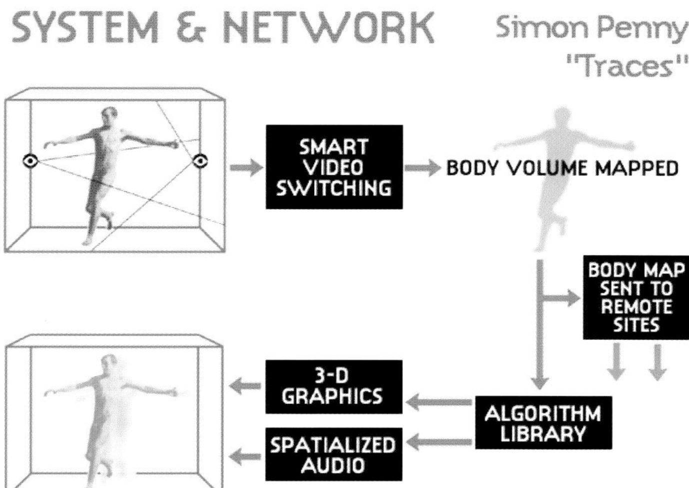

are generated in real time based on the users' behavior. Unlike other VR projects, I have no interest here in illusionistic texture mapped models, the illusion of infinite virtual space or building "virtual worlds." All attention is focused on the ongoing bodily behavior of the user.
Traces will be a telematic, networked experience. But creating an illusion of close proximity (like in the work of Paul Sermon) is not the goal. Rather, there is an emphasis on the highly technologically mediated nature of the communication. The users never see each other, only the highly mediated results of each others' behavior. The user interacts with gossamer spatial traces which exhibit the dynamics and volumes of bodies, but are translucent and ephemeral.

Collaborators: Andre Bernhardt, Jeffrey Smith, Jamie Schulte and Phoebe Sengers.
Traces is developed with the support of GMD as the Cyberstar winning project and the support of Carnegie Mellon University.

In *Traces* werden so gut wie alle klanglichen und visuellen Erfahrungen auf der Basis des Benutzerverhaltens in Echtzeit generiert. Anders als bei anderen VR-Projekten habe ich hier kein Interesse an illusionistischen Texture-Mapping-Modellen, an der Illusion eines unendlichen virtuellen Raums oder am Aufbau „virtueller Welten". Die gesamte Aufmerksamkeit konzentriert sich auf den Verlauf des körperlichen Verhaltens des Anwenders.
Traces wird eine telematische, vernetzte Erfahrung sein. Es geht aber nicht darum, die Illusion von körperlicher Nähe zu schaffen, sondern der Schwerpunkt liegt auf der technologisch vermittelten Natur der Kommunikation. Die Benutzer sehen einander nie direkt, sie sehen nur das vermittelte Ergebnis des Verhaltens des jeweils anderen. Der Benutzer interagiert mit spinnwebfeinen räumlichen Spuren, die die Dynamik und das Volumen der Körper zum Ausdruck bringen, aber durchscheinend und ephemer sind.

Mitarbeit: Andre Bernhardt, Jeffrey Smith, Jamie Schulte und Phoebe Sengers.
Traces wurde als Gewinner des Cyberstar mit Unterstützung des GMD sowie der Carnegie Mellon University entwickelt.

Simon Penny (AUS) is an artist, theorist and teacher in the field of Interactive Media Art. His art practice consists of interactive and robotic installations, which have been exhibited in the US, Australia and Europe. He is Associate Professor of Art and Robotics at Carnegie Mellon University where, among other things, he teaches Gizmology, Robotic Art Studio and Theory of Interactive Art. He established the Electronic Intermedia Program at the University of Florida 1990–93, curated Machine Culture at Siggraph '93 in Anaheim CA and edited the anthology *Critical Issues in Electronic Media* (SUNY Press 1995). Simon Penny (AUS) ist Künstler, Theoretiker und Lehrer im Bereich der interaktiven Medienkunst. Seine praktische Kunstpraxis hat interaktive und Roboter-Installationen hervorgebracht, die in Australien, den USA und Europa zu sehen waren. Er ist Associate Professor für Kunst und Robotik an der Carnegie Mellon University, wo er unter anderem Gizmology (etwa: Kleinzeugkunde), Robotic Art Studio und Theorie der Interaktiven Kunst lehrt. Er hat 1990–93 das Electronic Intermedia Program an der University of Florida eingerichtet, war Kurator des Machine-Culture-Bereichs der Siggraph 93 in Anaheim, Kalifornien, und hat die Anthologie *Critical Issues in Electronic Media* herausgegeben (SUNY Press, 1995).

EASEL

Daniel Rozin

Easel looks like a painting easel with a blank canvas stetched on a frame mounted to it. The painter uses a small paintbrush in the same manner a painter would. Instead of solid colors, the brush applies live video from cameras positioned nearby. Each new stroke of the brush brings a new coat of "current video" to the canvas. The painter can select between a few live video sources by dipping the paintbrush into a few paint cans that are mounted on the easel. The computer that runs the *Easel* software is hidden in the background and there is no computer screen in sight.

At the heart of *Easel* are a video camera and a video projector aimed at the canvas. The camera is sensitive to infrared light only, and the projector projects the computer screen. The paintbrush's bristles are made of fishing wire that serve as fiber optics and emit infrared light through the canvas. The infrared light is captured by the camera that transfers it to the computer via a video digitizing board. A second video camera is connected to the computer and inputs a picture of the surrounding view. The computer mixes both video sources according to a few simple algorithms, and the result is sent through the projector back to the canvas. The effect is an illusion that the images are being applied by the brush. Sensors in the paint cans switch between video sources for the input of the second video board.

Easel is interesting aesthetically both as a work in progress and as a final piece. As a work in progress every new stroke of the brush brings a new coat of video to the canvas; since there is no erasing, the background is always some previous video. The changing proportions between new and old strokes change the viewers' perception of positive and negative spaces. As the piece is completed various patches of video blend into a soft collage with multiple levels of transparency, a hint of three-dimensionality is present due to the layering effect of the

Easel sieht aus wie eine große Malerstaffelei mit einer leeren Leinwand, die auf einen fest an der Staffelei montierten Rahmen gespannt ist. Der „Maler“ verwendet einen kleinen Pinsel genau auf die gleiche Art wie ein echter Maler. Anstelle von Farbe trägt der Pinsel allerdings Live-Videos von in der Nähe aufgestellten Kameras auf. Jeder neue Pinselstrich bringt eine neue Schicht des „laufenden Videos“ auf die Leinwand. Der Maler kann zwischen mehreren Videoquellen wählen, indem er seinen Pinsel in unterschiedliche an der Staffelei befestigte „Farbtöpfe“ taucht. Der Computer, durch den *Easel* angesteuert wird, ist im Hintergrund versteckt, es ist kein Monitor sichtbar.

Das Herz von *Easel* bilden eine Video-Kamera und ein auf die Leinwand gerichteter Videoprojektor. Die Kamera nimmt nur Infrarotlicht auf, der Projektor gibt den Inhalt des Computerbildschirms wieder. Die Haare des Pinsels bestehen aus optischen Fasern, die IR-Licht auf die Leinwand abstrahlen. Diese IR-Strahlung wird von der Kamera eingefangen, die die Daten über einen Video-Digitizer an den Rechner weiterleitet. Eine zweite Videokamera beliefert den Computer mit Bildern aus der Umgebung. Mit Hilfe einiger einfacher Algorithmen mischt der Computer die beiden Videoquellen, und das Ergebnis wird über den Projektor auf die Leinwand geworfen. Dabei entsteht die Illusion, als würden die Bilder durch den Pinsel aufgetragen. Sensoren in den Farbtöpfen schalten zwischen den verschiedenen Video-Quellen für das zweite Bild um.

Easel ist sowohl als Work-in-Progress als auch als fertige Arbeit von ästhetischem Interesse. Als Work-in-Progress bringt jeder neue Pinselstrich auch eine neue Videoschicht auf die Leinwand, und da es kein Löschen oder Radieren gibt, bleibt auf dem Hintergrund immer etwas von den früheren Videoschichten zurück. Die unterschiedlichen Proportionen der alten bzw. neuen Pinselstriche ändern auch die Wahrnehmung des Betrachters von positiven und negativen Räumen. Wenn das Stück fertig ist, verschmelzen zahlreiche „Video-Flicken“ zu einer sanften Collage mit vielen unterschiedlichen Transparenzebenen, ein Hauch von Dreidimensionalität entsteht durch die Schichtung der Video-Ebenen. Der Inhalt eines Stückes, das auf der „Staffelei“ entsteht, ist nicht vorgegeben. Da aber die Videoquellen rund um den Maler plaziert sind, ergibt sich natürlich eine gewisse Thematik. Der erste Kreis liegt am nächsten: Eine Kamera, die auf den Künstler selbst gerichtet ist und so ein Selbstportrait oder die Abbildung von nahegelegenen Objekten erlaubt. Der zweite Kreis wäre dann eine Videokamera, die die Umgebung einfängt, etwa das Zimmer. Der dritte Kreis könnte eine Live-Zuspielung aus dem Fernsehen oder eine Kamera sein, die aus dem Fenster sieht. Mit diesen drei Eingabekreisen kann der Künstler ein Bild schaffen, das einen be-

coats of video. The content of a piece painted with *Easel* is not set. However the placement of the video sources does imply a set of expanding circles around the painter. The first circle is the closest. It is a camera pointed at the artist allowing him/her to portray themselves or any objects near by. The second circle is a video camera pointing at the surrounding environment such as the room. The third circle is a live feed from TV or a camera pointed out the window. Using these three inputs the artist can create a picture that reflects a certain moment in time at a certain location and state of mind.

This piece was created with funding by Interval Research Corp. and NYC-ITP.

stimmten Moment an einem bestimmten Ort unter bestimmten Bedingungen widerspiegelt.

Diese Arbeit wurde mit Förderung von Interval Research Corp. und NYC-ITP realisiert.

DANIEL ROZIN (USA) STUDIED INDUSTRIAL DESIGN AT THE BEZALEL ACADEMY IN JERUSALEM AND TOOK PART IN THE INTERACTIVE TELECOMMUNICATIONS PROGRAM AT NYU. HE GRADUATED BOTH TIMES WITH HONORS. HE HAS WORKED AS A DESIGNER FOR VARIOUS COMPANIES DESIGNING COMPUTER INPUT DEVICES AND PERIPHERALS AND HAS RECEIVED THE ROTHSCHILD AWARD, AMONG OTHERS, FOR HIS WORK. HE IS CURRENTLY RESEARCH DIRECTOR AND ASSISTANT PROFESSOR FOR THE NEW YORK UNIVERSITY'S TELECOMMUNICATION PROGRAM. ▬ Daniel Rozin (USA) studierte Industrial Design an der Bezalel Akademie in Jerusalem und nahm am Interactive Telecommunications Program der NYU teil. Beide Studien absolvierte er mit Auszeichnung. Als Designer war er bei verschiedenen Unternehmen am Design von Eingabe- und Peripheriegeräten beteiligt und erhielt dafür u. a. den Rothschild-Preis. Zur Zeit ist er Forschungsleiter und Assistenzprofessor des Telecommunication Program der New York University.

AUGMENTED REALITY FICTION

Stefan Schemat / Michael Joyce / Hiroki Maekawa / Dominica Freyer / Burki Carstens / Mike Felsmann / Isabella Bordoni / Roberto Paci Dalò

arf (Augmented Reality Fiction) or the Construction of a Medium

Our arf technology is used to create a new narrative medium. arf makes it possible to represent the stories connected with a certain place directly on location. In this way the story of the released prisoner Franz Biberkopf in Döblin's *Berlin Alexanderplatz* can be experienced in Rosenthal, on the outskirts of the city, at the location where it took place in the novel.
However, our medium not only works with a direct reference to actual places, it also takes the physiology of the users into account. This means that the energy and speed of movement are registered and thus interactively control the acoustic event, which becomes more hectic or calmer accordingly. This not only highlights the story, but also enables the participants to direct how it continues themselves. In other words, the arf-author must learn to write on the physiology of the human being.
Over the course of time, an extensive cinematic language has been developed to transport plots, characters and moods beyond the screen. If one considers that arf works alongside the actually existing world as a backdrop with acoustic stimulations (e.g. music, sounds, dialogues), while taking the energy of the movements and thus also the emotional state of the user into account as well, then it may become somewhat clearer, how complex this kind of "cinematic language" must be.
The auditive narrative means that arf can make use of are mobile and static sounds and 3D sounds, which are used for orientation and navigation. The Flat-Sounds can be used analogously to an off-voice in film, to represent the inner dialogue that is constantly taking place within each person. In this 3D environment, it is particularly the non-3D stream of consciousness sounds that develop a very peculiar effect.
When a participant then encounters a mobile 3D voice, it is like meeting a—solely audible—ghost. This virtual character may lead, startle or confuse the participant. These ghost-like voices are intuitively intelligible. This raises the anthropological question of why human beings invented ghosts.

arf (Augmented Reality Fiction) oder di Konstruktion eines Mediums

Mittels unserer *arf*-Technologie entstand ein neue erzählerisches Medium. Durch arf wird es möglich direkt auf einem Ort die Geschichten abzubilden, die mit ihm verbunden sind. So kann die Geschich des entlassenen Zuchthäuslers Franz Biberkopf au Döblins *Berlin Alexanderplatz* in der Rosenthaler Vorstadt mittels arf dort nacherlebt werden, wo si auch im Roman angesiedelt ist.
Unser *augmented reality*-Medium arbeitet aber nicht nur mit dem direkten Bezug zu den realen Orten, sondern bezieht auch die Physiologie des Users mit ein. So wird die Bewegungsenergie und -geschwindigkeit aufgenommen und steuert inter aktiv das akustische Geschehen, welches hektisch oder entsprechend ruhiger wird. So wird nicht nur eine Geschichte untermalt, sondern der Teilnehmende steuert selber ihren Fortgang. Der arf-Auto muß also lernen, auf der Physiologie des Mensche zu schreiben.
Um im Kino Handlungen, Charaktere und Stimmungen über die Leinwand hinaus zu transportieren, wurde im Laufe der Jahre eine umfangreiche Filmsprache entwickelt. Wenn man nun bedenkt, daß *arf* neben der real existierenden Welt als Kulisse mit akustischen Reizen (z. B. mit Musik, Geräuschen und Dialogen) unter Einbeziehung de Bewegungsenergie und damit auch des emotiona len Zustandes des Benutzers arbeitet, wird ansatzweise deutlich, welche Komplexität eine entsprechende „Filmsprache" haben muß.
Auf der Ebene der auditiven erzählerischen Mittel hat *arf* mobile und statische Klänge sowie 3D-Sounds, die der Orientierung und Navigation dienen, zur Verfügung. Die Flat-Sounds können analo zur Off-Stimme im Film verwendet werden, um de in jedem Menschen ständig ablaufenden inneren Dialog darzustellen. In diesem 3D-Environment en falten gerade die Nicht-3D-Stream-of-Conciousnes Sounds eine ganz eigentümliche Wirkung.
Begegnet dem Teilnehmer nun eine mobile 3D-Stimme, so erscheint ihm ein – nur hörbarer – Geist. Dieser virtuelle Charakter kann ihn führen, ihn erschrecken oder verwirren. Diese geisterhafte Stimmen sind intuitiv verständlich. Dadurch wirft sich die anthropologische Frage auf, warum Menschen Geister erfunden haben.

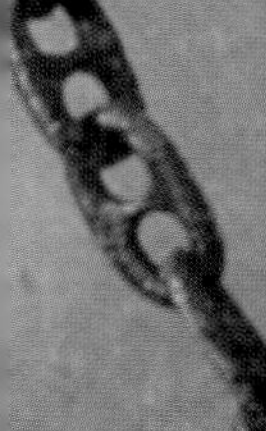

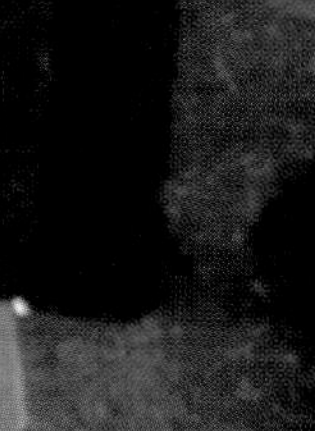

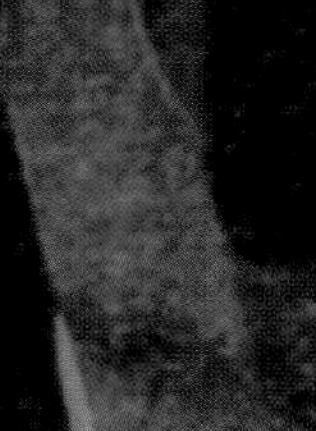

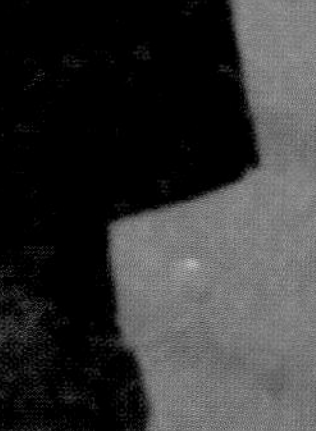

HAZE EXPRESS

Christa Sommerer / Laurent Mignonneau

HAZE Express is an interactive computer installation that develops the metaphor of traveling and watching landscapes passing by through the window of vehicles such as trains, cars and air planes. When looking at a landscape at high speed, one does not really know very much about this landscape, how it looks in detail or how people live in it, for example. The passing landscapes become mere images, accumulations of forms, shapes and colors, like a haze of impressions.

HAZE Express is an interactive computer installation that performs the recombination, development and evolution of seemingly random images in a way that is reminiscent of how we see images through the window of a train.

In the interactive journey with *HAZE Express* the viewer can watch the passing images, stop them and look at their composition in more detail. The way he moves his hand on the train window surface will influence how the landscape behind becomes composed: non-deterministic evolutionary image composition linked to interaction will always provide new and unique image elements that become part of a semi-realistic and semi-virtual trip through data landscapes.

Sitting in one of the *HAZE Express*'s comfortable chairs, the viewer can look out of the window and move his hand on the window surface. When he slides his hand from the left to the right, the images will slide in the same direction, uncovering continuous landscapes, composed of organic and abstract image scenes.

The location of where the viewer touches the window as well as the frequency and speed of his hand's movement will influence what kind of image elements will be created.

Genetic selection is used to always provide new image elements that are selected by the viewer's interaction.

The faster the hand slides horizontally on the window surface, the faster the landscape scrolls in the same direction. Images can also be simply stopped by creasing the hand's movement while remaining with the hand on the window surface.

Developed for International Academy of Media Arts and Sciences (IAMAS), Japan.

HAZE Express ist eine interaktive Computerinstallation, die sich metaphorisch mit dem Reisen und d Landschaftsbeobachtung durch ein (Bahn-, Bus-, Flugzeug-)Fenster auseinandersetzt. Blickt man b hoher Geschwindigkeit auf eine Landschaft, so erfährt man nicht wirklich viel über sie; man kann n ahnen, wie sie in ihren Details aussieht, wie die Menschen in ihr leben usw. Die vorbeiziehende Landschaft wird zum reinen Bild, zu einer Anhäufung von Formen und Farben, zu wie durch einen Dunstschleier wahrgenommen Eindrücken.

Bei der interaktiven Computerinstallation *HAZE Express* erinnert die Neukombination, Entwicklung und Evolution von scheinbar zufälligen Bildern an das Betrachten einer Landschaft aus einem Zugfenster.

Bei der interaktiven Reise mit dem *HAZE Express* betrachtet der Besucher die vorbeiziehenden Bilde er kann sie anhalten und ihre Komposition im Detail betrachten. Die Handbewegungen, die er auf der Fensterfläche macht, beeinflussen die Zusammensetzung der dahinter erscheinenden Bilder: Eine nicht-deterministische Bildkomposition, die mit der Interaktion verknüpft ist, bietet ständig neue und einzigartige Datenelemente, die Teil ein halb realistischen, halb virtuellen Reise durch die Datenlandschaften werden.

In einem der bequemen Stühle des *HAZE Express* sitzend kann der Besucher aus dem Fenster sehen und die Hand an der Fensterfläche bewegen. Schiebt er die Hand von links nach rechts, bewegt sich auch die dahinterliegende Landschaft in dies Richtung und enthüllt neue Landschaftsteile, die aus organischen und abstrakten Bildzsenen zusam mengesetzt sind.

Je nachdem, wo der Betrachter das Bild berührt u welche Frequenz seine Handbewegungen aufweisen, verändert sich die Art der zu erstellenden Bild elemente. Eine genetische Auswahl sorgt dafür, da immer neue Bildelemente durch die Interaktion m den Handbewegungen der Betrachter generiert werden. Je schneller sich die Hand horizontal bewegt, um so schneller läuft auch die Landschaft in die gleiche Richtung. Die Bilder können angehalte werden, indem einfach die Handbewegung gestoppt wird, auch wenn die Hand nicht von der Scheibe genommen wird.

Christa Sommerer (A) studied biology and botany in Vienna, completed studies at the Academy of Fine Arts in Vienna and post-graduate studies at the Staedelschule in Frankfurt. She is currently professor at the International Media Academy in Gifu (Japan) and artistic director of ATR Advanced Telecommunication Research Laboratories in Kyoto (Japan). Laurent Mignonneau (F) studied sculpting in Angouleme and completed post-graduate studies at the Stàdelschule in Frankfurt. He is currently Artist in Residence at the International Media Acadèmy in Gifu (Japan) and artistic director at ATR Advanced Telecommunication Research Laboratories in Kyoto (Japan).

Christa Sommerer (A) studierte Biologie und Botanik in Wien, schloß ein Studium an der Akademie der Bildenden Künste in Wien sowie ein Postgraduate-Studium an der Frankfurter Staedelschule an. Gegenwärtig ist sie Professorin an der Internationalen Medienakademie in Gifu (Japan) sowie künstlerische Leiterin von ATR Advanced Telecommunication Research Laboratories in Kyoto (Japan). Laurent Mignonneau (F) studierte Bildhauerei in Angoulême und schloß ein Postgraduate-Studium an der Staedelschule Frankfurt an. Derzeit ist er Artis-in-Residence an der Internationalen Medienakademie in Gifu (Japan) sowie Künstlerischer Leiter bei ATR Advanced Telecommunication Research Laboratories in Kyoto (Japan).

prix ars electronica 99

.NET
INTERACTIVE ART
COMPUTER ANIMATION
VISUAL EFFECTS
DIGITAL MUSICS
u19/CYBERGENERATION

WHAT EXACTLY IS COMPUTER ANIMATION? WHAT ARE VISUAL EFFECTS?

WAS IST EIGENTLICH COMPUTER-ANIMATION? UND WAS SIND VISUAL EFFECTS?

How are these different? How is excellence in these defined? Which pieces of computer graphics work best reflect these "definitions?" And how exactly does one compare work coming from a high-end production house to a six-week student project to an independent artist's piece?

How are these different? How is excellence in these defined? Which pieces of computer graphics work best reflect these "definitions"? And how exactly does one compare work coming from a high-end production house to a six-week student project to an independent artist's piece?

I have spent half of my life working with computers—always related to computer graphics (even if only in "intent") and always for the purpose of animation. "So what?," you ask (and "Rightfully so," I say). Well, I am 41.

Granted this additional, small piece of information isn't interesting in itself either (unless you are a friend of my still young children and enjoy the thrill of imagining someone so "archaic") but, together with the first line, this changes the perspective on me and on my comments. It provides "context." It allows perhaps an openness, an understanding, thought possibilities that weren't previously there. Half of 41 is 20 years (in integers). That's a long time in the history of computers. There have been many changes.

I write all of that not because I think it's important to know about me, but because I do believe that understanding the importance of "context" is essential. What is the Prix Ars Electronica? What are the categories? What are the works? How are they compared? How are they judged? What results are being presented here?

The Prix Ars Electronica was created to gather, acknowledge, honor and make accessible to others (through the Ars Electronica Festival and the Ars Electronica Center) the current state of digital media creativity. That's a sentence packed with intent. Gathering work is in itself a huge job, but it is a worthy one as it is exactly through this collected

Worin unterscheiden sie sich? Wie definiert man den Begriff "herausragend"? Welche computergrafischen Werke reflektieren diese "Definition" am besten? Und wie vergleicht man die aufwendigen Produkte eines High-End-Produktionshauses mit einem in sechs Wochen entstandenen Studentenprojekt oder dem Werk eines unabhängigen Künstlers?

Ich habe mein halbes Leben mit der Arbeit mit Computern zugebracht – und immer im Zusammenhang mit Computergrafik (wenn auch teilweise nur von der Zielsetzung her) und immer mit dem Hintergrund der Animation. „Na und?", werden Sie fragen (und zu Recht, wie ich anmerke). Nun – ich bin 41.

Ich gebe zu, daß dieses kleine Stückchen Information als solches auch nicht gerade interessant ist (außer für die Freunde meiner noch jungen Kinder, für die die Vorstellung von jemandem so „Archaischen" vielleicht aufregend sein kann), aber zusammen mit dem ersten Satz ändert dies doch die Perspektive meines Standpunktes und meiner Kommentare – sie erhalten einen „Kontext", der eine Offenheit erlaubt, Verständnis, gedankliche Möglichkeiten, die es ohne ihn nicht gäbe. Die Hälfte von 41 ist – gerundet – 20, und das ist eine lange Zeit in der Geschichte der Computer, da hat es viele Veränderungen gegeben.

Ich schreibe all dies nicht etwa, weil der Leser etwas über mich wissen soll, sondern weil ich überzeugt bin, daß es wichtig ist, Verständnis für die Zusam-

body of work that the re-definition of the medium and the re-evaluation of excellence within that happens.

The methods and means of "computers" makes them at times a medium, at times a tool, at times a process and at times a result (and often all of the aforementioned rolled into one). That means that these "media" evolve continuously. As do the categories and judging criteria of the Prix Ars Electronica honoring the "top work."

This statement discusses the "Computer Animation" and "Visual Effects" categories, submissions, jury and results. So, first and foremost, what exactly is computer animation? What are visual effects? How are they different? Which pieces of computer graphics work best reflect these "definitions?"

Although most of us have at least an intuitive response to these questions, a proposed re-definition of their answers is exactly what is asked for of the world at large when the annual Prix Ars Electronica competition is opened. It was also the wonderful task set before the jury serving both these categories, in the form of a large and widely ranging body of submitted work. These written words are in many ways a reflection of my view of the three day "conversation" that transpired within and through this body of work amongst jury members Maurice Benayoun (France), Rob Legato (USA), Barbara Robertson (USA) and myself, Ines Hardtke (Canada).

The definition of computer animation can be large, small or somewhere in between. For me (implicitly and explicitly on the "larger" end of things), "animation" remains "the art of giving life to something that would otherwise not have any". Adding the word "computer" to this obviously implies the use of a computer somewhere in this process of "animation." But, for a computer animation competition honoring top work in the field (as opposed to an animation festival doing "the same"), a computer must not only be implicated but must be an essential (and so irreplaceable) component of the achievement or manifestation of "result."

Although "visual effects" are often animated, this category can loosely be defined as being driven by pre-determined (existent) "action" (as opposed to the "animation" category which determines "action"). Perhaps "adding" life as distinct from "giving" life. This definition moves the judging away

menhänge zu haben. Was ist der Prix Ars Electronica? Was sind diese Kategorien? Wie können sie verglichen werden, wie beurteilt? Welche Ergebnisse werden hier vorgestellt?

Der Prix Ars Electronica wurde geschaffen, um den aktuellen Stand der Kreativität in den digitalen Medien zu dokumentieren, zu bewerten, zu honorieren und (in Zusammenarbeit mit dem Ars Electronica Festival und dem Ars Electronica Center) anderen zugänglich zu machen. Schon das Zusammentragen der Werke ist eine umfangreiche Aufgabe, aber es ist lohnend, weil gerade diese *Sammlung* von Werken eine Neudefinition des Mediums und eine Bewertung dessen ermöglicht, was mit und in ihm geschieht.

Die mit dem Begriff „Computer" verbundenen Methoden und Mittel lassen uns diesen manchm eher als Medium begreifen, manchmal als Werkzeug, manchmal als Prozeß und manchmal auch a Ergebnis – und nicht selten treffen alle diese Termini gemeinsam zu. Dies bedeutet, daß sich da „Medium" kontinuierlich weiterentwickelt – wie ja auch die Kategorien und Beurteilungskriterien des Prix Ars Electronica, der die Spitzenleistungen auszeichnet.

Dieser Aufsatz diskutiert die Einreichungen, Ergebnisse, Juryentscheidungen und Kategorien zu „Computeranimation" und „Visual Effects". Dabei stellt sich zunächst die Frage, was denn eigentlich Computeranimation ist, was Visual Effects sind. Und worin unterscheiden sie sich? Welche Werke der Computergrafik geben diese „Definitionen" am besten wieder?

Obwohl jeder von uns zumindest intuitiv auf diese Fragen antworten könnte, so ist doch jedes Jahr be der Ausschreibung des Prix Ars Electronica eine generelle Neudefinition für die breite Öffentlichke erforderlich. Es war eine wunderbare Aufgabe für die Jury, diese beiden Kategorien anhand einer bre ten Palette eingereichter Werke beurteilen zu dürfen, und dieser Text spiegelt in vielerlei Hinsicht meine Einschätzung der dreitägigen „Konversation wider, die sich rund um die vielfältigen Werke zwischen den Jurymitgliedern Maurice Benayoun (F), Rob Legato (USA), Barbara Robertson (USA) und mi Ines Hardtke (CDN), entsponnen hat.

Die Definition des Begriffs „Computeranimation" kann weit oder eng gefaßt sein oder irgendwo in der Mitte liegen. Für mich, die ich eher auf der „weitgefaßten" Seite der Dinge stehe, bleibt „Animation" immer „die Kunst, einer Sache Leben einzuhauchen, das sonst keines hätte". Die Beifügung des Begriffs „Computer" bedeutet dabe offensichtlich, daß der Einsatz des Computers irgendwo in diesem „Animationsprozeß" eine Rolle spielt. Aber bei einem Computeranimationspreis, der die Spitzenarbeiten auf diesem Gebiet auszeichnen will (im Gegensatz zu einem reinen Animationsfestival, das aus seiner Sicht „das gleiche" vorhat), darf der Computer nicht bloß ein implizites Werkzeug sein, sondern muß eine essentielle (und damit unersetzliche) Komponente des

from "content" and towards the more "technical" given that the effect itself and more so its integration into the action is what now, by definition, is "important". Notably, the word "computer", although not explicit in the title, is almost exclusively implicit to this "adding" - although there do remain some optical printers out there in the world, their numbers and use (sadly in many ways) are dwindling. The visual effects here are assumed to be digital.
Does this split of giving versus adding life, computer animation versus visual effects make sense? I suppose so. It is another way of "seeing" and comparing work in this very large computer graphics field. Do I think that this split will remain valid? Not likely. In computer graphics there will hopefully remain movement and evolution. There will always be trends. There will always be a mass of effort around the "limitations" as well as around the newly provided, boundary-breaking tools and methods. And, often our limitations are exactly our current day definitions, our understanding, our implementations, our ways of thinking and perceiving. Soon, with all of the work being done in the integration of sound and visual, the categories of "music" and "animation" will not be sufficient. With all that is happening in the "interactive" world we will soon be obliged to widen and re-define our notion of "life" I think. Let's hope so.
For now though, the categories of Computer Animation and Visual Effects stand as they are. And we the jury screened almost 300 pieces in the former and 65 in the latter. We did move a couple of pieces between the categories based on the nature of the work.

What are the prizes for? What is the "result"?

The Prix Ars Electronica Computer Animation and Visual Effects category each have a top award/first prize - the Golden Nica, two second prizes and up to twelve honorable mentions possible. What, then, are these prizes for?
The prizes and honorary mentions are for excellence in the field, in the category. Period.
What is excellence? Well, excellence is certainly something that everyone has access to—conceptually, technically, through its application, through the content. And all of this together is in order to

Werkes bzw. des erzielten „Ergebnisses" darstellen. Auch wenn die „Visual Effects" häufig auf Animation basieren, kann man diese Kategorie definieren als von einer vorgegebenen – d. h. bereits existenten – Handlung bestimmt (im Gegensatz zur „Animation", die diese Handlung selbst bestimmt). Vielleicht könnte man auch sagen „Leben hinzufügen" im Gegensatz zu „zum Leben erwecken". Diese Definition verschiebt die Bewertung weg vom Inhalt hin zu den eher „technischen" Aspekten, weil jetzt der Effekt selbst – und noch stärker seine Integration in die Handlung – per definitionem wichtig wird. Und wenn der "Computer" hier auch nicht explizit im Titel steht, so ist er doch für das „Hinzufügen" essentiell, denn wenn es auch noch einige wenige traditionelle optische Ausgabegeräte in dieser Branche gibt, so ist ihre Zahl und ihre Anwendung rückläufig (was in vieler Hinsicht bedauerlich ist). Die Visual Effects werden hier also als digital verstanden.
Macht nun diese Trennung in „Leben spenden" und „Leben hinzufügen" – Computeranimation gegen Visuelle Effekte – überhaupt Sinn? Ich glaube schon: Es ermöglicht eine andere Betrachtungs- und Beurteilungsweise der Arbeiten in diesem riesigen Feld der Computergrafik. Bleibt diese Trennung für die Zukunft gültig und aufrecht? Das halte ich nicht für wahrscheinlich. In der Computergrafik wird es hoffentlich auch weiterhin Bewegung und Entwicklung geben, Trends und Tendenzen. Es wird sicherlich immer ein Menge Anstrengungen rund um die „Grenzbereiche" wie rund um die neuen, grenzüberschreitenden Werkzeuge und Methoden geben, und nur zu häufig liegen diese Grenzen in unseren gegenwärtigen Definitionen, in unserem Verständnis, unseren Umsetzungen, unserer Art des Denkens und Wahrnehmens begründet. Betrachtet man die Bemühungen der Integration von Bild und Klang, so wird klar, daß die Kategorien „Musik" und „Animation" bald nicht mehr ausreichen werden, und bei allem, was in der „interaktiven" Welt passiert, werden wir bald gezwungen sein, auch unseren Begriff von „Leben" zu erweitern und neu zu definieren – glaube und hoffe ich.
Gegenwärtig jedenfalls haben wir uns mit den Kategorien Computeranimation und Visual Effects auseinanderzusetzen. Und die Jury hat fast 300 Werke in der ersteren und 65 in der letzeren Kategorie begutachtet, wobei einige Stücke von einer Kategorie in die andere verschoben wurden, weil dies der Natur des Werks besser entsprach.

Wofür werden die Preise vergeben? Was ist das „Ergebnis"?

Beide Kategorien des Prix Ars Electronica – Computeranimation und Visual Effects – haben je einen Hauptpreis, die Goldene Nica, zwei Auszeichnungen und bis zu zwölf Anerkennungen zu vergeben. Doch wofür werden diese Preise zuerkannt?
Die Preise und Anerkennungen werden für heraus-

achieve excellence of result—the actual manifestation of the original idea or concept. "Excellence" always (always!) is suited to context. And, any context can be mastered. Any context can have its boundaries pushed on. Any context can serve as a springboard for creativity (and for excellence within that).

What is the selection process?

So, how does one identify, determine, compare and ultimately judge "excellence" in this? For the jury we agreed that true excellence is one that begins with excellence of idea and is carried through to excellence of result. This is tough. It is certainly a tall order. And, no, perhaps contrary to popular belief, this notion of excellence is accessible to all. It is not limited or defined by "means." There actually is no such thing as excellence of "means"—excellent application within means yes, but not excellence of means. That necessarily implies, in order to rightfully compare a commercial product from a top production house to a six-week student project, that contexts of submissions cannot be judged and/but must be made "clear." And, if the idea was "wonderful" but the means were not there to manifest it then perhaps there was no excellence of idea in the first place.

What were the results?

Only "content" is not enough. Only "design" is not enough. Only "idea" is not enough. And, doing for the sake of doing, is not enough.
The idea has to be for some content—unless the idea is one of pure research (and even then it must be made accessible). Rendering or execution can be limited by "means" but not by care or manner. Anything that anyone does can be done well or not. This may sound simplistic but it obviously isn't "simple" (otherwise more people would "do it").
The pieces that truly are excellent are—again—excellent in idea, in technique, in application of technique, in content, in presentation. The piece is integral with itself. It is consistent with itself. It starts, is carried through and ends "excellently."
Notably, some people drop the ball along the way (putting it bluntly).
Notably, some people have ideas that don't match

ragende Leistungen auf diesem Gebiet zuerkannt. Punkt. Was bedeutet „herausragend"? Nun, herausragende Leistungen kann wirklich jeder erzielen – konzeptionell, technisch, durch Anwendung oder durch Inhalt. Und all dies zusammen ist erforderlich, um ein wahrhaft hervorragendes Ergebnis zu erreichen – die Manifestation der ursprünglichen Idee oder des Konzeptes. „Hervorragend" ist ein Werk immer (immer!) innerhalb seines kontextuellen Zusammenhangs. Und jeder Kontext kann dabei seine Grenzen erweitern, jeder Kontext kann als Sprungbrett für Kreativität dienen (und dabei bis zum Außergewöhnlichen vorstoßen).

Wie findet der Auswahlprozeß statt?

Wie identifiziert man, bestimmt man, vergleicht man, beurteilt man letztlich das „Herausragende"? Diese Jury war sich einig darin, daß wahrhaft hervorragende Werke mit einer hervorragenden Ideebeginnen und diesen ihren Qualitätsanspruch bis zum Endergebnis durchhalten. Das ist zweifellos schwierig, zweifellos eine große Aufgabe. Aber – vielleicht im Gegensatz zur landläufigen Meinung diese Form der Meisterschaft kann von jedermann erreicht werden. Sie wird nicht von den „Mitteln" definiert oder eingeschränkt. Es gibt nämlich keine „Qualität der Mittel" – eine Qualität der Anwendung innerhalb der Mittel, das wohl, nicht aber „hervorragende Mittel" als solche. Wenn man also ein kommerzielles Produkt eines großen Produktionshauses mit einer in sechs Wochen entstandenen studentischen Seminararbeit gerecht und fair zu vergleichen hat, bedeutet dies, daß der Entstehungszusammenhang der Einreichungen nicht bewertet werden kann, wohl aber deutlich gemacht werden muß. Und wenn die Grundidee hervorragend erscheint, aber die Mittel für eine ebenso gute Umsetzung nicht ausgereicht haben, dann muß man davon ausgehen, daß die Idee vielleicht doch nicht ganz so exzellent war.

Welche Ergebnisse zeigten sich?

„Inhalt" allein ist nicht genug. Schönes „Design" allein ist nicht genug. Eine „gute Idee" allein ist nicht genug. Und ein Tun um des Tuns willen ist ebenfalls nicht genug.
Die Grundidee muß einen bestimmten Inhalt tragen, außer sie wäre ein reiner Forschungsansatz, und selbst dann muß dies deutlich und faßbar werden. Die Durchführung oder das Rendering kann durch die zur Verfügung stehenden Mittel beschränkt werden, aber nicht durch fehlende Sorgfalt oder Fertigkeit. Was immer jemand tut, kann er (oder sie) gut oder weniger gut tun. Das mag jetzt sehr simpel klingen, aber es ist offensichtlich doch nicht so einfach, denn sonst würden mehr Leute das durchhalten.
Die wirklich herausragenden Werke sind – es sei hier wiederholt – in jeder Hinsicht herausragend: i

the rendering, execution, means, ability and/or capacity. Notably, some execute well and present it not at all. Work can't be narcissistic. People can't stop and say "What this is is so wonderful that everyone will obviously 'see'." Well, if it isn't accessible, it can never be "obvious."
Notably, some do not have a sense of the history of the field. Although relatively young in itself, it is old enough now to have seen much innovation and creativity—many excellent ideas and manifestations thereof. I have never understood working in a void. I always want to know what has been done in order to go and do what hasn't. Some people obviously don't share this notion and at times throughout the screenings, redundancy of idea was obvious.
Notably, some assume—perhaps given that this appears to be a "visual" category—that sound or music are not important. This is wrong. They are important. They are actually essential. They must be integral to the piece.
And, most noteworthy, many did things "right"... resulting in wonderful discussions and debates around the submissions and, of course, an amazing list of prize winners and honorable mentions.
For the computer animation category, the jury was actually able to get to the point where individual members "mattered." Differences in definitions, interests, aesthetics, understanding needed to be presented, explained, defended, and accepted. This results in the "appropriate" (correct?) range of pieces being selected as "winners". This results in the "correct" distribution of prizes. The list or prize order can never please only one person or even any person ("personally"). All jury members need to be able to live with it, to find it "fair", and to be proud of the whole. All people responsible for the pieces on the computer animation list truly can be proud.
For the Visual Effects category this unfortunately wasn't the case. I in no way mean to take away from the prize winning and honorably mentioned submissions—which certainly deserve their merit—but, in general, the quality of the presentation of the submissions (more than the submissions themselves) was poor. People often, usually falsely, assumed understanding of context, of whole, of idea, of purpose, of method when it truly wasn't apparent.
So, that said, here are this year's winners ...

ihrer Idee, in ihrer Technik, in der Anwendung dieser Technik, in ihrem Inhalt, in ihrer Präsentation. Das Stück ist ein in sich geschlossenes Ganzes, es ist in sich konsistent, es beginnt hervorragend, es bleibt hervorragend, es endet hervorragend.
Es fällt auf, daß manche Leute – grob gesprochen – unterwegs ihr Ziel aus den Augen verlieren.
Es fällt auf, daß manche Leute Ideen haben, die nicht zur Durchführung oder zur Ausführung, nicht zu ihren Mitteln, zu ihren Fähigkeiten und/oder Möglichkeiten passen.
Es fällt auf, daß manche wunderbar ausführen und dies dennoch nicht präsentieren können. Die Arbeit kann und darf nicht narzißtisch sein. Man kann nicht an einem bestimmten Punkt aufhören und sich sagen: „Nun, dies ist so wunderschön, daß es jedem ins Auge fallen wird", denn wenn es nicht zugänglich, nicht faßlich ist, dann kann es auch niemals „augenfällig" sein.
Es fällt auf, daß einigen das Gefühl für die Geschichte dieses Kunstbereichs fehlt. Obwohl das Genre noch relativ jung ist, so ist es doch alt genug, eine Menge an Innovation und Kreativität getragen zu haben – viele ausgezeichnete Ideen und ihre Umsetzung. Ich habe nie verstanden, wie man in einem Vakuum arbeiten kann. Ich möchte immer wissen, was getan wurde, um irgendwohin zu gelangen, und warum. Einige Einreicher teilen diese Ansicht nicht, und es wurde bei der Betrachtung der Werke bisweilen eine starke Redundanz der Ideen sichtbar.
Es fällt auf, daß offenbar einige – in der Annahme, dies sei eine „visuelle" Kategorie – Ton und Musik für unwichtig halten. Das ist falsch. Sie sind wichtig, mehr noch, sie sind essentiell. Und sie müssen ein integrierter Bestandteil des Werkes sein.
Und am meisten fällt auf, daß viele alles „richtig" gemacht haben ... was zu wunderbaren Diskussionen und Debatten um die Einreichungen geführt hat und zu einer erstaunlichen Liste von Preisträgern und Anerkennungen.
Bei der Computeranimation kam die Jury sogar an jenen Punkt, an dem jedes einzelne Jurymitglied als Individuum Bedeutung erlangte: Unterschiede in der persönlichen Definition, in den Interessen, der Ästhetik, im Verständnis mußten präsentiert werden, erklärt, verteidigt und akzeptiert. Und daraus ergab sich die „angemessene" (und korrekte?) Auswahl jener Werke, die als „Gewinner" anzusehen waren, daraus ergab sich die „gerechte" Verteilung der Preise. Keine Liste von Preisträgern kann nur einer Person gefallen oder auch jedermann („persönlich"). Alle Jurymitglieder mußten sie akzeptieren, sie „fair" finden und auf das Gesamtergebnis stolz sein. Und stolz sein können alle Einreicher, die sich in der Preisträgerliste der Computeranimation wiederfinden.
Im Bereich der Visual Effects war dies leider nicht der Fall. Ich möchte in keiner Weise die Leistungen der Preisträger und der Anerkennungen schmälern – die alle diese Ehre verdienen –, wenn ich darauf

The Prix Ars Electronica Golden Nica for Computer Animation

Bunny directed by Chris Wedge and produced at Blue Sky Studios (USA)

The Prix Ars Electronica Computer Animation Awards of Distinction

A Bug's Life directed by John Lasseter and Andrew Stanton, produced by Pixar (USA)
Snack and Drink directed by Bob Sabiston and Tommy Pallotta, produced by Flat Black Films (USA)

The Prix Ars Electronica Honorary Mentions in Computer Animation

In the Computer Animation category, the jury chose to award all honorary mentions. Actually choosing to do this wasn't difficult, given that we had more pieces that we wanted to honor than "mentions." We ended up coming up with quite an elaborate "system" to describe our choices, preferences and sense of import for the pieces allowing for a list of work that felt "fair"—meaning reflected each member's participation and resulted in an overall "jury" list.
This year the honorary mentions go to ...
Bad Night directed by Emre and Lev Yilmaz of Protozoa (USA)
Bike directed by Dietmar Offenhuber of AEC Future-Lab (Austria)
Bingo directed by Chris Landreth of Alias|Wavefront (Canada)
En Dérive directed by Patrice Mugnier/Heure Exquise (France, a student work)
Fly Band! directed by Seiji Shiota and Tohru Patrick Awa of Polygon Pictures (Japan)
Ghostcatching directed by Paul Kaiser, Shelley Eshkar and Bill T. Jones of Riverbed (USA)
Polygon Family directed by Jun Asakawa and Toshifumi Kawahara of Polygon Pictures (Japan)
Ronin Romance Classics directed by Bruce Pukema of Ronin Inc. (USA)
Stationen directed by Christian Sawade-Meyer (D)
Tightrope directed by Daniel Robichaud of Digital Domain (USA)
Ultima Forsan directed by William Le Henanff (France)

hinweise, daß die Qualität der Präsentation der Einreichungen (mehr noch als die Einreichungen selbst) generell eher schwach war. Die Einreicher habe oft – und meist zu Unrecht – angenommen, der Kontext, das Ganze, die Idee, der Zweck oder di[e] Methode sei ohnehin offensichtlich, wenn dies kei[-]neswegs der Fall war.
Und nachdem das alles gesagt ist, hier die diesjäh[ri]gen Preisträger:

Die Goldene Nica für Computeranimation des Prix Ars Electronica

Bunny von Chris Wedge und produziert von Blue Sky Studios (USA)

Die Auszeichnungen für Computer Animation des Prix Ars Electronica

A Bug's Life von John Lasseter und Andrew Stanton[,] produziert von Pixar (USA)
Snack and Drink von Bob Sabiston und Tommy Pallotta, produziert von Flat Black Films (USA)

Die Anerkennungen für Computer Animation des Prix Ars Electronica

Im Bereich der Computeranimation hat die Jury di[e] mögliche Höchstzahl an Anerkennungen ausgesprochen, und dies war keineswegs schwierig, wei[l] wir mehr anerkennenswerte Stücke hatten, als un[s] Anerkennungen zur Verfügung standen. Wir habe[n] letztlich ein ziemlich ausgefeiltes „System" ausgearbeitet, um unsere Auswahl zu beschreiben, unsere Präferenzen und die subjektive Wertigkeit zu definieren, was zu einer Werkliste geführt hat, die wir als „fair" ansehen und die das persönliche Eng[a]gement jedes einzelnen Jurymitgliedes in dieser Gesamtliste widerspiegelt.
Die Anerkennungen des Jahres 1999 gehen an:

Bad Night von Emre und Lev Yilmaz von Protozoa (USA)
Bike von Dietmar Offenhuber vom AEC Future-Lab (A)
Bingo von Chris Landreth von Alias|Wavefront (CDN)
En Dérive von Patrice Mugnier, Studentenarbeit/ Heure Exquise (F)
Fly Band! von Seiji Shiota und Tohru Patrick Awa vo[n] Polygon Pictures (J)
Ghostcatching von Paul Kaiser, Shelley Eshkar und Bill T. Jones von Riverbed (USA)
Polygon Family von Jun Asakawa und Toshifumi Kawahara von Polygon Pictures (J)
Ronin Romance Classics von Bruce Pukema von Ronin Inc. (USA)
STATIONEN von Christian Sawade-Meyer (D)
Tightrope von Daniel Robichaud von Digital Domai[n] (USA)
Ultima Forsan von William Le Henanff (F)
Un Temps pour elle von Erwin Charrier – eine Studentenarbeit/Heure Exquise (F)

Un Temps pour elle directed by Erwin Charrier/Heure Exquise (a student work, France)

The Prix Ars Electronica Golden Nica for Visual Effects

What Dreams May Come produced by Digital Domain, Mass.illusion and POP (USA)

The Prix Ars Electronica Visual Effects Awards of Distinction

A viagem by Alain Escalle (France)
Guinness "Surfer" by Computer-Film Company (GB)

The Prix Ars Electronica Honorary Mentions in Visual Effects

This year the honorary mentions in the Prix Ars Electronica Visual Effects category were awarded to ...
Alaris "Aliens" by Juan Tominic Muller of Daiquiri Spainbox (Spain)
Lottery "Fantasy" by Manuel Horrillo Fernandez of Daiquiri Spainbox (Spain)
Photoreal Digital Cars: Metal Desert and Metal City by Ray Giarratana of Digital Domain (USA)
No Way by Geoffrey Guiot, Bruno Lardé and Jérôme Maillot/Heure Exquise (France, a student work)
Original Copies by Miles/Murray/Sorrell of Fuel (GB)
Virus by Phil Tippett and Craig Hayes of Tippett Studios (USA)

In conclusion ...

If an idea is worth realizing, then it is worth realizing well. If you don't know the work in the above list, please try and see it. These are ideas exceptionally well realized. Individually and together, they currently define computer animation and visual effects. They are our top-of-line present. They point towards our future. And they will become part of our wonderful history.
It was an honor and a pleasure to have been on this year's jury—to have had access to such a wonderful body of work; to sit, discuss, debate with my distinguished co-jurors; to have had the chance to meet firsthand the amazing group of people responsible for the Prix Ars Electronica competition. To all of you I say thank you and congratulations.

Die Goldene Nica für Visual Effects des Prix Ars Electronica

What Dreams May Come, produziert von Digital Domain, Mass.illusion und PoP (USA)

Die Auszeichnungen für Visual Effects des Prix Ars Electronica

A viagem von Alain Escalle (F)
Guinness „Surfer" von CFC / Computer-Film Company (UK)

Die Anerkennungen für Visual Effects des Prix Ars Electronica

In diesem Jahr wurden folgende Anerkennungen für Visual Effects des Prix Ars Electronica vergeben:
Alaris „Aliens" von Juan Tomicic Muller / Daiquiri Spainbox (E)
Lottery „Fantasy" von Manuel Horrillo Fernandez / Daiquiri Spainbox (E)
Photoreal Digital Cars: Metal Desert & Metal City von Ray Giarratana von Digital Domain (USA)
No Way von Geoffrey Guiot, Bruno Lardé, Jérôme Maillot – eine Studentenarbeit/Heure Exquise (F)
Original Copies von Miles/Murray/Sorrell von Fuel (UK)
Virus von Phil Tippett und Craig Hayes von Tippett Studios (USA)

Zum Abschluß

Wenn eine Idee es wert ist, realisiert zu werden, dann ist sie es wert, *gut* realisiert zu werden. Wer die Werke der obigen Liste nicht kennt, sollte sie sich unbedingt ansehen. Diese Ideen wurden ausnehmend gut umgesetzt. Sowohl als einzelne wie in ihrer Gesamtheit definieren sie den gegenwärtigen Stand der Computeranimation und der Visual Effects. Sie stellen die gegenwärtige Spitze des Genres dar, sie sind zukunftsweisend und werden Teil unserer wunderbaren Geschichte sein.
Es war eine Ehre und ein Vergnügen, Mitglied der diesjährigen Jury zu sein – Zugang zu haben zu einer so großartigen Gesamtheit an Werken, zu sitzen und zu diskutieren, mit meinen geehrten Mitjuroren zu debattieren, Gelegenheit zu haben, die erstaunliche Gruppe von Leuten kennenzulernen, die für den Prix Ars Electronica verantwortlich sind. Ihnen allen drücke ich meinen Dank und meine Glückwünsche aus.

BUNNY

Chris Wedge / Blue Sky Studio

"It's a suspense story. A case of mistaken identity, with a twist that I think has a lot of heart to do it," says Chris Wedge. When asked why a rabbit? Wedge answered, "I was always doodling rabbits, I think because I was fascinated by the character of Uncle Wiggly and the animation in those old illustrations from the 1930's. That was definitely an influence. I wanted to create something in that rich storybook style—realistic, yet fantasy."

In fact, the short, which began as an effort to stretch the limits of Blue Sky Studios' proprietary lighting software, has such a warm, filmic, photorealistic style that it belies the computer technology that made it possible. Through the use of a software technique called radiosity, which is a complete simulation of how natural light works, Wedge and his crew were able to create an unparalleled dimensionality and organic realism never before attempted in a computer-animated film.

"In a real environment there is usually more than one single color of light illuminating a scene," Wedge explained. "There are all these sympathetic hues—yellow bouncing off a yellow wall, greens being reflected from trees outside, blue from the sky; colours we may not even be aware of unless they're missing. Recreating that ambient illumination in the computer gives us a richness of live action photography and the versability to make anything happen."

Still, pioneering this new technique wasn't easy. The technical team began by setting up a master lighting program that would be fairly consistent throughout the film. "That got us 90 percent of the way there," explained Dave Walvoord, who served as digital effects supervisor of the film. "But the real trick came when you'd be looking at a shot and think—oh man! the stove is just popping out way too much and we really want the attention on *Bunny*. That's when radiosity stopped being our friend and started working against us."

Walvoord said the team couldn't tweak the lightning to correct the brightness of the stove because with radiosity, that little change affected the whole global lighting structure. Ironically, this problem is exactly what happens on a live-action set. "In the studios, they're always fighting radiosity," Walvoord said, smiling, "But they can stick out their hands and

„Es ist eine spannende Geschichte. Ein Fall von Irrtum in der Identität, mit einer Wendung, die mein Ansicht nach doch zu Herzen geht", meint Chris Wedge. Auf die Frage, warum ausgerechnet ein Hase, antwortet Wedge: „Ich habe schon immer Hasen gekritzelt, wahrscheinlich weil ich von der Figur des Uncle Wiggly und den Illustrationen der 30er Jahre fasziniert war. Das hat mich sicher beei[nflußt]. Und ich wollte irgend etwas in diesem reichen Märchenbuch-Stil produzieren – realistisch und doch voll Phantasie."

Tatsächlich hat dieser Kurzfilm – der eigentlich als Versuch begonnen hatte, die Fähigkeiten der Blue Sky Studios im Bereich der Lichteffekte zu erweite[rn] – einen so warmen, filmischen fotorealistischen St[il], daß er die Computertechnik verleugnet, die ihn eigentlich erst möglich gemacht hat. Durch die Verwendung einer Softwaretechnik, die man als „Radiosity" bezeichnet und die eine umfassende Simulation des Verhaltens von natürlichem Licht ermöglicht, waren Christ Wedge und sein Team in der Lage, eine bisher unerreichte Tiefe und einen organischen Realismus zu erzielen, wie sie noch ni[e] in einem computeranimierten Film erzielt wurden.

„In einer realen Umgebung gibt es normalerweise mehr als nur eine Lichtfarbe, die eine Szene beleuchtet", erklärt Wedge. „Es existieren da die viele[n] mitschwingenden Farbtöne, gelbes Licht, das von einer gelben Wand abstrahlt, Grüntöne, die von Bäumen draußen reflektiert werden, Blautöne aus dem Himmel – Farben also, die wir möglicherweis[e] erst dann wahrnehmen, wenn sie fehlen. Wenn wi[r] dieses Umfeldlicht im Computer nachstellen, gibt uns das den Farbreichtum der realen Fotografie u[nd] die Flexibilität, wirklich alles geschehen zu lassen."

Allerdings war es nicht leicht, als Pionier dieser neuen Technik aufzutreten. Das Technikerteam begann damit, einen Hauptlichtplan zu erstellen, der durch den ganzen Film hindurch ziemlich konsistent bleiben sollte. „Das waren schon einmal 90 Prozent des Weges", erklärt Dave Walvoord, der als Digital Effects Supervisor am Film mitgearbeitet hat. „Aber die eigentliche Arbeit beginnt dann, wenn man sich eine Szene ansieht und feststellen muß: O je, der Herd sticht viel zu sehr heraus, und wir wollten doch die gesamte Aufmerksamkeit au[f] Bunny konzentrieren ... In diesen Situationen hörte Radiosity auf, unser Freund zu sein, und begann, gegen uns zu arbeiten."

Walvoord erklärt, daß das Team nicht einfach das Licht ein wenig verändern konnte, um den Herd au[s] der Helligkeit zu bekommen, weil im Radiosity-Verfahren jede noch so kleine Veränderung sofort die globale Lichtstruktur betrifft. Ironischerweise i[st] dies eines jener Probleme, die auch bei Live-Filmaufnahmen aufzutreten pflegen. „Auch in den Studios kämpfen sie ständig mit Reflexlicht", sagt Walvoord mit einem Lächeln, „aber die können einfach die Hand ausstrecken und schnell herausfin-

figure out where the shadow is coming from. It's a little more complicated in the computer." The team ended up putting the computer-equivalent of "bounce cards" and "flags" in the programming, blocks that would add or take away indirect light. "And sometimes, we just had to throw physics out the window and do what looked right," Walvoord stated.
Nina Bafaro, one of two lead animators that included Doug Dooley, said that although extensive reference material of the real rabbits and moths was used, both characters are highly stylized to capture the storybook quality of Wedge's vision. That vision is what changed Bafaro's mind about computer animation. "I came from a traditional animation background and didn't like computers," she said. "But when I saw Bunny—even early on, before she had fur, I knew that Blue Sky was the only computer-animation studio I could work for. The company has a real respect for traditional animation roots."
Bafaro, who with Dooley was responsible for the majority of the scenes in the film, said she was especially sensitive to the characters' physical presence, adding "with the moth, the focus was on giving weight to the body, almost as if it is a struggle for him to stay airborne. Bunny was this crotchety, bitter, old woman character, so her movements had to be feeble and full of effort—but with quick expressive rabbit ears and body movements."
Jim Bresnahan, who also animated for the film, said getting physical substance to read on screen has a lot to do with timing and physics. "A good animator has to be a bit of a scientist as well as an actor," Bresnahan explained adding "what's unique about *Bunny* and Blue Sky animation in general, is an attention to character development. We aren't just out there moving limbs up and down like puppeteers. We try to understand the character's history and motivation. It is that aspect of a real performance that gives our work a lot of heart and believability."
The score is also an original—composed by Tom Waits and Kathleen Brennan who have collaborated on a number of films including *Dead Man Walking*, *One From The Heart*, (which garnered an Academy nomination), *Night on Earth* and *American Heart* to name a few. The music for *Bunny*, has an emotional

den, woher der Schatten kommt. Im Computer ist das ein wenig komplizierter." Schließlich wurden sogar Computeräquivalente zu den traditionellen Lichtablenkschirmen und Reflexionsflächen aufgestellt, um indirektes Licht wegzunehmen oder umzuleiten. „Und manchmal haben wir einfach die ganze Physik über Bord geworfen und das getan, was richtig ausgesehen hat."
Nina Bafaro – gemeinsam mit Doug Dooley Hauptanimatorin – berichtet, daß trotz der Verwendung von ausführlichem Referenzmaterial echter Hasen und echter Motten beide Charaktere stark stilisiert wurden, um die von Chris Wedge angestrebte märchenhafte Anmutung zu erzielen. Diese Vision Wedges hat auch Bafaros Einstellung zur Computeranimation verändert: „Ich komme vom traditionellen Trickfilm und mochte Computer nicht", sagt sie. „Aber als ich Bunny dann gesehen habe, und das noch in einer frühen Phase, nämlich bevor sie ihr Fell bekam, da wußte ich, daß Blue Sky das einzige Computeranimationsstudio ist, für das ich arbeiten könnte. Dieses Unternehmen hat wirklich Respekt vor der Tradition und den Wurzeln der Animation."
Jim Bresnahan, der auch Animationen zum Film beigetragen hat, meint, daß es viel mit Timing und Physik zu tun habe, wenn eine animierte Figur auf dem Bildschirm gut rüberkommt. „Ein guter Animator muß ein wenig Wissenschaftler und ein wenig Schauspieler sein", erklärt er und fügt hinzu: „Was an Bunny so einmalig ist – und an Blue-Sky-Animationen allgemein –, ist das Augenmerk, das auf die Entwicklung einer Figur gelegt wird. Wir bewegen nicht einfach Glieder hin und her wie ein Puppenspieler seine Marionette. Wir versuchen, die Geschichte und die Motivation unserer Gestalten zu verstehen. Und dieser Aspekt einer realen Darstellung gibt unseren Arbeiten so viel Herz und Glaubwürdigkeit."
Die Originalmusik des Films wurde von Tom Waits und Kathleen Brennan komponiert, die bei etlichen Filmen zusammengearbeitet hatten, darunter *Dead Man Walking*, *One From the Heart* (was eine Oscar-Nominierung nach sich zog), *Night on Earth* und *American Heart*, um nur einige zu nennen. Die Musik zu *Bunny* hat eine emotionale Spannweite, die von einem ungewöhnlichen hymnenartigen Akkordeon-Solo bis zu einem Instrumentalchaos reicht, das an ein sich einstimmendes Orchester erinnert. Waits leiht einem von ihm selbst geschriebenen Text zum Abspann seine berüchtigte knirschende Stimme.
„Der Schlüssel zu *Bunny*", stellt Wedge schließlich fest, „liegt darin, daß es zuallererst eine Filmerfahrung und eine Geschichte ist. Wir sind einfach technikverrückt geworden, aber der Film wurde so angelegt, daß er diese Tatsache verschleiert. Es gibt keine Plastikoberflächen, nichts, was den typischen Computer-Eindruck hervorruft, und auch keine besonde-

range that journeys from an unusual accordion hymn-like solo to an instrumental chaos most reminiscent of an orchestra warming up. Waits lends his infamous gravelly vocal style to lyrics he wrote for the ending credit roll.

"The key to *Bunny*," Wedge concludes, "is that it is a film experience and a story first. We just happened to go insane with the technology, but it is designed to hide the fact. There are no plastic surfaces, nothing that has a defined computer signature and no particulary graphic special effects. We don't want people to think too hard about what went into creating it. We just want them to sit back and enjoy it."

ren grafischen Effekte. Wir wollen nicht, daß die Leute allzusehr darüber nachdenken, was dahinte steckt. Wir wollen einfach, daß sie sich zurücklehnen und den Film genießen."

CHRIS WEDGE (USA) IS HEAD OF THE DEVELOPMENT DEPARTMENT AND ONE OF THE FOUNDERS OF BLUE SKY STUDIOS. HE ACHIEVED INTERNATIONAL RECOGNITION FOR THE CHARACTER ANIMATION IN THE FILM *JOE'S APARTMENT* (AWARD OF DISTINCTION PRIX ARS ELECTRONICA). WEDGE BEGAN AS A CARTOON ANIMATOR, WORKED ON THE DISNEY PRODUCTION *TRON* AND HAS ANIMATED MANY PRIZE-WINNING COMMERCIAL VIDEOS. HIS WORKS HAVE BEEN DISTINGUISHED AT ALL THE MAJOR INTERNATIONAL FESTIVALS. ▬ Chris Wedge (USA) ist einer der Gründer von Blue Sky Studios und Leiter der Entwicklungsabteilung. Mit der Charakteranimation im Film *Joe's Appartement* (Auszeichnung Prix Ars Electronica) gewann er internationale Anerkennung. Wedge begann als Trickanimator, wirkte an der Disney-Produktion *Tron* mit und hat zahlreiche preisgekrönte Werbevideos animiert. Seine Arbeiten wurden bei allen großen internationalen Festivals

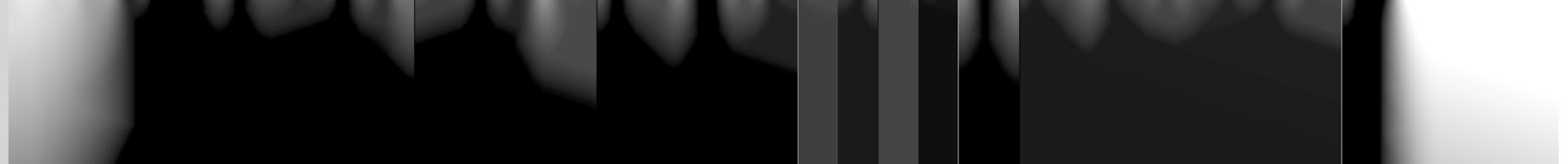

A BUG'S LIFE

John Lasseter / Andrew Stanton / Pixar

As *Toy Story* was entering its final year of production in 1994, John Lasseter and his team began actively exploring ideas for their next feature project. A film involving insect characters had been discussed and seemed a natural, because it could utilize the strengths and advantages of computer animation. The spark of the idea for *A Bug's Life* came one day as Andrew Stanton and Joe Ranft were having lunch. They began talking about the classic Aesop fable, The Ant and the Grasshopper, in which a starving grasshopper, fiddle in hand, drops in on a family of ants and begs for a bite to eat. When the grasshopper confesses that he spent the summer months making music, the industrious ants turn him away and suggest that he spend the winter dancing. Aesop's conclusion was "there's a time to work and a time to play." Stanton and Ranft concluded that it might make for a pretty interesting scenario if the grasshopper, being much bigger than the ants, decided to just take the food. Their active imaginations began racing and they laughed at the humorous possibilities.

Lasseter shared their enthusiasm and helped flesh out the idea.

Bringing the colourful cast of characters from *A Bug's Life* to the screen required the collective talents of more than sixty animators. Unlike traditional Disney features, where one supervising animator and a team are assigned to work on a particular character, animators at Pixar would typically work on many if not all of the characters during the course of production. With a large cast of bugs that included 13 main characters and six supporting players, each one posing its own set of challenges, and scenes often involving as many as eight or nine characters, this was an extremely difficult film to work on from an animation standpoint. From a purely technical standpoint, *A Bug's Life* represents a major advance over its predecessor, *Toy Story*. New tools and procedures had to be created specifically to meet the demands of this production while the experience gained on their first film allowed the Pixar team to take the art form to the next level of accomplishment in all areas. The production itself had ten times the computing power of *Toy Story*,

Als *Toy Story* 1994 in sein letztes Produktionsjahr ging, begannen John Lasseter und sein Team bereits, Ideen für ihr nächstes Filmprojekt zusam menzutragen. Ein Film mit Insekten als Darstelle war andiskutiert worden und schien auch auf de Hand zu liegen, weil dabei die Stärken der Computeranimation am besten zum Tragen kommen könnten.

Der eigentliche Anstoß zu *A Bug's Life* kam allerdings an jenem Tag, an dem Andrew Stanton un Joe Ranft beim Mittagessen auf Äsops klassische Fabel von der Ameise und der Heuschrecke zu sp chen kamen, in der ein verhungernder Grashüpfe die Fiedel in der Hand – bei einer Ameisenfamilie anklopft und um etwas zu essen bittet. Als der Grashüpfer gesteht, daß er den Sommer mit Mu zieren verbracht hat, schicken ihn die fleißigen Ameisen weg und schlagen ihm vor, daß er im W ter tanzen solle. Äsops Moral der Geschichte war daß es eine Zeit zum Spielen und eine für die Ar gäbe. Stanton und Ranft kamen zum Schluß, daß dies ein ziemlich interessantes Szenario ergeben könne, wenn sich die Heuschrecke – sehr viel grö als die Ameisen – das Futter einfach nehmen würde. Ihre stets wache Phantasie fing an Blüte treiben, und sie hatten viel Spaß mit den humor len Möglichkeiten.

John Lasseter teilte ihren Enthusiasmus und half mit, der Idee das nötige Fleisch zu geben.

Um die farbenfrohen Charaktere von *A Bug's Life* auch auf den Schirm zu bekommen, mußten übe 60 talentierte Animatoren zusammenarbeiten. Anders als bei traditionellen Disney-Trickfilmen, jeweils ein Supervisor und sein Team einer einzig Figur zugeteilt sind, wirken die Animatoren bei Pixar im Laufe der Produktion normalerweise an vielen – wenn nicht sogar allen – Gestalten mit. einer dermaßen umfangreichen Käfer-Besetzung liste mit immerhin 13 Hauptdarstellern und sech Nebenrollen, die jeweils ganz spezielle Herausfo rungen stellten – und das in Szenen mit bis zu ac oder neun „Darstellern" –, war dieser Film vom A mationsstandpunkt extrem schwierig.

Vom rein technischen Standpunkt stellt *A Bug's L* gegenüber seinem Vorgänger *Toy Story* einen gro ßen Schritt vorwärts dar. Neue Werkzeuge und A läufe mußten speziell entwickelt werden, um de Anforderungen dieser Produktion gerecht zu wer den, während es andererseits die Erfahrung aus dem ersten Film dem Pixar-Team erlaubte, die Kunstform in jeder Hinsicht auf die nächsthöher Leistungsebene zu bringen. Die Produktion selbs verschlang die zehnfache Rechnerleistung von *To Story*, mit 1000 Prozessoren in der RenderFarm, d rund viermal so schnell arbeiteten wie beim erst Film. Aber diese Faktoren wurden durch die enor

vith 1,000 processors in the RenderFarm operating ıbout four times faster than the ones on the last ilm. But those factors were counterbalanced by the ·normous complexity of the film. For example, the nost difficult scenes in *A Bug's Life* still required over oo hours per frame to render. The average shot locked in at about 15 hours of render time."

oy Story proved that we could do anything if we put ut minds to it," says Lasseter. "It reinforced my belief hat it's not the technology that's important; the tory and the characters need 100% of our focus. All he technology is derived from what's needed in the tory. The foundation of the way we work is that art hallenges technology, then technology inspires the art.

Komplexität des Films wieder aufgewogen. So benötigten die schwierigsten Szenen in *A Bug's Life* noch immer über 100 Stunden zum Rendering eines einzigen Kaders, und das Rendern selbst durschschnittlicher Einstellungen dauerte noch immer gut 15 Stunden pro Kader.

„*Toy Story* hat bewiesen, daß wir alles machen können, wenn wir es uns einmal in den Kopf gesetzt haben", sagt Lasseter. „Und meine Überzeugung, daß es nicht auf die Technologie ankommt, ist wieder bestärkt worden: Die Geschichte und die Charaktere brauchen hundert Prozent Aufmerksamkeit. Die Technologie wird von dem abgeleitet, was wir für die Geschichte brauchen. Die Grundlage unserer Arbeit besteht darin, daß die Kunst die Technologie herausfordert, und dann die Technologie die Kunst inspiriert."

John Lasseter (USA) made motion picture history in 1995 as the director of *Toy Story*, the first-ever computer-animated feature film. He has written and directed a number of short films and television commercials at Pixar, including *Luxo Jr.* (a 1986 Oscar nominee), *Red's Dream* (1987), *Tin Toy*, which won the 1989 Academy Award, for Best Animated Short Film. Andrew Stanton (USA) has been a member of the Pixar Animation team since 1990. He went on to receive an Oscar nomination in 1996 as one of the four screenwriters who collaborated on the landmark computer animated phenomenon, *Toy Story*.

John Lasseter (USA) schrieb 1995 als Regisseur des ersten abendfüllenden computeranimierten Films *Toy Story* Filmgeschichte. Er hat zahlreiche Kurzfilme und Werbespots bei Pixar produziert, darunter *Luxo jr.* (1986 für den Oscar nominiert), *Red's Dream* (1987), *Tin Toy* (Oscargewinner 1989 als bester Kurztrickfilm). Andrew Stanton (USA) ist seit 1990 Mitglied des Pixar Animation-Teams. Er wurde 1996 als einer der vier Autoren des Meilensteins der Computeranimation *Toy Story* für einen Oscar nominiert.

SNACK AND DRINK

Bob Sabiston / Tommy Pallotta / Flat Black Films

Snack and Drink is the latest in a series of animated documentary shorts from Flat Black Films. It features Ryan Power, a six-foot tall thirteen-year-old in Austin, Texas. Ryan has the condition of autism: "an absorption in self-sentered subjective mental activity, especially when accompanied by marked withdrawal from reality." Filmmakers Bob Sabiston and Tommy Pallota follow Ryan to a local convenience store to purchase a "snack and drink." Along the way Ryan describes his fascination with a set of six animated kid's cartoon tapes starring Fieval, the mouse character from *An American Tail*.

Ryan is a particularly appropriate subject for our animation technique. The dreamlike and fractured nature of our images match the subject matter of his dialog very well. Ryan is a remarkable and engaging kid—we feel fortunate to have met and been able to film him. His mother initially invited us to do the interview—she told us that her son was autistic and obsessed with cartoon animation. It was her feeling that seeing himself animated would have a profound effect on him. One afternoon in December 1998 we went to Ryan's house to meet and film him. At first he would not consent to being interviewed. Two strangers with a camera probably made him nervous. He disappeared into the back of the house for a while, and we chatted with his mother and sister. Eventually he reappeared and announced that he was going to 7-11, a convenience store around the corner from his house. We asked if we could accompany him, and he said ok. The whole incident was spontaneous—yet the situation perfectly suited our needs and seemed to relax Ryan enough to talk to us at length. A few days ago I dropped off the finished tape at his mother's house—Ryan has since moved back to El Paso. He has not seen *Snack and Drink* yet—we are all eager to hear about his reaction to the film.

Snack and Drink is part of our ongoing software/art

Snack and Drink ist der jüngste einer Serie von an mierten Dokumentar-Kurzfilmen von Flat Black Films. Der Film beschäftigt sich mit dem 13jährige 1.80 m großen Ryan Power, der in Austin, Texas, le Ryan leidet an Autismus – einer „Absorption in ei sich um sich selbst drehende, subjektiv geistige Aktivität, besonders wenn sie von ausgeprägtem Rückzug aus der Realität begleitet wird". Bob Sabiston und Tommy Pallotta folgen Ryan zu eine nahegelegenen Laden, um „einen Snack und eine Drink" einzukaufen. Auf dem Weg erzählt Ryan vo der Faszination, die sechs Zeichentrickfilme auf ih ausüben, darunter auch *Feivel der Mauswanderer*. Ryan hat sich als besonders geeignet für unsere Animationstechnik erwiesen. Die traumgleiche u zersplitterte Qualität unserer Bilder paßt sehr gu zum Thema seines Dialogs. Ryan ist ein bemerker wertes und sehr einnehmendes Kind – wir sind froh, seine Bekanntschaft gemacht und ihn gefil zu haben. Seine Mutter hat uns zum Interview ei geladen – sie hatte uns berichtet, ihr Sohn sei Au und von Zeichentrickfilmen völlig besessen. Sie glaubte, daß es einen tiefen Eindruck auf ihn machen würde, sich selbst in einer Animation zu sehen. Eines Nachmittags im Dezember 1998 fuh ren wir also zu Ryans Haus, um ihn zu besuchen. Zuerst wollte er sich nicht interviewen lassen – zwei Fremde mit einer Kamera machten ihn offer sichtlich nervös. Er verschwand eine Weile ins Hinterhaus, und wir unterhielten uns mit seiner Mutter und seiner Schwester. Irgendwann taucht er wieder auf und gab bekannt, er werde zu „7 - 1 gehen, einem Lebensmittelladen gleich um die Ecke. Wir fragten, ob wir ihn begleiten dürften, u er sagte, es sei ok. Die Situation hatte sich sponta ergeben und paßte dennoch perfekt zu unseren Wünschen, außerdem schien sie Ryan hinreichen zu entspannen, so daß er ausführlich mit uns sprach.

Vor einigen Tagen habe ich das fertige Band bei s ner Mutter vorbeigebracht – Ryan ist inzwischen wieder in El Paso. Er hat *Snack and Drink* noch nic gesehen, aber wir sind alle gespannt darauf, von seiner Reaktion auf den Film zu hören.

roject. Flat Black Films is actively developing a nethod of doing animation which retains maximum espect for the individual artist. Simultaneously we re developing software tools to enable artists to xpress themselves in new ways. The work that esults from introducing artists to these new tools is lways fresh—they are continually challenged to dapt their aesthetic sensibilities to the new tools. Many mistakes are left in the final work—they show he learning process at work and ultimately ontribute to the strength of the piece.

Snack and Drink ist Teil eines größeren Software/ Kunst-Projekts. Flat Black Films entwickelt eine Animationsmethode, die den einzelnen Künstler so sehr respektiert wie möglich. Gleichzeitig entwickeln wir Software-Werkzeuge, die es dem Künstler ermöglichen, sich auf neue Weise auszudrücken. Die Werke, die sich daraus ergeben, daß wir Künstler mit diesen neuen Werkzeugen bekannt machen, sind stets von besonderer Frische – sie leben von der Herausforderung, die ästhetische Sensibilität diesen neuen Werkzeugen anzupassen. Viele Fehler werden in der fertigen Arbeit belassen, denn sie zeigen den Lernprozeß am Werk selbst und tragen letztlich zur Stärke des Stückes bei.

Bob Sabiston (USA) born 1967. Between 1985 and 1991 he studied at the MIT Media Laboratory, receiving a Bachelor of Science and a Masters degree in computer graphics research. He has twin interests in the visual arts and computer programming. Tommy Pallotta (USA) graduated with a degree in Philosophy. Eschewing traditional film methods since his feature, Pallotta has worked exclusively in video and digital formats. He is co-founder of Conduit Digital Festival. Bob Sabiston (USA), geb. 1967. Von 1985 bis 1991 studierte er am MIT Media Laboratory, graduierte zum Bachelor of Sciences und zum Master (Computergrafik). Seine Interessen liegen gleichermaßen in der Kunst und der Computerprogrammierung. Tommy Pallotta (USA) hat Philosophie studiert. Hält sich seit seinem ersten Film von traditionellen Methoden fern und arbeitet ausschließlich in Video- und digitalen Formaten. Mitbegründer des Conduit Digital Festival.

POLYGON FAMILY

Jun Asakawa / Toshifumi Kawahara / Polygon Pictures

Polygon Family is a family of four, performing an ordinary daily life with an expression of delicate habit and gesture.
Polygon Pictures was one of the first companies to apply realistic television aspects to its work, producing five short CG animation pieces expressly for TV, built upon different themes.
Polygon Family is one of these short CG animation pieces.
The project was named "Digital Adult Sesame", because we wanted to highlight the fact that the contents could be enjoyed by adults as well as children.
On the technical side, we came up with an original project management system called DWARF (Digital Work in process & Asset Routing Foundation).
Up until that point, such mammoth projects, which involved many people working simultaneously on large quantities of data over a long period of time, had been overseen by people, which inevitably entailed considerable human resources costs and inefficiencies.
DWARF computerizes this process, thus realizing a sophisticated production management system in sync with the future of CG production.

Die vierköpfige *Polygon Family* lebt ein gewöhnli-
oches Alltagsleben und verfügt über ein ausgefei
tes Bewegungs- und Gestenrepertoire.
Polygon Pictures war eines der ersten Unternehmen, das die realistischen Größenverhältnisse de
Fernsehens auf seine Arbeit angewendet hat, indem es fünf computeranimierte Kurzfilme zu unt
schiedlichen Themen ausdrücklich für das Fernse
hen produziert hat. *Polygon Family* ist eines diese
kurzen CG-Animationsstücke.
Das Projekt wurde als „Digitale Sesamstraße für
Erwachsene" bezeichnet, weil wir die Tatasche
unterstreichen wollten, daß der Inhalt von Erwac
senen wie von Kindern genossen werden kann.
Auf der technischen Seite haben wir dafür ein eig
nes Projekt-Management-System entwickelt, das
DWARF heißt (Digital Work in Process & Asset
Routing Foundation). Bis zu diesem Zeitpunkt wu
den Mammutprojekte dieser Art, bei denen gleic
zeitig eine Vielzahl von Mitarbeitern über einen l
gen Zeitraum an einer enormen Menge von Date
arbeiten, von Menschen überwacht, was in jeden
Fall beträchtliche Kosten und einiges an Ineffizier
nach sich zog. DWARF computerisiert diesen Proz
und stellt ein ausgefeiltes Produktionsmanagement-System zur Verfügung, das mit der Zukunft
der CG-Produktion im Einklang steht.

Toshifumi Kawahara (J) born 1950, received an MA from the Art and Design Department of the University of California at video and computer graphics. After graduating and returning to Japan, worked for Takenobu Igarashi Design studio, and then founded the computer graphics studio, Polygon Pictures, Inc. in 1983. At present, President of Polygon Pictures, Inc. Managing Director of Multimedia Research Center (MRC)/ National Institute. Jun Asakawa (J), born 1952, is a freelance film director for movies, TV-programs and commercials.

Toshifumi Kawahara (J), geb. 1950, graduierte am Art and Design Department der University of California Los Angeles (UCLA) zum MA. Nach dem Studienabschluß und der Rückkehr nach Japan arbeitete er für Takenobu Igarashi Design, bis er 1983 das Computergrafikstudio Polygon Pictures gründete, dessen Präsident er bis heute ist. Daneben ist er Leiter des Multimedia Research Center (MRC) am National Institute. Jun Asakawa (J), geb. 1952, ist freiberuflicher Regisseur für Filme, TV-Progra[illegible] und Werbespots.

UN TEMPS POUR ELLE

Erwin Charrier / Heure Exquise

A seaside bathed by the sun, a young woman moves into the light, time is accelerating in front of the lens of the camera, unrolling the film of a life.
This short film shows us a young woman coming to an island to film an eclipse. When the camera starts to roll, time accelerates all around her faster and faster. So she walks in this magic universe.
This student film was made at the SUPINFOCOM CGI school in 1998. The idea came to me while going through the pages of a fashion magazine. The flaring style and the "burnt" look of these photographs attracted me so much that I wanted to reproduce this kind of image with CG tools. I then made a scenario around those strong images that I had in my mind.
The subtle variations of the of lighting create a tropical and paradisiac climate. I wanted the audience to feel the heat as if standing in the sun.
In my opinion, this short film is more finalized in terms of lighting. I like to use light to erase, colour, heat or freeze an object. I think the quest for realism in CG should be achieved by a very deep and thorough work on lighting rather than work on the complexity of the objects.
Because of the character animation, which is really not my specialty, I preferred to focus all my efforts on the atmospheres of the shots to fine tune the picture. The whole film was made with 3DSmax2.
I then knew that I could not obtain ultra-realistic pictures, so I tested a graphic line halfway between photography and classical CG pictures. Since I had to work on a small hardware configuration, I had to experiment, find technical tricks, turn arounds, and eventually develop a new approach. This is something that people working on higher-end hardware would not venture into.

Ein sonnendurchfluteter Strandabschnitt, eine junge Frau im Licht, die Zeit beschleunigt sich vor dem Verschluß der Kamera und entrollt den Film eines Lebens.
Dieser Kurzfilm zeigt uns eine junge Frau, die auf eine Insel kommt, um eine Sonnenfinsternis zu filmen. Während die Kamera zu laufen beginnt, beschleunigt sich die Zeit um sie herum mehr und mehr, und sie wandelt in einem magisch anmuten den Universum.
Diese Studentenarbeit entstand 1998 an der SUPI FOCOM-Computergrafik-Schule. Die Idee kam mir, als ich die Seiten eines Modemagazins durchblätterte. Der leuchtende Stil und der überbelichtete Look der Fotos haben mich so fasziniert, daß ich diese Art von Bildern mit computergrafischen We zeugen reproduzieren wollte. Daraufhin begann ic ein Szenario um meine Phantasie-Bilder aufzubauen.
Die subtilen Variationen der Beleuchtung schaffer einen paradiesisch-tropischen Höhepunkt. Ich wo te, daß das Publikum die Hitze fühlen könnte, als stünde es selbst in der Sonne. Ich arbeite gerne m Licht, um zu löschen, zu färben oder um ein Objek heiß oder kalt erscheinen zu lassen. Ich glaube, da sich der erwünschte Realismus in der Computergrafik eher durch eine intensive Auseinandersetzung mit der Beleuchtung denn durch eine beson dere Komplexität der Objekte erzielen läßt. Da die Character-Animation nicht gerade zu meinen Stär ken zählt, habe ich all meine Anstrengungen auf c Feinabstimmung der Einstellungen gerichtet. Der gesamte Film entstand mit Hilfe von 3Dsmax2. Mi war klar, daß ich keine ultra-realistischen Bilder erreichen konnte, deswegen bemühte ich mich ur eine grafische Linie, die irgendwo zwischen Fotografie und „klassischen" CG-Bildern liegt. Da mir nur eine beschränkte Hardware-Ausstattung zur Verfügung stand, mußte ich experimentieren, mir technische Tricks und „Hintertürchen" einfallen la sen und bisweilen sogar einen völlig neuen Ansat finden – etwas, das sich jemand, der mit High-End Hardware arbeitet, nicht unbedingt antun würde.

Erwin Charrier (F), 24, started to play with CGI only four years ago at home. He discovered a passion for photography and cinema very late at school, but now he's trying to catch up. He has been working since one year at Mac Guff Ligne, a French CGI company based in Paris, where he does some mattepaintings, CG plants and lots of cool stuff. *Un Temps Pour Elle* is his first film. Erwin Charrier (F), 24, begann erst vor vier Jahren, sich zuhause mit CGI zu beschäftigen. Während seiner Schulzeit hatte er spät eine Leidenschaft für Photographie und Kino entwickelt, aber jetzt versucht er aufzuholen. Seit einem Jahr arbeitet er bei Mac Guff Ligne, einer französischen CG-Firma mit Sitz in Paris, wo er Matte Paintings herstellt, computergrafische Pflanzen und etliche andere coole Sachen. *Un Temps*

GHOSTCATCHING

Paul Kaiser / Shelley Eshkar / Bill T. Jones

Ghostcatching is a virtual dance collaboration created by digital artists Paul Kaiser and Shelley Eshkar in collaboration with dancer/choreographer Bill T. Jones. Kaiser and Eshkar made the visual and sound composition; Jones choreographed and performed the dance. In addition, Michael Girard and Susan Amkraut (authors of the Character Studio software) corrected the motion capture data and contributed to the choreographic composition.

Ghostcatching finds its place in the unexpected intersection of dance, drawing, and computer composition. The work is made possible by advances in motion capture, a technology that tracks sensors attached to a moving body. The resulting data files reflect the position and rotation of the body in motion, without preserving the performer's mass or musculature. Thus, movement is extracted from the performer's body.

Captured phrases become the building blocks for the virtual composition. As data, the phrases are edited, re-choreographed, and staged for a digital performance in the 3D space of the computer.

Here, the body of Bill T. Jones is multiplied into many dancers, who perform as three-dimensional drawings. Their anatomies are intertwinings of drawn strokes, which are in fact painstakingly modeled as geometry on the computer—never drawn on paper. So, we may ask: What is human movement in the absence of the body? Can the drawn line carry the rhythm, weight, and intent of physical movement? What kind of dance do we conceive in this ghostly place, where enclosures, entanglements, and reflections vie with the will to break free?

Ghostcatching ist eine virtuelle Tanzszenerie, die aus der Zusammenarbeit der mit digitalen Medi arbeitenden Künstler Paul Kaiser und Shelley Esh mit dem Tänzer und Choreographen Bill T. Jones entstand. Kaiser und Eshkar schufen die visuelle und klangliche Komposition, Jones choreographi te und tanzte die Bewegungsszenen. Weiters hal Michael Girard und Susan Amkraut (die Autoren Character Studio Software) die Motion-Capture-Daten korrigiert und an der choreographischen Komposition mitgewirkt.

Ghostcatching ist ein Mix aus Tanz, Zeichnung u Computer-Komposition. Das Werk wurde durch d Fortschritte in Motion Capture möglich, einer Tec nik, die an einem Körper befestigte Sensoren verfolgt. Die daraus resultierenden Datenfiles reflek ren die Position und Rotation des Körpers in der Bewegung, ohne dabei die Masse oder Muskulat des Akteurs zu übernehmen – die Bewegung wir also gewissermaßen aus dem Körper des Mitwirkenden extrahiert.

Die aufgenommenen Bewegungsphrasen werde zu Bausteinen der virtuellen Komposition. Die Daten werden editiert, neu choreographiert und digitale Aufführung im 3D-Raum des Computers inszeniert.

Hier wurde der Körper von Bill T. Jones in zahlreic Tänzer multipliziert, die sich als dreidimensional Zeichnungen bewegen. Ihre Anatomie besteht a sich ineinanderschlingenden Zeichnungsstriche die ihrerseits mühsam im Computer erstellt wurden – sie wurden niemals auf Papier gezeichnet. Wir stellen also die Frage: Was ist menschliche Bewegung ohne den dazugehörigen Körper? Kan eine gezeichnete Linie den Rhythmus, das Gewic und die Absicht einer physischen Bewegung tran portieren? Welche Art von Tanz erleben wir in die sem geisterhaften Raum, wo Umhüllung, Versch gung und Reflexion im Widerstreit stehen mit d Willen auszubrechen?

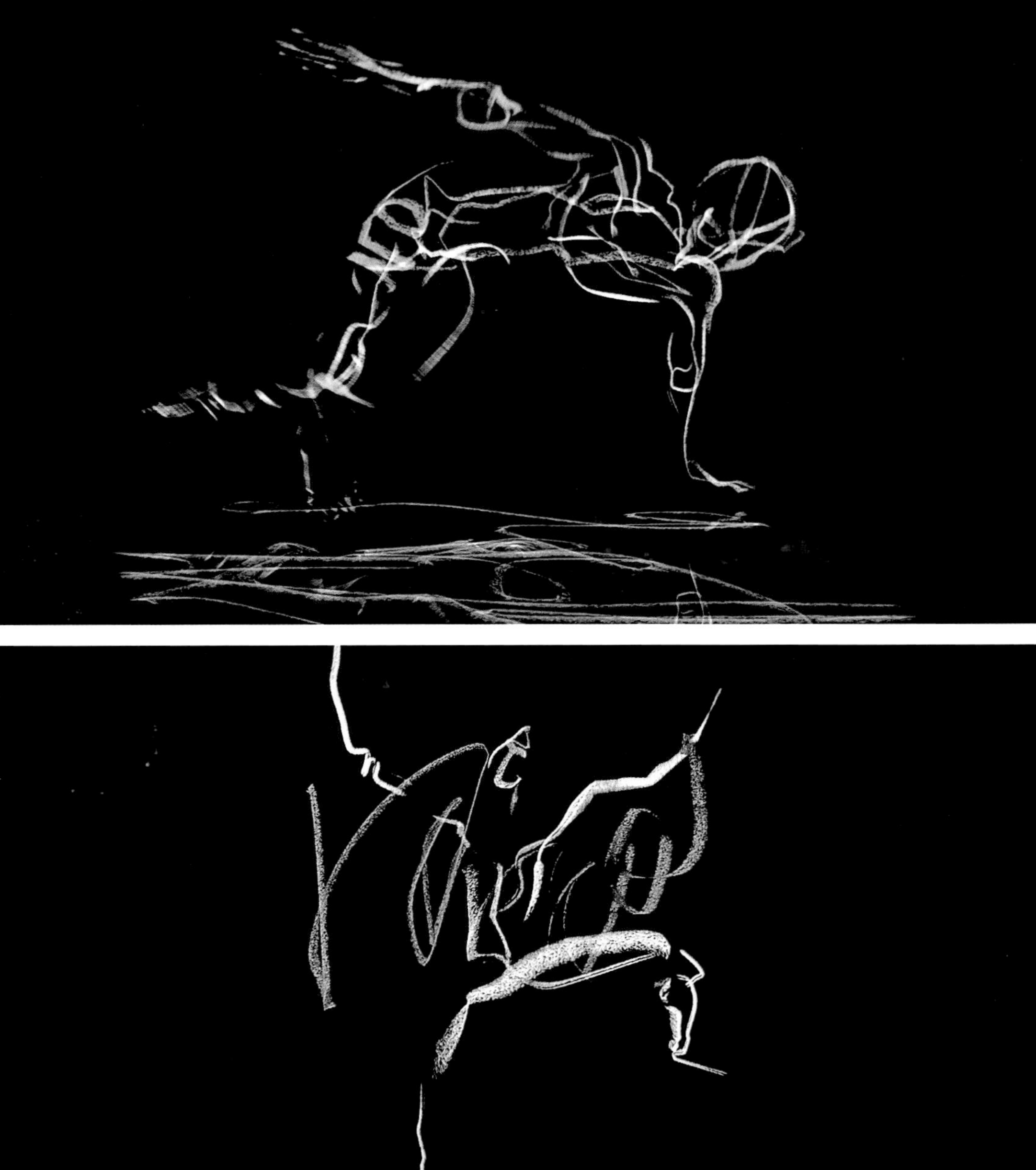

Paul Kaiser (USA) and Shelley Eshkar (USA) are the artistic directors of the Multimedia Studio Riverbed in New York. Kaiser has been distinguished with a Computer World /Smithsonian Award and received a Simon Guggenheim fellowship. Eshkar is an experimental animator and holds lectures at renowned art schools in the USA. For *Ghostcatching* they worked together with the dancer and choreographer Bill T. Jones, who works internationally and has received numerous awards.

Paul Kaiser (USA) und Shelley Eshkar (USA) sind künstlerische Leiter des Multimedia Studios Riverbed in New York. Kaiser wurde mit einem Computer World / Smithonian Award ausgezeichnet und erhielt ein Simon-Guggenheim-Stipendium. Eshkar ist experimenteller Animator und hält Vorlesungen an renommierten Kunstschulen der USA. Für Ghostcatching arbeiteten sie mit dem international tätigen und vielfach ausgezeichneten Tänzer und Choreographen Bill T. Jones zusammen.

BINGO

Christopher Landreth / Alias|Wavefront

The making of the animated short film *Bingo* was a unique exercise in production, software development, and storytelling. The production team for *Bingo* needed to accomplish at least two simultaneous goals. First, we needed to help design, test and verify CG software while the latter was under development—software which would eventually become Alias|Wavefront's animation program Maya. Second, we had a goal of experimenting with the storytelling and imagery that CG animation is uniquely capable of producing. For these reasons, *Bingo* is both highly refined as a piece of character animation and distinctly experimental in its narrative.

Bingo experiments with narrative form in at least one important way: it is, to my knowledge, the first animation which is entirely based on a theatrical short play,written for the stage. The play itself, entitled *Disregard This Play*, is an absurdist, surreal drama performed by a theatre company from Chicago, the Neo-Futurists. The dialogue soundtrack in *Bingo* was recorded directly from a performance of this play, and the animated imagery was created after this recording, completely based on this theatrical performance.

"By means of shrewd lies, unremittingly repeated, it is possible to make people believe that heaven is hell—and hell heaven. The greater the lie, the more readily it will be believed."
Adolf Hitler, from *Mein Kampf*

I have talked about implementing software techniques and experimenting with narrative as "goals" in producing *Bingo*. But most importantly for me, my goal in creating *Bingo* was to tell a story largely driven by the statement above—one which has troubled me both for the evil it conveys, and for the stunning accuracy it expresses about human nature. When I saw the Neo-Futurists performing *Disregrad This Play*, I saw a crystallization of this statement which I felt could be given power through the art of computer animation. *Bingo* shows a consequence when one lacks self-empowerment. We see the absurd, darkly humourous but disturbing effect that a lie, "unremittingly repeated" has on an otherwise intelligent and mannered person, and that person's

Die Herstellung des compu teranimierten Kurzfilms *Bingo* stellte uns in Produk tion, Software-Entwicklung und im Erzählerischen vor eine einzigartige Aufgabe. Das Produktionsteam muß zumindest zwei Ziele gleic zeitig erreichen: Einerseits sollte CG-Software entwickelt, getestet und noch während der Entwicklung verifiziert werden – Softwa die irgendwann zum Alias|Wavefront-Animation programm Maya werden wollte. Andererseits hat ten wir uns vorgenommen, mit einer Erzählebene und Bildwelten zu experimentieren, wie sie nur d Computergrafik zu schaffen in der Lage ist. Aus di sen Gründen ist *Bingo* sowohl ein höchst raffinie tes Beispiel für Character-Animation als auch in s ner Erzählweise sehr experimentell.

Bingos erzählerische Besonderheit liegt zumindes in einem Punkt: Meines Wissens ist es die erste Animation, die zur Gänze auf einem kurzen Theaterstück basiert, das für die Bühne konzipiert wurde. Das Stück selbst – *Disregard This Play* („Beacht Sie dieses Stück nicht") ist ein absurd-surreales Drama, das von den Neo-Futurists – einer Theater compagnie aus Chicago – aufgeführt wird. Der Soundtrack der Dialoge in *Bingo* wurde direkt bei einer Aufführung dieses Stückes mitgeschnitten, und die animierte Bildwelt entstand ausschließlic auf Basis dieser Theateraufführung.

„Durch geschickte Lügen, unablässig wiederholt, i es möglich, die Leute glauben zu machen, der Him mel sei die Hölle und die Hölle der Himmel. Je dre ster die Lüge, desto eher wird ihr Glauben geschenkt werden." A. Hitler, *Mein Kampf*

Ich habe über die Implementierung von Software-Techniken und über die Erzählung als „Ziele" bei *Bingo* gesprochen. Aber am wichtigsten war für mich, eine Geschichte im Sinne des obigen Zitats erzählen – eines Zitats, das mich ob des Bösen, da es vermittelt, irritiert und das mich gleichzeitig wegen der Schärfe seiner Beobachtung der menschlichen Natur erstaunt. Als ich die Neo-Futuristen bei der Aufführung von *Disregard This Play* sah, erkannte ich einen Kristallisationspunkt dieser Aussage und fühlte, daß man ihr durch die Kunst der Computeranimation noch mehr Gewich verleihen könnte.

Bingo zeigt eine mögliche Konsequenz fehlenden Selbstvertrauens. Wir sehen, welch absurden, schwarzhumorigen und gleichzeitig störenden Effekt eine „unablässig wiederholte" Lüge bei eine im Grunde intelligenten und wohlerzogenen Pers

self-perception. To me, the main character in *Bingo* has free will: he is free to walk away from that stage where he is confronted by the other characters. He is also free to tell these characters who he really is, if not "Bingo the Clown." That he does neither, and eventually accepts the absurd conclusion that he is a clown, is on a deep level infuriating to watch. It also mirrors an equally absurd, often inexplicable vulnerability that I have seen in people (including myself) to accept inaccuracies or "unremittingly-repeated lies" about our self-identities. I wanted to give voice to that perception in *Bingo*.

auslösen kann und wie diese Person sich selbst wahrnimmt. Für mich hat der Hauptpdarsteller in *Bingo* einen freien Willen: Er kann jederzeit die Bühne verlassen, auf der er mit den anderen Charakteren konfrontiert wird. Er hat auch die Freiheit, diesen Figuren zu sagen, wer er ist, wenn er denn nicht Bingo der Clown ist. Daß er weder das eine noch das andere tut und irgendwann einfach die absurde Schlußfolgerung akzeptiert, ein Clown zu sein, läßt den Betrachter auf einer ganz tiefliegenden Ebene Wut empfinden. Es spiegelt eine ebenso absurde und häufig unerklärliche Bereitschaft wider, die ich bei Leuten (auch bei mir selbst) erfahren habe – Ungenauigkeiten oder „unablässig wiederholte Lügen" über ihre eigene Identität hinzunehmen. Dieser Wahrnehmung wollte ich in *Bingo* Ausdruck und Stimme verleihen.

CHRIS LANDRETH HAS BEEN AN ANIMATOR AT ALIAS/WAVEFRONT SINCE JANUARY 1994. IT'S HIS JOB TO DEFINE, TEST AND ABUSE ANIMATION SOFTWARE, IN-HOUSE, BEFORE IT IS RELEASED TO THE PUBLIC. IN ADDITION TO WELL-MANNERED SOFTWARE, THIS HAS RESULTED IN THE PRODUCTION OF ANIMATED SHORT FILMS, INCLUDING *THE END* (1995) AND *BINGO* (1998). BOTH FILMS HAVE WON RECOGNITION AND AWARDS WORLDWIDE. *THE END* WAS NOMINATED FOR AN ACADEMY AWARD IN 1996 FOR "BEST ANIMATED SHORT FILM". Christopher Landreth ist seit Januar 1994 Animator bei Alias|Wavefront. Seine Aufgabe ist es, Animationssoftware zu definieren, im Hause zu testen und zu mißbrauchen, bevor sie für das Publikum freigegeben wird. Außer einer sich anständig verhaltenden Software hat dies mehrere animierte Kurzfilme mit sich gebracht, darunter *the end* (1995) und *Bingo* (1998). Beide Filme haben internationale Anerkennung und Preise gewonnen, *the end* wurde 1996 sogar für einen Oscar (Best Animated Short Film) nominiert.

ULTIMA FORSAN

William Le Henanff

This project was my graduation project for my Master of Arts at the National Center of Comics and Image. Over the course of five months, my work consisted of doing the scriptwriting, story-board and production. The original music is by David Georgelin, student at the Louis Lumière cinema school, Paris.

The story takes place during the Second World War, in 1942, above the town of Lorient. The encounter is between a pilot of the Royal Air Force and the captain of a submarine. During the night a submarine comes back home after a long journey. A group of Lancasters must destroy this submarine base of the underground bunkers of Keroman.
I wanted to show these two army corps, more exposed during the Second World War, each one with its toy, as in the dreams of child.
The greatest difficulties were the creation of the different environments (air/sea) and representing the atmosphere of a bombardment (inside the airplane).
I worked a lot with lighting and used the sun of an environment shader to do explosions.

(*Ultima Forsan* translates as
"may be the last ... hour")

Ich habe dieses Projekt als Diplomarbeit für meinen Master of Art am National Center of Comics and Image gemacht. Über fünf Monate arbeitete ich am Skript, am Drehbuch und an der eigentlichen Produktion. Die Musik zum Film stammt von David Georgelin, einem Studenten der Kinoschule von Louis Lumière, Paris.
Die Geschichte spielt 1942 – während des Zweiten Weltkrieges – in der Nähe des Ortes Lorient und zeigt die Begegnung zwischen einem Piloten der Royal Air Force und einem U-Boot-Kapitän. Während der Nacht kehrt das U-Boot nach langer Fahrt heim. Gleichzeitig nähert sich ein Geschwader von Lancasters, das den Auftrag hat, die Bunker der U-Boot-Basis von Keroman zu zerstören. Ich wollte diese beiden Gruppen von Militärs – die zu den exponiertesten des Krieges gehört haben – jeweils mit ihrem Spielzeug zeigen, wie sie im Traum eines Kindes erscheinen könnten.
Das Schwierigste war wohl, unterschiedliche Umgebungen (Himmel und Meer) zu schaffen und die Atmosphäre des Bombardements aus der Sicht der Flugzeugkanzel wiederzugeben. Ich habe viel mit Lichtquellen und Beleuchtungseffekten gearbeitet und die Explosionen mit Hilfe von Sonnen- und Schattenmasken erzeugt.

(*Ultima Forsan* heißt übersetzt etwa
„Vielleicht die letzte ... Stunde")

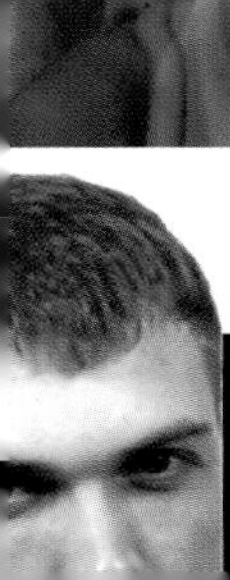

WILLIAM LE HENANFF (F) ATTENDED THE DUT-INFOCOM FOR COMPUTER GRAPHICS IN LANNION, WORKED FOR VARIOUS COMPANIES AS COMMUNICATIONS ENGINEER, CUTTER AND EDITOR FOR SHORT FILMS AND TELEVISION MAGAZINES AND AS A COMPUTER GRAPHICS ARTIST; IN THIS FUNCTION HE WAS INVOLVED IN SEVERAL FILM PRODUCTIONS. ▬ William Le Henanff (F) besuchte die DUT-Infocom für Computergrafik in Lannion, arbeitete bei verschiedenen Unternehmen als Kommunikationstechniker, Cutter und Gestalter von Kurzfilmen und Fernsehmagazinen und als Computergrafiker und

EN DÉRIVE

Patrice Mugnier / Heure Exquise

The film, which is more than just a story, evokes a few moments torn from the apathy of a city. The harbor city, this small seaside capital of a Mediterranean country, has been abandoned by most of the inhabitants. A journalist on the radio reports of chaos, confusion, a state of emergency in the city. A man at a window looks out at the sea, hears the noises of the city—and fears the worst ...
A ship docks, and it may be the last one.
The title of the film—*En dérive* ("Drifting") reflects a multifaceted feeling:a country losing control, in the midst of a process of political dissolution, dominated by latent violence; the gliding movement of the camera passing over the ocean to the site of the drama and stopping at the protagonist of the story; the man's feeling of drifting as he sits at the window with nowhere to flee—except to the horizon of the sea.
The film's computer generated images were created with a 3D program. The computer generated image, that is neither animation nor painting nor cinema, opens up an amazing space, in which the real and the imaginary collide. For me, *En dérive* is a first attempt in this direction.

Der Film, der mehr als eine bloße Geschichte ist, evoziert einige der Apathie einer Stadt entrissene Momente. Die Hafenstadt, diese kleine, am Meer gelegene Hauptstadt eines Mittelmeerstaates, ist von den meisten ihrer Bewohner verlassen worden. Im Radio berichtet ein Journalist vom Chaos, von der Verwirrung, vom Ausnahmezustand, die in der Stadt herrschen. Ein Mann am Fenster blickt aufs Meer, hört die Geräusche der Stadt – und befürchtet das Schlimmste. ...
Ein Schiff legt ab, vielleicht ist es das letzte.
Der Titel des Films – *En Dérive* („Treibend") – spiegelt ein vielschichtiges Gefühl wider: das Entgleiten eines Staates, der sich in einem politischen Auflösungsprozeß befindet, in dem unterschwellige Gewalttätigkeit herrscht; die gleitende Bewegung der Kamera, die über das Meer hin zum Ort des Dramas streicht und dabei an den Protagonisten der

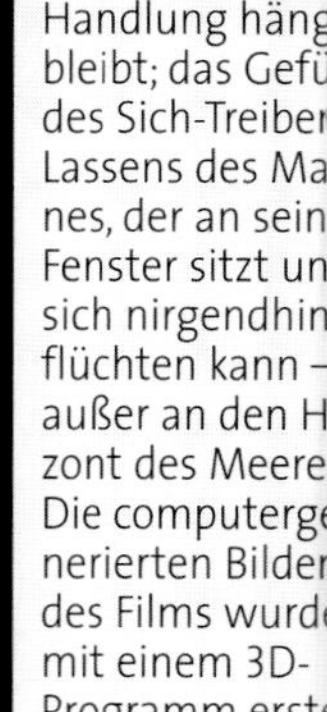

Handlung häng bleibt; das Gefü des Sich-Treiber Lassens des Ma nes, der an sein Fenster sitzt un sich nirgendhin flüchten kann – außer an den H zont des Meere Die computerge nerierten Bilder des Films wurd mit einem 3D-Programm erste
Das computergenerierte Bild, das weder Animati noch Malerei noch Kino ist, eröffnet einen erstau chen Raum, in dem das Reale und das Imaginäre aufeinanderprallen. *En Dérive* ist für mich ein ers Versuch in diese Richtung.

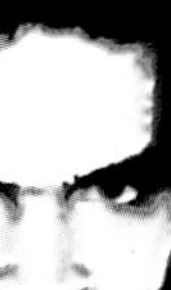

PATRICE MUGNIER (F) IS AN ARCHITECT AND CREATED THE FILM IN THE COURSE OF TRAINING AT THE ATELIER IMAGE ET INFORMATIQUE (AII). HE ALSO WORKED AS A STAGE SET DESIGNER AND AS ASSISTANT TO THE EXHIBITION DIRECTOR AT THE CENTRE GEORGES POMPIDOU. HE IS CURRENTLY WORKING ON ANOTHER FILM PROJECT AND AS A FREELANCE GRAPHICS ARTIST, AS WELL AS TEACHING COMPUTER GRAPHICS.

Patrice Mugnier (F) ist Architekt und hat den Film im Rahmen einer Ausbildung am Atelier Image et Informatique (AII) hergestellt. Er arbeitete auch als Bühnenbildner und Assistent des Ausstellungsleiters am Centre Georges Pompidou. Derzeit arbeitet er an einem weiteren Filmprojekt und als freischaffender Grafiker

BIKE – A ROADMOVIE

Dietmar Offenhuber

3D done in Softimage 3D—designed as a loop sequence, the story is constructed by switching the point of view. Soundtrack done in Mathematica – Frequencies were computed by mathematical functions and layered with short analog noise impacts.

Collaborator: Markus Decker

Die 3D-Elemente wurden in Softimage 3D als Endlosschleife geschrieben, die Geschichte selbst wird aus der Veränderung des Betrachter-Standpunkts entwickelt.
Der Soundtrack entstand in Mathematica, wobei die Grundfrequenzen aus mathematischen Funktionen errechnet und mit kurzen analogen Geräuschteilen überlagert wurden.

Mitarbeit: Markus Decker

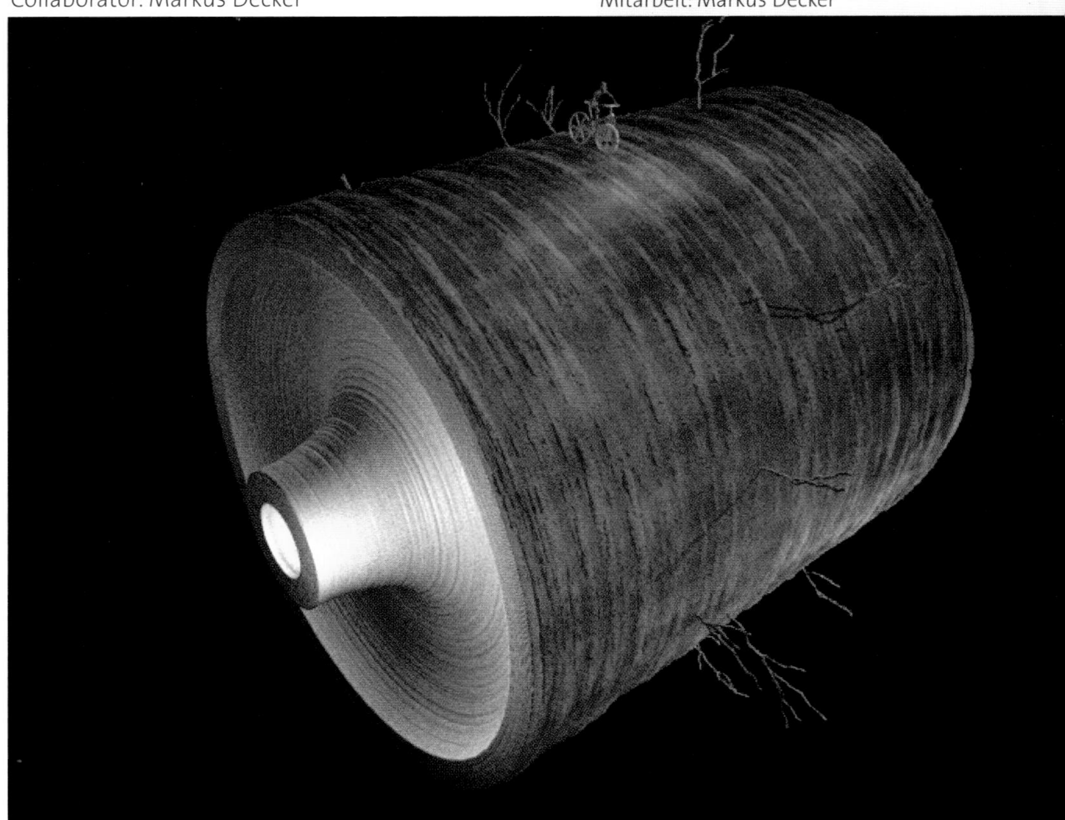

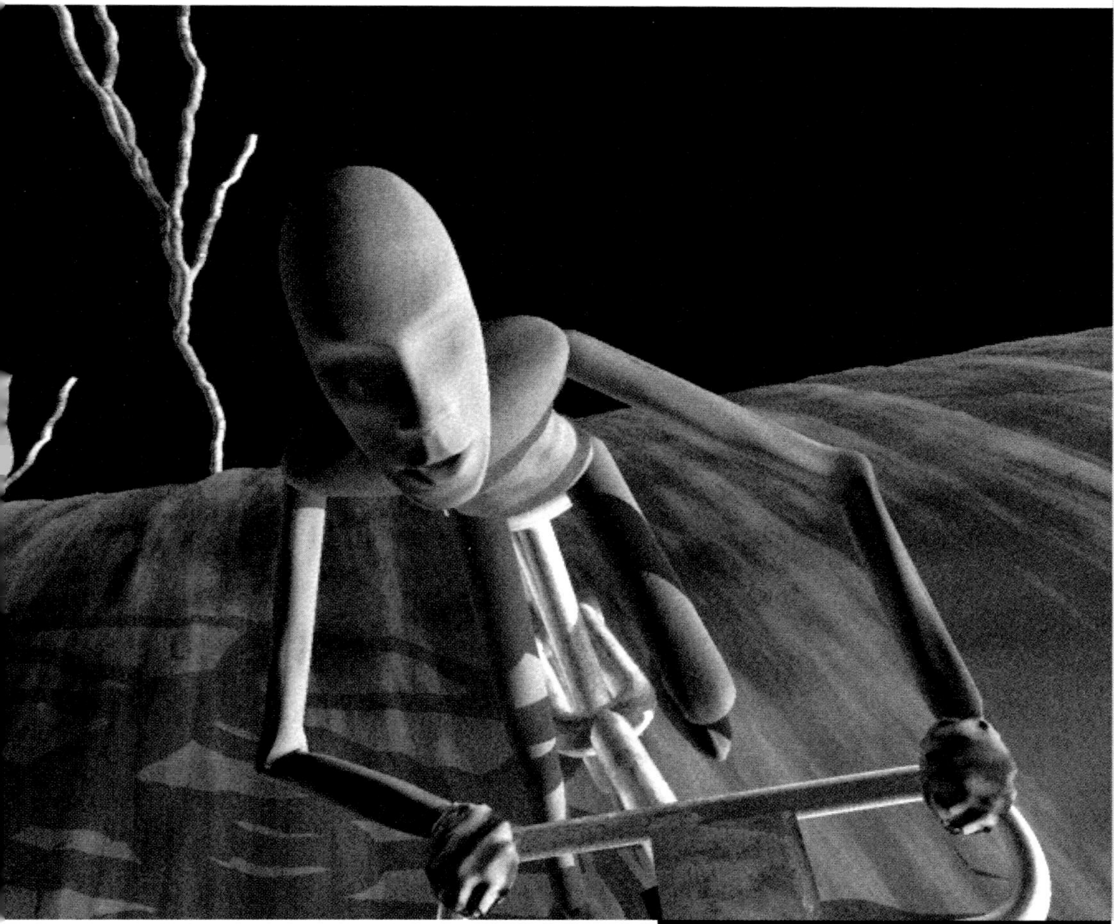

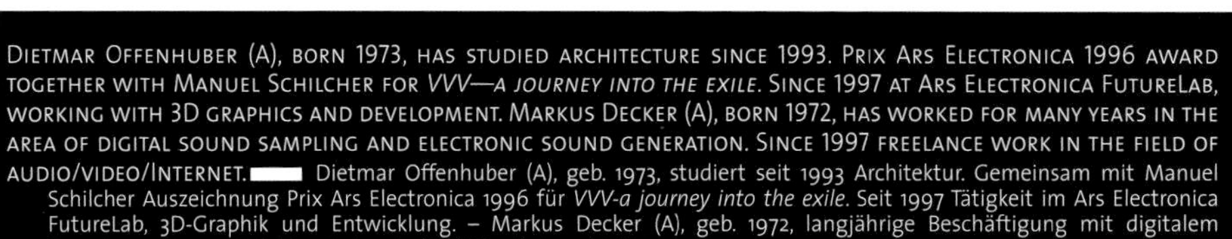

Dietmar Offenhuber (A), born 1973, has studied architecture since 1993. Prix Ars Electronica 1996 award together with Manuel Schilcher for *VVV—a journey into the exile*. Since 1997 at Ars Electronica FutureLab, working with 3D graphics and development. Markus Decker (A), born 1972, has worked for many years in the area of digital sound sampling and electronic sound generation. Since 1997 freelance work in the field of audio/video/Internet. Dietmar Offenhuber (A), geb. 1973, studiert seit 1993 Architektur. Gemeinsam mit Manuel Schilcher Auszeichnung Prix Ars Electronica 1996 für *VVV-a journey into the exile*. Seit 1997 Tätigkeit im Ars Electronica FutureLab, 3D-Graphik und Entwicklung. – Markus Decker (A), geb. 1972, langjährige Beschäftigung mit digitalem

RONIN ROMANCE CLASSICS

Bruce Pukema

Each of the longer form pieces that I do is an attempt to learn the craft of animation. What I feel are weaknesses in the last animation gives me an excuse to produce another in hopes of addressing these weaknesses. So far I have as many ideas as I have weaknesses. As I observe my progress it has come to me that I had better come up with a lot more ideas. The broad narrative in the animation is the structure. The "little moments" are added to keep me amused as I attempt to stave off the boredom of animating in a computer. The frustration of never being pleased with what I produce is offset by my growing fascination with animation.
The technical end of our production is fairly simple. I use Softimage running on a SGI 2 Extreme with an R4000. Due to a lack of equipment I try to "edit in the camera" as much as possible. The final edit was done on a Flame courtesy of Lamb & Company.

Jedes meiner längeren Stücke ist nur ein Versuch, das Handwerk der Animation zu erlernen. Das, wa ich als die Schwächen der jeweils letzten Animati ansehe, gibt mir eine Ausrede, eine neue zu mach – in der Hoffnung, die Schwächen auszuräumen. Bisher habe ich so viele Ideen wie Schwächen, un wenn ich mir meine Fortschritte so ansehe, dann sollte ich besser noch sehr viele Ideen auf Lager haben.
Das Erzählerische dieser Animation liegt in der Struktur. Einige kleine zusätzliche Momente habe ich hinzugefügt, um mich zu unterhalten und der Langeweile des Animierens am Computer zu entg hen. Die Frustration, niemals mit dem zufrieden z sein, was ich produziere, wird langsam von der ständig wachsenden Faszination, die die Animati auf mich ausübt, verdrängt.
Die technische Seite unserer Produktion ist zieml einfach. Ich verwende Softimage, das auf einer SC Extreme mit einer R4000 läuft. Aus Mangel an Equipment versuche ich, so viel wie möglich scho „in der Kamera zu schneiden". Die Schlußbearbeitung erfolgte mit freundlicher Unterstützung von Lamb & Company auf einem Flame.

BRUCE PUKEMA HAS A BFA IN FINE ARTS AND HAS TAUGHT ART AND SPANISH FOR SIX YEARS. HE HAS WORKED AS ARTIST/ART DIRECTOR FOR THE NBC TELEVISION AFFILIATE IN MINNEAPOLIS FOR TEN YEARS. THE LAST SIX YEARS HAVE BEEN SPENT AS OWNER/PRESIDENT OF RONIN ANIMATION.

Bruce Pukema (USA) graduierte zum BFA aus bildender Kunst und hat sechs Jahre lang Spanisch und Kunst unterrichtet. Zehn Jahre lang war er als Künstler und künstlerischer Leiter an der NBC Television Filiale Minneapolis tätig. Seit sechs Jahren ist er Eigentümer und Geschäftsführer von Ronin Animation.

TIGHTROPE

Daniel Robichaud / Digital Domain

Tightrope is a 5 minute, all CG-animated short film, written and directed by Daniel Robichaud, with Stephane Couture and Bernd Angerer serving as lead animators. The film was produced by Scott Ross and Digital Domain. Edward Kummer was the film's executive producer, and Vala Runolfsson was associate producer.

The allegorical story finds our central character, The Jester, moving along a tightrope through a mystical, cloud-like milieu. His open face reveals inquisitive eyes. For The Jester, life is a joy to behold.

Suddenly, he comes upon another man moving towards him – on the same tightrope. The other man, The Suit, has an ominous gray demeanor. His face is obscured by a dark mask.

The Jester extends a hand in friendship which is rebuffed by The Suit – who then attempts to knock The Jester off the tightrope.

The Jester reveals an assortment of magical tricks which he plays upon The Suit. Not to be outdone, The Suit responds with a desperate act which has possibly dire consequences for them both.

Tightrope ist ein fünfminütiger, gänzlich computeranimierter Kurzfilm, unter der Regie von Dani Robichaud. Hauptanimateure waren Stephane Couture und Bernd Angerer. Der Film wurde von Scott Ross und Digital Domain produziert. Execu Producer war Edward Kummer, Associate Produc Vala Runolfsson.

Die allegorische Geschichte beginnt damit, daß unsere Hauptgestalt, der Narr, auf einem gespan ten Hochseil durch eine mystische, wolkenähnlic Umgebung wandert. Sein offenes Gesicht zeigt einen neugierigen, forschenden Blick. Für den Narren ist das Leben eine Lust.

Plötzlich begegnet er einem anderen Mann, der auf ihn zubewegt – auf demselben Hochseil! De zweite Mann, „Der Anzug" genannt, ist ein düste Wesen, sein Gesicht ist von einer dunklen Maske bedeckt.

Als freundliche Geste streckt der Narr eine Hand aus, die jedoch von seinem Gegenüber, das plötz versucht, ihn vom Seil zu stoßen, zurückgewiese wird.

Der Narr setzt sein ganzes Repertoire an Zaubertricks ein, um dem Mann im Anzug beizukommen, doch um den stillen Zweikampf nicht z verlieren, antwortet dieser mit einem verzweifel Akt, der möglicherweise für beide schlimme Folg haben wird ...

DANIEL ROBICHAUD (CDN) STUDIED GRAPHICS DESIGN AT THE UNIVERSITY OF QUEBEC, WORKED FOR NATIONAL CANADIAN TELEVISION AND AT "THE FILM & TAPE WORKS" IN CHICAGO. HE JOINED DIGITAL DOMAIN IN 1994 AS DIGITAL EFFECTS SUPERVISOR AND HAS WORKED ON *APOLLO 13*, *THE FIFTH ELEMENT*, *TITANIC* AND OTHERS. SCOTT ROSS (USA) IS GENERAL DIRECTOR OF DIGITAL DOMAIN AND THE PRODUCER OF *TIGHTROPE*; STEPHANE COUTURE (CDN) AND BERND ANGERER (A) WERE INVOLVED IN THE PRODUCTION OF *TIGHTROPE* AS LEAD CHARACTER ANIMATORS.

DANIEL ROBICHAUD (CDN) STUDIERTE Grafikdesign an der University of Quebec, arbeitete beim nationalen kanadischen Fernsehen, und bei „The Film & Tape Works" in Chicago. 1994 kam er als Digital-Effects-Supervisor zu Digital Domain und arbeitete unter anderem an *Apollo 13*, *The Fifth Element* und *Titanic* mit. Scott Ross (USA) ist Generaldirektor von Digital Domain und Produzent von *Tightrope*. Stephane Couture (CDN) und Bernd Angerer (A) waren als Lead Character Animators an der Produktion von *Tightrope*

STATIONEN

Christian Sawade-Meyer

In recent years I have come to realize how much people differ in the ways they think and that these differences increase with age. It is difficult to keep one's own goal in mind, which is itself only vaguely defined. One seeks the path to contentment and personal recognition.
One loses a great deal of energy along the way, because the surroundings constantly exercise influence and perspectives are often blocked.
Preserving and successfully maintaining imagination and visions is a tedious task in this environment that is stuck in a rut.
The film shows an emotional segment of this path with the possible ending that the desired goal is not quite attained and one loses one's energy.
I have not reprogrammed the 3D Studio.
I have used the available techniques simply to tell this story.
The look is most important to me, and I have tried to avoid typical 3D aesthetics.

The odyssey of life through a monotonous, hardly fertile world with its misleading influences. A creature, dragging a full crate of plants behind it, makes its way through an expansive wasteland.
The strange creature hopefully digs a hole for a plant in the ground. Here is where the plants carried in the crate are to flourish. As soon as the second plant is in its place in the much too barren ground, the first surrenders to the dryness and wilts. Feeling desperate and helpless, the creature must give up the second plant as well. A glance at the horizon shows nothing but wasteland far and wide.
Nevertheless, it goes on, dragging the crate behind, aimless but still hopeful. Lost in thought, the strange creature tramples over a decayed signpost. Suddenly it discovers another sign in the distance. With renewed hope, it heads for this sign and finds itself facing a forest full of signs. Instead of finding a path, though, it seems more in danger of losing its orientation completely among all the confusing signposts.
Finally, unnerved it pushes the signs away furiously. Thrashing and running, it pushes a path through the confusion. With a loud scream it falls to the ground, having tripped over a large rock. As it comes to again, it realizes it has found something important—a bubbling spring of water. Hope!

In den letzten Jahren ist mir bewußt geworden, w stark sich Menschen durch Denkweisen unterscheiden und daß mit dem Alter diese Differenze zunehmen. Das eigene Ziel im Auge zu behalten, was an sich aber auch nur vage definiert ist, ist s schwer. Man sucht den Weg zur Zufriedenheit ur nach der persönlichen Anerkennung.
Auf diesem Weg verliert man sehr viel Energie, da das Umfeld ständig Einfluß nimmt und oftmals Perspektiven verbaut.
Phantasie und Visionen für sich zu bewahren unc erfolgreich zu behaupten, ist in dieser festgefahrenen Umwelt recht mühsam.
Der Film zeigt einen emotionalen Ausschnitt dies Weges, mit dem möglichen Ende, daß man das ersehnte Ziel knapp verfehlt und seine Energie ve liert.
Ich habe das 3D-Studio nicht neu programmiert. habe die zugänglichen Techniken benutzt, um ei fach eine Geschichte zu erzählen. Wert gelegt ha ich auf den Look und die Vermeidung allzu typischer 3D-Ästhetik.

Die Odyssee des Lebens durch eine eintönige, we fruchtbare Welt mit ihren irreführenden Einflüss Ein Wesen, eine vollgepackte Pflanzenkiste hinter sich herziehend, auf dem Weg durch eine weite Öde.
Voller Hoffnung gräbt das fremdartige Wesen ei Pflanzloch in den Boden. Hier sollen die in der Kis mitgebrachten Pflanzen gedeihen. Kaum findet c zweite Pflanze im viel zu trockenen Boden ihren Platz, muß sich die erste der Trockenheit ergeben und verdorrt. Verzweifelt und machtlos muß das Wesen auch die zweite verloren geben. Ein Blick zum Horizont zeigt weit und breit nur Öde.
Trotzdem zieht es, mit der Kiste im Schlepp, ziello aber hoffnungsvoll weiter. In Gedanken versunke trampelt der Fremdling über einen morschen Wegweiser. Plötzlich entdeckt er in der Ferne ein weiteres Zeichen. Mit neuer Hoffnung geht er da auf zu, und es eröffnet sich ihm ein Wald voller Schilder. Doch anstatt einen Weg zu finden, droh durch die verwirrenden Richtungsweiser völlig di Orientierung zu verlieren.
Nervlich am Ende, stößt er wütend die Schilder b seite. Er schlägt um sich und bahnt sich rennend einen Ausweg aus dem Gewirr. Mit einem lauten Aufschrei stürzt er zu Boden. Ein großer Fels ließ i stolpern. Als er wieder zur Besinnung kommt, me er, daß er etwas Wichtiges gefunden hat – eine sprudelnde Wasserquelle – Hoffnung!

CHRISTIAN SAWADE-MEYER (D), BORN 1974, HAS BEEN WORKING ON THREE-DIMENSIONAL IMAGES SINCE 1995. STATIONEN WAS CREATED DURING THE SECOND AND THIRD SEMESTERS OF HIS CURRENT STUDIES IN COLLABORATION WITH UDO BADE (MUSIC/SOUND) AND TOBIAS ALPERT (STORY CONSULTANT). A FASCINATION WITH ARTIFICIAL NATURALNESS COMPELS HIM TO REALIZE HIS OWN STORIES. AN IMPORTANT ASPECT OF THIS IS MERGING TRADITIONAL INFLUENCES WITH NEW TECHNIQUES. FOLLOWING THE AWARD OF A GERMAN YOUNG TALENT PRIZE IN 1998 (FOR GEFANGEN), THIS IS THE FIRST INTERNATIONAL AWARD FOR HIS SECOND WORK. ▬ Christian Sawade-Meyer (D), geb. 1974, arbeitet seit 1995 an dreidimensionalen Bildern. STATIONEN entstand im 2. und 3. Semester seines gegenwärtigen Studiums als eine Zusammenarbeit mit Udo Bade (Music/Sound) und Tobias Alpert (Story Consultant). Die Faszination an der künstlichen Natürlichkeit ist sein größter Antrieb, eigene Geschichten digital umzusetzen. Wichtig ist dabei das Verschmelzen von traditionellen Einflüssen mit neuen Techniken. Nach der Verleihung eines deutschen Nachwuchspreises 1998 (für GEFANGEN) ist dies die erste internationale Honorierung für seine zweite Arbeit.

THE FLY BAND!

Seiji Shiota / Tohru Patrick Awa / Polygon Pictur

The FLY BanD! is a funky music group from New York. With the distinguished feeling of rhythm and groove, they make great sounds using daily goods as musical instruments. Polygon Pictures was one of the first companies to apply realistic television aspects to its work, producing five short CG animation pieces expressly for TV, built upon different themes. *The Fly BanD!* is one of these short CG animation pieces.
The project was named "Digital Adult Sesame", because we wanted to highlight the fact that the contents could be enjoyed by adults as well as children.
On the technical side, we came up with an original project management system called DWARF (Digital Work in process & Asset Routing Foundation).
Up until that point, such mammoth projects, which involved many people working simultaneously on large quantities of data over a long period of time, had been overseen by people, which inevitably entailed considerable human resources costs and inefficiency.
DWARF computerizes this process, thus realizing sophisticated production management system in sync with the future of CG production.

Die *FLY BanD!* ist eine etwas seltsame Musikgrup und kommt aus New York. Mit ihrem ausgepräg Gefühl für Rhythmus und Groove macht sie tolle Klänge, wobei sie alltägliche Dinge als Instrumen verwendet.
Polygon Pictures war eines der ersten Unternehmen, das die Größenverhältnisse des Fernsehens auf seine Arbeit angewendet hat, indem es fünf computeranimierte Kurzfilme zu unterschiedlich Themen ausdrücklich für das Fernsehen produzi hat. *The FLY banD!* ist eines dieser kurzen CG-Animationsstücke.
Das Projekt wurde als „Digitale Sesamstraße für Erwachsene" bezeichnet, weil wir die Tatasche unterstreichen wollten, daß der Inhalt von Erwachsenen wie von Kindern genossen werden kann.
Auf der technischen Seite haben wir dafür ein ei nes Projekt-Management-System entwickelt, das DWARF heißt (*Digital Work in Process & Asset Routing Foundation*). Bis zu diesem Zeitpunkt wu den Mammutprojekte dieser Art, bei denen gleic zeitig eine Vielzahl von Mitarbeitern über einen gen Zeitraum an einer enormen Menge von Dat arbeiten, von Menschen überwacht, was in jeder Fall beträchtliche Kosten und einiges an Ineffizie nach sich zog. DWARF computerisiert diesen Pro und stellt ein ausgefeiltes Produktionsmanagement-System zur Verfügung, das mit der Zukunf der CG-Produktion im Einklang steht.

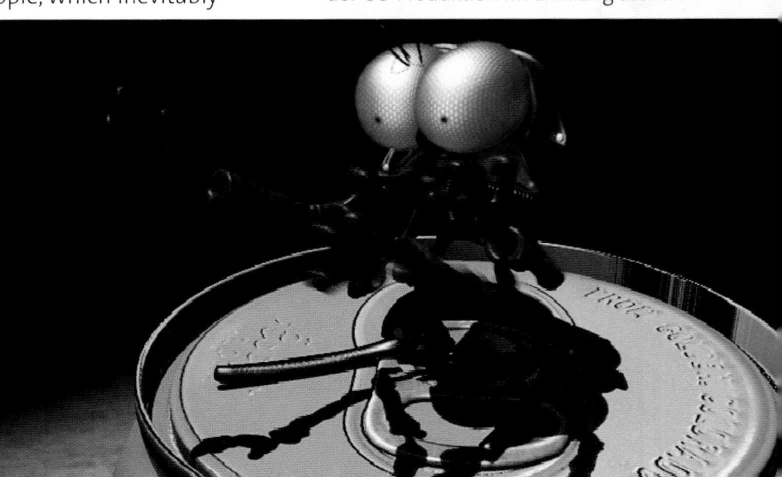

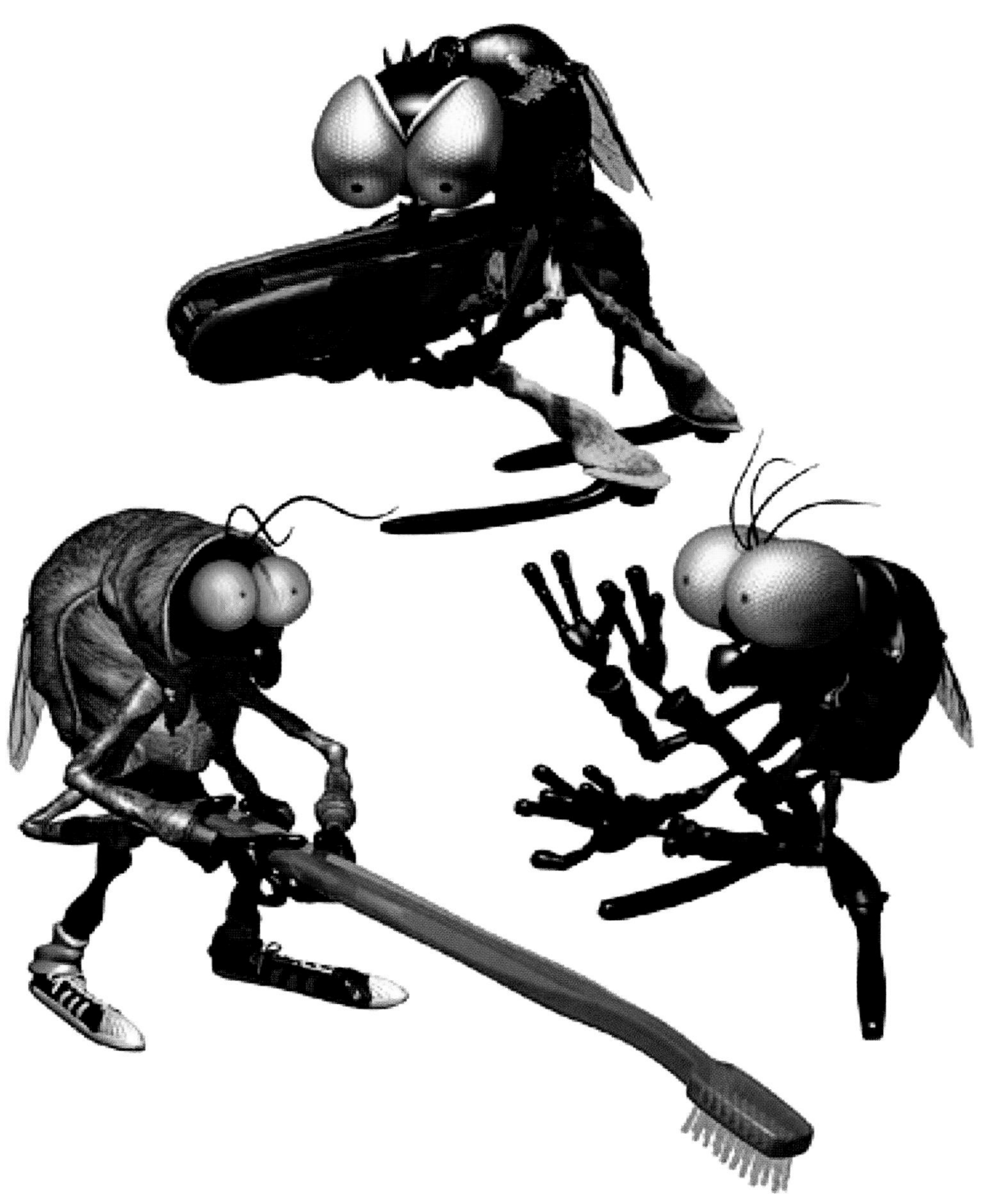

SEIJI SHIOTA (J), BORN 1971, STUDIED COMPUTER GRAPHICS AND DESIGN AT THE TECHNICAL FACULTY OF THE CHIBA UNIVERSITY IN JAPAN. COMPUTER GRAPHICS ARTISTS AT POLYGON PICTURES SINCE 1994. TOHRU PATRICK AWA (J), BORN 1971 IN SANTA MONICA, USA, STUDIED COMPUTER GRAPHICS AND DESIGN AT THE TECHNICAL FACULTY OF THE CHIBA UNIVERSITY IN JAPAN. HAS WORKED SINCE 1995, ALTHOUGH WITH SEVERAL INTERRUPTIONS, AS A DIRECTOR FOR POLYGON PICTURES.

Seiji Shiota (J), geb. 1971. Ausbildung in Computergrafik und Design an der technischen Fakultät der Chiba University in Japan. Seit 1994 Computergrafiker bei Polygon Pictures. Tohru Patrick Awa (J), geb. 1971 in Santa Monica, USA. Ausbildung in Computergrafik und Design an der technischen Fakultät der Chiba University in Japan. Arbeitet mit Unterbrechungen seit 1995 als

BAD NIGHT

Emre Yilmaz / Lev Yilmaz

A young lad receives a telephone call which stirs up an unexpected challenge to his ego. He briefly indulges in self–absorbed mental meandering in the evening air. Sadly, in the process he fails to notice a series of highly improbable, if not miraculous, opportunities before him.

Although the concept & message of *Bad Night* is based purely on whiny psychological humor, it was created using innovative techniques in performance animation (motion capture animation).

Taking cues from the look & movement of Balinese shadow puppets, Emre and Lev made the characters by filming co-workers and friends in various poses and expressions. This video was then scanned and imported into Photoshop where the actors were cut and pasted into virtual "puppets". The lifeless puppets were animated using ALIVE motion capture software. Various movements were controlled by joysticks.

Ein junger Mann erhält einen Anruf, der eine unerwartete Herausforderung an sein Ego darstellt. Ganz in sich selbst versunken begibt er sich auf einen abendlichen Spaziergang, nur übersieht er dabei leider eine Menge sich bietender – höchst unwahrscheinlicher, wenn nicht gar wundersamer – Gelegenheiten.

Obwohl das Konzept und die Aussage von *Bad Night* ausschließlich auf einem etwas weinerlichen psychologischen Humor basieren, wurde das Werk unter Einsatz innovativer Techniken in der Performance-(Motic Capture)-Animation geschaffen.

Für die Imitation des Aussehens und der Bewegu balinesischer Schattenpuppen haben Emre und Freunde und Mitarbeiter in verschiedenen Posen und mit unterschiedlichem Ausdruck gefilmt. Dieses Video haben sie in Photoshop importiert, die Akteure ausgeschnitten und auf virtuelle „Puppen" übertragen wurden. Diese unbelebten Puppen wurden ihrerseits mit Hilfe der ALIVE Motion-Capture-Software animiert, wobei zahlre che der Bewegungen auch über Joystick gesteue wurden.

Lev and Emre Yilmaz are a two brother team who have been making trouble since they were kids given a Super 8 camera by their unsuspecting mom. Emre Yilmaz is a puppeteer/animator working at Protozoa, a San Francisco based animation studio. His work areas include puppeteering, character design, character setup, applying motion capture to non-human character, and internet animation. Lev Yilmaz came to Protozoa in February 1998, when a quick collaboration with brother Emre won Best Performance Animation at the World Animation Celebration that month. ▬ Lev und Emre Yilmaz sind ein Brüderpaar, das Ärger seit dem Tag macht, an dem ihre nichtsahnende Mutter den Kindern eine Super-8-Kamera geschenkt hat. Emre Yilmaz arbeitet als Puppenspieler und Animator bei Protozoa, einem Animationsstudio in San Francisco, wo sein Arbeitsbereich neben der Arbeit mit den Puppen auch das Design der Charaktere und Motion Capture an nicht-menschlichen Darstellern sowie Internet-Animation umfaßt. Lev Yilmaz kam im Februar 1998 zu Protozoa, und ein schnelles Kooperationsprojekt mit seinem Bruder wurde noch im selben Monat

THE ARTISTRY OF "WHAT DREAMS MAY COME"

Künstlerische Aspekte von „Hinter dem Horizont"

Vincent Ward / Stephen Simon / Barnet Bain
Mass.illusions / POP / Digital Domain

It's hard visualizing the Afterlife, even with the world's master artists guiding the way. Bringing director Vincent Ward's inspired vision to life on screen in *What Dreams May Come* demanded the utmost from several effects houses, including Mass.illusions, Pacific Ocean Post (POP), Digital Domain, Illusion Arts, CIS, and Cinema Production Services, Inc.

Visual Effects Producer/Supervisor Ellen M. Somers was formerly Boss Film's Head of Production for eight years (where she originally met Ward on the ill-fated *Alien3*) and Warner Digital's VP Head of Production. Somers was actually planning to take some time off after the demise of Warner Digital when Dreams' producer, Interscope Pictures, persuaded her to come in on the production side in March 1997 and make an evaluation of the effects that would be needed to complete the film.

Somers' persistence would be a key ingredient in the overall success of *What Dreams May Come*'s visuals. The entire effects package had already been awarded to Mass.illusions (*Judge Dredd*), which was being bankrolled by troubled mini-major Cinergi. But in September 1997, on the eve of production, Cinergi was sold to Disney and backed out of Mass.illusions. Suddenly, Somers was in the uniquely difficult position of having to bring in other effects houses to save the picture before cameras had started rolling!

Somers attempted to split the work up along biblical lines. POP took over 118 shots spanning the Victorian landscapes of "Marie's World" and "Bridge City", the astounding "Venetian Library", and the ship graveyard and inverted cathedral. The tabletop miniatures for the hellish environments were built by Mike Joyce's Cinema Production Service, Inc. Digital Domain took on 54 shots ranging from character animation to reconstructing an entire poppy-laden landscape.

Es ist schwer, das Leben nach dem Tode in Bilder umzusetzen, selbst wenn die größten Künstler der Welt versuchen, den Weg zu weisen. Es erforderte die höchsten Anstrengungen von mehreren Effektfirmen, darunter Mass.illusions, Pacific Ocean Post (POP), Digital Domain, Illusion Arts, CIS und Cinema Production Services, Inc., bis die inspirierten Visionen des Regisseurs Vincent Ward in *What Dreams May Come* („Hinter dem Horizont") zum Leben auf der Leinwand erwachten.

Ellen M. Somers, Visual Effects Producer/Supervisor, war zuvor acht Jahre Produktionsleiterin bei Boss Film (wo sie beim wenig erfolgreichen *Alien3* auch Ward kennengelernt hatte) und Produktionschefin bei Warner Digital gewesen. Eigentlich hatte Somers sich eine Ruhepause nach dem Abschied von Warners gönnen wollen, als die Produzenten von *Dreams*, Interscope Pictures, sie im März 1997 überredeten, doch bei dem Film einzusteigen und die erforderlichen Effekte zu bewerten, die zur Fertigstellung des Films nötig werden würden. Somers' Hartnäckigkeit sollte sich zu einem der

/ass.illusions' contribution would be visualizing
9% of the "Painted World", some 58 shots depicting
wild, floral landscape comprised of running
igment, which is Chris Neilson's introduction to the
fterlife. It was critical that this sequence evoked a
trong response, or audiences would tune out of the
ilm before its emotional one-two punch could ever
onnect. Ward, who had trained as a painter, intuited
hat the Afterlife should be both familiar and alien,
nd drew inspiration from the German Romanticists,
specially the lush imagery of Casper David
riedrich.

or three months before filming began, visual re-
earchers delved into countless art libraries search-
ng for illustrations in the vein of the images Ward
ad in mind. Ultimately, Friedrich and other 19th
entury masters helped define and communicate

Hauptingredienzien beim allgemeinen Erfolg der Bildwelt von *What Dreams May Come* entwickeln. Das gesamte Effekte-Paket war bereits an Mass.illusions (*Judge Dredd*) vergeben worden, das von Cinergi, dem krisengeschüttelten Zwerg unter den Großstudios, finanziert wurde. Aber als kurz vor Produktionsbeginn Cinergi im September 1997 an Disney verkauft wurde und aus Mass.illusions ausstieg, war Somers in der außergewöhnlich schwierigen Lage, andere Effekthäuser hereinnehmen zu müssen, um einen Film zu retten, von dem noch kein Meter gedreht war.

Somers versuchte, die Arbeit entlang biblischer Linien aufzuteilen. POP übernahm 118 Einstellungen, darunter die viktorianischen Landschaften aus „Maries Welt" und „Bridge City", die umwerfende „Venezianische Bibliothek", den Schiffsfriedhof und die umgedrehte Kathedrale. Die Minitaurmodelle für die Höllenumgebung wurden von Mike Joyces Cinema Production Service, Inc., beigesteuert. Digital Domain wiederum halste sich 54 Einstellungen auf, die von Character Animation bis zur

Ward's vision to a whole range of artisans, from production designer Eugenio Vanetti to cinematographer Eduardo Serra and dozens of visual effects artists.

"We actually hired Josh Rosen as the Art Director for Mass.illusions and installed him in that community. Although all the people working on the project at Mass.illusions, even the software people, were painters themselves, Josh's art direction had that certain feel we were looking for. Josh was an amazing find—he was a software developer we found on sabbatical in Italy doing illustrative work for a book, and on the side, he was off painting frescoes, you know? We also hired Sid Dutton of Illusion Arts and Michael Lloyd to do matte paintings. And basically, we went to POP because there were certain artists there that I knew would match Vincent's criteria, like Deak Ferrand, who became an incredibly instrumental person on the film. So finding the right type of personnel was a bit like finding a needle in a haystack."

Somers' support itself may have played a key role in keeping Mass.illusions' team—including Visual

Rekonstruktion einer mit Mohnblumen übersäte Landschaft reichten.

Der Beitrag von Mass.illusions bestand aus 99% „Gemalten Welt", 58 Einstellungen, die eine wilde Blumenlandschaft aus noch fließenden Farbpigmenten zeigten, die Chris Neilsons erste Begegnung mit dem Leben nach dem Tode einrahmt. E war absolut entscheidend, daß diese Sequenz die Kinogänger emotional fesselt, denn sonst würde sie sich aus dem Film verabschieden, noch bevor emotionale Schlagkraft des Werkes überhaupt ei Chance hätte, sich zu entfalten. Ward – selbst ausgebildeter Maler – hatte intuitiv erfaßt, daß das Leben im Jenseits anheimelnd-bekannt und doch gleichzeitig fremd wirken mußte, und hatte seine Inspiration von den deutschen Romantikern, beso ders von Caspar David Friedrich, bezogen.

Noch vor Drehbeginn durchwühlten die Bildprod zenten zahllose Kunstbibliotheken – stets auf der Suche nach Illustrationen im Sinne jener Bilder, d Ward vorschwebten. Und schließlich halfen die G mälde Friedrichs und anderer Künstler des 19. Jah hunderts, die Vision Wards zu definieren und in d Köpfen aller bildnerischen Mitarbeiter zu veranke vom Production Designer Eugene Vanetti zum Kameramann Eduardo Serra und zu Dutzenden v Visual-Effects-Künstlern.

„Wir haben Josh Rosen als Art Director für

Mass.illusions angeworben und ihn in diese Position eingesetzt. Obwohl alle bei Mass.illusions mit dem Projekt beschäftigten Mitarbeiter – selbst die Softwareleute – eine künstlerische Ausbildung hatten, bot doch erst Joshs künstlerische Leitung die Gewähr, daß das von uns gesuchte Gefühl hinübergebracht werden könnte. Josh war ein absoluter Glückstreffer – ein Softwareentwickler, den wir während eines Urlaubsjahres in Italien aufgespürt hatten, wo er Illustrationen für ein Buch gezeichnet und nebenbei Fresken gemalt hat. Wir haben auch Sid Dutton von Illusion Arts und Michael Lloyd angeheuert, um Hintergrundgemälde zu produzieren. Und schließlich gingen wir vor allem deshalb zu POP, weil ich wußte, daß dort einige Künstler beschäftigt waren, die Vincents Kriterien genau erfüllen würde, etwa Deak Ferrand, der später wirklich eine Integrationsfigur in dieser Produktion wurde. Insgesamt war die Suche nach dem richtigen Personal aber so etwas wie die Suche nach der Nadel im Heuhaufen."

Somers' Unterstützung hat eine wichtige Rolle dabei gespielt, das Team von Mass.illusions – darunter die Visual Effects Supervisors Joel Hyneck und Nicholas Brooks, die Produzentin Donna Langston sowie die Softwareentwickler Pierre Jasmin und Pete Litwinowitcz – so lange im Projekt zu halten, bis sie bewiesen hatten, daß ihre bislang unerprobte Strategie für die Effekte der „Gemalten Welt" tatsächlich funktionierte. Andere hatten einen traditionelleren Ansatz vorgeschlagen, etwa eine Bluebox-Aufnahme der Schauspieler und ihre Einbettung in eine digitale Landschaft, die über Multi-Ebenen oder 3D-Matte-Gemälde erstellt werden sollte. Das hätte wohl auch funktioniert, aber es hätte Ward nicht die geforderte Freiheit und jenes Gefühl der Wirklichkeit gegeben, das er so verzweifelt gesucht hat.

Als Motion Control und Bluebox-Verfahren ausgeschieden worden waren, weil Ward und der Kameramann Eduardo Serra komplexe und sehr flüssige Kamerabewegungen im Glacier National Park in

Effects Supervisors Joel Hyneck and Nicholas Brooks, line producer Donna Langston and software creators Pierre Jasmin and Pete Litwinowitcz—on the project long enough to prove that their untested strategy for the Painted World's effects would work. Others had posited a more traditional approach involving shooting the actors against greenscreen and comping them into a digital landscape created via multiplane or 3-D matte paintings, which might have worked, but would not have given Ward the freedom he demanded and the sense of reality he desperately sought.

Having discarded motion control and greenscreen while Ward and cinematographer Eduardo Serra planned complex and very fluid camera moves in Montana's Glacier National Park, Somers' team relied on traditional tracking and Lidar surveys of the location to recreate camera motion and locate objects so the shots could later be immersed in running pigment. Lidar is basically a radar survey, typically used in building dams and so on, which gave us 'a burst' —or cloud—of points, resulting in a 3-D wireframe

of the landscape. Then by doing a traditional survey of the markers we placed on location, we could line up this wire frame with the shot and basically recreate both camera move and topography."
Amazingly, every single shot in the "Painted World" began as a photographic plate, yet ended up looking like it had been freshly hand-painted by a 19th century master. But since Robin Williams and Cuba Gooding Jr. had to remain unretouched, they were painstakingly extracted from every shot. Then a new edge-detection system created by Mass.illusion and dubbed "machine vision" was applied to the now clean plates to further deconstruct each shot into between fifteen and thirty maps, which were then treated with particle systems brushstrokes to create the "Painted World" effect. But applying dripping, swirling paint to thousands of flowers and leaves demanded both procedural and manual control. Then Mass.illusions built a toolkit of a number of brushstrokes, so they could control the color, separation, thickness and dynamics of the paintstrokes themselves through certain handles, which allowed them to create paint rolling down blades of grass in certain shots. The amazing thing about this process is that we could have a crane on a 30' camera track, moving in every possible axis known to the cinematographic man, and then basically apply brush strokes to every leaf and every detail in that scene!

Montana planten, verließ sich Somers' Team auf traditionelles Tracking und auf Lidar-Aufnahmen des Drehorts, um die Kamerabewegung und Objekte zu verorten, damit die Einstellungen später in die fließende Farbe getaucht werden konnten. „Lidar ist so etwas Ähnliches wie eine Radaraufnahme – man verwendet es beispielsweise beim Deichbau –, und wir erhielten dadurch eine Punktwolke von Daten, die als Grundlage eines dreidimensionalen Drahtmodells der Landschaft diente. Mit Hilfe der traditionellen Markierungspunkte vor Ort konnten wir dann dieses Gittermodell mit der Einstellung abgleichen und so die Kamerabewegungen und die Topographie nachbauen."
Erstaunlicherweise begann tatsächlich jede einzelne Einstellung in der „Gemalten Welt" als Photographie, auch wenn sie letztlich so aussieht, als wäre sie soeben von einem Meisters des 19. Jahrhunderts frisch in Öl gemalt. Aber nachdem Robin Williams und Cuba Gooding Jr. unretouchiert bleiben mußten, wurden sie mühsam aus jeder einzelnen Aufnahme herausgefiltert. Danach wurde mittels eines von Mass.illusions geschaffenen Kantenerkennungssystems jede Aufnahme in 15 bis 30 Ebenen zerlegt, die wiederum mit Partikelsystem-Pinselstrichen bearbeitet wurden, um den Effekt einer gemalten Welt zu erzielen. Tausende von Blüten und Blättern mit tropfender, fließender Farbe zu betupfen verlangte nach prozeduraler ebenso wie manueller Steuerung.
„Mass.illusions hat dann ein Werkzeugset aus diversen Pinselstrichen zusammengestellt, das es erlaubte, die Farbe, Trennung, Dicke und Dynamik der Pinselstriche als solche über Art Handgriffe zu steuern, womit man bei einigen Einstellungen beispielsweise Farbe über einzelne Grashalme hinunterlaufen lassen konnte. Das Erstaunliche daran ist, daß wir an einem Zehn-Meter-Kran eine Kamera hängen haben, die sich in jeder dem Kameramann nur erdenklichen Ebene bewegt, und daß wir trotzdem jedes einzelne Blatt, jedes einzelne Detail in dieser Szene mit individuellen Pinselstrichen bearbeiten können! Das ist schon genial."

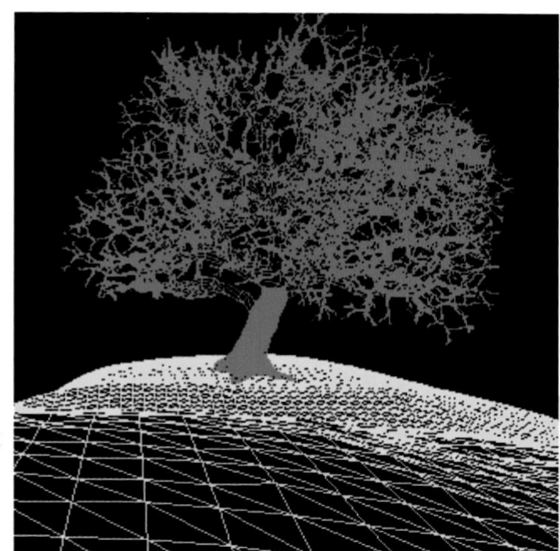

)igital Domain's Visual :ffects Supervisor Kevin Mack :reated the "Painted World's")nly indigenous species, the Painted Bird", as a 3-D ınimated element which was supplied to Mass.illusions for compositing. DD handled an ıdditional 54 shots, including full landscape econstruction on the sequence in which Chris flies hrough a field of poppies, and adding a ghostly blur o Cuba Gooding Jr. But their "main event scene," ıccording to Somers, "was the Autumn Tree, which)lows apart as Chris connects with Annie and ealizes things are horribly wrong." The "Autumn ree" wasn't constructed as a model, it was actually grown organically using a series of algorithms in what's called an L system.

he remarkable imagery of *What Dreams May Come* s a testament to the determination of a small group)f filmmakers and effects artists to convincingly)ortray paradise and damnation on celluloid. It also epresents a synthesis between two very different ırtforms. "One thing the filmmaker and the painter ıave in common is they're trying to describe the world," Ward concludes. "I would like to think that his film has actually opened another perceptual way for artists to view the world and a completely different range of options of how to describe it. I ıope ultimately that artists will choose to work in ive-action film paintings—not matte paintings— ınd perhaps we have initiated that.

Kevin Mack, Visual Effects Supervisor bei Digital Domain, hat das einzige nur in der „Gemalten Welt" vorkommende Lebewesen beigesteuert, den „Gemalten Vogel", der als 3D-animiertes Element zur Komposition an Mass.illusions weitergegeben wurde. Daneben hat DD noch weitere 54 Einstellung bearbeitet, darunter die Landschaftsrekonstruktion in jener Sequenz, in der Chris durch das Mohnfeld fliegt, und Cuba Golding Jr. eine geisterhafte Unschärfe hinzugefügt. Aber ihre wichtigste Szene, so Somers, „war der ‚Herbstbaum', der auseinanderfällt, als Chris Verbindung zu Annie bekommt und merkt, daß irgendetwas schrecklich falsch gelaufen ist. Der Herbstbaum wurde nicht als Modell gebaut, sondern man hat ihn organisch wachsen lassen durch eine Serie von Algorithmen innerhalb eines sogenannten L-Systems."

Die bemerkenswerte Bildwelt von *What Dreams May Come* legt Zeugnis ab von der Entschlossenheit einer kleinen Gruppe von Filmschaffenden und Effektkünstlern, das Paradies und die Verdammung überzeugend auf Zelluloid darzustellen. Der Film ist auch eine Synthese zweier sehr unterschiedlicher Kunstformen. „Eins haben Filmemacher und Maler gemeinsam: Beide versuchen die Welt zu beschreiben", schließt Ward. „Ich stelle mir gerne vor, daß dieser Film Künstlern einen neuen Weg eröffnet, die Welt zu sehen, und eine völlig neue Palette von Möglichkeiten, sie zu beschreiben. Ich hoffe, daß sich letztlich Künstler dazu entschließen werden, mit Live-Action-Filmgemälden zu arbeiten statt mit stehenden Hintergrundgemälden – und vielleicht haben wir das ja initiiert."

What Dreams May Come. Director: Vincent Ward. Producers: Stephen Simon and Barnet Bain. VFX Art Director: Joshua Rosen. VFX Supervisors: Joel Hynek and Nicholas Brooks. VFX Line Producer: Donna Langston. Software Creators: Pierre Jasmin, Peter Litwinowicz. 3D Supervisor: Mike Schmitt. In collaboration with the VFX companies: Pacific Ocean Post, Mass.illusion, Digital Domain, Giant Killer Robots, Mobility, Shadowcaster and Lunarfish. What Dreams May Come („Hinter dem Horizont"). Regie: Vincent Ward. Produzenten: Stephen Simon und Barnet Bain. VFX Art-Director: Joshua Rosen. VFX Supervisors: Joel Hynek und Nicholas Brooks. VFX Line Producer: Donna Langston. Software Creators: Pierre Jasmin, Peter Litwinowicz. 3D-Supervisor: Mike Schmitt. Unter der Mitwirkung folgender VFX-Firmen: Pacific Ocean Post, Mass.illusion, Digital Domain sowie

GUINNESS "SURFER"

CFC – Computer Film Company

For several long seconds the camera lingers on a man's face. He is waiting. At last we cut to handheld footage following the man and his three companions, all carrying surfboards. They hurl themselves into a heaving ocean. The ultimate wave has arrived. It starts to roll and we see that the men are not alone. The spirit of the wave is physically embodied in enormous white horses which are charging through the water with them. Above, below and inside the wave men and horses surge thrillingly forward.
This astonishing visual effect was created by The Computer Film Company for the latest Guinness television commercial, "Surfer", which first aired on 17th March 1999.
Acclaimed director Jonathan Glazer has collaborated with CFC before, initially with the Nike "Parklife" commercial. The company also produced some alarmingly realistic effects for his controversial music video for U.N.K.L.E., "Rabbit in Your Headlights." "It was the painterly quality that CFC's designers brought to one of the U.N.K.L.E. shots that gave me the confidence I needed that they could handle this work," recalls Glazer. "I wanted something that was mythological and yet utterly real. Working with such contrasting elements, one liquid, one muscular and solid, they produced of the most extraordinary compositing work I've seen."
Rumour has it that the brief for the commercical was daunting enough to frighten off some other effects houses but, says Senior Visual Effects Designer Paddy Eason, "The scary jobs are the ones that make all this worth doing."
A number of ways of achieving the creative team's vision were considered, including doing it all as CG, or using real waves but CG horses, both of which would haven given the team greater control but, as Eason notes, "We are very aware that the kind of happy accidents you get in the real world, the natural movements of waves and horses, will always give you a better shot. So our final choice was to use real waves and horses, where necessary adding CG water and the odd CG horses leg." Dominic Parker, head of 3D, adds: "We wanted to find a way of conveying the chaotic and violent dynamic of the film using CG elements to fill in the gaps from the shots—underwater hooves, bubbles, surf, spray, and spume."
The film celebrates the pleasures in store for those

Etliche lange Sekunden hindurch verweilt die Kamera auf dem Gesicht eines Mannes. Schließlic schneiden wir um auf eine Handkamera, die den Mann und seine drei Gefährten verfolgt, die alle Surfbretter tragen. Sie werfen sich in den aufgewühlten Ozean, und dann kommt endlich die We aller Wellen. Sie beginnt zu rollen, und wir erkennen, daß die Männer nicht allein sind. Der Geist d Welle materialisiert sich in riesigen weißen Pferd die mit den Surfern durch das Wasser toben. Ober halb, unterhalb und innerhalb der Welle stürmen Menschen und Pferde nach vorne.
Dieser erstaunliche visuelle Effekt wurde von The Computer Film Company für den neuesten TV-Werbespot von Guinness produziert, der unter de Titel *Surfer* erstmals am 17. März 1999 ausgestrah wurde.
Der gefeierte Regisseur Jonathan Glazer hatte bereits zuvor mit CFC zusammengearbeitet, und zwar am *Parklife*-Spot für Nike. Die Company hatt auch einige bestürzend realistische Effekte für se umstrittenes Musikvideo *Rabbit in Your Headlight* für U.N.K.L.E. produziert. „Es ist die malerische Qu lität, die die Leute von CFC bei einer der U.N.K.L.E.-Einstellungen zustandebrachten, die mir das nöti Vertrauen gab, daß sie auch diese Aufgabe erfüllt könnten", erinnert sich Glazer. „Ich wollte etwas, d zugleich mythologisch und doch real anmutet. Be der Arbeit mit so kontrastierenden Elementen – eines flüssig, eines muskulös und fest – haben sie eines der erstaunlichsten Kompositionswerke geschaffen, das ich je gesehen habe."
Gerüchteweise wird berichtet, daß schon das Exposé für den Werbespot anspruchsvoll genug war, einige andere Effekt-Häuser abzuschrecken, aber, so berichtet der Senior Visual Effects Design Paddy Eason, „die abschreckenden Jobs machen d ganze erst spannend."
Es wurden verschiedene Möglichkeiten zur Umset zung der Visionen des kreativen Teams angedacht darunter auch die Variante, alles durch Computergrafik zu erstellen oder aber echte Wellen und co putergenerierte Pferde zu benutzen. Beides hätte dem Team mehr Steuerungsmöglichkeiten gegeben, aber – sagt Eason – „wir sind uns dessen bewußt, daß die kleinen Zufälle in der realen Welt die natürlichen Bewegungen von Pferden und Wellen einfach immer die besseren Aufnahmen ergeben. Deshalb haben wir letztlich beschlossen echte Pferde und echte Wellen zu verwenden und wo nötig – CG-Wasser und das eine oder andere Pferdebein hinzuzufügen." Dominic Parker, der Leiter der 3D-Abteilung, fügt hinzu: „Wir wollten einen Weg finden, die chaotische und fast gewalt tätige Dynamik des Films zu verwenden und die Computergrafik zum Füllen der Lücken im gedreh ten Material verwenden – Hufe unter Wasser, Blasen, Gischt und Schaum."
Der Film feiert die Freuden, die jener harren, die z warten verstehen, nur – den Luxus des Wartens

repared to wait, hough waiting was ot a luxury available the team at CFC. Although we'd bviously done some anning, there's only much you can do in dvance with this sort material," says achael Penfold, Senior sual Effects Producer CFC, "The surfers ere shot in Hawaii and we'd given the crew as uch information as possible beforehand about hat we hoped for, but we really had no idea what e would get—the size of the waves, the weather, much was beyond our control. Once we had a ugh cut, we used it to decide what we needed om the 3 day studio shoot of horses, tip-tanks and ray. We shot these elements at very high speed sing a Photosonics camera, so we had thousands of et of film which we used to create a library of nages which the team could draw on."

ne footage was shot, composited and had FX added colour before being transformed into black and hite, so that the final look is not stark but has a nge of mercurial greys, helping convey the chaos urrounding the surfers.

ne project was headed at CFC by Paddy Eason and an Glass, though the finished film drew on skills om right across CFC's areas of FX expertise. "The mposting was done by Paddy, Adrian de Wet and yself," explains Glass, "We used Cineon running on licon Graphics machines. Keylight (keying software, eveloped in house but now commercially available) as invaluable during this process." Silicon Graphics so supported Matador, which Gavin Toomey and ex Payman used for the paint work. Dominic Parker nd Richard Clarke worked on the 3D elements using oudini, Maya & Renderman, and the final conform nd grade was completed on Domino by Tom ebenham.

konnte sich das CFC-Team nicht erlauben. „Obwohl wir natürlich einige Planungen gemacht hatten, kann man bei dieser Art Material nur begrenzt im voraus planen", sagt Rachael Penfold, Visual Effects Producer bei CFC. „Die Surfer wurden in Hawaii aufgenommen, und wir hatten der Crew so viel an Vorabinformation über unsere Wünsche gegeben, wie wir konnten, aber wir wußten nicht wirklich, was wir erhalten würden – das Wetter, die Wellengröße und vieles andere lag außerhalb unserer Kontrolle. Als wir den ersten Rohschnitt hatten, wurde auf dessen Basis festgelegt, was wir von den dreitägigen Studioaufnahmen mit den Pferden in Kipp-Becken und mit Sprühmaschinen brauchten. Diese Elemente wurden mit einer Photosonics-Hochgeschwindigkeitskamera aufgenommen, so daß wir etliche hundert Meter Film hatten, von denen eine Bildbibliothek zusammengestellt wurde, aus der sich das Team bedienen konnte."

Außenaufnahmen, Montage und Effekte wurden in Farbe hergestellt, bevor das Produkt in schwarzweiß umgewandelt wurde. Dies läßt den Spot nicht so hart erscheinen, sondern gibt ihm eine Palette von quecksilberartigen Grautönen, die das Chaos, das rund um die Surfer herrscht, noch unterstreichen.

Das Projekt wurde bei CFC von Paddy Eason und Dan Glass geleitet, wenn auch das Produkt letztlich in allen Bereichen von den Special-Effects-Erfahrungen von CFC zehrt. „Die Komposition wurde von Paddy, Adrian de Wet und mir gemacht", erklärt Glass. „Wir haben Cineon auf Silicon Graphics Maschinen eingesetzt. Keylight (eine im Hause entwickelte, jetzt aber auch kommerziell erhältliche Key-Software) war bei diesem Prozeß von unschätzbarem Wert." Silicon Graphics unterstützte auch Matador, das Gavin Tommer und Alex Payman für die Malarbeiten eingesetzt haben. Dominic Parker und Richard Clarke haben an den 3D-Elementen gearbeitet (mit Houdini, Maya und Renderman), und die endgültige Abgleichung und Fertigstellung erfolgte durch Tom Debenham mit Hilfe von Domino.

CFC The Computer Film Company

E COMPUTER FILM COMPANY (CFC) WAS FOUNDED IN 1984 IN LONDON. CFC PIONEERED THE WORLD'S FIRST DIGITAL FILM SCANNING, AGE PROCESSING AND RECORDING SERVICE AT FULL CINEMA QUALITY, FOR WHICH THE COMPANY HAS RECEIVED TWO TECHNICAL ACADEMY WARDS® FROM THE ACADEMY OF MOTION PICUTURE ARTS AND SCIENCES. ▬ Computer Film Company (CFC) wurde 1984 in London gründet. Sie war das erste Unternehmen, das digitale Filmscans, Bildverarbeitung und Spezialdienstleistungen in voller Kinoqualität anbot, für die Firma auch zweimal den Technischen Academy Award der Academy of Motion Picture Arts and Sciences erhielt.

A VIAGEM
Alain Escalle

1543. A Portuguese ship drops anchor for the first time before Japan, marking the beginning of an expansion into the Far East; new trade routes are opened up and there is an intensive cultural exchange.
This event was captured on a large collection of painted wall panels illustrated by a Japanese artist, which thus create an antique snapshot of the encounter between two worlds on wooden panels embossed with gold-leaf. The pictures reflect their amused, amazed and sometimes confused impressions of these people from the West, with their odd customs and long noses, bringing strange animals with them and unknown objects like guns.

The Design and Electronic Realization of the Film *A viagem*

The work *A viagem*, generated in film resolution, was commissioned for the Portuguese Pavilion at the Lisbon Expo 98 and was created by the same team that had made *Cités antérieures: Bruges* in 1995 (Director: Christian Boustani, Images and Special Effects: Alain Escalle).
The technical and visual realization was intended to be done on the basis of a storyboard, which proved to be an elaborate and time-consuming project (nine months post-production!), with tasks ranging from color studies based on color cards before the shooting started (directed by Christian Boustani, lasting for two weeks), directing the special effects during the shooting, to the creation of the graphic elements and directing the post-production team comprising about twenty people.
The film uses several different kinds of computer graphic elements: 2D objects (computer generated decorative elements in the tradition of Japanese screens), pure 3D effects and elements from existing film material in both higher and lower resolutions.
The film elements were divided into two groups:
1. The overall views and other settings requiring a high resolution, 42 minutes altogether, which were scanned in with 2K at Cinesite, London, and
2. the settings for which a normal video resolution was sufficient (amounting to five hours of picture material, scanned by After Movies).
The 2D elements were prepared by an assistant and

„1543. Zum ersten Mal läßt ein portugiesisches Schiff vor Japan den Anker fallen, und dies marki den Beginn einer Expansion in den Fernen Osten neue Handelsrouten werden eröffnet und ein int siver kultureller Austausch findet statt.
Das Ereignis wurde auf einer großen Sammlung von gemalten Wandschirmen festgehalten, illustriert von japanischen Künstlern, die damit eine antiken Schnappschuß der Begegnung zweier W ten auf blattvergoldeten Holzpaneelen festgeha haben. Die Bilder reflektieren ihre amüsierten, erstaunten und bisweilen verwirrten Eindrücke v diesen Menschen aus dem Westen, mit ihren eig artigen Gebräuchen und ihren langen Nasen, die seltsame Tiere mitbringen und so unbekannte G genstände wie die Gewehre."

Zur Bildgestaltung und elektronische Realisierung des Films *A viagem*

Das in Filmauflösung generierte Werk *A viagem* eine Auftragsarbeit für den portugiesischen Pavillon auf der Lissabonner Expo 98 und wurde von jenem Team geschaffen, das 1995 bereits *Cit antérieures: Bruges* realisiert hatte (Leitung: Christian Boustani, Bilder und Special Effects: Ala Escalle).
Auf der Basis eines Storyboards sollte die technische und visuelle Umsetzung des Films stattfind was sich als umfangreiches und langwieriges Pr jekt erwies (neun Monate Post-Production!), wo die Aufgaben von Farbstudien anhand von Farbk ten vor den Dreharbeiten (Leitung: Christian Boustani, Dauer: zwei Wochen) über die Leitung Spezialeffekte während der Aufnahmen bis zur Schaffung der grafischen Elemente und der Leit des rund zwanzigköpfigen Post-Production-Tean reichten.
Der Film verwendet mehrere Arten von compute grafischen Elementen: 2D-Objekte (auf dem Com puter erzeugte Dekorelemente in der Tradition ja nischer Paravents), reine 3D-Effekte und Element aus dem sowohl in hoher wie niedriger Auflösur vorliegenden Filmmaterial.
Die Filmelemente wurden in zwei Gruppen eing teilt:
1. Die Gesamtansichten und andere Einstellunge die hohe Auflösung erforderten, insgesamt 42 Minuten, die mit 2K bei Cinesite, London, eing scannt wurden, und 2. jene Einstellungen, bei de normale Videoauflösung ausreichend war (insge samt 5 Stunden Bildmaterial, eingescannt bei Af Movies).

Die 2D-Elemente wurden von mir und einem As stenten über fünf Monate hinweg vorbereitet. S bildeten die grafische Einheit des Films und versorgten meine mit der Komposition beschäftigt Computergrafiker, die auf zwei *Inferno*- und zwe

myself over a period of five months. They provided the basis for the graphical unity of the film and were given to the computer graphics artists, who worked on the composition with two *Inferno* and two *Flame* computers. These were linked for this project with the post-production company TRIX, which is well known in the field of rides and animation. Altogether there were six people working day and night for almost four months on the compositing.
Pure 3D elements were inserted at various places in the film. These are essentially simple 3D models animated and textured with *Inferno/Flame*. These elements include the ship (which was sometimes also derived from a model filmed with motion control), the sea monster (whose decomposition in a wave was created as an animation using *Inferno*), the breaking vessel (the saffron it contains was made as a particle animation with *Inferno* and with individual sparks like *Sapphire* and *5d monters*), and the flying deer at the end of the film. They were created within two months by eight people using the programs *Explore* and *Softimage*. A typical setting like the one at the beginning is relatively long and very complex - the realization of the first minute consumed about two months of work on a *Flame*

Flame-Rechnern arbeiteten, die für diese Gelegenheit von der eher im Ride- und Animationsbereich bekannten Post-Production-Firma TRIX zusammengehängt wurden. Insgesamt haben sechs Leute über fast vier Monate Tag und Nacht am Compositing gearbeitet.
Reine 3D-Elemente wurden an verschiedenen Stellen des Films eingesetzt und sind im wesentlichen einfache 3D-Modelle, die mit *Inferno/Flame* animiert und texturiert wurden. Zu diesen Elementen gehören das Schiff (das manchmal auch aus einem mit Motion-Control gefilmten Modell abgeleitet wurde), der Seedrache (seine Dekomposition in eine Welle wurde mittels *Inferno* geschaffen), das zerbrechende Gefäß (der Safran, den es enthält, entstand als Partikelanimation mit *Inferno* und mit einzelnen Sparks wie *Sapphire* und *5d monters*) und die fliegenden Hirsche vom Schluß des Films. Sie wurden mit den Programmen *Explore* und *Softimage* von acht Leuten innerhalb zweier Monate geschaffen. Eine typische Einstellung wie jene am Anfang des Films ist ziemlich lang und sehr komplex – die Realisierung der ersten Minute verschlang rund zwei Monate Arbeit auf einer *Flame*-Maschine.

Die Szene setzt sich wie folgt zusammen:

1. Allgemeine Ansicht des Hafens von Lissabon (sie wurde zur Gänze aus niedrig aufgelösten Elementen im Zentrum des Hafens zusammengesetzt, wobei der Hafen als solcher auch hochauflösend dargestellt wurde, nachdem er zuvor aus Elementen in

machine. The scene is composed as follows:
1. General view of the Lisbon harbor ... (this was composed entirely of low resolution elements in the middle of the harbor, whereby the harbor itself was represented in high resolution after being first composed of elements in normal video resolution), ... which fades into:
2. a camera panning over the facade of a building (a virtual camera pan in the machine [*Flame*] over the facade, which is a retouched photo of a historical building in Lisbon. The roof is a 3D model rendered and textured in *Flame*. The people were inserted in the picture at the end.)
This is linked with:
3. a pan through the crowd and across the marketplace. (This is a conventional film camera pan put together from three shots done with motion control for financial reasons, because we did not have enough extras. On the whole, the point was to balance the three shots, multiply the crowd and create a virtual decor with *Inferno* based on the graphic elements. In turn, this was to be faded into the three-dimensional space of the camera pan [virtual camera of *Flame*].)
This fades into:
4. Crossing the panel screen and a flashback to the ship traveling to Japan (movement and virtual decor created with *Flame/Inferno* on the basis of graphic elements [sky, clouds and ocean are animations], and the ship, which is a pure 3D element [*Explore*], is copied in).
Tying into this is:
5. The arrival in the scientist's cabin (created entirely in the virtual space of *Inferno/Flame*, beginning with photographic elements and a high resolution scan of the person).
The computer graphic work of the film thus uses very different techniques, which are the result of an intensive study of the technological possibilities, although there is something handcrafted about the application, which I prefer, because it conveys more emotion with the work and makes the images look less synthetic.

normaler Video-Auflösung komponiert worden war), die überleitet in:
2. Eine Kamerafahrt über die Fassade eines Gebäu des (virtuelle Kamerafahrt in der Maschine [*Flam* über die Fassade, welche ein retuschiertes Foto eines historischen Bauwerks in Lissabon ist. Das Dach ist ein in *Flame* gerendertes und texturierte 3D-Modell. Die Personen werden zum Schluß in d Bild eingesetzt.) Dies verknüpft sich mit:
3. einer Fahrt durch die Menge und über den Mar platz. (Dies ist eine gewöhnliche Film-Kamerafahr die sich aus drei Aufnahmen zusammensetzt, we wir nicht genug Statisten hatten, und aus finanzi len Gründen mit Motion Control durchgeführt wurde. Insgesamt ging es darum, die drei Aufnah

men abzugleichen, die Menge zu vervielfältigen und mit *Inferno* ein virtuelles Dekor auf der Basis der grafischen Elemente zu erzeugen, das seinerseits in den dreidimensionalen Raum den Kamera fahrt eingeblendet wird [virtuelle Kamera von *Flame*].) Dies blendet über zu:
4. Überquerung des Paravents und Flash-back auf das Schiff auf der Fahrt nach Japan (Bewegung u virtuelles Dekor in *Flame/Inferno* auf der Basis gra scher Elemente erzeugt [Himmel, Wolken und Me sind Animationen] und Schiff einkopiert, das ein nes 3D-Element ist [*Explore*]).Daran schließt sich
5. Die Ankunft in der Kabine des Wissenschaftlers (zur Gänze im virtuellen Raum von *Inferno/Flame* erzeugt, ausgehend von fotografischen Elemente und von der hochauflösend eingescannten Perso
Die computergrafische Arbeit des Films verwende also sehr unterschiedliche Bearbeitungstechniken die sich aus einem intensiven Studium der techn logischen Möglichkeiten ergeben haben, wobei d Anwendung etwas Handwerkliches an sich hat, w ich auch deswegen bevorzuge, weil es mehr Gefü bei der Arbeit vermittelt und die Bilder weniger s thetisch aussehen läßt.

Alain Escalle (F), born 1967, studied Applied Arts, cinema and video from 1983 to 1989. At first he worked as an assistant infographist on Peter Greenaway's video-danse *M for man*. Director and digital creator since 1991, he is developing a visual and graphic work on moving pictures with new technologies. Because of this exploration of images between traditional cinema and animation, he has worked with other directors on several projets like *Cities of the past: Brugge*, or *A viagem* (directed by Christian Boustani). Alain Escalle (F) geb. 1967, studierte 1983 bis 1989 Angewandte Kunst, Filmwissenschaft und Video. Er arbeitete zunächst als Assistent der Computergrafik an Peter Greenaways Tanzvideo *M for man*. Seit 1991 ist er Regisseur und digitaler Künstler und entwickelt mit Hilfe der neuen Technologien eine Bildsprache, die zwischen traditioneller Kinematografie und Animation zu vermitteln versucht. Dabei arbeitet er auch mit anderen Regisseuren zusammen, etwa bei Projekten wie *Cities of the Past:*

LOTTERY "FANTASY"

Manuel Horrillo Fernandez / Daiquiri / Spainbox

As an ad for the Spanish Lotteries Organization, the Lottery *Fantasy* spot is a depiction of a wonderworld where dreams may come true.
The most important challenge for the Daiquiri/-Spainbox team was an artistic one: to create and visualize a world which has no reference in real life and succeed in realizing pictures both surrealistic and magic, but at the same time easily understandable in an advertising language.
There were no major problems in the technical field except for the lighting: all backgrounds were shot in broad daylight, and we had to be very careful with lighting and matching the refraction of the light in the shots with the 3D lights.
Among the tools used for the post-production and visual effects were: Softimage, for the "Fantasia" boat, the fans, the water for the firemen (with Dinamation) and the sea under the Fantasia (with Natural FX from Arete), the trumpets, the castles and the funfair with the cars.
Alias and Maya were used to model and animate the sailboats, the carrousel with diamonds, and the marbles set at the beginning of the spot.
We worked with 3D Equalizer too and rendered with Mental Ray. Final compositing was realized on Flame and Henry.
The whole team was composed of 14 3D artists and editors working for 2 months.

Als Werbespot für die spanische Lottogesellschaf ist *Fantasy* die Darstellung einer Wunderwelt, in Träume wahr werden können.
Die größte Herausforderung für das Team von Daiquiri/Spainbox war künstlerischer Art, galt es doch, eine Welt zu schaffen und visuell darzustellen, die in der Realität keine Entsprechung hat, ur dabei surrealistisch-magische Bilder zu realisiere die dennoch in der Kürze der Werbesprache leich verständlich sind.
Im technischen Bereich gab es keine Probleme, abgesehen vom Licht: Alle Hintergründe waren b vollem Sonnenschein aufgenommen, und wir mußten die Lichteffekte und Reflexionen der 3D-Modelle recht vorsichtig anpassen.
Wir verwendeten u. a. Softimage, und zwar für d *Fantasia*-Boot, das Meer (mit Natural FX von Aret für die Trompeten, die Schlösser und den Vergnügungspark mit den Wagen.
Alias und Maya wurden zur Modellierung und Ar mation der Segelboote, des Karussels mit den Di manten und für die Kugeleffekte am Beginn des Spots verwendet.
Wir haben auch mit 3D Equalizer gearbeitet und mit Mental Ray gerendert. Das abschließende Compositing erfolgte auf Flame und Harry. Insgesamt waren vierzehn 3D-Künstler und Mitarbeiter zwei Monate an der Produktion des Spots beschäftigt.

Manuel Horrillo Fernandez (E) was a graphics artist and illustrator and worked as an assistant in the field of journalism and as a computer graphics artist in Paris. He later became involved in the advertising branch and founded the post-production company Daiquiri Digital Pictures with J. T. Muller in 1990 and the visual effects company HD Spainbox in 1992.

Manuel Horrillo Fernandez (E) war Grafiker und Illustrator und arbeitete als Assistenz im journalistischen Bereich sowie als Computergrafiker in Paris. Später war er in der Werbebranche tätig und gründete mit J. T. Muller 1990 das Postproduction Unternehmen Daiquiri Digital Pictures sowie 1992 die Visual Effects

ORIGINAL COPIES

Fuel / Peter Miles, Damon Murray, Stephen Sorrell

Over the last six months Fuel have produced, edited and directed a series of short films under the title *Original Copies*. Lasting approximately 25 minutes, the films are a continuous succession of messages and comments, using a mixture of graphics, live action and computer animation.
Original Copies features: A seductive sequence of pornographic stills combined with moving type to form a riddle about AIDS; an animated text narrated by Patrick Moore explaining the Heisenberg Theory of Change, illustrated by live action sequences of Fuel in motion; a series of live-action portraits of young video game players under intense concentration during a game; and a narrated DNA text that suggests the extent of genetic control in the future—live-action footage of teenage kissers cut with film of a pit bull terrier trained to hang from the branch of a tree to strengthen it's jaw lock. A collaboration with Juergen Teller, Kate Moss and writer Shannan Peckham produced a five minute section called *Can I Own Myself*, which asks questions about the authorship and ownership of images. The combination of Teller and Moss, utilised for the first time on video, allows the viewer to question the commercial and moral applications of an image.
Their films have been screened at onedotzero '97 and '98, at the ICA, the Cardiff International Animation Festival '98, Rotterdam Film Festival '99 and at the Lux cinema.

Im Lauf der letzten sechs Monate hat Fuel eine Serie von Kurzfilmen unter dem Titel *Original Co*
produziert, gestaltet und herausgebracht. Mit ei
Gesamtdauer von rund 25 Minuten sind diese Fi
eine kontinuierliche Abfolge von Nachrichten un
Kommentaren und verwenden eine Mischung au
Grafik, Live-Action und Computeranimation.
Original Copies umfaßt: Eine verführerische Sequenz pornografischer Standbilder kombiniert m
bewegter Schrift, die ein Kreuzworträtsel zum Thema AIDS bildet; einen animierten Text von Patrick Moore, der die Heisenbergsche Theorie de
Veränderung erläutert, illustriert mit Live-Action-Sequenzen von Fuel in Bewegung; eine Serie von Live-Action-Portraits hochkonzentrierter junger Videogame-Spieler während des Spiels; und eine
erzählten Text über DNA und das Ausmaß der ge
tischen Steuerung unserer Zukunft – Live-Action-Bilder von küssenden Jugendlichen mit eingeble
deten Bildern eines Pit-Bull-Terriers, der darauf trainiert ist, seine Bißkraft durch Hängen an eine
Ast zu steigern.
Die Zusammenarbeit mit Jürgen Teller, Kate Mos
und dem Schriftsteller Shannan Peckham ergab eine fünfminütige Sequenz mit dem Titel *Can I Own Myself*, die Fragen nach der Urheberschaft u
nach dem Eigentum an Bildern aufwirft. Die erst
mals im Video eingesetzte Kombination von Telle
und Moss erlaubt dem Betrachter, die kommerzie
und moralische Anwendung von Bildern zu hinte
fragen.
Die Filme von Fuel wurden bei onedotzero '97 un
'98, bei der ICA, beim Cardiff International Animation Festival '98, dem Rotterdamer Film Festival '99 sowie bei Lux Cinema gezeigt.

ACTIVITY

Fuel are Peter Miles, Damon Murray and Stephen Sorrell. They formed their design group in 1990 while still at the Royal College of Art, where they produced the first four issues of their magazine, *Fuel*. They have since published another three magazines and in October 1996 a book published by Booth-Clibborn Editions, entitled *Pure Fuel*. Now signed to The Artists Company, they have produced TV commercials for The *Australian* newspaper in Sydney and directed a pop promo for The Pecadiloes on A&M Records.

Fuel – das sind Peter Miles, Damon Murray und Stephen Sorrell. Sie haben ihre Design-Gruppe 1990 noch als Studenten am Royal College of Art gegründet, wo sie die ersten vier Ausgaben ihrer Zeitschrift *Fuel* heraus-

PHOTOREAL DIGITAL CARS: METAL DESERT & METAL CI

Ray Giarratana / Digital Domain

The use of CG cars at Digital Domain was first employed as a technique in the Plymouth "Neon" automotive advertising campaign of 1996, which presented a number of playful "Neons" bouncing off of an unseen trampoline.
Conventional wisdom had the cars being shot practically, and then manipulated digitally; however, working for director Terry Windell of A Band Apart, visual effects supervisor Fred Raimondi came to the conclusion that the most artistic and cost-effective way to achieve this "effect" was to build and animate the cars digitally. Raimondi's thought process went something like this: "What does computer graphics do best? The answer: shiny metallic things. Ding—a car is a big shiny metallic thing, so it should be natural!" With this in mind, he brought CG supervisor Eric Barba and Digital Domain's Lightwave team on-board to recreate the photo-real look that was crucial to making the spot work. Relying on extremely high-resolution models, the team created all the textures, down to the safety-glass decal on the windows, that allow the viewer to distinguish reality from fiction—and, in this case, practical from CG. According to Raimondi, "lighting the cars became the key element in the process. When real cars are lit, they use a Fisher box, which actually isn't as much lighting the car as it is reflecting a big white card onto the car. So what we had the artists do was, instead of putting light sources over the car, we had them put a big white card over the car. We then light that card and, like magic, we had a great CG car." The basic concept of CG cars took its next step into the mainstream with Dodge "Time" and "Time 2." Using a technique similar to that employed in the "Neon" spot, director Terry Windell, this time paired with visual effects supervisor Ray Giarratana, had Eric Barba and his Lightwave team creating first, a Dodge Viper; and then, for "Time 2", two additional digital vehicles.
With the 1999 Pontiac campaign for GM and creative agency DMB & B, *Metal City* and *Metal Desert*, director Ray Giarratana sought to create a highly stylized and entirely CG environment with a photo-real CG car. In particular, the goal of this campaign was to create digital camera moves intended to "mime" the

Computeranimierte Autos wurden bei Digital Domain erstmals als Technik für die Plymouth-„Neon"-Werbekampagne des Jahres 1996 eingesetzt, als eine Anzahl verspielter „Neons" von eine unsichtbaren Trampolin hüpften.
Der konventionelle Ansatz sah vor, die Autos norm zu drehen und dann digital zu manipulieren; bei d Arbeit mit dem Regisseur Terry Windell von A Ban Apart allerdings kam der Visual-Effects-Supervisor Fred Raimondi zu dem Schluß, daß dieser „Effekt" am künstlerischsten wie kostengünstigsten zu erreichen wäre, wenn man die Autos zur Gänze digital baut und animiert.
Raimondis Gedankengänge waren etwa so: „Was kann die Computergrafik am besten? Antwort: Glänzende metallische Dinge darstellen. Pling! – E Auto ist ein großes glänzendes metallische Objekt deswegen müßte das ganz natürlich sein!"
Gesagt, getan – er holte Eric Barba als CG Supervisor und das Lightwave-Team von Digital Domain an Bord, um jenen fotorealistischen Look zu erzeugen, der für den Spot unerläßlich war. Mit Hilfe vo Modellen in extrem hoher Auflösung erstellte das Team alle Texturen, bis hin zum Sicherheitsglas-Aufkleber an den Fenstern, an denen der Seher no malerweise Realität von Fiktion unterschieden kann, beziehungsweise in diesem Fall Auto von Computergrafik. Laut Raimondi war „die Ausleuchtung der Autos das entscheidende Element im Produktionsprozeß. Wenn ein reales Auto fotografiert wird, dann erfolgt das in einer Fisher-Box, in der nicht so sehr der Wagen als vielmehr eine weiße Pappe beleuchtet wird, die dann vom Wage reflektiert wird. Anstatt also das Computermodell des Autos über Lichtquellen anzuleuchten, ließen wir die Künstler ebenfalls einen ‚weißen Karton' über das Fahrzeug legen. Dieser wurde dann ange strahlt – und wie durch Zauberei hatten wir ein großartiges CG-Auto."
Das Grundkonzept der CG-Autos wurde für Dodge „Time" und „Time 2" noch einen Schritt weiterentwickelt. Mit einer Technik, die jener des „Neon"-Spots ähnelte, ließ der Regisseur Terry Windell – diesmal im Team mit dem Visual-Effects-Supervisc Ray Giarratana – Eric Barba und seine Lightwave-Mannschaft zunächst einen Dodge Viper konstruieren, dann, für „Time 2", zwei weitere digitale Fahrzeuge.
Mit der 1999er Pontiac-Kampagne *Metal City* und *Metal Desert* für GM und die Kreativagentur DMB & B versuchte der Regisseur Ray Giarratana eine durchgestylte und ausschließlich computergrafische Umgebung um ein fotorealisisches CG-Auto zu bauen. Das Hauptziel bei dieser Kampagn war es, digitale Kamerabewegungen einzuführen, die die Charakteristiken einer „echten" Aufnahme

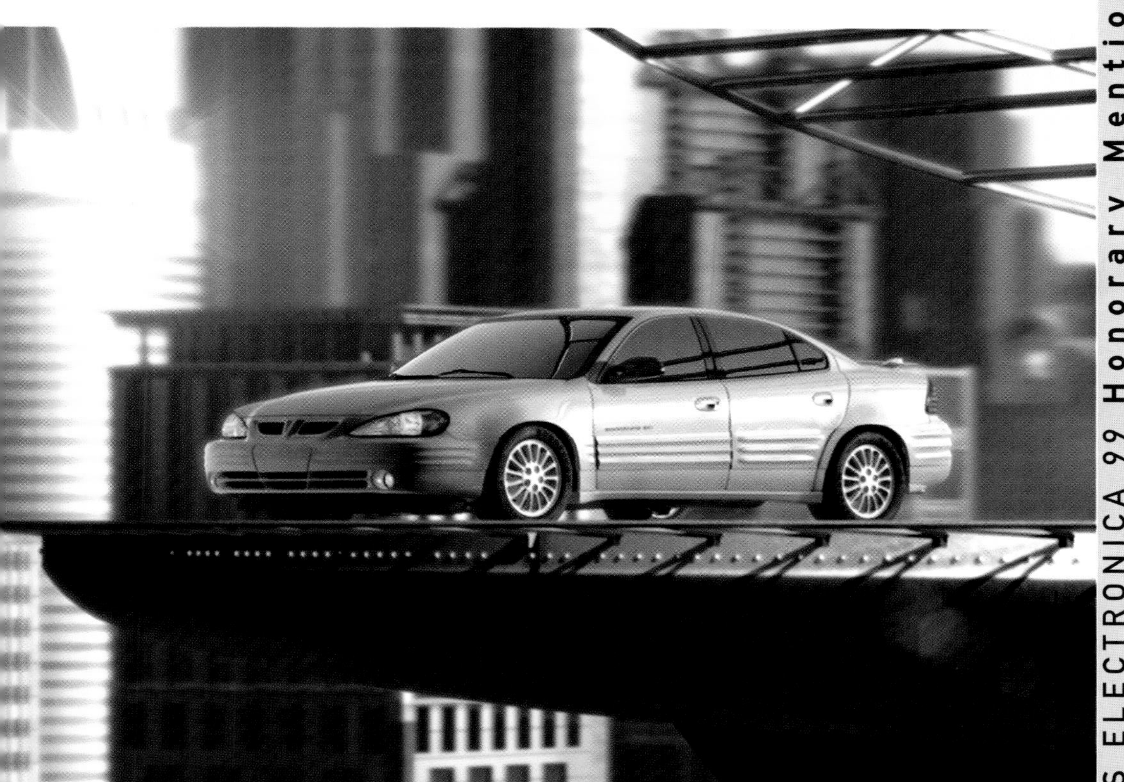

aracteristics of practical photography. In so doing, arratana, with digital director of photography Eric arba and CG Supervisor Wayne England, succeeded pushing the animation to the next level—tricking e viewer into believing that a practical vehicle had een shot and composited into a digital universe.

nis latest series of commercials is, in many respects, e culmination of the efforts of Digital Domain to ing CG cars to life; and perhaps, most importantly, ey represent the increased flexibility that digital naging provides in the creation of advertising nages.

imitieren. Dabei schaffte Giarratana es in Zusammenarbeit mit dem Leiter der digitalen Fotografie Eric Barba und dem GC Supervisor Wayne England, die Animation wiederum auf die nächsthöhere Entwicklungsebene zu heben: Dem Betrachter wird suggeriert, er sähe ein wirkliches Auto, das gefilmt und in ein digitales Universum hineinkomponiert wurde.

Diese neueste Serie von Werbespots ist in vieler Hinsicht der Gipfelpunkt der Bemühungen von Digital Domain, CG-Autos zum Leben zu bringen, und sie ist vor allem ein Beispiel für die gesteigerte Flexibilität, die durch die digitale Bildverarbeitung bei der Schaffung von Werbung möglich geworden ist.

Ray Giarratana (USA) is director and visual effects supervisor at Digital Domain. His responsibilities as director and/or visual effects supervisor have included advertising campaigns for Coca Cola (*Skydiver*, Panda *Picnic*), Budweiser (*Recycled Ants*, *Tongue Lashing*), for Mercedes Benz (*Rhinos*) and the visual effects for Michael Jackson's video *Ghost*. Ray Giarratana (USA) ist Regisseur und Visual Effects Supervisor bei Digital Domain. In seinen Verantwortungsbereich als Regisseur und/oder Visual Effects Supervisor fallen Werbekampagnen für Coca Cola (*Skydiver*, *Panda Picnic*), Budweiser (*Recycled Ants*, *Tongue Lashing*), für Mercedens Benz (*Rhinos*) sowie die Visual Effects für

NO WAY

Geoffrey Guiot / Bruno Lardé / Jerôme Maillot / Heure Exquis

In the fourth year of computer graphics studies at the Supinfocom the students are required to realize a film of several minutes in length using computer generated images.
Geoffrey Guiot had already thought of a story the year before, which centered around the idea of having real people act in a computer generated environment.
He was soon joined by Bruno Lardé and Jerôme Maillot (who was responsible for the post-apocalyptic atmosphere), and the team was complete.
The three started working in September 1997 and were soon granted permission to skip lectures. They met at Bruno's, where they had gathered their computers.
Geoffrey, who had already done several videos with Nicolas Carsel, brought him to the team to ensure the continuity of dialogue in the story.
Geoffrey was also the one who took care of all the filming. In addition, he made arrangements with the small community in the north of France, where he was living at the time, to let them use the community's multipurpose hall.
Work continued until June 1998. The filming, done with Hi8, was done parallel to montage. The team only had very limited resources available to them; they had no blue box, in particular, so extracting the images was very time-consuming.
When the work was presented to a jury of professors and professionals, it was awarded the highest marks and especially captured the attention of Emmanuel Prevost, the producer at Gaumont Multimedia. He was willing to produce the film, which had started as a video, and take it into cinema distribution.
During the summer and fall of 1998 Geoffrey and Emmanuel have been working on adapting the film for this purpose.

Im vierten Jahr der Computergrafik-Ausbildung a
der Supinfocom müssen die Studenten einen ein
Minuten langen Film mit computergenerierten B
dern realisieren.
Geoffrey Guiot hatte sich schon im Jahr zuvor ei
kurze Geschichte ausgedacht, wobei die zentrale
Idee darin bestand, echte Menschen in einer com
putergenerierten Umgebung agieren zu lassen.
Bald stießen Bruno Lardé und Jerôme Maillot (de
für die post-apokalyptische Atmosphäre verantwortlich ist) dazu, und das Team war komplett.
Im September 1997 begannen die drei mit ihrer A
beit, und sehr schnell wurde es ihnen gestattet,
Vorlesungen fern zu bleiben. Sie trafen sich also
Bruno, wo sie ihre Computer versammelt hatten
Geoffrey, der bereits einige Videos mit Nicolas
Carsel realisiert hatte, holte diesen in die Mann-
schaft, um die Dialogkontinuität der Geschichte
sicherzustellen.
Geoffrey war es auch, der sich um alle Aufnahme
kümmerte. Er erreichte es auch, daß die kleine Ge
meinde im Norden Frankreichs, in der er damals
wohnte, ihm die Mehrzweckhalle zur Verfügung
stellte.
Die Arbeit dauerte bis in den Juni 1998. Die Dreh
beiten, die mit Hi8 realisiert wurden, fanden para
lel zur Montage statt. Das Team verfügte nur übe
äußerst begrenzte Mittel, vor allem hatten sie ke
Blue Box, und deshalb war das Extrahieren der Bi
der besonders langwierig.
Als die Arbeit einer Jury aus Professoren und Pro
präsentiert wurde, erhielt sie die beste Note und
erregte vor allem die Aufmerksamkeit von Emma
nuel Prevost, dem Produzenten bei Gaumont Mu
media.
Letzterer war bereit, den Film, der als Video bego
nen hatte, zu produzieren, um ihn auch in den Ki
vertrieb nehmen zu können.
Sommer und Herbst 1998 waren Geoffrey und
Emmanuel damit beschäftigt, den Film für diese
Zweck zu adaptieren.

Geoffrey is currently working in a team with Nicolas as a director for video clips and commercials for Première Heure and Why Us. Bruno and Jerôme are professional computer graphics artists, who regularly work for Première Heure. ▬ Geoffrey arbeitet zur Zeit im Team mit Nicolas als Regisseur für Videoclips und Werbespots für Première Heure und Why Us. Bruno und Jerôme sind professionelle Computergrafiker geworden, die

ALARIS "ALIENS"

Juan Tomicic Muller / Daiquiri Spainbox

Two aliens, picking up samples of terrestrial life on earth, get confused by the new train between Madrid and Valencia and mistake the train for their own space-craft.
Created in 1999, this is an advertising spot for RENFE, the Spanish Railway Company.
The Daiquiri/Spainbox team, in charge of the post-production and 3D visual effects, computer generated almost all the elements of the spot: the aliens, the ladybird, the grass where it lands, the aliens' attack, the aliens' weapons and accessories, the railway station and the train in some shots.
The work has been implemented using Softimage, Maya and Alias software, plus a specially developed Daiquiri/Spainbox software for enhancing the response of the characters to light.
Compositing was done on Henry and Flame.

Zwei Außerirdische – gerade damit beschäftigt, Proben irdischen Lebens einzufangen – werden v neuen Schnellzug zwischen Madrid und Valencia verwirrt, weil sie ihn für ihr Raumschiff halten ...
Dieser 1999 geschaffene Kurzfilm ist ein Werbesp für die spanische Eisenbahngesellschaft RENFE.
Das Team von Daiquiri/Spainbox, das für die Post Production und die 3D-Visual Effects zuständig w hat fast alle Elemente des Werbespots auf dem Computer generiert: die Außerirdischen, den Marienkäfer, das Gras, auf dem er vor dem Eingre fen der Außerirdischen landet, die Waffen und Accessoires der Aliens, den Bahnhof und in einige Einstellungen auch den Zug.
Das Werk wurde mit Softimage, Maya und Alias generiert, dazu kam eine von Daiquiri/Spainbox selbst entwickelte Software, die die Reaktion der Charaktere auf Lichteffekte verbessert. Die Komp sitionsarbeit erfolgte auf Henry und Flame.

JUAN TOMICIC MULLER (E) STUDIED IN SANTIAGO DE CHILE AND IN BRUSSELS, WORKED ON COSTA GAVRAS PRODUCTIONS AND ALICE COOPER'S SOUTH AMERICAN TOUR, BECAME VISUAL EFFECTS DIRECTOR FOR RTL LUXEMBURG AND LATER FOR TELSON IN MADRID. AFTER 1987 HE BECAME A PARTNER IN VIDEOCAMINO IN MADRID AND FOUNDED THE POST-PRODUCTION COMPANY DAIQUIRI DIGITAL PICTURES WITH M. H. FERNANDEZ IN 1990 AND THE VISUAL EFFECTS COMPANY HD SPAINBOX IN 1992.

Juan Tomicic Muller (E) studierte in Santiago de Chile und Brüssel, arbeitete bei Produktionen von Costa Gavras und bei der Südamerika-Tour von Alice Cooper mit, wurde Visual Effects Director bei RTL Luxemburg und später bei TELSON in Madrid. Ab 1987 war er Teilhaber bei Videocamino in Madrid und gründete mit M. H. Fernandez 1990 das Postproduction-Unternehmen Daiquiri Digital Pictures sowie 1992 die Visual Effects Firma HD Spainbox.

VIRUS
Phil Tippett & Craig Hayes / Tippett Studio

Our entry consists of excerpts of our visual effects work for the 1998 Universal film *Virus*. *Virus* tells the story of a giant marauding, extraterrestrial lifeform that manifests itself aboard a Russian science vessel in an attempt to battle the human "virus" which struggles to prevail against it. Tippett Studio used computer graphic technologies to met the challenge of perfectly creating a CG version to match the full scale puppet of Goliath, this giant, complex, robot which was comprised of over eleven hundred parts. Many technologies were used to model, light, composite, and animate the subtle, yet powerful performance of Goliath, one of the most complex CG characters ever created. Tippett Studio was contacted halfway through principal photography to match the practical Puppet with the CG version. Craig Hayes supervised the visual effects and scrutinized the puppet, taking comprehensive measurements prior to commencing the complex and detailed model which even reflected the K-Y jelly and red food coloring smeared on the puppet. The Art Department worked up textures and surfaces for Goliath working with the programming department to develop a variety of shaders.
With all the moving parts there was the potential for Goliath to appear too busy, so we monitored the pantomime to insure that it kept looking like what it was—a multi-ton metal object charging around. Getting all the subtle little bits on sixteen-frame push-in shots of Goliath was a challenge, because we had to capture the live-action lighting precisely. Because the files were so huge, Julie Newdoll, our lighting supervisor spent weeks figuring out a way to render and light Goliath. Footage of the full-sized prop on set, while useful as lighting reference, often handicapped the animation as really huge things can't be choreographed very well.

Unsere Einreichung besteht aus den Visual Effect für den 1998 von Universal herausgebrachten Fil *Virus*. *Virus* erzählt die Geschichte einer riesigen marodierenden außerirdischen Lebensform, die a einem russischen wissenschaftlichen Raumschiff auftaucht, um den „menschlichen Virus" zu bekämpfen, der sich heftig gegen den Angriff wehr Tippett Studio hat alle Register der Computergra gezogen, um eine perfekte CG-Version zu schaffe die in allen Details der lebensgroßen Puppe des Goliath entspricht, einem riesigen komplexen Roboter, der aus über 1.100 Teilen besteht.
Viele Techniken wurden eingesetzt, um die subtil und doch machtvolle Figur des Goliath zu modell ren, zu beleuchten, einzubinden und animieren – eine der komplexesten CG-Figuren, die je geschaf fen wurden. Tippett Studio wurde etwa nach der Hälfte der Dreharbeiten kontaktiert, um die Pupp mit ihrer CG-Version in Einklang zu bringen. Craig Hayes hat die Visual Effects überwacht und die Puppe umfassend vermessen, bevor er mit dem Aufbau des komplexen und detaillierten Comput Modells begann, bei dem selbst die auf das Mod geschmierten Gel-Schichten und die rote Lebensmittelfarbe nachgebildet wurden. Das Art Department hat danach die Texturen und Oberflächen des Goliath ausgearbeitet, wobei in Zusammenarbeit mit der Programmierabteilung eine Anzahl von Schattierungsprogrammen entwickelt wurden.
Bei der Vielzahl von beweglichen Teilen bestand d Gefahr, daß der animierte Goliath allzu geschäfti wirken könnte, weshalb wir großes Augenmerk d auf gelegt haben, daß er als das erscheint, was er ist – ein mehrere Tonnen schweres herumtobend Metallobjekt. All die subtilen Details der 16-Kader Einschub-Aufahmen nachzustellen war eine schwierige Aufgabe, weil wir die Lichteffekte der Live-Action-Aufnahmen genau reproduzieren mu ten. Da die Datenmenge ins Riesenhafte anwuch verbrachte unsere Beleuchtungs-Supervisorin Jul Newdoll Wochen damit, eine Möglichkeit der Beleuchtung und des Renderings für Golia auszuarbeiten. Die Live-Aufnahmen der Requisite am Set waren zwar einerseits als Lichtreferenz wichtig, andererseits haben sie die Animation oft behindert, weil so riesige Dinge nicht unbedingt leicht zu choreografieren sind.

TIPPETT STUDIO
picture: VIRUS page 1 of 1
part: vGoliath r20, front
date: 971015 scale: 1:15 D. Woolsey

en our challenge was to composite the CG Goliath odel, matching the look of surrounding shots that ere filmed with an animatronic creature equipped th strobe lights, laser beams, and a spot light on s head. First, each shot required creating 2D light ams and strobe flashes, which interactively lit the nders and the plate. Then, we used CG and photo- aphic elements—dust, steam, fire and even electric cs to make the shots convincing and for dynamic fect.

Unsere nächste Herausforderung war die Einbindung des CG-Goliath-Modells in die Live-Aufnahmen, wobei wir eine Übereinstimmung mit der mit Stroboskoplicht, Laserstrahlen und einem Spotscheinwerfer auf dem Kopf ausgestatteten Puppe erzielen mußten. Zuerst wurden für jede Einstellung 2D-Lichtstrahlen und Stroboskop-Blitze gestaltet, die interaktiv die gerenderten Kader ausleuchteten, dann setzten wir computergenerierte und fotografische Elemente ein – Staub, Dampf, Feuer und sogar elektrische Lichtbögen –, um die Aufnahmen überzeugend und dynamisch wirken zu lassen.

PHIL TIPPETT (USA), FOUNDER OF BERKELEY-BASED TIPPETT STUDIO, IS A DIRECTOR OF ANIMATION AND PRODUCER OF VISUAL EFFECTS. HE WAS, AMONGST OTHERS, RESPONSIBLE FOR COMPUTER ANIMATION IN *STAR WARS*, *JURASSIC PARK* AND *ROBOCOP*. HE HAS RECEIVED TWO ACADEMY AWARDS FOR *THE RETURN OF THE JEDI* AND FOR *JURASSIC PARK*. CRAIG HAYES (USA) IS AN ACADEMY AWARD-WINNING SPECIAL EFFECTS SUPERVISOR, ART DIRECTOR AND PARTNER AT TIPPETT STUDIO. FOR *JURASSIC PARK* HE DEVELOPED THE REVOLUTIONARY "DID" (DIGITAL INPUT DEVICE).

Phil Tippett (USA), Gründer des Tippett Studio (Berkeley, Kalifornien), ist Regisseur für Animationen und Produzent von Visual Effects. Er war unter anderem für die Computeranimationen in *Star Wars*, *Jurassic Park* und *Robocop* verantwortlich. Für *Rückkehr des Jedi* und für *Jurassic Park* hat er jeweils einen Oscar erhalten. Oscar-Preisträger Craig Hayes (USA) ist Special Effects Supersvisor, Art Director und Partner bei Tippett Studio. Für *Jurassic Parc* hat er das revolutionäre „DID"

prix ars electronica 99

.NET
INTERACTIVE ART
COMPUTER ANIMATION
VISUAL EFFECTS
DIGITAL MUSICS
u19/CYBERGENERATION

Kodwo Eshun

MUSIC FROM THE BEDROOM STUDIOS

Musik aus dem Schlafzimmerstudio

In 1996, the composer Bob Ostertag pointed to the paradox that had driven the Prix Ars Electronica for Computer Music to a point of crisis: "... as computers' presence in music has mushroomed from nearly invisible to downright unavoidable, so the range of music considered to be Computer Music has become increasingly fixed and rigid. Why this emergence of Computer Music, instead of an openness to all the musics which computers make possible?"

1996 wies der Komponist Bob Ostertag auf das Paradoxon hin, das den Prix Ars Electronica für Computermusik an einen Krisenpunkt geführt hatte: „Während sich der Computer in der Musik vom unsichtbaren zum geradezu unvermeidbaren Handwerkszeug entwickelt hat, ist das Spektrum jener Musik, die als Computermusik betrachtet wird, zunehmend rigid und festgefahren geworden. Wie kommt es zur Entstehung einer ‚Computermusik' anstatt einer Offenheit sämtlichen durch Computer ermöglichten Musikarten gegenüber?"

Changing the Prix Category from Computer Music to Digital Musics acknowledges this "openness to all the musics which computers make possible." Focusing on digital innovation, the 1999 Jury embarked on a mission to immerse itself in the soundworlds of 720 entries. We listened eagerly for new ways of listening. Nothing would have pleased us more than to hear the new Todd Dockstader or the new Bernard Parmegiani, but the vast bulk of electroacoustic and acousmatic entries showed no such iconoclasm. As the judge and composer Laetitia Sonami said, "There's a certain arrogance that comes with the language which says that to be recognised you have to follow that language and nobody questions it. There's no self regeneration. Because it's an academic world , it can live on its own. In this case, there's no commercial imperative, so you can keep this kind of bubble going."

Like a Cavalier king only too aware of the new dispensation, the ancien regime of electroacoustic music has automatically assumed a noblesse oblige for itself, awarding itself an undeserved authority at the cost of cultural irrelevance. But Sonami's argument applies across the board; there was just as

Die Änderung der Kategorie des Prix Ars Electro von „Computermusik" zu „Digitaler Musik" anerkennt diese „Offenheit gegenüber sämtlichen d Computer ermöglichten Musikarten". Mit dem Schwerpunkt auf digitaler Innovation ist die Jur des Jahres 1999 aufgebrochen, in die Klangwelt von 720 Einreichungen einzutauchen. Wir haben aufmerksam nach neuen Formen des Hörens gelauscht, und nichts hätte uns mehr gefreut, als neuen Todd Dockstader oder den neuen Bernard Parmegiani zu hören – allein, die große Menge e troakustischer und akusmatischer Einreichunge zeigte keine solchen Ikonoklasmen. Die Jurorin u Komponistin Laetitia Sonami stellte fest: „Es lieg eine gewisse Arroganz in der Ausdrucksweise, d da behauptet, um anerkannt zu werden, müsse man dieser Ausdrucksweise folgen, und nieman hinterfragt das. Es gibt keine Selbstregeneriereu und weil es eine akademische Welt ist, kann sie und in sich selbst leben. In diesem Fall gibt es ke nen kommerziellen Imperativ, und deswegen ha sich diese Art von Blasen weiter am Leben."

Wie ein König, der sich seines Gottesgnadentun nur zu sehr bewußt ist, hat das *Ancien Régime* d

much formulaic music produced outside academia as inside. Today, graphical software packages such as GRM Tools or SoundHack with their menu upon menu of options enthrall producers, generating a situation where the track and the composition become a predictable outcome of programmes like SuperCollider. This year's Jury included the producer-engineers Jim O'Rourke and Robin Rimbaud aka Scanner, both of whom were especially attuned to digital transparency where signature sounds are directly attributable to particular software.

Many entries, for example relied on digital signal processing. The gorgeous shuttling, tumbling, shingling sound of GRM Shuffler VST mode was heard repeatedly. "I'm getting allergic to people processing things just because they can," O' Rourke complained more than once. "It doesn't matter what they put in at point A because it's just the sound of the process." On the one hand the proliferation of software has a democratizing effect. Because the late 90s minimal techno producer uses the same software in his bedroom studio as an acousmatic composer at her university studio, both become digital musicians, Powerbook composers.

On the other hand, the latest GRM upgrade matters less than a distinctive sonic thought process. So the approaches to the virtual studio become even more crucial and the clash between ways of hearing becomes a battle between the noises of art and the musics of sound.

In its gleeful glide between horror n' humour, its split second slide between a grin and a groan, the Jury recognised a new digital aesthetic in the music video *Come to Daddy*, unanimously awarding the Golden Nica to its English video director Chris Cunningham and the influential English electronic producer Richard James/Aphex Twin. Filmed on Thamesmead Estate in South East London where Stanley Kubrick shot *Clockwork Orange*, *Come to Daddy* is the first in Cunningham's classic trilogy of videos, followed by 1998's superkinetic Squarepusher video *C'mon my Selector* and 1999's ultralascivious *Windowlicker* video, again for Aphex Twin. The Cunningham-James collaboration is characterised by what composer-conductor Naut Humon calls a sound driven aesthetic of extreme digital mutation, one which speaks to the artificial in us, as it veers from micro engineered rapid-edit rhythms to brutalizing psychotic music with a visceral virtuosity.

elektroakustischen Musik eine Noblesse-oblige-Attitüde um ihrer selbst willen eingenommen und sich eine unverdiente Autorität beigemessen, auf die Gefahr hin, in kultureller Irrelevanz zu versinken. Aber Sonamis Argument trifft auch auf andere Bereiche zu: Es gab genauso viel formelhafte Musik außerhalb wie innerhalb der Akademien. Die heutigen grafischen Software-Werkzeuge wie GRM Tools oder Soundhack verlocken die Produzenten mit ihren unzähligen Menüs voller Optionen; sie führen dazu, daß die Komposition und die Tonspur vorhersagbar werden und sich nicht mehr von dem unterscheiden, was ein Programm wie SuperCollider hervorbringt. Der diesjährigen Jury gehörten die beiden Produzenten und Toningenieure Tim O'Rourke und Robin Rimbaud aka Scanner an, die beide ganz besonders empfindsam sind für eine digitale Transparenz, in der die einzelnen Klangsignaturen ohne weiteres einer bestimmten Software zuzuordnen sind.

Viele Einreichungen basierten zum Beispiel auf digitaler Signalverarbeitung. Der großartige schüttelnde, purzelnde, klingelnde Klang des GRM Shuffler VST-Mode war immer und immer wieder zu hören. „Ich werde allergisch gegen Leute, die einfach Dinge bearbeiten, bloß weil sie das eben können", hat O'Rourke sich mehr als einmal beschwert. „Es ist egal, was sie am Punkt A einsetzen, weil ohnehin nur der Prozeßklang übrig bleibt." Die Verbreitung der Software hat nun einerseits einen demokratisierenden Effekt: Wenn am Ende der 90er Jahre ein kleiner Techno-Produzent in seinem Mini-Studio in der Garçonniere die gleiche Software verwendet wie eine akusmatische Komponistin in ihrem Universitätsstudio, so werden beide digitale Musiker, Powerbook-Komponisten.

Andererseits ist das letzte GRM-Upgrade weniger wichtig als ein eindeutiger klanglicher Denkprozeß, und deswegen wird die Art und Weise, wie man sich dem digitalen Studio nähert, immer entscheidender, und das Aufeinanderprallen zwischen verschiedenen Arten des Hörens wird eher zu einer Schlacht zwischen den Geräuschen der Kunst und der Musik des Klangs.

In seinem fidelen Hin und Her zwischen Horror und Humor, in den Bruchteilen von Sekunden, die zwischen Grinsen und Grausen standen, hat die Jury im Musikvideo *Come to Daddy* eine neue digitale Ästhetik entdeckt und die Goldene Nica einstimmig seinem englischen Video-Regisseur Chris Cunningham und dem einflußreichen englischen Elektronik-Produzenten Richard James / Aphex Twin zuerkannt. *Come to Daddy* – aufgenommen im Thamesmead-Areal in South East London, wo Stanley Kubrick sein *Uhrwerk Orange* gedreht hat – ist der erste Teil von Cunninghams klassischer Video-Trilogie, gefolgt vom superkinetischen Squarepusher-Video *C'mon my Selector* (1998) und dem überaus lasziven *Windowlicker*-Video (1999), ebenfalls für Aphex Twin. Die Zusammenarbeit von Cunningham und James läßt sich durch das charakterisieren, was der Komponist und Dirigent Naut

When programmes become immediately recognisable, it's easy to hear how the software is manipulating its user. A key approach in 90s digital music obstructs this tendency by amplifying the point of breakdown into a new digital irritainment, an immanent disobedience that maximises the moment when the CPU reaches 100% and your Powerbook crashes. Back in the 60s, Hendrix exploited the immanent potential of the guitar feeding back through the amps, turning the noise of destruction into art. Today's Powerbook composers are doing the same as they turn electronic catastrophe into music, training us to enjoy the sound of failure and the art of the accident.

"What I like is when digital doesn't work," says Robin Rimbaud. Across the audio-spectrum, producers are arranging digital error into new granular synthetic tones, turning accidents into new texturhythms, opening all the sound files until the graphic user interface gives up the ghost. This tendency was pioneered by Aphex Twin and by the winners of the 1999 Distinction: Vienna's Mego label. Rather than splitting the prize between the two Mego entries: Christian Fennesz's *Hotel Parall.lel* and Pita aka Peter Rehberg's *Seven Tons for Free Remaster Version 1.2*, the Jury broke with Ars Electronica convention, agreeing with O' Rourke's suggestion that the Distinction should be awarded to the Mego label as a whole.

Sonically speaking Rehberg's *Seven Tons for Free Remaster Ver.1.2* consists of pulsing, hissing, flapping sinewave tones, arranged on an early 8 bit 520 Powerbook. In the *Hotel Paral.lel* CD you hear a micro-pulsing variation where sounds transform in and out of recognition, pulling you in and out of perceptual focus. A tinny guitar becomes a scratch which blurts into an ear shredding sinewave that modulates into high pitched whines that become a new kind of brand new improved tinnitus. Since the mid 90s, Mego has defined what O'Rourke calls a "brand new punk computer music, a punk aesthetic, like do it yourself, press your own records, get your own distribution going."

They achieved this firstly by mutating the real-time sinewave synthesis strategies familiar from academic computer music, and secondly "by taking it out of the context of art music as O' Rourke argued, a move "that should be recognised just as much as the music." As Robin Rimbaud explained, "There's a recognition of a wider world, where I get the feeling

Humon eine „klanggesteuerte Ästhetik der extremen Mutation" nennt, eine Ästhetik, die das Artifizielle in uns anspricht, während sie von mikro technisch konstruierten Rhythmen in eine brutalisierende psychotische Musik mit einer Virtuosität aus dem Bauch heraus übergeht.

Wenn Programme unmittelbar erkennbar werden, ist es nicht weiter schwierig herauszuhören, wie di Software ihren Anwender manipuliert. Einer der Schlüsselansätze der 90er Jahre blockiert diese Tendenz, indem der Punkt des Zusammenbruchs ir ein neue digitale anhaltende Irritation umgewandelt wird, in eine immanente Unfolgsamkeit, die jenen Moment maximiert, an dem der Prozessor seine 100prozentige Auslastung erreicht und das Powerbook abstürzt. In den 60ern erforschte Jimi Hendrix das immanente Potential der Gitarrenrüc kopplung durch den Verstärker, indem der das Geräusch der Destruktion zur Kunst erhob. Die heu tigen Powerbook-Komponisten machen das gleich indem sie die elektronische Katastrophe in Musik verwandeln und uns dazu bringen, den Klang des Versagens, die Kunst des Unfalls zu genießen.

„Mir gefällt es, wenn das Digitale nicht funktioniert", sagt Robin Rimbaud. Quer durch das Audio-Spektrum arrangieren Produzenten digitale Irrtümer in neue körnige synthetische Töne, verwandeln Un- und Zufälle in rhythmische Texturen öffnen alle Sound-Files, bis die grafische Benutzeroberfläche den Geist aufgibt. Vorreiter dieser Tendenz waren Aphex Twin und die Preisträger de diesjährigen Auszeichnung: das Wiener Mego-Lab Anstatt den Preis zwischen den beiden Mego-Einreichungen *Hotel Parall.lel* von Christian Fenne und Pitas – d. h. Peter Rehbergs – *Seven Tons for Fr Remaster/Version 1.2* aufzuteilen, hat die Jury mit den Konventionen des Prix Ars Electronica gebrochen und sich O'Rourkes Vorschlag angeschlosser die Auszeichnung dem Mego-Label als ganzem zuzuerkennen.

Klanglich gesehen besteht Peter Rehbergs *Seven Tons for Free Remaster/Version 1.2* aus pulsierende zischenden, klappenden Sinuswellen-Tönen, die a einem frühen 8-bit 520er Powerbook arrangiert werden. Auf der *Hotel Paral.lel*-CD hört man eine mikropulsierende Variation, in der die Klänge sich das und aus dem Erkennbaren bewegen und um den Wahrnehmungspunkt des Hörers verschiebe Eine blecherne Gitarre wird zu einem Kratzen, da in eine trommelfellsprengende Sinuswelle ausbricht, die bis zu einem hochtönenden Geheul ansteigt, das zu einer neuen Art allerneuesten ve besserten Tinnitus wird. Seit Mitte der 90er Jahre hat Mego das definiert, was O'Rourke „eine ganz neue Punk-Computermusik" nennt, eine „Punk-Ästhetik des Do-it-yourself: Presse deine eigenen Platten und bring deine eigene Distribution in Gang".

Dies erzielten sie erstens durch eine Mutation de Echtzeit-Sinuswellensynthese-Strategien, die ma aus der akademischen Computermusik kennt, ur zweitens dadurch, „daß sie das aus dem Zusam-

vith electroacoustic music that there's nothing utside it."

he second Distinction unanimously went to the eteran New York based Japanese composer Ikue Aori for *Birth Days*, her stunning 3 part Alesis drum nachine suite. Performed live, Mori's virtuosity nables her to draw cross- and counter olyrhythmelodies from the most basic factory resets, arranging these into an enchanting udiomaze of a composition. Mori's rhythmatic vizardry underlined the extent to which rhythm emains the next frontier for Ars Electronica in 2000 nd beyond.

pproaching producers from the overlapping worlds f turntabilization, hiphop,and electronica for the 999 Prix, the judges encountered a spectrum of esistance ranging from indifference to antagonism. ears of insularity have created the sense that Prix rs Electronica was no different from the Bourges estival, another elite competition in which composers award prizes to other composers.

nd so an influential duo like Autechre would not be noved, insisting there was nothing special about vhat they did. Such extreme self-deprecation conrasted with the majority of entries where, inadvertntly or deliberately, compositional statements often ecame an alibi for underwhelming music. Complex xplanations detailing how MetaSynth software canned visual data to generate audio often raised opes which their music failed to satisfy. O'Rourke poke for the Jury when he noted that "If somebody nakes a big deal about where they're coming from nd then I don't hear it then I'm gonna hold it gainst them." Separated from its program, much cousmatic music sounded indistinguishable from Hollywood sound design but drained of the drama f, for example, John Frizzell's music for *Alien esurrection*.

he key exception here was Montreal based artists ollective The User. Their manifesto succinctly explained how their *Symphony for Dot Matrix Printers* eshapes "ambient technology" into a "musical tructure that" doubles as "a critique of technology" n the form of a parody of an archetypal office unit. rchitect Thomas Macintosh and composer Emanuel Aaden's *Symphony for Dot Matrix Printers* impressed he Jury enough to earn an Honorary Mention. "Dot natrix printers," they explain, "are turned into nusical 'instruments' while a computer network

menhang der Kunst-Musik gerissen haben", wie O'Rourke argumentiert hat, ein „Schachzug, der als solcher ebenso anerkannt werden muß wie die Musik." Robin Rimbaud erklärte: „Sie erkennen darin eine größere Welt an, während ich sonst bei der elektroakustischen Musik immer den Eindruck bekomme, außerhalb gäbe es nichts."

Die zweite Anerkennung ging einstimmig an die in New York beheimatete japanischen Komponisten-Veteranin Ikue Mori für *Birth Days*, ihre beeindruckende dreiteilige Suite für Alesis drum Machine. Live vorgetragen, gelingt es Mori dank ihrer Virtuosität, aus den einfachsten Werks-Voreinstellungen einander kreuzende und gegenläufige „Polyrhythmelodien" zu generieren und diese in einen bezaubernden Kompositions-Audio-Irrgarten zu arrangieren. Moris rhythmische Zauberei unterstreicht einmal mehr, in welchem Maße der Rhythmus die Herausforderung der Ars Electronica im Jahr 2000 und darüber hinaus sein wird.

Als die Jury-Mitglieder Produzenten aus den einander überschneidenden Welten von Plattentellerdrehern, Hiphop und Electronica auf den Prix 99 ansprachen, begegneten sie einem Spektrum des Widerstands, das von Indifferenz bis zur offenen Ablehnung reichte. Jahre des Inseldaseins haben den Eindruck hervorgerufen, der Prix Ars Electronica unterscheide sich in keiner Weise vom Festival von Bourges, auch so einem Elite-Wettbewerb, wo Komponisten anderen Komponisten die Preise zuerkennen.

Und so konnte ein einflußreiches Duo wie Autechre nicht überzeugt werden, weil sie darauf bestanden, daß an dem, was sie tun, nichts Besonderes sei. Solch eine extreme Selbstabwertung kontrastiert allerdings mit der Mehrheit der Einreichungen, bei denen – bewußt oder unbewußt – die kompositorischen Begleitnotizen oft als Alibi für eine eher „unterzeugende" Musik herhalten mußten. Komplexe Erklärungen, die detailliert darlegen, wie die MetaSynth-Software visuelle Daten scannt, um ein Audio-Produkt zu erzeugen, erweckten häufig Hoffnungen, die die Musik dann in keiner Weise befriedigte. O'Rourke hat die Meinung der gesamten Jury ausgedrückt, als er bemerkte: „Wenn jemand großes Getue darum macht, woher er kommt, und ich das aber nicht hören kann, dann ist das für mich ein Argument gegen ihn." Wenn man die akusmatische Musik getrennt von ihrem Programm hernahm, war sie oft nicht vom Sound-Design à la Hollywood zu unterscheiden – mit dem einen Unterschied, daß ihr die Dramatik von – beispielsweise – John Rizzells Musik zu *Alien Resurrection* fehlte.

Die wichtigste Ausnahme war hier das in Montreal beheimatete Künstlerkollektiv The User. Ihr Manifest erklärte kurz und bündig, wie ihre *Symphony for Dot Matrix Printers* die „Ambient-Technologie" in eine „musikalische Struktur umsetzt", die gleichzeitig als „Technologiekritik" in Form einer Parodie auf die archetypische Büroeinheit auftritt. Die *Symphony for Dot Matrix Printers* des Architekten Thomas

system, typical of a contemporary office becomes the 'orchestra' used to play them. The orchestra is 'conducted' by a network server which reads from a composed 'score'." Not only did their ideas amplify their project; more importantly their installation overcame the decontextualizing effect of the video player, an effect which fatally drained all the other pieces of their site specific impact.

Late 90s digital music tends towards the pragmatic rather than programmatic. Programmatic statements are disguised; a misspelling like Mego group Farmers Manual album title *fsck* or Mouse on Mars compositions such as *X-Flies* or *Tamagnocchi* says as much as any manifesto. In fact a misspelling that makes you disbelieve your eyes is an entire manifesto, one compressed and abbreviated, encrypted and delivered under the Trojan Horse of derision and sarcasm.

Of the 12 Honorary Mentions, the Jury was especially pleased to award an Honorary Mention to Berlin producer Stefan Betke for his *Pole* project. *Pole* uses the simple Waldorf filter to generate the mesmerising pop, crackle and snap of his *Pole 2* CD. The implied rhythm of its enwombing bass skank acknowledges and extends the massively influential techno-dub continuum pioneered by Berlin's Basic Channel/ Chain Reaction label throughout the 90s.

Cologne duo Mouse on Mars—electronic composers Jan St Werner and Andi Toma—earned an Honorary Mention for the bewitching micro-engineered texturhythms of their sumptuous 1997 album *Autoditacker*. Emotionally, Mouse on Mars exemplify the joy of a toy, what another Honorary Mention, the electroacoustic composer Rose Dodd termed *kinderspel*, the animistic life of toys in a child's playroom. Their melodies spangled and twinkled, wriggled and burst. Like the younger hypermelodic sister to *Hotel Paral.lel*, *Autoditacker's* restless variation reveled in insectile complexity. Running too much information through the inputs produces the bursting effect of frictional forms in ceaseless life.

German producer Bernhard Günter's suite *The Ant Moves/The Black and Yellow Carcass/ A little Closer* was another popular choice for an Honorary Mention. As Robin Rimbaud pointed out, "He influenced an awful lot of compositions that have happened in the last 5 or 6 years." The extreme quietness of Günter's microsonic pieces demanded an extreme concentration to the processed natural

Macintosh und des Komponisten Emanuel Made beeindruckte die Jury hinreichend, um eine Anerkennung zu verdienen. „Nadeldrucker", so erkläre sie, „werden in musikalische ‚Instrumente' verwa delt, während ein Computernetzwerk – typisch f das Büro der Gegenwart – zum ‚Orchester' wird, diese Instrumente spielt. Das ‚Orchester' wird vo einem Netzwerk-Server ‚geleitet', der von einer komponierten ‚Partitur' abliest." Ihre Ideen habe nicht nur ihr Projekt verstärkt, sondern ihre Insta tion überwand auch den dekontextualisierenden Effekt des Video-Abspielgeräts, der alle anderen Stücke ihres spezifischen Eindrucks beraubt hat.

Die digitale Musik der späten 90er Jahre neigt dazu, eher pragmatisch als programmatisch zu s Programmatische Bezüge werden getarnt; ein „Schreibfehler" wie im Album-Titel *fsck* der Mego Gruppe Farmers Manual, oder „Mouse on Mars"-Kompositionen wie *X-Flies* oder *Tamagnocchi* sag ebensoviel aus wie ein Manifest. Eine bewußte Falschschreibung, die dich deinen Augen nicht mehr trauen läßt, ist ein komplettes Manifest, ko primiert und abgekürzt, verschlüsselt und als Trojanisches Pferd voller Spott und Sarkasmus hi terlassen.

Die Jury freute sich besonders, eine der zwölf Anerkennungen dem Berliner Produzenten Stefa Betke für sein *Pole*-Projekt zuzuerkennen. *Pole* ve wendet den simplen Waldorf-Filter, um das fast hypnotisierende Ploppen, Knacken und Klicken se ner *Pole 2*-CD zu erzeugen. Der implizite Rhythm seines einhüllenden Basses anerkennt und erwei tert jenes sehr einflußreiche Techno-Dub-Kontinuum, das das Berliner Label Basic Channel / Ch Reaction durch die ganzen 90er Jahre vertreten

Das Kölner Duo Mouse on Mars – die elektronischen Komponisten Jan St. Werner und Andi Tom erhielten eine Anerkennung für die bezaubernde mikrotechnischen Strukturhythmen ihres aufwe digen Albums *Autoditacker* (1997). Emotional ges hen, demonstrieren Mouse on Mars exemplarisc die Freude am Spielzeug oder, wie eine andere Anerkennungspreisträgerin – die elektroakustisc Komponistin Rose Dodd – es ausgedrückt hat, an „Kinderzimmer", am Eigenleben des Spielzeugs i Spielraum eines Kindes. Ihre Melodien sprühten und funkelten, wandten sich und explodierten. W ein jüngerer hypermelodischer Bruder von *Hotel Paral.lel* schwelgte *Autoditakers* rastlose Variatior der Komplexität eines Ameisenhaufens. Wenn zu viel Information durch den Input gejagt wird, füh das zum explodierenden Effekt der Reibungsform in einem nie endenden Leben.

Die Suite des deutschen Produzenten Bernhard Günter, *The Ant Moves / The Black and Yellow Carcass / A little Closer*, fand ebenfalls Anklang und wurde mit einer Anerkennung bedacht. Robin Rimbaud: „Er hat eine Vielzahl von Kompositione beeinflußt, die in den letzten fünf oder sechs Jah entstanden sind." Die extreme Ruhe von Günters mikroklanglichen Stücken erforderte eine besonc

unds occurring at the far edge of hearing. Listen-g to the act of listening, your attention zoomed to the electronics of everyday life, the hums of diators, the tock of clocks. At micro-perceptible vels, the borders between silence and accident came porous. At one point O'Rourke asked Naut umon to turn off his Power Book and the sonic ents obscured by the machine's hum loomed idibly into earshot.

the other extreme, composer Zbiegniew Karkow-i's and Masami Akita's (Merzbow) *Metabolic Speed rception* used the granular Internet sounds of Dial- Connection to generate a riverrun of harmonic ertones in the noise tradition of Merzbow and Lou ed's Metal Machine Music. Like many composers, rkowski and Akita used the internal sounds of ftware, but unlike them, knowing this only added the fascination of their music.

gital processes generate new kinds of chaos; usic organizes this into what Felix Guattari termed chaosmos. 1999 was the year in which the Prix Ars ectronica heard the chaosmos, the year in which nger and unknowing returned to the unstable edia of digital musics.

re Konzentration auf die bearbeiteten Naturklänge, die am äußersten Ende des Hörbereichs angesiedelt sind. Wenn man dem Akt des Zuhörens zuhörte, so versank die eigenen Aufmerksamkeit in die Elektronik des Alltags, ins Summen der Radiatoren, ins Ticken der Uhren. Auf der Ebene der Mikro-Wahrnehmung wurden die Grenzen zwischen Stille und Zufälligkeit plötzlich durchlässig. Irgendwann ersuchte O'Rourke Naut Humon, doch sein Powerbook abzudrehen, und plötzlich sprangen die bisher vom leisen Summen der Maschine übertönten Klangereignisse in den Bereich des gut Hörbaren.

Am anderen Extrem verwendete *Metabolic Speed Perception* der Komponisten Zbiegniew Karkowski und Masami Akita (Merzbow) die granulären Internet-Klänge von Einwählverbindungen, um einen Fluß harmonischer Obertöne zu generieren, die in der Geräuschtradition von Merzbow und Lou Reeds „Metal Machine"-Musik stehen. Wie viele andere Komponisten verwendeten auch sie die internen Klänge der Software, aber anders als bei den meisten erhöhte dieses Wissen in diesem Fall die Faszination ihrer Musik.

Digitale Prozesse generieren neue Formen des Chaos; die Musik organisiert dies zu dem, was Felix Guattari „Chaosmos" genannt hat. Das Jahr 1999 war jenes, in dem der Prix Ars Electronica den Chaosmos gehört hat, das Jahr, in dem die Gefahr, das Unbekannte in das instabile Medium der digitalen Musik zurückgefunden hat.

COME TO DADDY

Aphex Twin (Richard D. James) / Chris Cunningham

Chris Cunningham was commissioned by Warp Records to write and direct the video for Aphex Twin's acclaimed *Come To Daddy* – the monstrous and indeed hilarious take on Prodigy-esque type music. *Come To Daddy* is the second video Cunningham has made for Warp, the first being Autechre's brooding *Second bad Vilbel*. After noting the extent of Cunningham's talent and taking into account the fact he was a massive Aphex Twin fan, he was the obvious man for the job.

Set on a run down East London council estate, where little old ladies and their dogs barely dare to roam, and evil techno spirits contort and explode from trashed TV sets, a gang of seemingly innocent children (who all turn out to be the spawn of the Twin's evil spirit – all bearing his bearded good looks) run riot through the estate, fighting and hurling whatever they can pick up at each other. "It's one of those videos where, if you can manage to see it, you can understand why it hasn't been on the telly much.

"It's a rush, this video," says James, slouching in Cunningham's Soho office. "It gets my ticker going. I don't think it's perverted. It's normal. It's only perverted if you're a lightweight."

"Usually I get sent tracks I hate," interjects Cunningham, "but I wrote this one in five minutes."

Select Magazine December 1997

Chris Cunningham erhielt von Warp Records den Auftrag, für Aphex Twins hochgelobtes *Come To Daddy* – jene monströse und dennoch fröhliche Persiflage der Musik vom „Prodigy"-Typ – ein Video zu schreiben und zu produzieren. *Come To Daddy* ist nach dem Streifen für Autechres *Second bad Vilbel* Cunninghams zweites Video für Warp. Neben Cunninghams offensichtlichem Talent machte ihn vor allem die Tatsache, selbst Aphex-Twin-Fan zu sein, zum idealen Mann für diesen Auftrag. Die Szenerie ist ein Gemeindebau im östlichen London, wo kleine alte Damen und ihre Hündchen sich kaum herumzustreifen getrauen und wo böse Techno-Geister aus weggeworfenen Fernsehapparaten ausbrechen. Dort treibt sich eine Bande scheinbar unschuldiger Kinder herum (die sich bald als Inkarnation der bösen Geister des Twins erweisen und auch sein Aussehen haben), sie ras wie wildgeworden durch die Anlagen, kämpfen u bewerfen sich gegenseitig mit allem, was ihnen unterkommt. „Es ist eines von jenen Videos, bei denen man – sofern man sie überhaupt zu sehe bekommt – verstehen kann, warum sie nicht öft in der Glotze zu sehen sind."

„Es ist absolut rasant, dieses Video", sagt James, in Cunninghams Büro in Soho herumhängt. „Es bringt mich richtig auf Touren. Ich glaube nicht, es pervers ist. Es ist normal. Pervers ist es nur, we du selbst ein Leichtgewicht bist."

„Normalerweise schickt man mir immer Bänder, ich nicht leiden kann", wirft Cunningham ein, „a das Buch für dieses hier habe ich in fünf Minute geschrieben."

Select Magazine Dezember 1997

Chris Cunningham's career as a music video director began in 1995 when he hooked up with the techno band Autechre and persuaded them to let him direct their promo. The piece was selected best low budget video by Music Week 1995. In August 1997 Chris collaborated with Richard D. James (the Aphex Twin) and directed the video for the single *Come to Daddy*. The video has since won a plethora of awards. Richard D. James (Aphex Twin) comes from a mining family in Cornwall. At an early age he became interested in electronics and attended courses. Today he is proud of having his studio in his bedroom. He loves to present himself as a "nice Cornish lad."

Chris Cunninghams Karriere als Musik-Video-Regisseur begann 1995, als er sich mit der Techno-Band Autechre zusammentat und sie überredete, ihn ihr Promotion-Video machen zu lassen. Das Stück wurde von *Music Week* zum besten Low-Budget-Video des Jahres 1995 gekürt. Im August 1997 arbeitete Chris mit Richard D. James (dem Aphex Twin) zusammen und führte beim Video zur Single *Come To Daddy* Regie. Das Video hat seither eine Unmenge von Auszeichnungen erhalten. Richard D. James (Aphex Twin) stammt aus einer Bergarbeiterfamilie in Cornwall. Schon in seiner Jugend interessierte er sich für Elektronik und besuchte Kurse. Heute ist er stolz darauf, sein Studio in seinem Schlafzimmer untergebracht zu haben. Er liebt es, sich als netter Kerl aus Cornwall („nice cornish lad") darzustellen.

MEGO / HOTEL PARAL.LEL / SEVEN TONS FOR FREE

Mego: Christian Fennesz / Peter Rehberg aka Pita

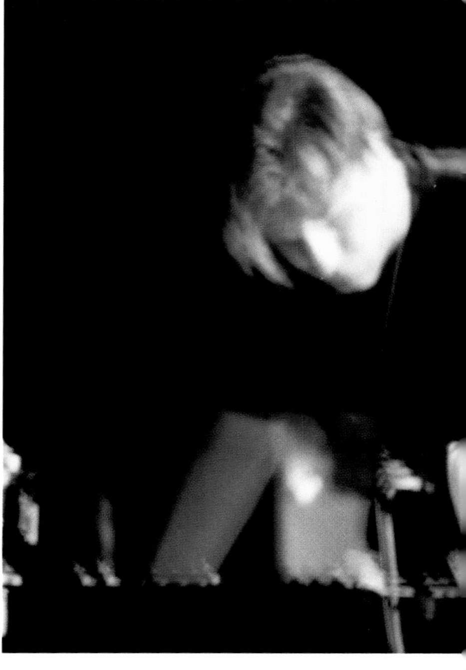

Mego likes to see itself as a platform for all kinds of information and communication carried via modern electronic media, whether it be a compact disc, MiniDisc, DVD, Internet, video, live PA or a vinyl record release. This is why extreme effort is put into packaging and artwork, as well as a glorious disregard for being pigeonholed into any one genre. It is our aim that Mego releases and ideas should be collected and experienced for many years to come and not be seen as some fodder for hopeless fashion victimized disc jockeys.
Mego opened its own Internet mail order shop called M.DOS in 1997. This features not only Mego releases but other labels worthy of investigation, and has become an online meeting place for the global electronic community.
Unlike most electronic based labels, Mego does make the effort to leave the cozy confines of the studio and play out live. With numerous performances (either as individual acts or as a full Mego "all nighter") in Munich, Frankfurt, Hamburg, Berlin (Interference), Karlsruhe (ZKM), Paris, Zurich, Barcelona (Sonar), London (LMC), Holland Festival 98, Stockholm, Lisbon, Rome, Milan, New York, LA, Chicago, Tokyo (ICC), as well as many outings in Vienna (Phonotaktik95+99, Hyperstrings, Word up, Wien Modern, etc..) and throughout Austria (Ars Electronica 97+99, Konfrontationen 98, Musikprotokoll 98).
© Mego

Mego sieht sich selbst gerne als Plattform für jed Art von Information und Kommunikation, die übe moderne elektronische Plattformen transportiert werden kann, sei es über CD, MiniDisc, DVD, Internet, Video, Live-Lautsprecher oder über die Vinyl-Schallplatte. Deshalb wird auch extrem viel Aufmerksamkeit auf Design und Verpackung gelegt und bewußt jede Form der Zuordnung zu einem Genre umgangen. Unser Ziel ist es, daß Mego-Produkte gesammelt und über Jahre hinweg gen sen werden und nicht als billiges Futter für hoffnungslos der Mode verfallene Diskjockeys dienen
Mego hat 1997 sein eigenes Internet-Mailorder-Geschäft unter dem Titel M.DOS eröffnet. Dort w den nicht nur Mego-Produkte, sondern auch and beachtenswerte Labels angeboten, und es ist zu einem Online-Treffpunkt der globalen elektronischen Community geworden.
Anders als die meisten Elektronik-orientierten Labe bemüht sich Mego, die gemütlichen Grenzen des Studios zu verlassen und „draußen" live zu spiele Zahlreiche Auftritte (entweder als individuelle Ac oder als ganze „Mego-Nächte") in München, Frankfurt, Hamburg, Berlin (Interference), Karlsruhe (ZK Paris, Zürich, Barcelona (Sonar), London (LMC), Holland Festival 98, Stockholm, Lissabon, Rom, Mailan

'otel Paral.lel, Fennesz' full-length debut, is a uzzling listen. Combining meticulously detailed :udio abuse with sparse rhythms, sweeping drones, ome beautifully crafted guitar textures, and andom discharges of digital noise, the album :raddles a range of conceptual territories simulta-eously. While not as immediately engaging as nstrument"—*Paral.lel* lacks the warmth of its redecessor and is a bit more thematically non-ommittal—it's also measurably more ambitious. In sense that seems to be the unifying theme of the Aego catalog, *Hotel Paral.lel* appears to go nowhere nd everywhere at once, careening off in a dozen ifferent directions with each track, but never noving beyond a certain base of musical ccessibility made significantly more ponderous by ne fact that the music is relentlessly abstract and evilishly subtle. A recent e-mail exchange offered ne following observation by the artist: "*Hotel* *aral.lel* is different from 'Instrument'—listen to it everal times. Best, Christian." Among the highest ecommendations I could offer for this disc is that ve had absolutely no difficulty in doing precisely nat. Rating: 8 *[sean cooper]*

Peter Rehberg a.k.a. Pita's first album, *Seven Tons For* *ree* was a monumental piece which was decisive in ne direction that Mego took as a label thereafter. evoid of any element of ornamentation, the album eatured endless repetitions of high frequency igital noises. Quite unlike 'minimal techno', all the ounds in this piece were reduced to pulse signals, istorted to unheard of extremes. These sounds ould have been seen as the ruins, or maybe the orpse of techno. Along with albums such as anasonic's *Vakio* and Ryoji Ikeda's +/-, this album ame to be known as a manifesto-like masterpiece." *Atsushi Sasaki)*

New York, Los Angeles, Chicago, Tokio (ICC) und viele Ereignisse in Wien (Phonotaktik 95+99, Hyper-strings, Word up, Wien Modern u. a.) und ganz Österreich (Ars Electronica 97 + 99, Konfrontationen 98, Musikprotokoll 98).
© *MEGO*

Hotel Paral.lel, Fennesz' Debüt in voller Länge, ist ein ungewohntes Hörerlebnis. Es kombiniert einen aus-geklügelten Mißbrauch des Studios mit knappen Rhythmen, weitausschwingendem Dröhnen, eini-gen wunderbar gemachten Gitarrentexturen sowie zufälligen Entladungen von digitalen Geräuschen – das Album beackert eine Vielzahl von konzeptuellen Gebieten gleichzeitig. Wenn auch nicht so unmit-telbar faszinierend wie *Instrument – Paral.lel* bietet nicht die Wärme des Vorgängers und ist thematisch etwas oberflächlicher –, ist es doch fühlbar ehrgei-ziger. Auf eine Art – die auch das Grundthema des Mego-Katalogs sein könnte – geht *Hotel Paral.lel* nirgendwo und überall gleichzeitig hin, düst bei jedem Track in ein Dutzend verschiedener Rich-tungen ab und verläßt doch nie eine bestimmte Basis musikalischer Zugänglichkeit, die dadurch sig-nifikant kraftvoll wird, daß die Musik unablässig abstrakt und teuflisch subtil bleibt. Ein kürzlich erfolgter E-Mail-Wechsel mit dem Künstler förderte folgenden Kommentar des Künstlers zutage: „*Hotel Paral.lel* unterscheidet sich von *Instrument* – manmuß es nur mehrmals hören. Herzlichst, Christian." Und zu den höchsten Empfehlungen, die ich dieser Platte geben kann, gehört, daß ich abso-lut kein Problem hatte, genau das zu tun.
Bewertung: 8
[sean cooper]

„Peter Rehberg alias ‚Pita's erstes Album *Seven Tons For Free* war ein monumentales Werk, das entschei-denden Einfluß auf die weitere Entwicklung von Mego als Label hatte. Frei von jedem ornamentalem Element umfaßte das Album endlose Wiederholung digitaler Hochfrequenzgeräusche. Anders als bei *Minimal Techno* waren die Klänge auf Impulssignale reduziert und bis in zu ungehörten Extremen ver-zerrt. Diese Klänge könnte man als die Ruinen – oder den Leichnam – des Techno ansehen. Zusam-men mit Albums wie Panasonics *Vakio* und Ryoji Ikedas +/- wurde dieses Album als ein manifest-ähnliches Meisterwerk bekannt."
(Atsushi Sasaki)

MEGO IS AN INDEPENDENT RECORD COMPANY BASED IN VIENNA WITH STUDIOS IN VIENNA AND BERLIN. RAMON BAUER AND PETER REHBERG TAKE CARE OF OPERATIONS IN VIENNA AND BEYOND, WHILE ANDI PIEPER MAINTAINS THE STUDIO IN BERLIN. CHRISTIAN FENNESZ HAS BEEN A GUITARIST WITH THE VIENNA BAND "MAISCHE" AND DEDICATED HIMSELF TO ELECTRONIC MUSIC SINCE THE EARLY 90S. Mego ist eine unabhängige Plattenfirma mit Hauptsitz in Wien und Studios in Wien und Berlin. Ramon Bauer und Peter Rehberg kümmern sich um die Abläufe in Wien und darüber hinaus, während Andi Pieper das Berliner Studio aufrechterhält. Christian Fennesz war Gitarrist bei der Wiener Band „Maische" und widmet sich seit den frühen 90er Jahren der elektronischen

BIRTHDAY

Ikue Mori

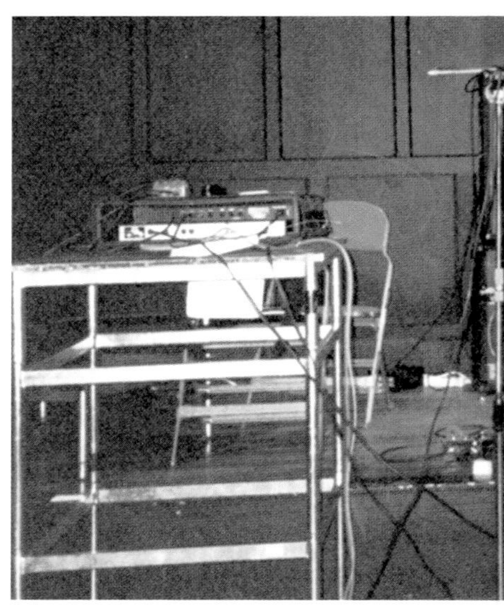

I program 3 drum machines, mutating their factory sounds to function not only as percussion but also as sound sources. At present I have 300 patterns randomly filled with texture/color, rhythmic patterns, pulse/beat, event/loud, event/quiet and melodies. The drum machines have 16(HRa,b) and 12(SR) key pads to assign the pitch, the voice and the mix, that can function in real time like a keyboard and are mixed with 2 multi processors controlled by keypads for immediate access to any program. In this piece the recordings of natural sounds (such as voice, feed back, outside noise, etc.) are manipulated by 2 processors and mixed into the background to create another layer of sound. The piece was made in three parts: 1. *Birthday* theme, 2. Growing up aggressively 3. Nostalgia, and live with no overdubs. The *Birthday* theme was created first with the pattern, in which the keypads are all assigned to triangle and pitched chromatically. Then a modified version of the melody was created with another drum machine with different voices playing together. The event and color patterns are created with certain voices programmed without quantizing. And then pre-recorded sounds from the player are mixed and manipulated by two multi processors, changing effects spontaneously with the progress of the music. They are the elements that add a depth to the music.

All the manually operated drum machines can work independently, creating combinations that are spontaneous and sometime unpredictable.

Ich programmiere drei Drum Machines und verä dere ihre werkseitige Einstellung so, daß sie nich nur als Perkussionsinstrumente, sondern auch a Klangquellen dienen. Derzeit habe ich 300 Must die beliebig mit Texturen/Farben, rhythmischen Mustern, Puls/Beats, lauten und leisen Events ur Melodien gefüllt sind. Die Drum Machines habe (HRa,b) und 12(SR)-Keypads, um Tonlage, Stimme und Mix einzustellen, die in Echtzeit wie ein Keyboard funktionieren und mit zwei Multiprozessc gemischt werden, die ebenfalls über Keypads für unmittelbaren Programmzugriff gesteuert werd In diesem Stück werden die Aufnahmen von Nat klängen (Stimme, Rückkoppelungen, Umweltgeräusche usw.) von zwei Prozessoren manipuliert und in den Hintergrund eingemischt, um eine w tere Klangebene zu schaffen. Das Stück entstanc drei Teilen: 1. Das *Birthday*-Thema; 2. Aggressives Aufwachsen; 3. Nostalgie; und wurde live ohne Overdubs gestaltet. Das *Birthday*-Thema entstar zunächst mit einem Muster, das alle Keypads Dreiecken zuordnet und die Tonhöhe chromatisc einregelt. Dann wurde eine modifizierte Version Melodie mit einer anderen Drum Machine und unterschiedlichen Stimmen geschaffen, die zusa menspielen. Die Ereignisse und Farbmuster wer mit bestimmten Stimmen gemeinsam unquanti ziert programmiert. Dazu werden vorab aufgenc mene Klänge aus einem Player eingemischt und über zwei Multiprozessoren manipuliert, was die Effekte spontan im Verlauf des Musikprozesse zu verändern erlaubt. Diese sind die Elemente, die d Musik die Tiefe verleihen.

Alle manuell bedienten Drum Machines können unabhängig voneinander eingesetzt werden, wodurch spontane – und bisweilen auch unvorh sehbare – Kombinationen entstehen.

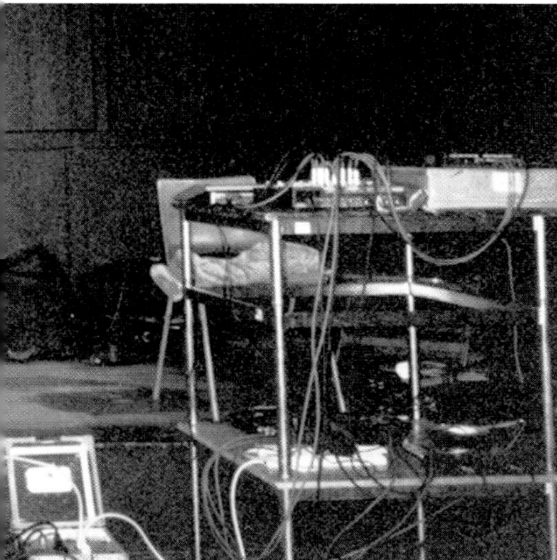

Ikue Mori moved to New York from Tokyo 1977, started playing drums, and formed the seminal New York No Wave band, DNA, with Arto Lindsay and Tim Wright, created a radical style of rhythm and noise, achieving legendary cult status in rock music. 1985 She started using drum machines in the unlikely world of improvisation. Using standard technology such as drum machine, she has created her own highly sensitive signature style.

Ikue Mori zog 1977 von Tokio nach New York, begann Schlagzeug zu spielen und gründete gemeinsam mit Arto Lindsay und Tim Wright die New Yorker No-Wave-Band „DNA", die einen radikalen Stil von Rhythmus und Geräusch schuf und bald Kultstatus erhielt. 1985 begann sie, Drum Machines in der ungewohnten Welt der Improvisation einzusetzen. Mit Standard-Technologie gelang es ihr dabei, einen höchst sensiblen persönlichen Stil zu finden.

CD 2

Stefan Betke

pole/stefan betke/crispydub pole/stefan
betke/crispydub pole/stefan betke/crispydub
pole/stefan betke/crispydub pole/stefan
betke/crispydub pole/stefan betke/crispydub
pole/stefan betke/crispydub pole/stefan
betke/crispydub pole/stefan betke/crispydub
pole/stefan betke/crispydub pole/stefan
betke/crispydub pole/stefan betke/crispydub
pole/stefan betke/crispydub pole/stefan
betke/crispydub pole/stefan betke/crispydub
pole/stefan betke/crispydub pole/stefan
betke/crispydub pole/stefan betke/crispydub
pole/stefan betke/crispydub pole/stefan
betke/crispydub pole/stefan betke/crispydub
pole/stefan betke/crispydub pole/stefan
betke/crispydub pole/stefan betke/crispydub
pole/stefan betke/crispydub pole/stefan
betke/crispydub pole/stefan betke/crispydub
pole/stefan betke/crispydub pole/stefan
betke/crispydub pole/stefan betke/crispydub
pole/stefan betke/crispydub pole/stefan
betke/crispydub pole/stefan betke/crispydub
pole/stefan betke/crispydub pole/stefan
betke/crispydub pole/stefan betke/crispydub
pole/stefan betke/crispydub pole/stefan
betke/crispydub pole/stefan betke/crispydub
pole/stefan betke/crispydub pole/stefan
betke/crispydub pole/stefan betke/crispydub
pole/stefan betke/crispydub pole/stefan
betke/crispydub pole/stefan betke/crispydub
pole/stefan betke/crispydub pole/stefan

pole/stefan betke/knusperdub pole/stefan
betke/knusperdub pole/stefan betke/knusperdu
pole/stefan betke/knusperdub pole/stefan
betke/knusperdub pole/stefan betke/knusperdu
pole/stefan betke/knusperdub pole/stefan
betke/knusperdub pole/stefan betke/knusperdu
pole/stefan betke/knusperdub pole/stefan
betke/knusperdub pole/stefan betke/knusperdu
pole/stefan betke/knusperdub pole/stefan
betke/knusperdub pole/stefan betke/knusperdu
pole/stefan betke/knusperdub pole/stefan
betke/knusperdub pole/stefan betke/knusperdu
pole/stefan betke/knusperdub pole/stefan
betke/knusperdub pole/stefan betke/knusperdu
pole/stefan betke/knusperdub pole/stefan
betke/knusperdub pole/stefan betke/knusperdu
pole/stefan betke/knusperdub pole/stefan
betke/knusperdub pole/stefan betke/knusperdu
pole/stefan betke/knusperdub pole/stefan
betke/knusperdub pole/stefan betke/knusperdu
pole/stefan betke/knusperdub pole/stefan
betke/knusperdub pole/stefan betke/knusperdu
pole/stefan betke/knusperdub pole/stefan
betke/knusperdub pole/stefan betke/knusperdu
pole/stefan betke/knusperdub pole/stefan
betke/knusperdub pole/stefan betke/knusperdu
pole/stefan betke/knusperdub pole/stefan
betke/knusperdub pole/stefan betke/knusperdu
pole/stefan betke/knusperdub pole/stefan
betke/knusperdub pole/stefan betke/knusperdu
pole/stefan betke/knusperdub pole/stefan
betke/knusperdub pole/stefan betke/knusperdu
pole/stefan betke/knusperdub pole/stefan
betke/knusperdub pole/stefan betke/knusperdu
pole/stefan betke/knusperdub pole/stefan
betke/knusperdub pole/stefan betke/knusperdu

STEFAN BETKE (D), BORN IN DÜSSELDORF AM RHEIN, BEGAN MAKING MUSIC AT THE AGE OF 14. MOVED TO COLOGNE A YEA LATER. MADE MORE MUSIC. MOVED TO BERLIN YEARS LATER. MORE MUSIC FOLLOWED. CD 1 WAS COMPLETED, CD FOLLOWED SOON AFTER. STILL LIVES AND WORKS IN BERLIN.

stefan betke (D), geboren im februar in düsseldorf a rhein. er fängt mit 14 an, musik zu machen. ein jahr später umzug nach köln. macht mehr musik. jahre später geht nach berlin. weitere musik folgt. CD 1 wird fertig CD 2 folgt schnell. lebt und arbeitet noch immer in berlin.

FIREFLIES ALIGHT ON THE ABACUS OF AL-FARABI II

Paul DeMarinis

60 foot long music wire with little dancing loops f mono-filament is stretched in an absolutely dark oom and illumined by an emerald laser beam. The oops dance on the harmonic nodes of the wire, roducing flickering points of light and aeolian harp-ke sounds. The piece relies on the adaptation of uman sensory systems to create an evolving xperience. The adaptation of the eye to the ionochrome light produces a variety of retinal olors, and prolonged listening to the drone creates n awareness of illusory acoustic images.

Eine 20 Meter lange Musiksaite mit kleinen tanzenden Schleifen aus Nylonfäden wird durch einen vollständig abgedunkelten Raum gespannt und mit einem Smaragdlaserstrahl beleuchtet. Die Schleifen tanzen auf den Obertonknoten der Saite, produzieren dabei flackernde Lichtpunkte und Klänge, die an die einer Äolsharfe erinnern. Das Stück benutzt die Fähigkeit des menschlichen Wahrnehmungssystems zur Anpassung, um ein umfassendes Erlebnis zu vermitteln. Die Anpassung des Auges an das monochrome Licht produziert eine Vielzahl von Farben auf der Netzhaut, und ein längerdauerndes Hören des Brummtons der Saite schafft ein Bewußtsein für illusorische akustische Bilder.

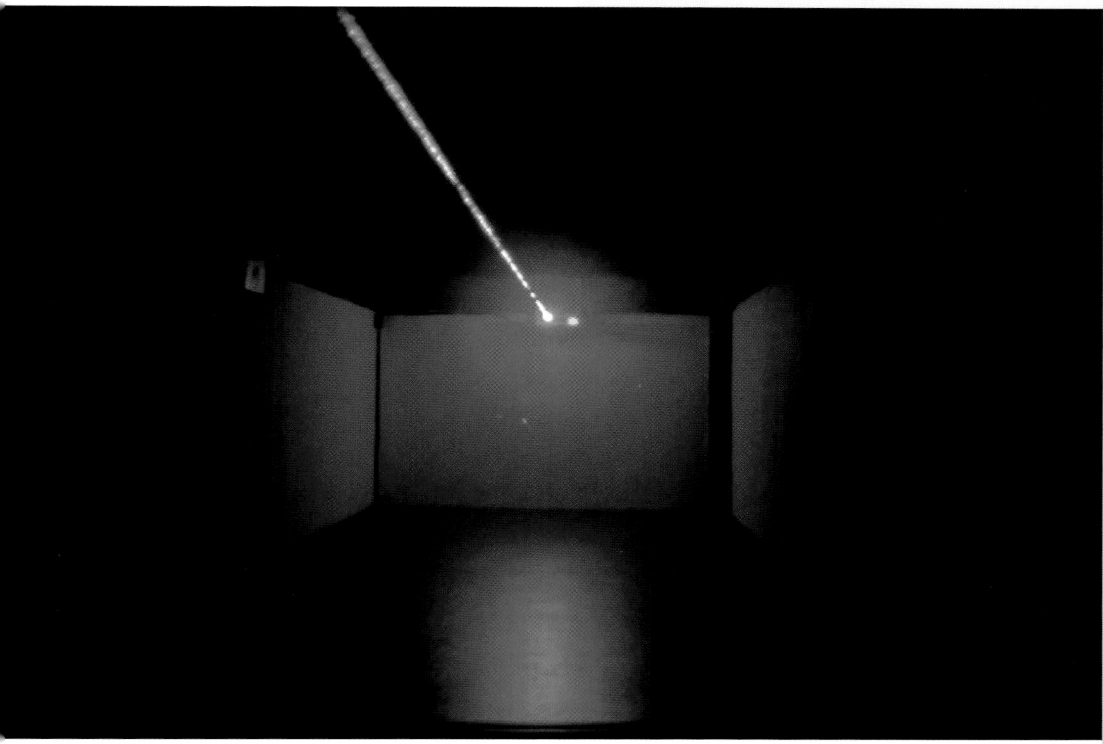

PAUL DEMARINIS (USA) HAS BEEN WORKING AS A MULTIMEDIA ELECTRONIC ARTIST SINCE 1971 AND HAS CREATED NUMEROUS PERFORMANCE WORKS, SOUND AND COMPUTER INSTALLATIONS AND INTERACTIVE ELECTRONIC INVENTIONS. HE HAS PERFORMED INTERNATIONALLY, AT THE KITCHEN, FESTIVAL D'AUTOMNE À PARIS, HET APOLLOHUIS IN THE NETHERLANDS AND AT ARS ELECTRONICA IN LINZ AND CREATED MUSIC FOR MERCE CUNNINGHAM DANCE CO. HIS INTERACTIVE AUDIO ARTWORKS HAVE BEEN SHOWN AT THE I.C.C. IN TOKYO, BRAVIN POST LEE GALLERY IN NEW YORK AND THE MUSEUM OF MODERN ART IN SAN FRANCISCO. HE HAS BEEN AN ARTIST-IN-RESIDENCE AT THE EXPLORATORIUM AND AT XEROX PARC AND HAS RECEIVED MAJOR AWARDS AND FELLOWSHIPS IN BOTH VISUAL ARTS AND MUSIC FROM THE NATIONAL ENDOWMENT FOR THE ARTS, N.Y.F.A. AS WELL AS PRIVATE FOUNDATIONS.

Paul DeMarinis (USA) arbeitet seit 1971 als Multimedia-Elektronikkünstler und hat zahlreiche Performances, Klang- und Computerinstallationen sowie elektronische Inventionen kreiert. Er ist u. a. bei The Kitchen, dem Festival d'Automne in Paris, am Het Apollohuis in Holland und bei Ars Electronica in Linz aufgetreten; er hat auch Musik für die Merce Cunningham Tanzcompagnie geschaffen. Seine interaktiven Audioarbeiten waren im I.C.C. in Tokio, in der Bravin Post Lee Gallery in New York und im Museum of Modern Art in San Francisco zu sehen. Er war Artist-in-Residence am Exploratorium und am Xerox PARC und hat Preise und Stipendien für visuelle Kunst und Musik vom National Endowment for the Arts, von der N.Y.F.A. und von privater Seite erhalten.

KINDERSPEL

Rose Dodd / Stephen Connolly

Kinderspel, for video and tape (November 1996) is experimental in its attempt to create an appropriate and collaborative musical and visual language. Our underlying ethos in both media was to give our imaginations full rein—to explore the boundaries of our respective domains and return to the origins of our creativity, viewing our artistic expression as child's play ("kinderspel") once more!

The tape part was created overall in response to the visual material. This affected the manner in which I went about identifying the appropriate character of sound material to be included. In essence I intended to create a sonic imitation, or likeness, of the visual material. In particular I was fascinated by the high-pitched register which the visual artist, Stephen Connolly, had created within his genre, and I set out to transplant this to the sonic dimension. The result is a sonic idiom which stretches at the boundaries of its own conventions.

The opening sound is a sample of a DAT machine as it forward winds/back winds; a sound common within the practices of electroacoustic music, but rarely used as a sample in its own right. Sampling is at a premium in *Kinderspel* and is used intentionally in a deliberate and rough way.

Kinderspel für Video und Band (November 1996) is insofern experimentell, als es versucht, eine geeig- nete kollaborative musikalische und visuelle Spra- che zu schaffen. Unser grundlegender ethischer A satz in beiden Medien war, der Phantasie die Züge schießen zu lassen, die Grenzen unserer jeweilige Bereiche niederzureißen und zum Ursprung unse Kreativität zurückzukehren – kurz, unsere künstler sche Ausdrucksweise wieder als Kinderspiel zu be trachten.

Der Tonband-Teil wurde zur Gänze als Reaktion au das visuelle Material geschaffen. Dies hatte vor allem Auswirkungen darauf, wie ich den jeweils passenden Charakter des zu verwendenden Klang materials festgelegt habe. Im wesentlichen habe ich versucht, eine klangliche Imitation des visuell Materials oder zumindest eine Ähnlichkeit zu pro duzieren. Ich war besonders von den „hohen Regi- stern" fasziniert, die der Bildkünstler Stephen Connolly innerhalb seines Genres geschaffen hat, und habe mich bemüht, das in die klangliche Dimension zu verpflanzen. Das Ergebnis ist ein klangliches Idiom, das die Grenzen seiner eigene Konvention überwindet.

Der Anfangsklang ist ein Sample einer DAT-Masc ne, die Band vor- und zurückspult, ein Klang, der i der Praxis der elektroakustischen Musik zwar hä fig vorkommt, aber selten selbst als Klangbasis v wendet wird. Sampling spielt in *Kinderspel* eine große Rolle und wird ganz bewußt unkonvention und rauh eingesetzt.

Rose Dodd (GB) completed her BA Hons. Music in 1990 at Dartington College of Arts, where she st composition with Frank Denyer. She then furthered her compositional studies with Diderik Wagenaar Royal Dutch Conservatoire, Den Haag. She is now working on her Doctorate in Electroacoustic Compo at the University of Newcastle upon Tyne, with a contributory thesis in Gender Issues and their re to Electroacoustic Technology. ▬ Rose Dodd (GB) graduierte 1990 mit einem BA Hons. Music am Dart College of Arts, wo sie Komposition bei Frank Denyer studiert hatte. Sie vertiefte ihre Kompositionsstudien bei D Wagenaar am Königlich Niederländischen Konservatorium in Den Haag. Sie arbeitet zur Zeit an ihrem Dokto elektroakustischer Komposition (Universität von Newcastle upon Tyne), wobei sie sich mit Gender-Problematik und

NAV

John Duncan / Francisco López

ɔhn Duncan and Francisco López propose to create new collaborative electroacoustic work that com-ines the unique approaches to sound of two out-tanding artists to create a synthesis that is greater ɿan the individual components. The goal is to cre-te a non-associative audio environment that is ɿonumental yet intimate in scale. Multi-channel udio spatialization and dramatically minimal light-ɿg conditions render the space both immense and ɿtimate, from one extreme to the other, from one ɿoment to the next, involving the audience in a ensual experience that is both private and public.
oth artists are known for performing in total dark-ess. For Duncan, this absence of visual stimuli is ffective—in fact essential—to eliminate as many eripheral distractions as possible, and to focus the stener's attention on internal, psychic responses to ɿe sound. For López, darkness serves to focus udience attention entirely on the sound itself, and n the environment that it creates.
ɔr this project, each of the artists gave audio ources and sourcefiles to the other, for use in proc-ssing and composing individually in their own tudios in Italy (Duncan) and Spain (López). The ɿodifications to these files were then recorded on D-R format and traded through the mail. The final ɿix was recorded in Duncan's studio, mastered with high-end audio D-A/A-D conversion process for dded depth and resonance.

John Duncan und Francisco López stellen ein neues kollaboratives elektroakustisches Werk vor, das die einzigartigen Klangansätze zweier hervorragender Künstler verbindet und eine Synthese schafft, die mehr ist als ihre Einzelteile. Ziel ist dabei, eine nicht-assoziative Audio-Umgebung zu schaffen, die einerseits monumental ist, andererseits aber eine gewisse Intimität aufweist. Die Multikanal-Raumverteilung und die dramatisch reduzierte Raumbeleuchtung lassen den Raum gleichzeitig immens und intim erscheinen, gehen von einem Augenblick zum nächsten von einem Extrem zum anderen und hüllen die Zuhörer in ein sinnliches Erlebnis, das gleichzeitig privat und öffentlich ist.
Beide Künstler sind dafür bekannt, daß sie gerne in völliger Dunkelheit auftreten. Für Duncan ist die Abwesenheit jeglicher visueller Stimuli wichtig – ja sogar unumgänglich –, um die Ablenkung von außen so gering wie möglich zu halten und die Aufmerksamkeit der Zuhörers auf ihre inneren, psychischen Reaktionen auf den Klang zu lenken. Für López dient die Dunkelheit dazu, das Publikum auf den Klang selbst und auf die Umgebung, die durch ihn geschaffen wird, einzustimmen.
Für dieses Projekt hat jeder der beiden dem anderen Klangquellen und Ursprungsdaten übergeben, um diese individuell in den jeweiligen Studios in Italien (Duncan) und Spanien (López) zu verarbeiten und zu komponieren. Die Veränderungen am Ausgangsmaterial wurde dann im CD-R-Format gespeichert und über Post ausgetauscht. Die endgültige Abmischung wurde in Duncans Studio aufgenommen und mit einem D-A/A-D-Wandler bearbeitet, um Tiefe und Resonanz hinzuzufügen.

JOHN DUNCAN IS WIDELY RECOGNIZED FOR HIS WORK IN PERFORMANCE, MUSIC, AND INSTALLATIONS BASED ON EMOTIONAL RESPONSES TO SENSORY DEPRIVATION AND STIMULI. OVER THE PAST EIGHTEEN YEARS, FRANCISCO LÓPEZ HAS BEEN DEVELOPING A POWERFUL AND CONSISTENT WORLD OF MINIMAL ELECTROACOUSTIC SOUNDSCAPES, "TRYING TO REACH AN IDEAL OF ABSOLUTE CONCRÈTE MUSIC." TO DATE, HIS PROLIFIC CATALOGUE COMPRISES 90 SOUND WORKS, WHICH HAVE BEEN RELEASED BY MORE THAN 40 RECORD LABELS. ▬ John Duncan ist weithin anerkannt für seine Performances, Musik und Installationen, die alle auf emotionalen Reaktionen auf sensorische Deprivation und Stimuli basieren. Im Lauf der vergangenen 18 Jahre hat Francisco López eine machtvolle und konsistente Welt aus minimalen elektroakustischen Klanglandschaften entwickelt, „ein Versuch, das Ideal einer absoluten Musique Concrète zu erreichen". Bis heute umfaßt ... ine umfangreiche Werkliste 90 Klangstücke, die auf mehr als vierzig Labels erschienen sind.

THE ANT MOVES / THE BLACK AND YELLOW CARCASS / A LITTLE CLOSER

Bernhard Günter

To enter a discussion about the concept of *The Ant Moves*, I will use the two following lines: the motto of my label "Thinking without words is the ultimate goal", and my private e-mail signature haiku "Elle fonderait / dans ma main / un peu de neige salie."
The first line expresses my wish to create a "language free zone" with my music, by using only non-referential sound materials and my refusal of any illustrative elements. This type of non-verbal, non-referential reflection is what characterizes my relationship with sound, painting, poetry, and art in general. I believe that since my work is the act of a human, it can (potentially) be transmitted to all other humans, without recourse to language.
The second line refers to both my first CD *Un Peu de Neige Salie* and to a haiku by Basho (an English translation would be "It would melt / in my hand / a little soiled snow", but I use only the French version, because the English one lacks the quality that it has in French, "snow" is female). It alludes to my preference for the small, non-spectacular, austere, as well as to the fact that my view of the world is a very zen-influenced one.
These notions have led me to a compositional strategy that is based on the sound itself. I start from sound material that I listen to very often and in a very attentive manner to find its internal qualities, tendencies, and potentials ... These are then enhanced by digital treatments to underline the direction the sound seems to want to go. Selected materials are then combined in various combinations that build the basis for the compositional form.In this process, silence is as important as sound, since I consider silence the "other" of sound, like in the relation of light and shadow ... The two unite to form the final "one."

Um in eine Diskussion über das Konzept von *The Ant Moves* einzutreten, möchte ich zwei kurze Te anführen: das Motto meines Labels „Thinking wit out words is the ultimate goal (Ohne Worte zu d ken ist das Endziel)", und den Signatur-Haiku me ner eigenen E-Mail: „elle fonderait / dans ma ma un peu de neige sale".
Der erste Text drückt aus, daß ich mit meiner Mu eine „sprachfreie Zone" schaffen möchte, indem nur nicht-referentielle Klänge verwende und den Einsatz von illustrativen Elementen ablehne. Dies Art non-verbaler, nicht-bezüglicher Reflexion cha rakterisiert auch meine Beziehung zum Klang, zu Malerei, Poesie und zur Kunst im allgemeinen. Ic glaube, mein Werk kann allen anderen menschli-chen Wesen (potentiell) mitgeteilt werden – ohn auf Sprache zurückgreifen zu müssen –, da es ein Akt eines menschlichen Wesens ist.
Der zweite Text bezieht sich einerseits auf meine erste CD *un peu de neige salie*, andererseits auf einen Haiku von Basho („er würde schmelzen / ir meiner Hand / ein wenig schmutziger Schnee", wobei ich die französische Version vorziehe, weil der Schnee weiblich ist). Der Text spielt an auf meine Vorliebe für das Kleine, Unspektakuläre, Strenge und darauf, daß meine Weltsicht stark vc Zen beeinflußt ist.
Diese Einstellung hat mich zu einer Komposition strategie geführt, die auf dem Klang selbst beruh Ich beginne mit Klangmaterial, das ich oft und se aufmerksam anhöre, um seine internen Qualität herauszufinden, seine Tendenzen und sein Poten tial, und diese werden dann durch digitale Verarb tung verstärkt, um die Richtung zu unterstreiche in die der Klang gehen zu wollen scheint. Ausgewählte Materialien werden dann in diversen Kombinationen zusammengestellt, die die Basis die eigentliche Form der Komposition bilden. Die Form bleibt bis zum letzten Augenblick flexibel u wächst wie ein Kristall. Was der Anfang war, kan gut auch zum Ende werden und umgekehrt. Bei diesem Prozeß ist die Stille ebenso wichtig wie derKlang – für mich ist sie einfach „die andere Seite" des Klangs, so wie der Schatten zum Licht gehört – und beide vereinigen sich letztlich zum Ganzen.

BERNHARD GÜNTER (D) BORN 1957. STARTED PLAYING DRUMS AT 12; CHANGED TO ELECTRIC GUITAR AT 17. IN 1980 MOV PARIS; ATTENDED LECTURES BY PIERRE BOULEZ AT IRCAM AND COLLÈGE DE FRANCE AND WORKED IN THE LIBRARIES OF CE POMPIDOU, TO AQUIRE CONTEMPORARY COMPOSITIONAL TECHNIQUES. PROVIDED MUSIC TO THE ENSEMBLE CHO GRAPHIQUE DE VITRY SEVERAL TIMES. 1986, RETURNED TO GERMANY. 1987, HE STARTED TO WORK ON MUSIC USIN COMPUTER. AFTER 4 YEARS OF PREPARATION AND ONE YEAR OF WORK, HE RELEASED HIS FIRST CD.

Bernhard Günt geboren 1957. Begann mit 12 Jahren Schlagzeug zu spielen, wechselte mit 17 zur E-Gitarre. 1980 Übersiedlung nach besucht Vorlesungen bei Pierre Boulez am IRCAM und am Collège de France, arbeitet in den Bibliotheken und am C Pompidou, um sich zeitgenössische Kompositionstechniken anzueignen. 1986 Rückkehr nach Deutschland. 1987 Arbeit am Computer. Nach vier Jahren Vorbereitung und einem Jahr Produktion erscheint seine erste CD.

CONSUMED

Richard Hawtin aka Plastikman

he album *Consumed* mines familiar areas, relying eavily on Hawtin's love affair with the minimal, yet vith this latest outing, *Plastikman* has offered and elivered spacious and uncluttered vistas not seen in revious incarnations. Time has provided Hawtin vith a refuge, freed from expectations and the emand of rigid formulas, Plastikman has been able o float free and explore the outer limits of his musi-al mind. Deep, luxurious and aquatic, *Consumed* alls somewhere between the laconic rumble of Aaurizio's electronic output, the lazy echo fed drive f King Tubby and the more familiar musical tricks of lastikman of old. Applying the less-is-more doctrine nd closely working and expanding the elements he as put into the mix, Hawtin has created an album n a grand scale, a piece of work that fills every vailable space with the minimum of effort. 5 + 5 = 000 if you see what I mean. This is the work of a onfident artist hitting his stride and coming out of he late 80's dance explosion intact and ready to rogress and take things further.
onsumed is a masterpiece, but like many great vorks, it's worth lies in its attempts to revolutionize. n album made for the head rather than the dance oor (but dispel any thoughts of "intelligent" techno ght now, this album is without contemporaries), nis album transports the listener further beyond ne lure of the strobe without them having to stand n a dance floor for five hours. The future sound of ne world today without a doubt.

Das Album *Consumed* beackert vertraute Gebiete, es stützt sich stark auf Hawtins Liebesaffäre mit dem Minimalen, und dennoch bietet das letzte Produkt von Plastikman weitläufige und geräumige Aussichten, die in früheren Inkarnationen nicht zu erkennen waren. Die Zeit hat Hawtin ein Refugium geliefert, ihn vom Erwartungsdruck und von der Nachfrage nach rigiden Formeln befreit. So war es Plastikman möglich, frei dahinzuschweben und die äußeren Grenzen seines musikalischen Geistes zu erforschen. Das tiefe, luxuriöse und flüssige *Consumed* situiert sich irgendwo zwischen dem lakonischen Rumpeln von Maurizios elektronischem Output, dem bedächtigen Echo-gesteuerten Drive von King Tubby und den etwas bekannteren musikalischen Tricks von Plastikman aus früheren Zeiten. Streng nach der Devise „Weniger ist mehr" und durch intensive Bearbeitung und Erweiterung der Elemente in seinem Mix hat Hawtin ein Album in großem Stil geschaffen, ein Werk, das jeden verfügbaren Raum mit einem Minimum an Anstrengung erfüllt. 5 + 5 = 1000, wenn Sie verstehen, was ich meine. Dies ist das Werk eines zuversichtlichen Künstlers, der seinen eigenen Weg heraus aus der Tanzexplosion der späten 80er gefunden hat und der bereit ist, weiterzugehen und Dinge weiterzuentwickeln.

RICHARD HAWTIN (CDN) AKA PLASTIKMAN HAS ALWAYS BEEN INTERESTED IN ELECTRONICS AND SYNTHESIZER. AMONG OTHER ACTIVITIES, HE FOUNDED THE LABEL "PLUS 8 RECORDS" AND HAS BEEN ACTIVE AS AN ORGANIZER OF TECHNO PARTIES AND FOUNDED HIS CURRENT LABEL "MINUS." Richard Hawtin (CDN) aka Plastikman interessierte sich schon immer für Elektronik und Syntheziser. Er gründete u. a. das Label „Plus 8 Records", betätigte sich als Organisator von Techno Parties

METABOLIC SPEED PERCEPTION

MAZK / Zbigniew Karkowski & Masami Akita

TCP dump,the raw data of internet traffic turned into audiofiles (soundhack) is the only sound material used in *Metabolic speed perception*. Several layers of this sound are then processed and filtered (vst plug-ins, super collider, peak) and edited (deck). No formal-theoretical or aesthetic considerations were employed in the creative process.

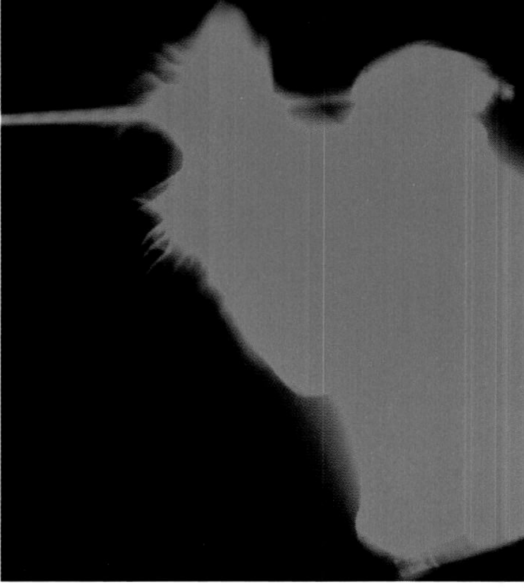

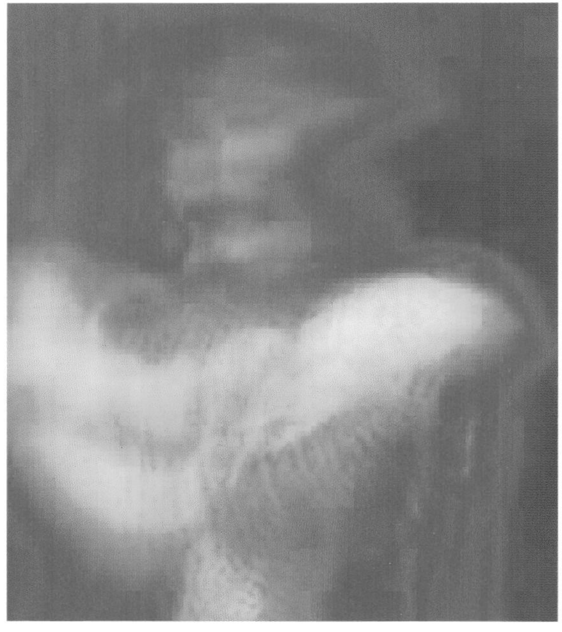

TCP-Dump, also die Rohdaten des Internet-Verke[illegible] in Audiofiles (Soundhack) umgewandelt, sind da[illegible] einzige Klangmaterial, das in *Metabolic speed per-ception* verwendet wird. Mehrere Lagen dieses Klangs werden bearbeitet, gefiltert (VST Plug-Ins, Super Collider, Peak) und geschnitten (Deck). Den kreativen Prozeß liegen keine formal-theoretisch[illegible] oder -ästhetischen Überlegungen zugrunde.

MAZK IS A DUO WHICH CONSISTS OF MASAMI AKITA, JAPANESE NOISE ARTIST (ALSO KNOW[illegible] MERZBOW) AND ZBIGNIEW KARKOWSKI, POLISH-BORN COMPOSER OF CONTEMPORARY [illegible] BASED IN TOKYO. THEY WORK WITH POWERBOOKS AND THEIR MUSIC CAN BE DESCRIB[illegible] "EXTREME DIGITAL ELECTRONICS." MAZK PERFORMS LIVE IN JAPAN AND HAS RELEASED [illegible] ENTITLED "SPL" ON OR LABEL IN THE UK. ▬ Das Duo MAKZ besteht aus Masami Akita, [illegible] japanischen Geräuschkünstler (auch bekannt als MERZBOW), und Zbigniew Karkowski, ein[illegible] Polen geborenen und in Tokio wohnhaften Komponisten zeitgenössischer Musik. Sie arbeite[illegible] PowerBooks, und ihre Musik läßt sich am besten mit „extreme digitale Elektronik" umschr[illegible] MAZK treten in Japan live auf und haben eine CD unter dem Titel SPL beim OR-Label in [illegible]

AUTODITACKER

Mouse on Mars

he titles of the LPs, even as provisional ones, are ıst as reckless as ever, but Valerie Trebeljahr's long vait is finally over. It's here, and as you will hear, this ime it sounds even more like exotic food, looking so ood you hardly dare taste it, let alone speak to it. As ou might already expect from the EP, Mouse on Aars are working hard on being even nicer. And the nore natural they sound, the more playful it is. Aelodies that make it seem probable that, after Aouse on Mars, computers will want to look more ke cuddly toys—and who could blame them—and ven more probable that by the time the world has igested their last album, it will fall back into a long, egenerative phase of general infantilism, which is ll the more probable for being desirable and would nake it possible to take everything seriously again.)K, earth, but this is the last time. Oh yes, and finally : is also probable that the stimulating dances on he spaceship Orion will in fact be danced again one ay and, most of all, that no one ever has to be mbarrassed again by anything, no matter how you pell it. For as Jan St. Werner once presciently ummarized the problems of the earth in an nterview: "If Wednesday is spelled with an s, then ou can use two n's; if Thursday has one r, then you ould spell it with three q's. And hey, I can imagine ncluding four g's, too. And the real question is vhether you spell crepe paper with a 'c' or a 'k' at the eginning." Pop for the 21st century, which will ertainly no longer be what it once was, but efinitely more pleasant. Thanks to Mouse on Mars.

Die Titel der neuen LP sind schon als vorläufige so halsbrecherisch wie immer, aber das lange Warten von Valerie Trebeljahr hat ein Ende. Sie ist da und klingt diesmal, wie ihr hören werdet, noch mehr nach exotischen Nahrungsmitteln, die so gut aussehen, daß man sich kaum traut, sie zu essen, geschweige denn anzusprechen. Wie die EP schon vermuten ließ, arbeiten Mouse On Mars hart dran, noch netter zu werden. Und, je natürlicher sie klingen, desto verspielter wird es. Melodien, die es wahrscheinlich werden lassen, daß Computer nach Mouse On Mars eher so aussehen wollen wie Kuscheltiere – und wer könnte ihnen das übelnehmen –, noch wahrscheinlicher, daß die Welt spätestens, wenn sie ihre neue Platte verdaut hat, in eine lange tiefe erholsame Phase des generellen Infantilismus verfällt, was um so wahrscheinlicher ist, als daß es wünschenswert wäre, und einen alles noch einmal ernst nehmen lassen würde. OK, Erde, aber ein letztes Mal jetzt. Ach ja, und endlich ist es auch wahrscheinlich, daß die stimulierenden Tänze auf Raumschiff Orion vielleicht doch eines Tages mal getanzt werden und daß einem vor allem nichts nie mehr peinlich sein müßte, egal wie man es schreibt. Denn, wie Jan Werner mal in einem Interview vorausschauend die Probleme der Erde zusammenfaßte: „Wenn sich Mittwoch mit zwei Ts schreibt, kann man drei Ps nehmen; wenn Donnerstag mit zwei Ns ist, kann man es mit fünf Ps schreiben. Ich könnte mir aber auch verdammt gut vorstellen, zwei Ls einzubauen. Und eigentlich ist doch die Frage, schreibt man Krepppapier am Anfang mit C oder mit K." Pop für das 21. Jahrhundert, das auch nicht mehr sein wird, was es mal war, aber mit Sicherheit angenehmer. Dank Mouse On Mars.

1993: ANDI TOMA (DÜSSELDORF) AND JAN ST. WERNER (COLOGNE) FOUND "MOUSE ON MARS." 1994: FIRST RELEASE WITH THE LONDON LABEL "TOO PURE." HAILED BY THE ENGLISH PRESS. ALBUM *VULVALAND*, FIRST PERFORMANCES IN ENGLAND. 1995: THE SECOND ALBUM, *IAORA TAHITI* IS ACCLAIMED BY NME AS ONE OF THE MOST IMPORTANT ALBUMS OF THE YEAR. 1997: THIRD ALBUM *AUTODITACKER*, PERFORMANCES IN AMERICA + JAPAN. 1998: FOUNDING OF THE LABEL "SONIG" AND SEPARATION FROM "TOO PURE." RELEASES OF THE ALBUMS *INSTRUMENTALS* AND *GLAM*. 1999: FOURTH ALBUM *NIUN NIGGUNG*.

1993: Andi Toma (Düsseldorf) und Jan St. Werner (Köln) gründen „Mouse on Mars". 1994: Erste Veröffentlichung beim Londoner Label „Too Pure". Werden von der Englischen Presse willkommen geheißen. Album *Vulvaland*, erste Auftritte in England. 1995: Zweites Album *Iaora Tahiti* wird von NME als eines der wichtigsten Alben des Jahres gefeiert. 1997: Drittes Album *Autoditacker*, Auftritte in Amerika + Japan 1998: Gründung des Labels „Sonig" und Trennung von „Too Pure". Veröffentlichungen der Alben *Instrumentals* und

SUPERBONUS

Terre Thaemlitz

Superbonus was recorded at Nantou Radio Studios in Nantou, Taiwan on January 21, 1999. *Superbonus* is an improvisational performance by Terre Thaemlitz (keyboards & electronics), accompanied by the jazz ensemble Funks Shui, featuring Tarcy Cheung (bass), Vincent Hui (dulcimer and percussion), Stephen Lin (snare kit) and Fang Min-Shu (additional keyboards and percussion). The near hour-long session was recorded spontaneously, being mastered on a discarded reel of tape found in the radio studio's engineering booth. The tape's diffuse quality and the bleed-through of previously recorded radio broadcasts adds to the character of this recording.

Superbonus is a simulacrum of improvisational jazz performance. Its primary objective is to present a digital representation of real-time performance techniques without involving any material engagement of such a performance.

Compositionally, *Superbonus* was programmed to reflect the styles of such contemporary jazz performers as The Necks, and keyboardist Evan Lurie. However, whereas these artists' works are a response to and/or deviation from years of training in formal composition strategies, Thaemlitz proposes that simulacra afford the digital composer a third option of forgoing formal music training in favor of directly addressing the music consumer's performance of desire in the jazz audio marketplace. The objective of *Superbonus* is not to suggest the replacement of live performance and traditional musicology, but to compose in a manner which consciously engages the digital distribution of music in a marketplace rooted in image management.

Superbonus wurde am 21. Januar 1999 in den Nantou Radio Studios in Nantou, Taiwan, aufgenommen. *Superbonus* ist eine Improvisations-Performance von Terre Thaemlitz (Keyboards & Elektronik), begleitet vom Jazz-Ensemble Funk Sh mit Tarcy Cheung (Bass), Vincent Hui (Dulcimer u Perkussion), Stephen Lin (Snare Kit) und Mang Mi Shu (Keyboards und Perkussion). Die beinahe einstündige Session wurde spontan mitgeschnitten, wobei als Masterband ein ausrangiertes Band die te, das sich in der Tontechnik des Studio gefunde hatte. Die diffuse Qualität des Bandes und das Durchklingen früherer Aufnahmen von Radiosendungen tragen wesentlich zum Charakter der Aufnahme bei.

Superbonus von Terre Thaemlitz ist ein Simulakru einer Jazz-Improvisation. Sein Hauptziel ist es, ei digitale Repräsentation von Performance-Technik in Echtzeit zu bieten, ohne eine solche Performan tatsächlich zu erfordern.

Als Komposition sollte *Superbonus* bewußt den S zeitgenössischer Jazzmusiker wie The Necks oder des Keyboarders Evan Lurie reflektieren. Während aber die Werke der erwähnten Künstler Ergebnis jahrelanger Ausbildung in formalen Komposition techniken sind, schlägt Thaemlitz vor, daß Simulakra dem digitalen Komponisten erlauben s len, einen dritten Weg außerhalb einer formalen Musikausbildung zu gehen und dabei das Wunsc verhalten des Konsumenten im Audiomarkt direk anzusprechen. Ziel von *Superbonus* ist es nicht, Li Aufführungen und traditionelle Musikwissensch zu ersetzen, wohl aber auf eine Weise zu kompon ren, die bewußt auf die digitale Distribution der Musik in einem im wesentlichen im Bildmanagement verwurzelten Markt abzielt.

Terre Thaemlitz (USA) is a musician, producer, DJ, remixer and owner of the label "Comatonse Recordings." was a member of the Analysis/Synthesis group at IRCAM and has collaborated on several interdisciplin projects (with Terrence McKenna and others). In 1991 he was awarded the Underground Grammy Award fr the House of Magic (Midtown Manhattan transsexual circuit). Terre Thaemlitz (USA) ist Musiker, Produ DJ und Remixer sowie Besitzer des Labels „Comatonse Recordings". Er war Mitglied der Analysis/Synthesis Gruppe IRCAM und arbeitete bei mehreren interdisziplinären Projekten (u. a. mit Terrence McKenna) mit. 1991 wurde ihm Underground Grammy Award from the House of Magic (Midtown Manhattan transsexual circuit) verliehen.

SYMPHONY FOR DOT MATRIX PRINTERS

[The User] / local area network orchestra

he *Symphony* project transforms banal office echnology into a system for musical performance. ot matrix printers are turned into musical "in- truments", while a computer network system, ypical of a contemporary office, becomes the orchestra" used to play them. The orchestra is conducted" by a network server which reads from a omposed "score." Each of the printers plays from a lifferent "part" comprised of notes and rhythms nade up of letters of the alphabet, punctuation narks and other characters. The resulting sounds are mplified and broadcast over a sound system, reating densely textured, rhythmically-driven nusic.

he system employed for the performance consists f one dozen dot matrix printers of various makes nd models, each driven by its own 8086 personal omputer. The PCs are connected to a Unix platform leXT server via two networks: one ethernet and one erial. Two pieces of custom software have been vritten to allow the control of the entire system rom the server. The individual PCs request their text ile "part" from the server via ethernet at the start of ach performance. The server then executes a com- nand file "score" which uses the serial network to all individual textfiles for each PC to print at precise imes. The inscription of the "score" and the "parts" n a modifiable fixed medium (ASCII text files) nables us to create performances which can be rchestrated, synchronized, and edited with a large neasure of flexibility and control. Without the cus- om hardware and software to operate the printers, he behaviour of these machines would be too andom to allow a rigorous compositional practice.

Das *Symphony*-Projekt verwandelt banale Bürotechnik in ein System für musikalische Performances. Nadeldrucker werden in „Instrumente" verwandelt, während ein Computernetzwerk, wie es für ein zeitgenössisches Büro typisch ist, zum „Orchester" wird, das sie spielt. Das „Orchester" wird von einem Netzwerkserver „dirigiert", der eine komponierte „Partitur" liest. Jeder der Drucker spielt einen unterschiedlichen „Part", der aus Noten und Rhythmen besteht, die aus den Buchstaben des Alphabets, Satzzeichen und anderen Zeichen zusammengesetzt sind. Die daraus resultierenden Klänge werden verstärkt und über eine Lautsprecheranlage ausgestrahlt, was eine dicht texturierte, rhythmusgetriebene Musik ergibt.

Das System für die Performance besteht aus einem Dutzend Nadeldrucker unterschiedlicher Hersteller, die jeweils von einem eigenen 8086er-PC angesteuert werden. Die PCs sind über zwei Netzwerke – Ethernet und seriell – mit einem Unix-gestützten NExT-Server verbunden. Zwei eigens geschriebene Programme erlauben die Steuerung des gesamten Systems vom Server aus. Die einzelnen PCs fordern ihren Text-"Part" zu Beginn jeder Aufführung über Ethernet vom Server an. Der Server führt dann eine „Partitur" aus Steuerbefehlen aus, die das serielle Netzwerk dazu verwendet, individuelle Textfiles aufzurufen, die von den einzelnen PCs zu genau definierten Zeitpunkten gedruckt werden. Da „Partitur" und „Parts" auf einem modifizierbaren festen Medium (ASCII-Textfiles) gespeichert werden, sind wir in der Lage, Performances zu schaffen, die mit einem erheblichem Maß an Flexibilität und Kontrolle orchestriert, synchronisiert und editiert werden können. Ohne die eigene Hard- und Software zur Ansteuerung der Drucker wäre das Verhalten der Maschinen allzu zufällig, als daß es eine rigorose Kompositionspraxis zuließe.

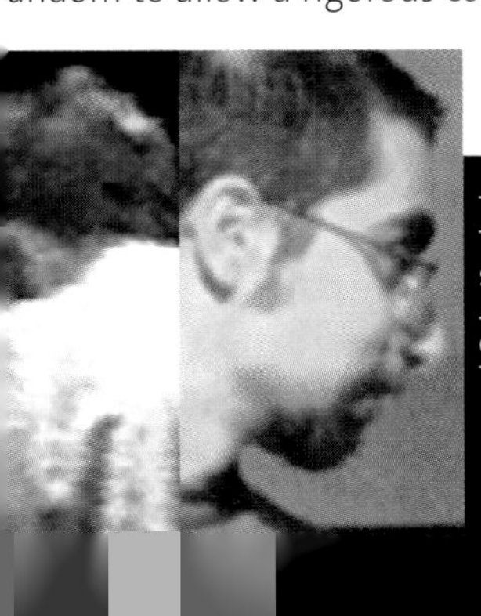

The term "user" objectifies and reduces individuality to an abstract and generic ideal. This reduction is employed wherever abstract rational methodology is applied to situations involving real people. In our society we employ the impersonal term "user" to justify the infliction of neon lighting, plastic cutlery and Muzak on a huge majority of our population. [The User] is an artists' collective formed of two members: architect Thomas McIntosh and composer Emmanuel Madan. Der Begriff „User" objektiviert und reduziert die Individualität auf ein abstraktes, auf eine spezielle Gruppe bezogenes Ideal. Diese Reduktion wird überall dort verwendet, wo eine abstrakte rationale Methodologie auf Situationen angewendet wird, in denen reale Leute vorkommen. In unserer Gesellschaft verwenden wir den unpersönlichen Begriff „User" oder „Nutzer", um die Anwendung von Neonlicht, Plastikbesteck und Muzak auf (und gegen) eine große Mehrheit unserer Bevölkerung zu rechtfertigen.

TEN

Tone Rec / Gaëtan Collet, Noëlle Collet, Claude Pailliot, Vincent Thierion

Tone Rec's music might sound like a serie of mistakes: each track has a line with starting and ending points, and between those moments anything can happen—and to echo Murray Walker, it usually does. Take *Pholcus* as a starting point; the opener kicks off with some metronomic clicks immersed in a pulsing high-end noise before being abruptly interrupted by reverberating chimes and piercing drums. Subsequent tracks see tone changes, volume changes, the introduction of brittle snapping for percussion. A track like *Voice Onset Time* consists solely of various grainy, looped drones intersecting over the course of 11 minutes. The loops are running in desyncronised ways to create unexpected rhythms. As an album, it keeps drawing you right into mix, as if the sounds are being generated inside your heart, then it'll suddenly makes out as if the music is coming from several buildings away, the frequency of the sounds changing accordingly.
This is not some contrived mathematical lab experiment; neither predeterminated structural model, nor theoretical approach for the music. Much of the band's music is basically a form of heavily deconstructed techno hardly inaccessible in its basic format, but highly innovative all the same.

From John Gibson's Article Nov 1998 Newcastle UK

Die Musik von Tone Rec könnte wie eine Reihe vo Fehlern klingen: Jede Spur hat eine Klanglinie mit einem Anfangs- und einem Endpunkt, und dazwi schen kann so ziemlich alles passieren – und, um mit Murray Walker zu sprechen, das tut es auch normalerweise.
Nehmen wir *Pholcus* als Ausgangspunkt: Eine Ein leitung fährt ab mit dem Ticken eines Metronom das in ein pulsierendes High-End-Geräusch einge taucht ist, bevor es abrupt von nachhallenden Glocken und einem durchdringenden Schlagzeug abgelöst wird. Die nachfolgenden Tracks zeigen Tonveränderungen, Lautstärkenvariationen und d Einführung eines brüchigen Schnappens als Perkussion.
Ein Track wie *Voice Onset Time* besteht ausschließ lich aus verschiedenen körnigen, in Schleifen laufenden Formen von Gebrumm, die einander im La von elf Minuten überschneiden. Die einzelnen Schleifen laufen unsynchronisiert ab und ergebe unerwartete Rhythmen.
Das Album selbst zieht einen ständig richtig in de Mix hinein, als würden die Klänge direkt im eigen Kopf generiert, dann plötzlich klingt es wieder so, als käme die Musik aus der Entfernung von einige Häuserblocks weiter, und die Frequenz der Klänge ändert sich dementsprechend.
Das ist nicht irgendein ausgeklügeltes mathemat sches Laborexperiment, es gibt auch kein vorgege benes Strukturmodell noch einen theoretischen A satz zur Musik. Der Großteil der Musik der Band i im wesentlichen ein stark dekonstruierter Techno in seiner grundlegenden Form nicht unzugänglic aber dennoch höchst innovativ.

Aus John Gibsons Artikel im November 1998, Newcastle,

Tone Rec consists of Claude Pailliot, Gaëtan Collet, Noëlle Collet and Vincent Thierion. The group has so far produced three albums and two vinyls and appears on several samplers from the label "sub rosa." Most recent activities include video music for Seton Smith in Paris, taking part in the Mille Plateaux Festival, Berlin, and dat politics together with Christian Fennesz / Mego in Lille. Tone Rec besteht aus Claude Pailliot, Gaëtan Collet, Noëlle Collet und Vincent Thierion. Die Gruppe hat bisher drei Alben und zwei Vinyls herausgebracht und ist auf mehreren Samplern des Labels „sub rosa" vetreten. Zuletzt Videomusik für Seton Smith in Paris, Teilnahme am Festival Mille Plateaux Berlin und bei dat politics gemeinsam mit Christian Fennesz / Mego in Lille.

TULPAS

Ralf L. Wehowsky (RLW)

ıave always seen my pieces in a permanent state ᶠ flux—the releases as a current manifestation of eas, which unfold, merge and collide with others in fferent ways before and afterwards. I have always ₃ed old material and completely reworked it.
ɴother aspect of my work refers to the question of ɔersonal artistic identity." I try to make a theme out ᶠ it by testing and developing different forms of ɔllaboration.
ılpas is a further exploration of these aspects of my ork: the idea of each piece being a preliminary ːrsion from a process which can result in another ːrsion—or something completely different—as well ; the idea of "my" pieces being an element in a con- nuous series of exchange (co)operations. (By the ay: I see none of my tracks as a "realisation" of ıese ideas—each one is created from genuine ıusical/aesthetical needs, which interfere with the ɜneral conceptual obligations in many different ays.) For *Tulpas* I invited only artists whose work I dmire and with whom I feel I have certain things in ɔmmon. Of course all of them also have their own dividual approach/methods of working, which are fferent from my own. Therefore I thought that ₃ing existing RLW tracks for the project would pro- ɔke an interesting exploration of these common ıd differing aspects. The approach and the results ere left up to the participants—referencing the ructure of an existing RLW composition, using its ɔunds, starting from the vision its atmoshpere voked, or "just" rearranging or remixing it ...
D 1 realises the basic idea with 7 interpretations of ıe peculiar composition, *Nameless Victims*, while D 2 refers to a general idea of RLW; CD 3 relates to ːveral actual aspects of my work, while CD 5 con- ːntrates on fundamental issues of my earlier work ıd CD 4 spins out related conceptual dispositions.

Ich habe meine Stücke immer als im Fluß befindlich angesehen – neue Fassungen sehe ich als eine ständige Manifestation von Ideen, die sich jedesmal auf andere Weise entfalten, verschmelzen, kollidieren. Ich verwende seit jeher älteres Material, das ich vollkommen umarbeite.
Ein anderer Aspekt meiner Arbeit bezieht sich auf die Frage der „persönlichen künstlerischen Identität". Ich versuche daraus ein Thema zu machen, indem ich verschieden Formen von Zusammenarbeit teste und entwickle.
Tulpas ist ein weiterer Schritt in der Auslotung dieser Aspekte meiner Arbeit: Jedes Stück ist eine vorläufige Version aus einem Prozeß, der zu einer anderen Version führen kann – oder zu etwas ganz anderem. Darüber hinaus sind „meine" Stücke Elemente einer kontinuierlichen Serie von Austausch-(Ko-)Operationen. Dabei sehe ich keinen meiner Tracks als die „Realisierung" dieser Gedanken an – jeder entsteht aus einem echten musikalisch/ästhetischen Bedürfnis heraus, das sich mit den konzeptionellen Verpflichtungen auf mannigfache Weise überschneidet.
Zu *Tulpas* habe ich nur Künstler eingeladen, deren Werk ich schätze und mit denen ich meinem Gefühl nach einiges gemeinsam habe. Natürlich haben sie alle ihre eigenen Ansätze und Arbeitsmethoden, die sich von meinen unterscheiden. Deshalb dachte ich mir, die Verwendung von existierenden RLW-Tracks für das Projekt könne einen interessante Einblick in diese Gemeinsamkeiten und Unterschiede geben. Der Ansatz und die Ergebnisse blieben den Mitwirkenden überlassen – ob sie sich nur auf die Struktur einer existierenden RLW-Komposition bezogen und ihre Klänge verwendeten oder von der Vision der von ihr ausgelösten Atmosphäre ausgingen oder sie „nur" neu oder als Remix arrangierten ...
CD1 realisiert die Grundidee mit sieben Interpretation derselben Komposition, *Nameless Victims*; CD2 bezieht sich auf den Grundgedanken von RLW; CD3 zeigt verschiedene aktuelle Aspekte meiner Arbeit auf; CD5 hingegen konzentriert sich auf fundamentale Anliegen meiner früheren Arbeit, während CD4 damit verbundene konzeptuelle Anlagen ausführt.

Ralf L. Wehowsky (D), born 1959, 1980 foundation of the experimental music ensemble P16.D4, 1984 foundation of the Selektion cooperative (label, films/videos, installations, books). 1992 first releases under own name (abbreviated RLW). Ralf L. Wehowsky (D), geb. 1959. 1980 Gründung des experimentellen Musikensembles P16D4. 1984 Gründung der SELEKTION-Kooperative (Label, Film/Video, Installationen, Bücher). 1992 erste Werke unter dem eigenen Namen, abgekürzt RLW.

prix ars electronica 99

.NET
INTERACTIVE ART
COMPUTER ANIMATION
VISUAL EFFECTS
DIGITAL MUSICS
u19/CYBERGENERATION

EARLY RETIREMENT F HOLLYWOOD'S DINOS ...

Frühpension für Hollywoods Dinos

At high speed and with more or less original ideas, the under-19s are well on their way to the next level of electronic lifestyle.

Mit rasantem Tempo und mehr o weniger originellen Ideen sind Unter-19jährigen auf dem Weg nächste Level des Electronic Lifest

The U19 entries included just about everything in the way of original productions that young minds can come up with to whip through a processor: the spectrum ranges from the digital children's drawings by the 6 to 11-year-olds through school children's first homepages and self-produced games all the way to sophisticated micro-mega productions by entire 3D teams and the comprehensively designed digital package by the outstanding winning crew.
Although the jury might have sometimes wished for more experimental daring and a bit more audacity, the award-winning products are certainly strongly indicative of the creative and expressive potential of young people in Austria. However, the fact that works were still entered primarily by boys is disturbing. The jury hopes that girls will have more courage to participate in the U19 competition in coming years.
Over the course of three days, the jury examined, tested and discussed a total of 600 freestyle computing productions in several runs. With this many entries, the competition is already at the top of the list of comparable competitions in the second year of its existence. The large number of participants shows that young people are taking advantage of opportunities for working digitally. In 1999 U19 is supported again by the Austrian Postal Bank (P.S.K.) and the Austrian Culture Service (*öks*). What the contents of the entries involves is a representation of the entrants' own very personal worlds, satire, violence, a presentation of practical information, pure aesthetics, self-presentation or a documentation of school activities, although the latter sometimes showed more of the teacher's hand than that of the young people who carried it out. It was notable that outstanding submissions were entered in the area of animation, which were created by young people between the ages of 15 and 19. The themes ranged from 3D animated construction plans to parodies and flamboyantly humorous adaptations of fairy tales, like *The Tortoise and the Rabbit* by Patrick Toifl (18). The 3D animation *Good Morning* by Alexander Kvasnicka (19) from Vienna is a parody of a complicated alarm

Eingereicht wurde bei U19 fast alles, was die jungen Gehirne so an Eigenproduktionen durch die Prozessoren jagen können: Die Spannweite reichte von digitalen Kinderzeichnungen der Sechs- bis Elfjährigen über erste Homepages von Schülern und selbstentwickelten Games bis zu ausgefeilten Micro-Mega-Productions ganzer 3D-Teams und dem durchdesignten digitalen Gesamtpaket der herausragenden Gewinner-Crew.
Auch wenn sich die Jury öfters ein bißchen mehr Mut zum Experiment und eine größere Portion Unverfrorenheit erhofft hätte, markierten die prämierten Produkte mit viel Kraft das kreative und ausdrucksstarke Potential der Jugend in Österreich. Bedenklich ist der Fact, daß die eingereichten Arbeiten immer noch vorwiegend von Burschen stammen. Die Jury wünscht sich für kommende Competitions mehr Mut seitens der Mädchen zur Teilnahme bei u19.
Während drei Tagen untersuchte, testete und besprach die Jury in mehreren Durchgängen insgesamt 600 Freestyle-Computing-Produktionen. Damit plazierte sich der Wettbewerb bereits im zweiten Jahr seiner Existenz an der Spitze der Liste vergleichbarer Ausschreibungen. Die große Anzahl an Teilnehmern beweist, daß die digitalen Arbeitsmöglichkeiten von Jugendlichen genützt werden. U19 wird auch 1999 von der Österreichischen Postspar-

lock machine for a sleepy head. Each of these two alented render-men was awarded an Honorary Mention.

n comparison with last year, there was an normous increase in the number of entries in the nusic sector. One senses the positive influence of nternationally recognized Austrian musicians in he experimental electronic and DJ scene. The unky *Mio topo* by Benedikt Schalk (16) and the nky Drum 'n Bass track *Scream* by Stefan Trischler

kasse (P.S.K.) und dem Österreichischen Kultur-Service (öks) unterstützt.

Inhaltlich geht es den Einreichern um die Darstellung ihrer ganz persönlichen Welten, um Satire, Gewalt, um Aufbereitung praktischer Informationen, um pure Ästhetik, um Selbstdarstellung oder um die Dokumentation schulischer Projekte. Diese zeigen gelegentlich die Handschrift der Lehrer und weniger die der ausführenden Jugendlichen. Auffallend war, daß im Bereich Animation hervorragende Beiträge eingereicht wurden, die von Jugendlichen im Alter zwischen 15 und 19 Jahren gestaltet wurden. Die Themenbandbreite bewegt sich zwischen 3D-animierten Konstruktionsplänen, Parodien und skurrilwitzigen Adaptionen von Märchen, wie The Tortoise and the Rabbit von Patrick Toifl (18). Die 3D-Anmiation Good Morning des Wieners Alexander Kvasnicka (19) parodiert eine umständliche Weckmaschine für Morgenmuffel. Die beiden begabten Render-men

(18) were also awarded Honorary Mentions for their quality.
Among the 6 to 11-year-olds, the exploration of the computer was mostly restricted to first attempts at graphics or simple experiments with Power Point. One outstanding product in this age group is the work by Sebastian Endt (10), who modeled his idea of a bright pink *Schweineherd* ("Pig Herd") in a simple 3D program. Another Honorary Mention was awarded to 8-year-old Stefanie Mitter for her graphic work *Clown*.
With the exception of the especially distinguished project *safe:reality*, the Net sector is still in an early phase of development. Notable here is the entry *SOS - Simple online Security* by Armin Weihbold (15): encrypted HTML files can be decrypted online using his Java script. In this way, he addresses a topical problem that is important to Internet users and implements it in a way that is thoroughly adapted the Web.
Among the many school homepages that were entered, the site by Franz Berger (18) for the HTL (secondary technical school) Braunau was awarded an Honorary Mention by the jury for the up-to-date and service-oriented presence of the school. The site demonstrates a useful Net application by young people. In general, however, neither the extent nor the implementation of contents and graphics among the submitted Web sites met the jury's expectations. In comparison with last year, there was a lack of innovative and humorous sites. There were unfortunately only a few entrants, who dared to go beyond private and fan homepages. Many of these sites left the jury with a somewhat isolated and reserved impression.
As a young talent, Markus Strahlhofer (19) is notably outstanding in the field of games. His continuing work, distinguished this year for the second time, indicates hope for more high quality games in the future. His VRML game *Area 51 - Back to the Surface* sets a high technical and graphical standard.
Among the many entries for interactive applications, the *Matura CD-Rom* from the classes 8a and 8b of the college preparatory school Akademiestrasse in Salzburg is remarkable for the reductive graphical design, text design and original navigation. Unlike many CD-Rom productions, of which the contents would be better placed on the Internet, the complete digital representation of a final year newspaper makes sense in this medium.
The driving force behind *Unser Tag* ("Our Day"), an interactive reading book, is Takuya Nimmerrichter (10). This is the second time that this young media freak has drawn attention to himself with a work that is remarkable for his age. Another of the 15

wurden mit je einer Anerkennung ausgezeichnet.
Im Vergleich zum letzten Jahr nahmen die Einreichungen im Musiksektor enorm zu. Spürbar ist der positive Einfluß der international starken österreichischen Musiker der experimentellen Electronic- und DJ-Szene. Das funkige Mia topo von Benedikt Schalk (16) und der schräge Drum ´n Bass Track Scream von Stefan Trischler (18) wurden für ihre Qualität ebenfalls mit einer Anerkennung belohnt.
Bei den 6- bis 11jährigen beschränkte sich die Auseinandersetzung mit dem Computer vorwiegend auf erste grafische Schritte bzw. auf einfache Versuche mit Power Point. Herausragendes Produkt in dieser Altersgruppe ist die Arbeit von Sebastian Endt (10), der seine Idee einer poppig pinken Schweineherde in einem einfachen 3D-Programm modellierte. Eine weitere Anerkennung erhielt die achtjährige Stefanie Mitter für ihre Grafik Clown.
Mit Ausnahme des speziell ausgezeichneten Projektes safe:reality befindet sich die Sparte Net noch im Anlaufstadium. Bemerkenswert ist SOS – Simple online Security von Armin Weihbold (15). Verschlüsselte HTML-Dateien können mit Hilfe seines Java-Scripts online entschlüsselt werden. Er greift damit eine aktuelle und für Internet-User wichtige Problematik auf und setzt sie webadäquat um.
Unter den vielen eingereichten Schulhomepages wurde außerdem die Site von Franz Berger (18) für die HTL Braunau von der Jury mit einer Anerkennung für die aktuelle und serviceorientierte Präsenz der Schule ausgezeichnet. Die Site demonstriert eine der sinnvollen Netzanwendungen von Jugendlichen. Im übrigen konnten weder der Umfang noch die inhaltliche und grafische Umsetzung der eingereichten Webseiten die Erwartungen erfüllen. Im Vergleich zum Vorjahr fehlten einige innovative, witzige Sites. Leider wagten sich nur wenige Einreicher über die Fan- und Privathomepage hinaus. Viele dieser Websites hinterließen bei der Jury einen etwas isolierten und zurückhaltenden Eindruck.
Im Feld der Games sticht das Nachwuchstalent Markus Strahlhofer (19) hervor. Zum zweiten Mal unter den Prämierten, läßt seine kontinuierliche Arbeit auch weiterhin auf hochwertige Spiele hoffen. Sein VRML-Spiel Area 51– Back to the Surface definiert einen hohen technischen sowie grafischen Standard.
Bei den vielen Einreichungen für interaktiven Anwendungen besticht die Matura-CD-Rom der 8a und 8b des Salzburger Gymnasiums Akademiestraße (eine Einzelarbeit) durch ihre reduzierte grafische Aufbereitung, Textgestaltung und originelle Navigation. Im Gegensatz zu vielen CD-ROM-Produktionen, die eigent-

Honorary Mentions goes to *Projekt Leben* ("Project Life") by Simon Oberhammer (18), as an outstanding hybrid between interaction and simulation. Very simple graphical signs representing living creatures are given the task of finding food and developing intelligence.

Golden Nica

(conspirat). On test flights through countless freestyle bytes, the jury repeatedly ran into this trademark of a young crew from Linz. The ten music tracks that were entered by this supposed band on CD set off the first rush of adrenaline on the second morning of the jury meeting: *Digital Noise*, it says on the CD cover. "An exciting mixture of digital interference noise and distorted voices—the Einstürzenden Neubauten of hard disks. At last, a digital act far removed from the techno-construction-set principle," was the tone of a statement from the jury. And wasn't there this strange device, a kind of flow heater, which was quite conspicuous as the only hardware object in the competition at a first general survey of the submissions? As it turned out, this satirical sabotage device with the promising name "Fuse Killer" also comes from the development department of (conspirat). When the device was first secretly tested in the basement of the ORF building in Linz, it did indeed "kill" a large section of the electricity supply in the broadcasting building. Finally the kind of freestyle kick the jury had been hoping for. Creative minds, throwing away the manual and starting, in their own way, to mercilessly maltreat and alienate the computer and technology, yet very purposefully and skillfully "misusing" it for their own stories. That was only the beginning: the breakthrough finally came with the (conspirat). computer animation *Personal Factory* by Raimund Schumacher and the experimental digital video *Bestanker on Tour* by Jürgen Oman. *Personal Factory*, the most professional and aesthetically assured submission in the U19 category, would stand out even in the flood of VIVA clips. In the end, the jury was not even surprised that they also have a Web site to promote their "label" (www.besu.ch/Phantomschmerz). (conspirat). was a hit at every level: artistic, multimedia, experimental and, most especially, very independent. The jury came to the conclusion that the team as a whole, with its ability to cover so many facets without becoming the least dilettantish, clearly deserved the Golden Nica. Their overall concept of open teamwork corresponds to the working methods of new media workers and makes fantastic use of the energies thus created.

lich vom Inhalt her im Internet besser aufgehoben wären, macht die abgeschlossene digitale Momentaufnahme einer Maturazeitung auf einem Datenträger Sinn. Als treibende Kraft hinter Unser Tag, einem interaktiven Lesebuch, steckt Takuya Nimmerrichter (10). Dieser junge Medienfreak schlägt bereits zum zweiten Mal mit einer für sein Alter bemerkenswerten Arbeit zu. Als auffallender Hybrid zwischen Interaktion und Simulation erhielt Projekt Leben von Simon Oberhammer (18) eine der 15 Anerkennungen. Einfachste grafische Zeichen, die Lebewesen repräsentieren, haben die Aufgabe, Nahrung zu finden und Intelligenz zu entwickeln.

Goldene Nica

(conspirat). Auf diesen Brand einer jungen Linzer Crew ist die Jury bei den Testflügen durch die unzähligen Freestyle-Bytes immer wieder gestoßen. Die zehn Musik-Tracks, die von der vermeintlichen Band auf CD eingetroffen sind, lösten am zweiten Sitzungsmorgen erstes Adrenalin bei der Jury: „Digitaler Lärm" heißt es auf der CD-Hülle. „Ein aufregender Mix aus digitalen Störgeräuschen und verzerrten Stimmen – die Einstürzenden Neubauten der Harddisks. Endlich ein digitaler Act weitab von Techno-Bausatz-Prinzip", so ein Jurystatement. Und war da nicht noch dieses seltsame Gerät, eine Art Durchlauferhitzer, das als einziges Hardware-Objekt des Wettbewerbes bereits bei der ersten groben Materialsichtung ins Auge gestochen ist? Wie sich herausstellen sollte, stammt das satirische Sabotage-Device mit dem vielversprechenden Namen „Fuse Killer" ebenfalls aus der Entwicklungsabteilung (conspirat). Beim ersten geheimen Test im Keller des ORF-Gebäudes in Linz wurde auch gleich die Stromversorgung großer Teile der Sendeanstalt abgeschossen. Endlich einer der erhofften Freestyle-Kicks. Kreative Köpfe, die die Handbücher wegwerfen und auf ihre Weise beginnen, den Computer und die Technik gnadenlos zu traktieren, zu entfremden und dennoch sehr gezielt und gekonnt für ihre Stories zu „mißbrauchen". Das war erst der Anfang: Den Durchbruch brachten schließlich die (conspirat).-Computeranimation Personal Factory von Raimund Schumacher und das experimentelle Digitalvideo Bestanker on Tour von Jürgen Oman. Personal Factory, der professionelle und ästhetisch sicherste Beitrag in der Kategorie U19, würde auch in der Flut der VIVA-Clips für Aufsehen sorgen. Daß die auch noch eine Website zur Promotion ihres „Labels" betreiben, hat die Jury dann nicht mehr erstaunt (www.besu.ch/Phantomschmerz).

Awards of Distinction

In addition to the Golden Nica, two Awards of Distinction, in the form of a multimedia Pentium Notebook, were also awarded in the competition. Aside from the group (conspirat). 18-year-old Alexander Fischl and Gregor Koschicek were the closest runner-ups for the prestigious Golden Nica. His overwhelming computer animation *Von Ignoranten, Betriebssystemen und Atomraketen* ("Ignoramuses, Operating Systems and Atomic Missiles") is outstanding for its nearly perfect depiction of a four-minute thriller about the Y2K bug, in other words the critical problem of changing the date in the year 2000. With this animation he met all the criteria that were especially important to the jury: original idea, humor, elements of surprise, power and use of individual components, and a strong feeling for his medium, the computer or computer networks respectively. In this case the criteria also included the high-quality sound design, the figurative language and the narrative strategy requiring no representation of persons and yet able to maintain the narrative tension until the very last moment. Equally persuasive were the adept use of the means available to him and the brilliant direction that gave the product as a whole its effectiveness. At the closing presentation, the quality of this complex 3D rendering project even impressed the computer animation and sound experts from California.

Among the many Web entries, *safe:reality* (www.cactis.org) by Philipp E. Haindl (18) emerged as a first-class work in terms of content and graphics and was deemed unequivocally worthy of an Award of Distinction. The high degree of "Webness" in his project is convincing, and thus it meets all the criteria that are important to the jury for an Internet work: the project can only be done on the net, in other words it is entirely designed for this medium, it involves the users and visualizes the users' participation, its aesthetic is based on the functions and limitations of the Web, and it makes use of the advantages of being non-local.

Haindl was one of the few entrants who proved able to combine digital processes, reflection and style in one product. For example, scripts running on the server in the background generate graphic elements from the user statements in the background.

Like many complex Web sites, *safe:reality* is not easily comprehensible, but a closer look reveals that it is outstanding for a number of reasons, not only because of its political topicality. Philipp Haindl takes the war in Kosovo as a starting point

(conspirat). hat zugeschlagen – auf allen Ebenen: künstlerisch, multimedial, experimentell und vor allem sehr eigenständig. Die Jury kam zum Schluß, daß das Gesamt-Team, welches so viele Facetten abzudecken vermag und dabei keine Spur von Verzettelung aufkommen läßt, die Nica unbestritten gewinnt. Ihr Gesamtkonzept der offenen Teamarbeit entspricht der Arbeitsweise von New Media Workers und nützt die dabei entstehenden Synergien großartig.

Auszeichnungen

Neben der Goldenen Nica wurden zwei Auszeichnungen in Form von je einem Multimedia-Pentium-Notebook vergeben.

Neben der Gruppe (conspirat). wurden die 18jährigen Alexander Fischl und Gregor Koschicek als heißeste Anwärter auf die prestigeträchtige Nica gehandelt. Seine umwerfende Computeranimation Von Ignoranten, Betriebsystemen und Atomraketen besticht durch nahezu perfekte Inszenierung eines vierminütigen Thrillers zum Thema Y2K-Bug, also dem brandheißen Problem der Datumsumstellung im Jahr 2000. Er erfüllt dabei alle Kriterien, auf die die Jury besonderen Wert gelegt hat: eigenständige Idee, Witz, Überraschungselemente, Kraft und Umsetzung der einzelnen Komponenten und ein starkes Bewußtsein für sein Medium, den Computer respektive die Rechner-Netzwerke. In diesem Fall gehören zu den Kriterien insbesondere das hochwertige Sounddesign, seine Bildsprache sowie seine narrative Strategie, die ganz ohne dargestellte Personen auskommt und dennoch bis zum letzten Moment die Spannung hält. Weiters überzeugten: der adäquate Einsatz der ihm zur Verfügung stehenden Mittel und die brillante Regie, welche zur Wirkung des Gesamtproduktes führt. In Anbetracht der Qualität dieses komplexen 3D-Rendering-Projektes staunten bei der Abschlußpräsentation auch die Computeranimations- und Sound-Jury-Experten aus Kalifornien.

Unter den zahlreichen Web-Einreichungen kristallisierte sich safe:reality (www.cactis.org) von Philipp E. Haindl (18) als inhaltlich und grafisch erstklassige Arbeit heraus und hat sich damit eine unumstrittene Auszeichnung verdient. Sein Projekt überzeugt durch hochgradige „Webness", also durch alle wichtigen Kriterien, die in den Augen der Jury für eine Internet-Arbeit wichtig sind: Das Projekt kann nur im Netz stattfinden, ist also wirklich auf dieses Medium zugeschnitten, es bezieht die User mit ein, visualisiert ihre Beteiligung, es

for reflecting on perceptions of reality in an anonymized abstract space—the Web—and has created an Internet site, where people interested in discussion and passing Net tourists can leave a statement about the war. This results in a dialogue that is intended to open new perspectives by being disconnected from the actual location of the respective user.
Looking back again at the best products, it may well be said that Hollywood's dinosaurs will have to come up with something good, if they want to avoid early retirement. The monopolies of the mainframes, expensive studios and mammoth companies are coming under increasingly determined attack.

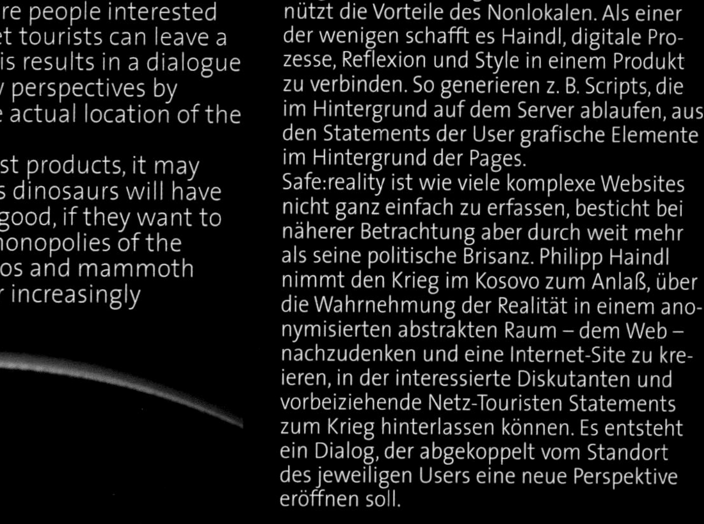

besitzt eine auf den Funktionen und Limitierungen des Web aufgebaute Ästhetik und nützt die Vorteile des Nonlokalen. Als einer der wenigen schafft es Haindl, digitale Prozesse, Reflexion und Style in einem Produkt zu verbinden. So generieren z. B. Scripts, die im Hintergrund auf dem Server ablaufen, aus den Statements der User grafische Elemente im Hintergrund der Pages.
Safe:reality ist wie viele komplexe Websites nicht ganz einfach zu erfassen, besticht bei näherer Betrachtung aber durch weit mehr als seine politische Brisanz. Philipp Haindl nimmt den Krieg im Kosovo zum Anlaß, über die Wahrnehmung der Realität in einem anonymisierten abstrakten Raum – dem Web – nachzudenken und eine Internet-Site zu kreieren, in der interessierte Diskutanten und vorbeiziehende Netz-Touristen Statements zum Krieg hinterlassen können. Es entsteht ein Dialog, der abgekoppelt vom Standort des jeweiligen Users eine neue Perspektive eröffnen soll.

Vor allem wenn man die besten Produkte noch einmal mit Abstand betrachtet, kann man sagen: Hollywoods Dinosaurierteams werden sich was einfallen lassen müssen, um der Frühpension zu entkommen. Die Monopole der Großrechner, teuren Studios und Mammut-Companies werden zunehmend hartnäckiger attackiert.

(CONSPIRAT).

RAIMUND SCHUMACHER/JÜRGEN OMAN

What is (conspirat).? It is difficult to pin it down, since this association is actually quite broad. People come and go, contribute their parts to the whole. (conspirat). produces texts, music, animations, installations, films, graphics and other types of actions, that often seem absurd at first glance. (conspirat). is simply a group of school students from the secondary technical school HTL 1 Linz, Goethestraße, from the department of graphics and communication design, who have set themselves the goal of being good. That means that there is no goal at all, but rather a perpetual and endless process that does not require planning. At school we discovered that we would prefer to implement experimental, sometimes insane and sometimes

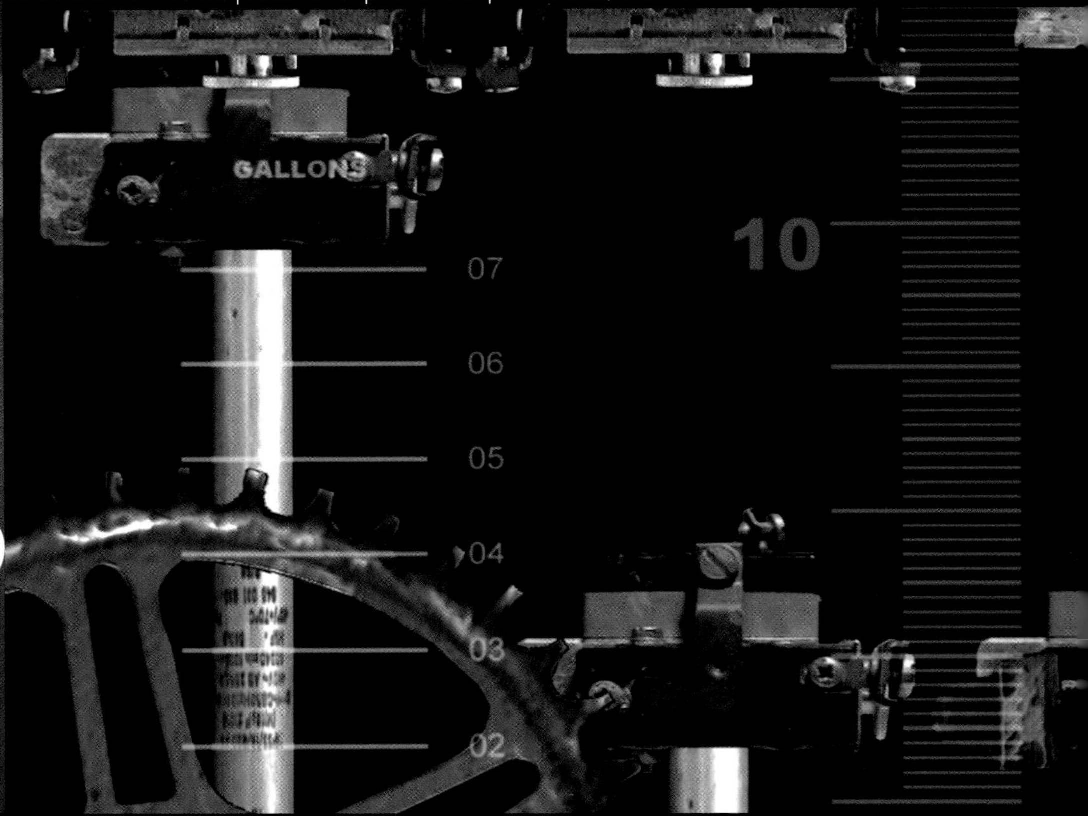

insanely idiotic works, which tend to deviate from the classical expectations of the teachers. The most recent projects have been an advertising campaign for the Euro with three spots and a background video for a phantomschmerz concert. A subgroup of (conspirat). is the music group "phantomschmerz" (http://besu.ch/phantomschmerz), which describes itself as a digital noise combo, meaning that sheet metal, barrels, disturbances and the wildest frequencies, but also classical musical instruments are sampled, composed together with the cheapest music hardware and given crazy texts. The (conspirat). works are rarely created in teamwork, because ultimately everyone has his own ideas. What we have in common, though, is a somewhat abnormal sense of humor that serves as a foundation for the projects.

(conspirat). besteht u. a. aus Raimund Schumacher, geb. 1979. Er besucht gegenwärtig die HTL für Grafik und Kommunikationsdesign in Linz. War schon im letzten Jahr mit dem Spiel „Würstelstand" unter den Anerkennungen bei Cybergeneration U19/Freestylecomputing. Jürgen Oman, geb. 1980, besucht derzeit ebenfalls die HTL für Grafik und Kommunikationsdesign in Linz. Seine Hauptinteressen liegen bei Film und Video und bei der Mitwirkung an der digitalen Lärmcombo „Phantomschmerz".

(conspirat). consists, among others, of Raimund Schumacher, born in 1979. He currently attends the secondary technical school for graphics and communication design in Linz, and received an Honorary Mention in the Cybergeneration U19/Freestyle Computing competition last year for the game "Würstelstand." Jürgen Oman, born in 1980, also attends the secondary technical school for graphics and communication design in Linz. His main interests are in film and video and he is a member of the digital noise combo "Phantomschmerz."

Was ist (conspirat).? Die Eingrenzung fällt schwer, ist diese Vereinigung doch ziemlich weitläufig. Leute kommen und gehen, tragen ihren Teil zum Ganzen bei. (conspirat). bringt Texte, Musik, Animationen, Installationen, Filme, Grafiken und Aktionen der anderen Art hervor, die auf den ersten Blick oft absurd wirken. (conspirat). ist einfach eine Gruppierung aus Schülern der HTL 1 Linz, Goethestraße, Abteilung Grafik- und Kommunikationsdesign, die es sich zum Ziel gesetzt haben, gut zu werden, das heißt, es gibt überhaupt kein Ziel, es ist ein immerwährender und endloser Prozeß, der keiner Planung bedarf. Wir haben in der Schule entdeckt, daß wir auch eher experimentelle, teils wahnsinnige und wahnsinnig blöde Arbeiten verwirklichen wollen, die jedoch manchmal von der klassischen Erwartungshaltung der Lehrer abweichen. Die letzten Projekte sind eine Euro-Werbekampagne mit 3 Spots und ein Hintergrundvideo für ein "phantomschmerz"-Konzert.
Eine Untergruppierung von (conspirat). ist die Musikgruppe "phantomschmerz" (http://besu.ch/phantomschmerz), die sich selbst als digitale Lärm-Combo bezeichnet, das heißt, es werden Blech, Tonnen, Störungen und ärgste Frequenzen, aber auch klassische Musikinstrumente gesampelt, auf billigster Musik-Hardware zurechtkomponiert und mit wahnwitzigen Texten versehen. Die (conspirat).-Arbeiten entstehen selten im Teamwork, da jeder letztendlich seinen eigenen Kopf hat. Was wir jedoch alle gemeinsam haben, ist ein etwas abnormaler Sinn für Humor, der als Grundlage für die Projekte dient.

VON IGNORANTEN, BETRIEBSSYSTEMEN UND ATOMRAKETEN

ALEXANDER FISCHL GREGOR KOSCHICEK

The year 2000. Object of many superstitious prophecies. Will it bring the dawn of a new era of humanity or perhaps the end of the world? Our animation is intended to draw attention to the dangers that could result from carelessness and ignorance. The malfunctioning of the computers controlling nuclear weapons.

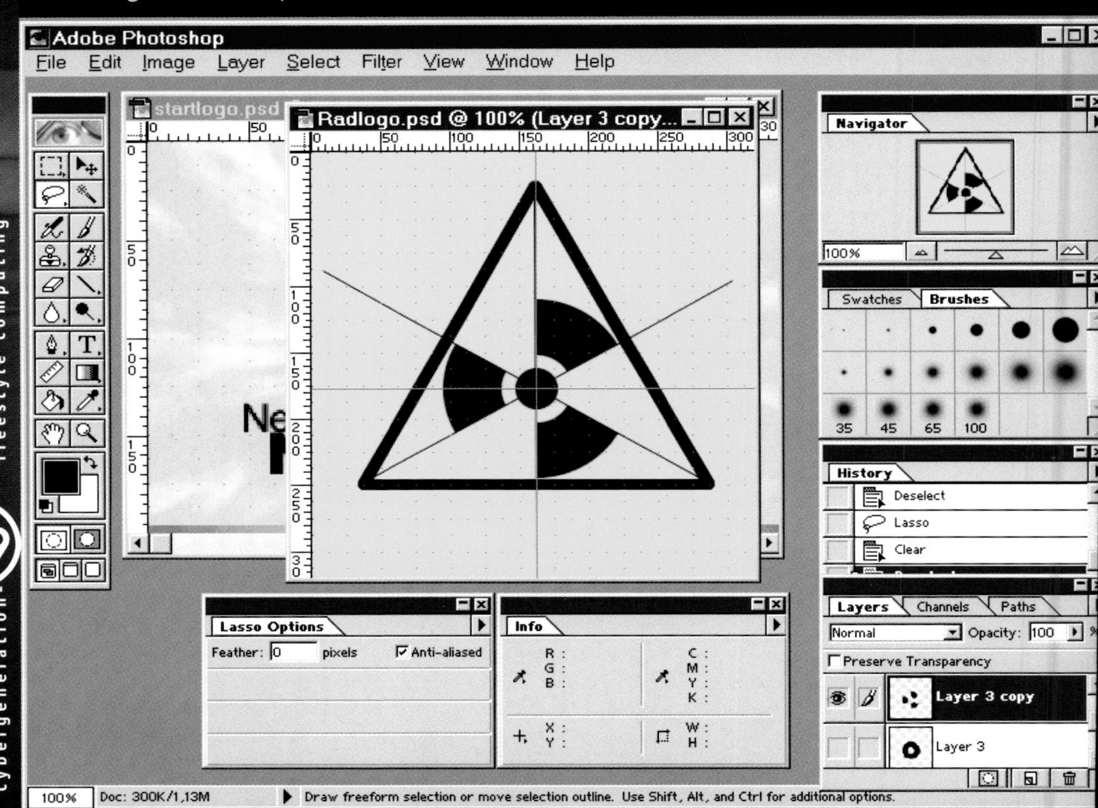

Everyone can decide for themselves what the video expresses, because it represents

a) a criticism of nuclear weapons,
b) a criticism of our trust in modern technologies,
c) a criticism of underestimating serious situations,
d) a parody of a certain operating system (the name has been changed).

The observer finds himself in a nuclear weapons base, several seconds before midnight. As he journeys through the events, he is accompanied by an interview that is intended to convey the actual year 2000 problem: an underestimation of and disregard for the dangers that could result from our technologies.

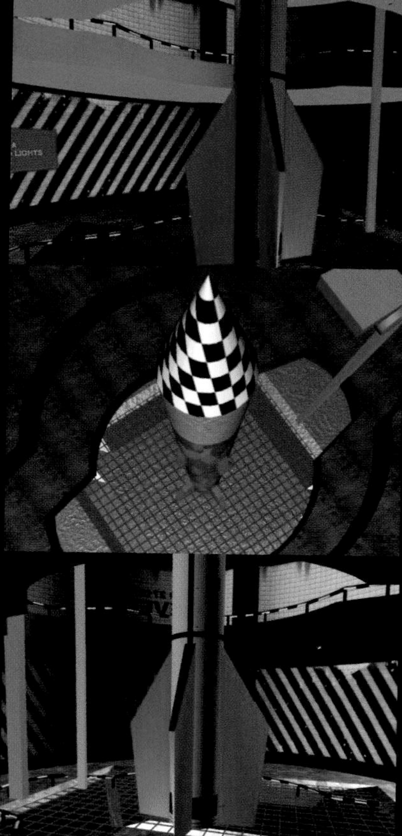

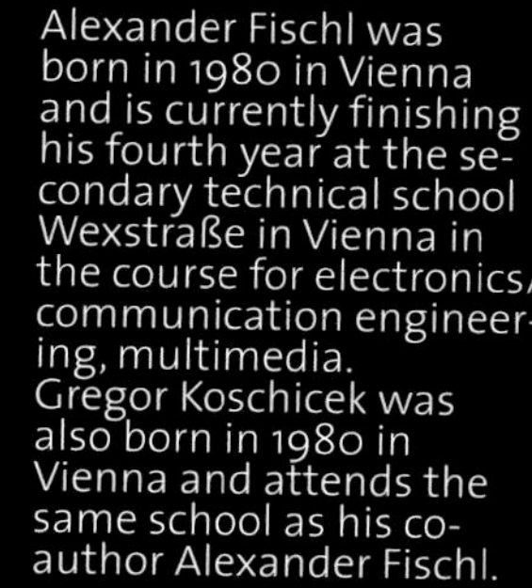

Alexander Fischl was born in 1980 in Vienna and is currently finishing his fourth year at the secondary technical school Wexstraße in Vienna in the course for electronics/ communication engineering, multimedia.
Gregor Koschicek was also born in 1980 in Vienna and attends the same school as his co-author Alexander Fischl.

Alexander Fischl, geb. 1980 in Wien, absolviert derzeit das vierte Schuljahr an der HTBLA Wexstraße in Wien in der Fachrichtung Elektronik/Nachrichtentechnik, Multimedia.
Gregor Koschicek wurde ebenfalls 1980 in Wien geboren und besucht dieselbe Schule wie sein Co-Autor Alexander Fischl.

Das Jahr 2000. Inhalt vieler abergläubischer Prophezeiungen. Wird es den Aufbruch in eine neue Ära der Menschheit bedeuten oder gar den Weltuntergang?
Unsere Animation soll auf eine der Gefahren aufmerksam machen, die durch Unachtsamkeit und Ignoranz entstehen könnte. Die Fehlfunktion von Computern, welche Kernwaffen kontrollieren.
Was das Video aussagt, kann jeder für sich entscheiden, denn es stellt

a) eine Kritik an Kerwaffen,
b) eine Kritik an unserem Vertrauen in moderne Technologien,
c) eine Kritik an der Unterschätzung ernster Situationen,
d) eine Persiflage auf ein gewisses Betriebssystem (Name geändert) dar.

Der Betrachter findet sich in einem Kernwaffenstützpunkt wieder; einige Sekunden vor Mitternacht. Während seiner Reise durch die Geschehnisse wird er von einem Interview begleitet, welches das eigentliche Jahr-2000-Problem

SAFER REALITY
SCREWING UP REALITY'S INTERFACE

PHIL E. HAINDL

http://www.cactis.org

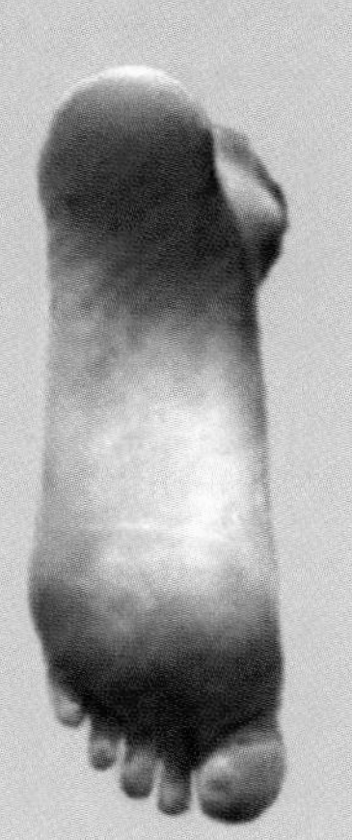

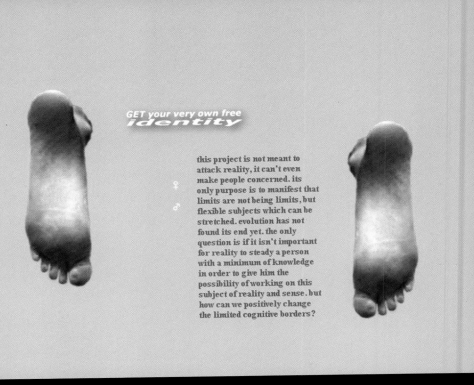

GET your very own free
identity

♀
♂

this project is not meant to attack reality, it can't even make people concerned. its only purpose is to manifest that limits are not being limits, but flexible subjects which can be stretched. evolution has not found its end yet. the only question is if it isn't important for reality to steady a person with a minimum of knowledge in order to give him the possibility of working on this subject of reality and sense. but how can we positively change the limited cognitive borders?

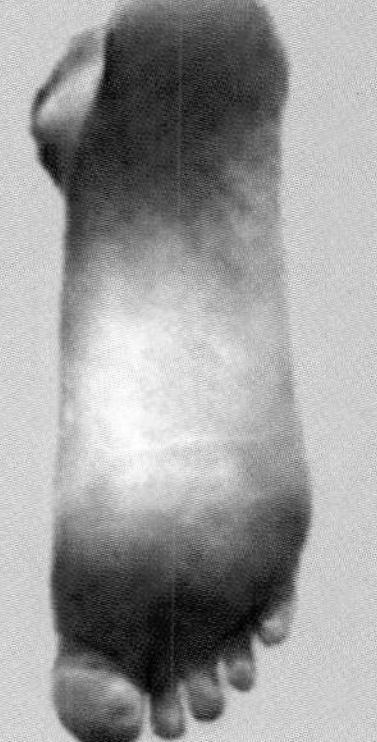

This Web project represents an homage to the perception of reality. It raises the question of the extent, to which we all depend on empirically developed reality or what the opportunities and chances are that stubborn and naive perception offers us.... Plato's Allegory of the Cave served as model for me, because I find it interesting in several respects.
Appropriate patterns of behavior are recommended to us human beings through education, society and conscience, which most of our naive fellow human beings gratefully accept. This ultimately led me to the question of what would happen if a person could express opinions and questions free from all considerations, conventions and adaptations....
...Thus it is/was possible, for example, to bring what has been happening in the war in Yugoslavia into an interactive discourse. Andrej Tisma, a friend of mine who lives in Novi Sad, described his daily struggle to escape the war. He told his story, how he protected his family, what he thinks about the NATO bombing - yet he did not forget to suggest other possible solutions for the Balkan problem. On the other side there was also an American who took part. He revealed his views on the solution to the conflict to the net community, whereby he also attempted to understand the Yugoslavian side. He did not know - and still does not know - that his discussion partner was someone directly affected, specifically Andrej, who was paying close attention and trying, for his part, to understand the statements of the other.

Phil E. Haindl was born in 1981 and lives in Leonding near Linz. He is currently finishing his final year at a college preparatory school in Linz. In his free time he is interested in philosophy and psychology.

Phil E. Haindl wurde 1981 geboren und lebt in Leonding bei Linz. Er besucht gegenwärtig die Maturaklasse des Bundesoberstufengymnasiums in Linz. In seiner Freizeit beschäftigt er sich mit Philosophie und Psychologie.

Webpage zur anonymen Kommunikation zwischen Menschen unterschiedlicher Kulturen, Ideologien und Standpunkte.

Dieses Web-Projekt stellt eine Hommage an die Wahrnehmung der Realität dar. Sie wirft die Frage auf, inwieweit wir alle von unserer empirisch entwickelten Realität abhängig sind bzw. welche Möglichkeiten und Chancen die „sture und naive" Wahrnehmung bietet. Als Vorbild galt mir Platons Höhlengleichnis, das ich in mehrerlei Hinsicht interessant finde. Durch Erziehung, Gesellschaft und Gewissen werden uns Menschen passende Verhaltensmuster „empfohlen", die die meisten unserer „naiven" Mitmenschen auch dankbar annehmen. So kam ich schlußendlich zur Frage, was denn nun passieren würde, könnte ein Mensch frei von jeglicher Rücksichtnahme, Konvention und Adaption an seine ideologischen Vorstellungen urteilen und fragen ...
So ist/war es beispielsweise möglich, die Kriegsgeschehnisse in Jugoslawien in einen interaktiven Diskurs einzubringen. Andrej Tisma, ein Freund von mir, der in Novi Sad lebt, schilderte seinen täglichen Kampf, dem Kriegsgeschehen zu entkommen. Er erzählt seine Geschichte, wie er seine Familie schützt, wie er denkt, was er von den NATO-Angriffen hält - er vergißt aber nicht, andere Lösungsvorschläge für das Balkan-Problem aufzuzeigen.
Auf der anderen Seite ein Amerikaner, der ebenfalls teilnahm. Er offenbarte der Netzgemeinde seine Ansichten von der Konfliktlösung, wobei er versuchte, die jugoslawische Seite zu verstehen. Er wußte nicht – und weiß noch immer nicht – daß sein Gesprächspartner ein betroffener, nämlich Andrej war, der wiederum

WEBPAGE DER HTL BRAUNAU

FRANZ BERGER (with help from Markus Leitner and Hans Blocher)
http://www.htl.at

Franz Berger was born in 1980, lives in Eberschwang in the Innviertel of Upper Austria, and attends the secondary technical school in Braunau am Inn. In addition to the conventional computer applications, he is also proficient in C++ and JavaScript.

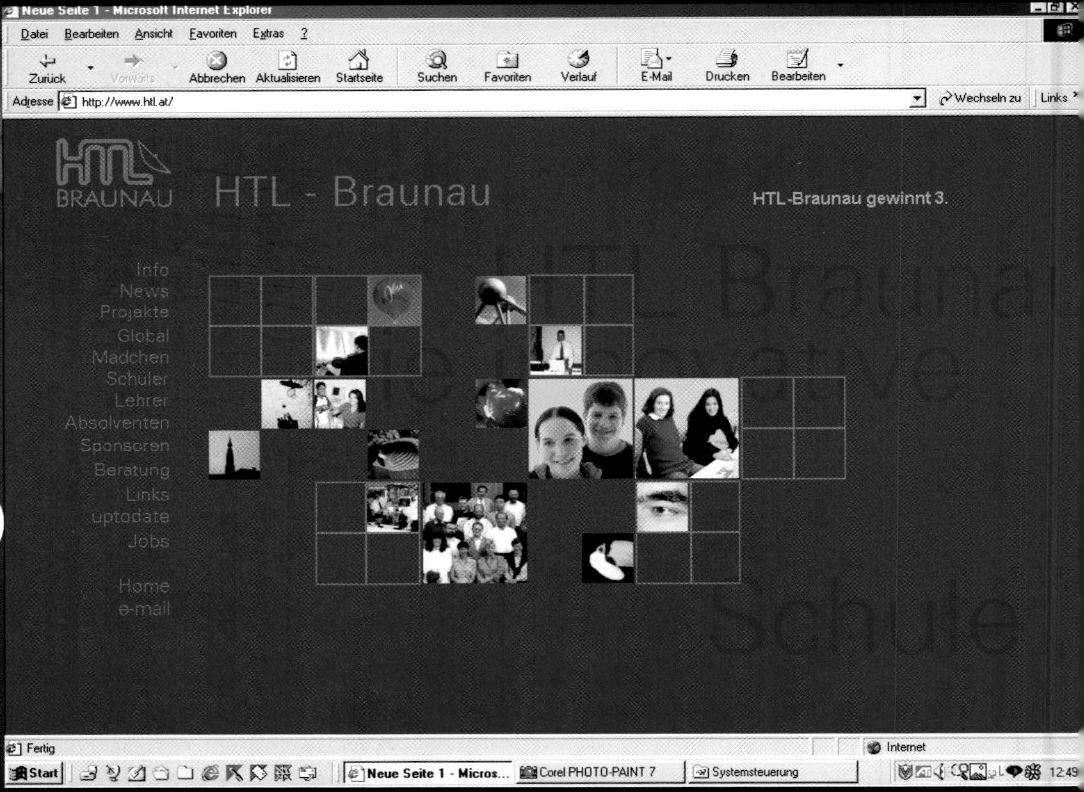

Franz Berger wurde 1980 geboren, lebt in Eberschwang im Oberösterreichischen Innviertel und besucht die HTL in Braunau am nn. Neben den herkömmlichen Computeranwendungen beherrscht er auch C++ und JavaScript.

The main task of my work was to completely revise the existing homepage for the secondary technical school Braunau and give it a new, attractive design and integrate interactive elements. The homepage is intended to represent the secondary technical school Braunau on the World Wide Web and provide everyone interested in it with an opportunity be informed about the school.

Die Hauptaufgabe meiner Arbeit bestand darin, die bereits bestehende Homepage der HTL Braunau komplett zu überarbeiten und mit einem neuen, ansprechenden Design zu versehen und interaktive Elemente einzubauen. Die Homepage soll dazu dienen, die HTL Braunau im World Wide Web zu vertreten und allen Interessierten die Möglichkeit zu bieten, sich über

SCHWEINEHERDE

SEBASTIAN ENDT

: represents a herd of pigs.
anding on a small hill and some of them are in the mud.
me to me when I was on an excursion and saw a herd of sheep.
: would be nice to be able to draw a herd like that myself on the
So I sat down and drew the picture of the herd of pigs entirely
except for the curly tails). At first I had a problem with the light
nake the pigs' shadows clearly visible. After working on it for
and after several renderings, it finally worked.

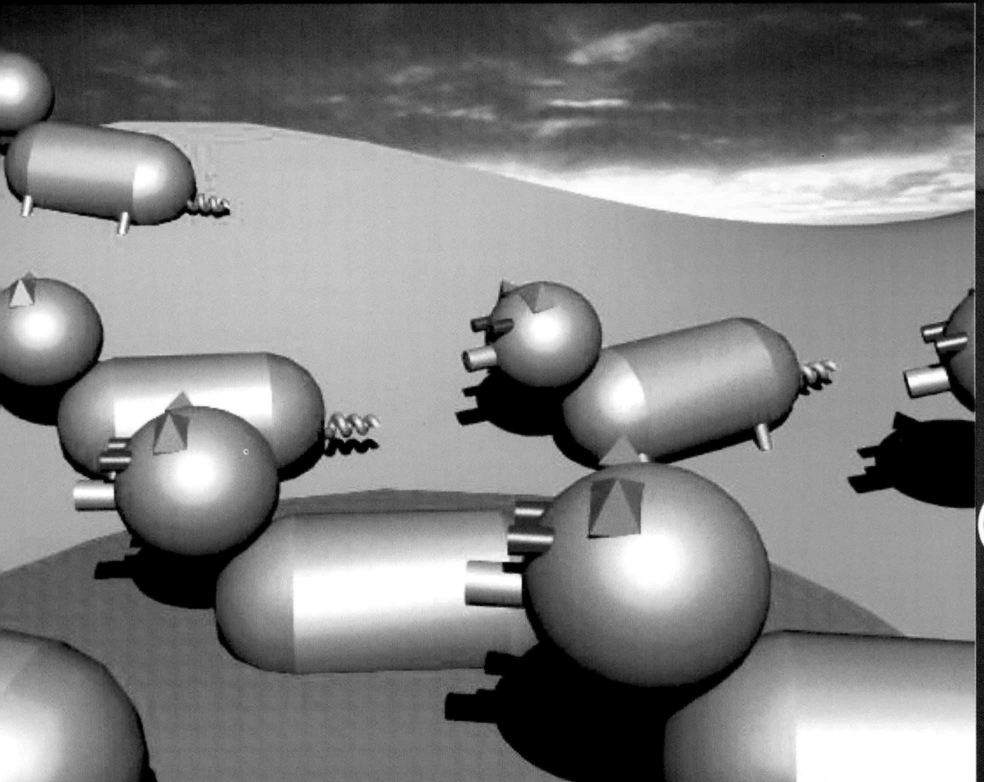

ellt eine Herde von Schweinen dar.
en auf einem kleinen Hügel und teilweise im Sumpf.
f die Idee, als ich bei einem Ausflug eine Herde Schafe sah.
daß es nett wäre, selbst am Computer so eine Herde zeichnen
Also setzte ich mich hin und erstellte völlig eigenhändig
s Ringelschwänzchen) das Bild der Schweineherde.
eiten hatte ich bei der Lichtquelle, um den Schatten
ne gut sichtbar zu machen. Doch nach längerem
und mehrmaligem Rendern klappte es.

Sebastian Endt was born in 1989 in Wels, where he also lives and attends the third grade at the grammar school Neustadt.

Sebastian Endt wurde 1989 in Wels geboren, wo er auch lebt und die dritte

MATURA CD DER 8A UND 8

SIMON GASSNER

Simon Gaßner was born in Zell am See and now lives in Salzburg. He is currently finishing his final year at the college preparatory school Akademienstraße in Salzburg.

The work was originally created as a supplement for the final year r
we had planned. Due to initial problems involved in working with a
students from different classes, though, I made the CD by myself in
It is planned to be released together with the final year newspaper
tains many articles, pictures and small programs created during ou
school. The CD has to be attractive as a memento of our school days
sell well, and it has to be attractive to sponsors, because it was mac
money from sponsors.

Simon Gaßner wurde in Zell am See geboren, lebt jetzt in Salzburg und absolviert zur Zeit die Maturaklasse des Gymnasiums Akademiestraße in Salzburg.

Die Arbeit entstand als eine Ergänzung zu unserer geplanten
Maturazeitschrift. Nach anfänglichen Problemen bei der Zusamme
der klassenübergreifenden Teams habe ich die CD als Einzelarbeit r
Sie wird voraussichtlich in Kombination mit der Maturazeitung
herausgegeben werden und beinhaltet zahlreiche Artikel, Bilder un
Programme, die während der Schulzeit entstanden sind. Die CD mu
Erinnerungswert haben, sie muß sich verkaufen lassen, und sie mu
Sponsoren attraktiv sein, weil sie mit Sponsore
realisiert wird.

GOOD MORNING

ALEXANDER KVASNICKA

This computer animation shows a preliminary version of a very complicated and involved, room-sized alarm clock machine in the style of a mad inventor. Although the animation is not overly long, it was still a bit much for my old Pentium 120 to handle. Since the final scene used nearly 20 Mb just as a MAX file, contained 400 objects with over 100 materials and just this took three minutes to open in 3D-Studio MAX, I was under a lot of pressure for the last few days. If I hadn't needed the computer for school every day, it would not have been a problem to just let it go through the rendering for a week, but as it was, I had a big problem.....

Diese Computeranimation zeigt eine vorläufige Version einer recht ausgeklügelten, raumfüllenden Weckmaschine im Stil von Daniel Düsentrieb.
Die Animation ist zwar nicht allzu lang, überforderte allerdings meinen alten Pentium 120 doch um einiges. Da die endgültige Szene als MAX-Datei allein fast 20Mb verbraucht, fast 400 Objekte mit über 100 Materialien beinhaltet und es alleine drei Minuten braucht, um sie in 3D-Studio MAX zu öffnen, war ich in den letzten Tagen einigermaßen im Streß. Hätte ich den Rechner nicht jeden Tag für die Schule gebraucht, wäre es kein Problem gewesen, ihn einfach eine Woche durchrendern zu lassen, doch so hatte ich ein großes Problem ...

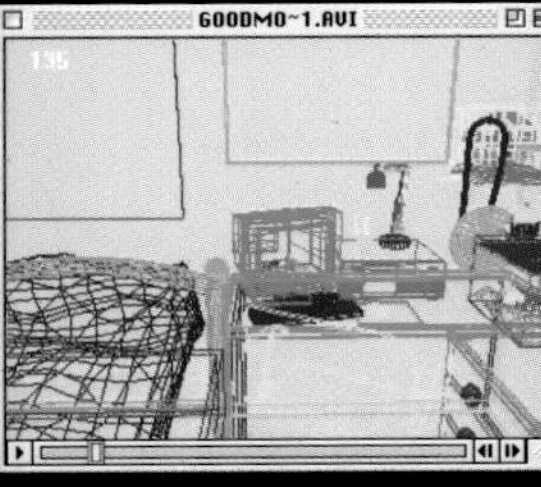

Alexander Kvasnicka was born in 1979 in Vienna, attends the course for business computer science at the secondary technical school for economics and engineering, and has worked in technical fields during practical training courses during school holidays. He is especially interested in film and computer animation.

Alexander Kvasnicka wurde 1979 in Wien geboren, besucht den Ausbildungszweig Betriebsinformatik an der HTL für Wirtschaftsingenieurwesen und hat während seiner Ferialpraktika im technischen Bereich gearbeitet. Seine besonderen Interessen liegen beim Film und der Computeranimation.

CLOWN

STEFANIE MITTER

We were at Ars Electronica Center and we were shown how you can draw on the computer with a mouse. There was a task bar with different signs and one with different colors. First I just tried it out and drew lines and surfaces. Then I clicked on a color with the mouse and started to draw a clown...

Wir waren im Ars Electronica Center, und dort hat man uns gezeigt, wie man auf einem Computer mit der Maus zeichnen kann. Es gab eine Task-Leiste mit verschiedenen Zeichen und eine mit verschiedenen Farben. Zuerst probierte ich es einfach einmal aus und zeichnete Striche und Flächen. Mit der Maus habe ich dann eine Farbe angeklickt und damit begonnen, einen Clown zu zeichnen ...

Stefanie Mitter was bor 1991 in Linz and attends grammar school Bruck-nerstraße. She sometim goes to the Ars Electron Center in her free time. would like to teach kind garten some day.

Stefanie Mitter wurde 1991 in Linz geboren un besucht die Volksschule Brucknerstraße. In ihrer Freizeit besucht sie mar mal das Ars Electronica Center. Sie möchte einn Kindergärtnerin werde

UNSER TAG

TAKUYA NIMMERRICHTER

Our Day" - My class wanted to make an interactive multimedia book on the computer. First we vanted to write a ghost story, but because the children in my class come from many different ountries and every child has a different story to tell, we decided to write about a day at school nd at home. Our teacher had us do the stories and pictures as homework, and some of the hildren have a computer at home. A friend of my father's helped us record the videos, because he as a digital video camera, but we made the videos ourselves. For the sound recordings I borrowed mini-disc recorder from my mother. My father helped us to adapt the pictures. The teacher didn't elp us, because she doesn't know so much about using a computer.

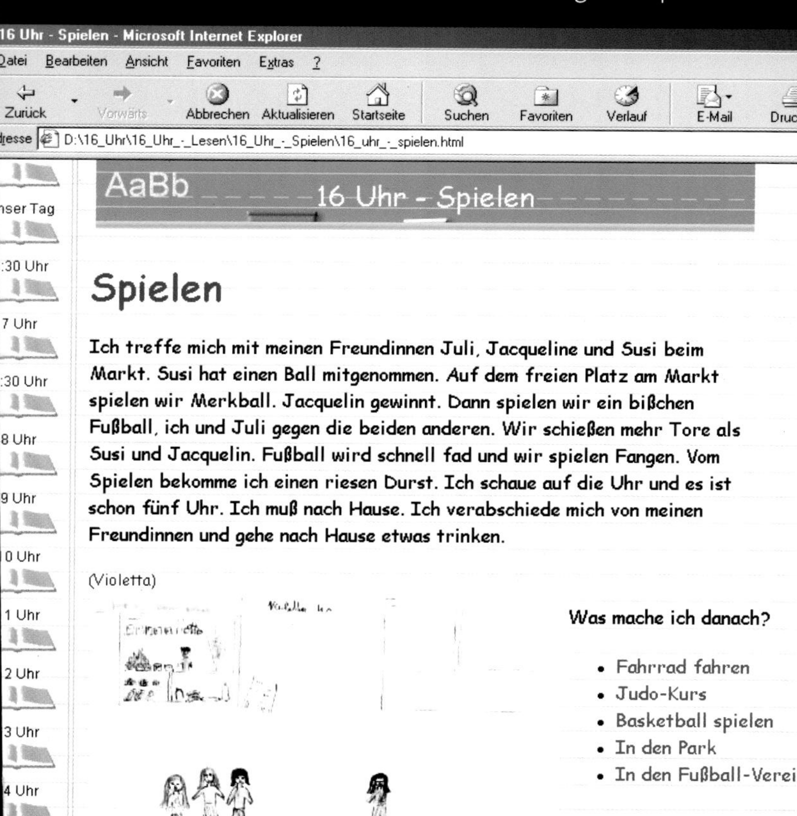

Takuya Nimmerrichter was born in 1989 and attends the Vereinsgasse grammar school in Vienna, where he also lives. Aside from judo and inline skating, his hobbies are computer, Lego Technik Cybermaster and his model train.

Takuya Nimmerrichter wurde 1989 geboren und besucht die Volksschule Vereinsgasse in Wien, wo er auch lebt. Seine besonderen Vorlieben sind neben Judo und Inline-Skaten der Computer, LEGO-Technik Cybermaster und seine Modelleisenbahn.

eine Klasse wollte auf dem Computer ein interaktives Multimediabuch herstellen. Zuerst woll- n wir eine Gespenstergeschichte schreiben, aber weil die Kinder unserer Klasse aus vielen ver- hiedenen Ländern kommen und jedes Kind eine andere Geschichte erzählen kann, haben wir s entschlossen, über unseren Tag in der Schule und zu Hause zu schreiben. Unsere Lehrerin hat s die Geschichten und Bilder als Hausaufgaben machen lassen, und einige Kinder haben mputer zu Hause. Beim Überspielen der Videos hat uns ein Freund meines Vaters geholfen, der e digitale Videokamera hat. Die Videos haben wir aber selber gemacht. Für die Tonaufnahmen be ich mir von meiner Mutter einen Mini-Disc-Recorder ausgeborgt. Beim Anpassen der Bilder uns mein Vater geholfen. Die Lehrerin hat uns nicht geholfen, weil sie sich mit dem Computer ht so gut auskennt.

PROJEKT LEBEN

SIMON OBERHAMMER

The program is based on the presupposition that intelligence emerges by itself, if one creates a system with simple rules that progressively complicate themselves or become ever more complex. Starting from this presupposition, I wanted to create a nice looking program involving the chaos aspect of artificial intelligence. After several ASCII-only versions, I found the tangle on the screen so attractive that I programmed a VGA version with simple graphics in simple surroundings.

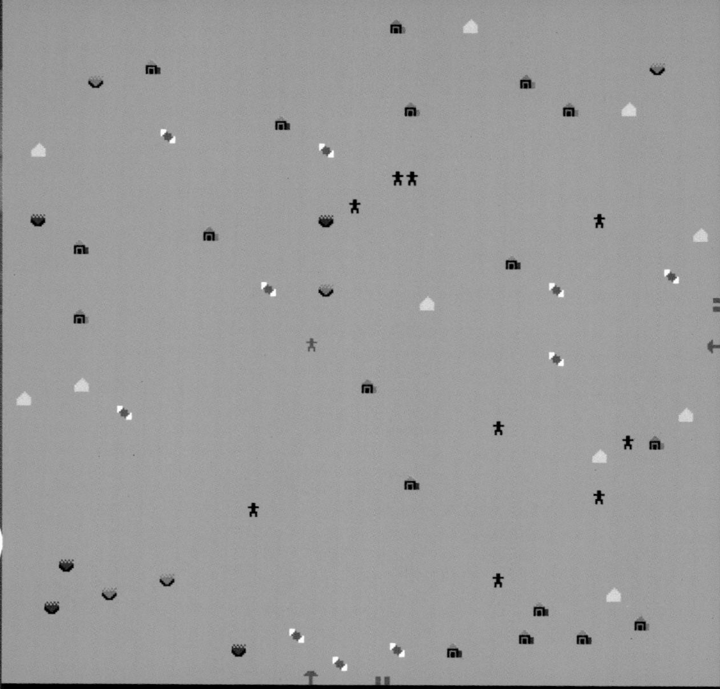

Nr. 1
Kein best. Ziel
Hunger: 45
Durst: 45
Hände frei
- - - - - - - -
Bekannte Stellen:
0 x Futtertrog
0 x Wassertrog
0 x Futterstelle
0 x Brunnen
0 x Fleischerei
0 x Steinbruch
=> Futtertrog(+Futter
=> Wassertrog(+Wasser
- - - - - - -
=> Futterstelle(-Flei
=> Brunnen(-Stein)
- - - - - - -
=> Fleischerei(+Fleis
=> Steinbruch(+Stein)
Use Cursorkeys:
« » Change Creature
Speed up/Slow Down
ESC beendet
Delay: 35000

Das Programm basiert auf der Annahme, daß sich Intelligenz von selbst ergibt, wenn man ein System mit einfachen Regeln erstellt, die sich selbst verkomplizieren bzw. das System selbst immer komplexer wird. Aus dieser Annahme heraus wollte ich ein „nett anzusehendes" Programm erstellen, das sich mit dem Chaos-Aspekt der Künstlichen Intelligenz beschäftigt. Nach einigen ASCII-only-Versionen fand ich das Gewusle auf dem Bildschirm so ansprechend, daß ich eine neue VGA-Version mit einfachen Grafiken in einem einfachen Umfeld programmierte.

Simon Oberhammer was born in 1981 in Schärding and attends the college preparatory school there. He is especially interested in graphic simulation and the field of artificial intelligence.

Simon Oberhammer wurde 1981 in Schärding geboren und besucht dort das Gymnasium. Sein besonderes Interesse gilt der grafischen Simulation und dem Gebiet der KI.

MIA TOPO

BENEDIKT SCHALK

vorked on this piece for about three months, including several terruptions. The first step was to prepare a sample with a drum achine…then I added a melody to the e-piano track with the program und Club 2.0 and underlaid it with a very soft Soft-Gong, a funk guitar riff d a slap bass. I made this soft, flowing sequence the main theme of the ece. Then I composed several variations to it and expanded the song by ning the different sequences together.

dem Stück arbeitete ich mit Unterbrechungen etwa drei Monate. Der e Schritt war, daß ich mit einer Drum-Machine einen Sample erstellte … n fügte ich mit dem Programm Sound Club 2.0 auf der E-Piano-Spur eine odie hinzu und unterlegte sie mit einem sehr weichen Soft-Gong, einem k-Gitarrenriff und einem Slap-Baß. Diese weiche, fließende Sequenz chte ich zum Hauptthema des Stücks. Dann komponierte ich dazu einige ationen und baute den Song aus, indem ich die verschiedenen Sequenzen nanderfügte.

Benedikt Schalk is 16 years old and attends a business secondary school in Vienna. He plays the drums and electric guitar and composes on the computer in his free time.

Benedikt Schalk ist 16 Jahre und besucht die Handelsschule in Wien. Er spielt Schlagzeug und E-Gitarre und komponiert in seiner Freizeit auf dem Computer.

AREA 51 BACK TO THE SURFACE

MARKUS STRAHLHOFER

Area 51 – Back to the Surface is a computer game based on a Web browser. Since I spend so much of my free time involved in 3D animations and working with video on the PC, and I also like to play various computer games with schoolmates over the Internet, I wanted to try to create a computer game myself. The present game can be downloaded free from the URL <www.inode.at/paradise>.

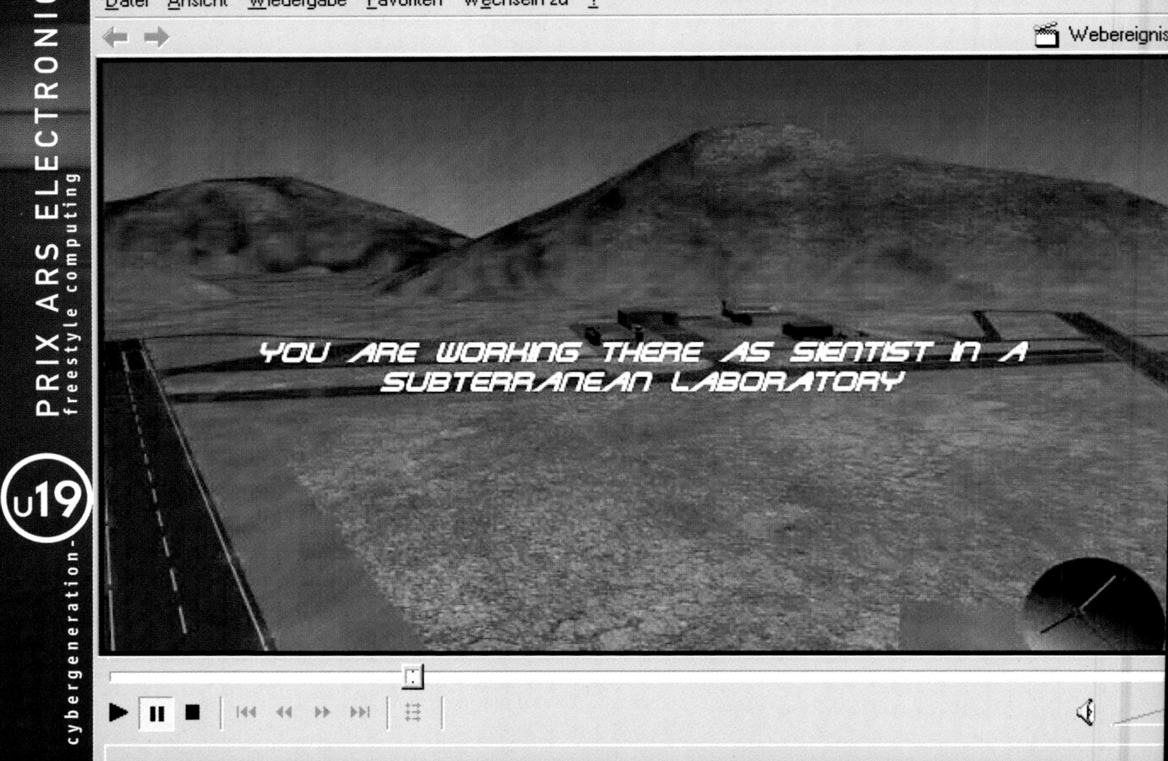

Area 51 – Back to the Surface ist ein Computerspiel auf der Basis eines Webbrowsers. Da ich mich in meiner Freizeit sehr viel mit 3D-Animationen und Videobearbeitung auf dem PC beschäftige und nebenbei das eine oder andere Computerspiel mit Schulkollegen über das Internet spiele, versuchte ich nun selber, ein Computerspiel anzufertigen. Das vorliegende Spiel kann von der URL <www.inode.at/paradise> gratis heruntergeladen werden.

Markus Strahlhofer, born 1980, lives in Vienna and attends the secondary technical school for mechanical engineering there, where he is in charge of school projects. During school holidays he has also been employed as a technician for a large electrical company.

Markus Strahlhofer, geboren 1980, lebt in Wien und besucht dort die HTL für Maschinenbau, wo er schulinterne Projekte leitet. In den Ferien war er unter anderem als Techniker bei Großunternehmen in der Elektrobranche tätig.

ORTOISE

AND THE RABBIT

PATRICK TOIFL

times have not completely passed me by, so after films like *Toy*
I wanted to make a computer animation, too.
v the finished version on video for the first time, I was shocked.
t 10,000 shillings in costs – and the animation was not even five
it really was fun. Modeling for three months, building scenes and
ndering for several months...., then it took several more weeks for

n nach Filmen wie *Toy Story, Antz* und *A Bug's Life* Lust, auch
nation zu machen. Ehrlich gesagt, hat mich das Ergebnis, als ich
Video sah, schockiert. Fünf Monate Arbeit, ungefähr 10.000
lie Animation dauert nicht einmal fünf Minuten ... Puh! Aber es
t. Drei Monate modellieren, Szenen bauen und letztlich
te rendern ..., dann brauchte es noch Wochen für die Musik,
nahmen und zuletzt noch vier Tage für den Schnitt. An dieser
hard Mahr danken, der mit seiner Musik wesentlich zur Wirkung

rick Toifl was born in 1980,
in Vienna and attends the
lege preparatory school IX,
ergasse. His desired future
ession: graphics artist and

Patrick Toifl wurde 1980
geboren, lebt in Wien und
besucht dort das
Bundesgymnasium IX,
Glasergasse. Sein
Berufswunsch: Grafiker und

SCREAM

STEFAN TRISCHLER

Scream was created in August 1997 with the program FastTracker and was the first song after *Exx-Files*, my first demo tape using my pseudonym "Exxon." Before that I made it to the Austrian finals for the European youth music competition SCYPE with the track *Paradise*. Quite unexpectedly I won the Endo-Techno contest conducted in conjunction with the steirischer herbst and was awarded a trip to Las Vegas for *Shmoof Operator* (from *Exx Files*). Since then I have started working with more professional sampling equipment and hope that I will soon be able to hold vinyl in my hands with one of my pieces on it.

Scream entstand im August 1997 im Programm FastTracker und war das erste Lied nach *Exx' Files*, meinem ersten Demo-Tape unter meinem Pseudonym „Exxon". Zuvor hatte ich mit dem Track *Paradise* das Österreichfinale des europaweiten Jugendmusikwettbewerbes „SCYPE" erreicht. Unerwartet kam der Sieg beim Endo-Techno-Contest im Rahmen des Steirischen Herbstes, als ich mit *Shmoof Operator* (aus *Exx' Files*) eine Reise nach Las Vegas gewann. Mittlerweile habe ich auf professionelleres Sampling-Equipment umgestellt und hoffe, bald ein Stück Vinyl mit einem meiner Stücke in Händen halten zu können.

Stefan Trischler, born 1980 in Vienna, started taking piano lessons when he was six years old, learned to play the drums when he was 12 and received his first music-capable computer when he was 14. Since then he has produced mostly Jungle (Drum `n' Bass) Music.

Stefan Trischler, geb. 1980 in Wien, erhielt seit seinem sechsten Lebensjahr Klavierunterricht, lernte mit 12 Schlagzeug und erhielt mit 14 seinen ersten musikfähigen Computer. Seitdem produziert er vorwiegend Jungle (Drum'n'Bass).

MPLE ONLINE SECURITY SOS

ARMIN WEIHBOLD

: basic idea for this encryption program was to secure access to Internet pages :hout using CGI scripts, which have to be stored in a special directory on the b server and cannot always be accessed. This gave me the idea of encrypting entire page and preparing it so that it can be decrypted with an ordinary wser capable of Java script 1.2. *SOS* encrypts .html files with the algorithm BC1 t I invented and outputs an html page with the encrypted original page and decryption routine in Java script.

Welcome to the Homepage of
the SOS - System and
the BC1 Algorithm!

Secure your Homepage without using CGI - Scripts!

lgorithm BC1 (Binary Comparision)

vorks on the basis of a binary comparision. That is if binary numbers are equal output 0 else 1. And this process is recursive.

```
)00   11111011
)11   10101000
----- ------------
)11   01010011
```

ncrypts four chars of the data at once. The comparision is as
s (one number represents one char) The example uses a
ord with length 6.

```
ta ->  1234
y  ->  1234
       2345
       3456
       4561
       5612
       6123
```

imes four new chars are to be encrypted the last bit of the
rd is shifted to the beginning.

ion

em, which stands behind this program is as followed:
st a possibility to encrypt (and decrypt) *.htm - files without CGI-BIN Skripts...so my idea was:

ıtm - file
OS.exe
get is the encrypted file, which can be easily opened and decrypted by an javascript 1.2 capable Browser.
the file, paste password and you can read the file again.

Code

Armin Weihbold was born in 1983 in Judenburg, currently lives in Mauthausen and attends the college preparatory school Khevenhüllerstraße in Linz. In his free time he is occupied with various programming languages and especially with online applications.

Armin Weihbold wurde 1983 in Judenburg geboren, lebt in Mauthausen und besucht das Bundesgymnasium Khevenhüllerstraße in Linz. In seiner Freizeit beschäftigt er sich mit diversen Programmiersprachen und im speziellen mit Online-Anwendungen.

;rundidee für dieses Verschlüsselungsprogramm war, den Zugang zu netseiten absichern zu können, ohne dabei CGI-Scripts zu benutzen, die in einem speziellen Verzeichnis auf dem Webserver ablegen muß und zu n man nicht immer Zugang hat. Daher hatte ich die Idee, die ganze Seite zu hlüsseln und so zu präparieren, daß man sie mit einem gängigen Java-Script higen Browser wieder entschlüsseln kann. *SOS* verschlüsselt .html-Dateien em selbsterfundenen Algorithmus BC1 und gibt eine .html-Seite mit der hlüsselten Originalseite und der Entschlüsselungsroutine in Javascript aus.

JURY
PRIX ARS ELECTRONICA 99

chairman of the jury

Hannes Leopoldseder – born 1940 in St. Leonhard; Ph.D., journalist for the Austrian Broadcastin Corporation since 1967, Managing Director of the Upper Austrian Region 1974—1998, ORF Informa tion Director since 1998. Co-founder of the Ars Electronica Festival and the Linzer Klangwolke i 1979, initiator of the Prix Ars Electronica competition in 1987. 1991 originated the idea of the Ar Electronica Center as a museum of the future in Linz. ▬ **Hannes Leopoldseder** – Geboren 1940 St. Leonhard, Dr.Phil., seit 1967 als Journalist beim Österreichischen Rundfunk tätig, 1974–1998 Landesintendant d ORF, Landesstudio Oberösterreich, seit 1998 ORF Informationsintendant. 1979 Mitbegründer der Ars Electronica ur der Linzer Klangwolke. 1987 Initiator des Prix Ars Electronica. 1991 Projektidee zum Ars Electronica Center als Museu der Zukunft in Linz.

2OG

.NET

Derrick de Kerckhove (CDN)

Director of the McLuhan Institute of Culture and Technology at the University of Toronto. His works on the effects of communication-media on the human nervous system include *Brainframes* and *The Alphabet and the Brain*.

Lisa Goldman (USA)

President, Construct. Before co-founding Construct in August 1995, Lisa was director of the Interactive Media Festival, an international competition held in June 1994 and June 1995 in Los Angeles. The Festival revolved around an exhibition reflecting the wide spectrum of disciplines and industries exploring interactive media. In addition to the gallery, there were live performances by the Blue Man Group and the Merce Cunningham Dance Company. From 1988 until the launch of the Festival in 1992, Lisa worked at Cunningham Communication, Inc., a top-rated high technology marketing firm in Palo Alto, California. She holds a degree in Fine Arts from Rice University in Houston, Texas and also studied at the Université de Paris IV, Sorbonne.

Joichi Ito (J/USA)

developer and producer in the areas of virtual reality and multimedia. Japan correspondent for Mondo 2000, Wired and others. Numerous publications, particularly on networks.

Declan McCullagh (USA)

is the chief Washington correspondent for Wired News and lives and works in Washington DC. An award-winning journalist, his articles have appeared in publications from *Playboy* magazine to the *Los Angeles Times*. McCullagh moderates "politech", a discussion list looking broadly at politics and technology, and the Association for Computing Machinery's Y2KRISKS forum. He has written the Y2K entry for Microsoft's *Encarta* encyclopedia, and has contributed to *Time* cover stories on topics such as Y2K and privacy.

Marleen Stikker (NL)

is co-founder and director of the Society for Old and New Media (1994). Having a background in philosophy she became director of the Summerfestival Amsterdam and initiated several media projects. In 1993 she founded De Digitale Stad (DDS), the first Digital City on the Internet. She was the "digital mayor" until 1996. Recently she co-founded Net4.nl, a net-based public broadcast organisation. She was involved in setting up of the European Cultural Backbone, a network of innovative media-cultural institutions in Europe in March 1999.

Interactive Art

Brian Blau (USA)

recently joined Silicon Graphics as the Graphics API Evangelist for Fahrenheit and OpenGL API's. Before joining SGI Brian was co-founder and Vice President at Intervista Software, an Internet startup building VRML and 3D web technologies and products. There he served in many roles, including software developer and manager of day-to-day engineering operations. Brian also worked at Autodesk Multimedia and the Institute for Simulation and Training, where he worked on desktop visual simulation systems and networked virtual realities. Brian also actively volunteers for SIGGRAPH. In 1996 he co-produced the acclaimed Digital Bayou interactive exhibition and he is currently producing the 1999 Computer Animation Festival and Electronic Theater.

Machiko Kusahara (J)

studied mathematics and history of science at Tokyo's International Christian University and is an Associate Professor of Media Art at the Faculty of Arts, Tokyo Institute of Polytechnics. She has been teaching computer graphics theory and media since 1986 and has published several books on computer graphics and A-Life. Her recent research has been centered around the transition of the nature of artistic creativity in interactive art, especially in relation to the concept of networking and A-Life.

Hans-Peter Schwarz (D)

studied visual communication at the University for Applied Science in Bielefeld, finishing 1973 as a qualified designer. 1982 doctorate summa cum laude for the title Dr. phil. from the Philipps-Universität. 1983—1990 curator at the Deutsches Architekturmuseum. 1990—91 project director for the conception of a new

museum for the history of the modern age in Frankfurt/Main. Since 1982 lecturer at the Universities of Marburg, Trier and Frankfurt, the University for pplied Science in Darmstadt and ıe State School of Design/Karlsıhe. Since 1992 director of the ledia Museum at the ZKM Center ır Art and Media in Karlsruhe. nce 1994 chair for the history of 't at the State School of Design/ arlsruhe (HfG). Since 1997 exteral project director for the them-:ic area of the EXPO 2000.

aul Sermon (GB)
ɔrn 1966. Studied at The Uniersity of Wales, with Professor Roy

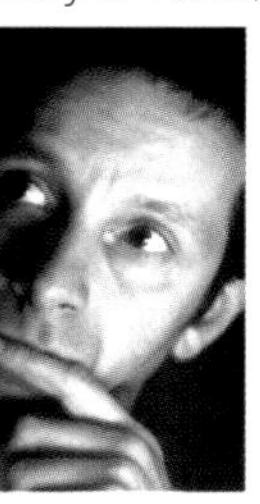

Ascott BA Hon's. Fine Art degree. Post-graduate MFA degree at The University of Reading, England, from Oct 1989 to June 1991. Awarded the Prix Ars Electronica Golden Nica", in the category of teractive art, for the hyper media stallation *Think about the People* ɔw (1991). Artist in Residence at ıe Center for Arts and Mediaechnology (ZKM) in Karlsruhe 993). Received the "Sparkey" ward from the Interactive Media estival in Los Angeles, for the teleatic video installation *Telematic reaming* (1994). Currently living in erlin, working as Associate Profesɔr for telepresence and telematic edia in the department of media 'ts at the Academy of Graphic ıd Book Arts in Leipzig. Exhibited orks in Great Britain, France, ustria, Belgium, Finland, Germany, olland, Canada, USA and Japan.

on Snoddy (USA)
ined GameWorks in March 1996 ; Vice President, Design from the /alt Disney Co. In 1993, Snoddy ɔunded the Walt Disney Virtual Reality Studio which is currently producing the Aladdin Virtual Reality ride. He also led the conceptual development and design of the ride system for the wildly popular Indiana Jones attraction. Prior to joining Disney, Snoddy was with Lucasfilm's THX division where he was instrumental in transitioning the THX sound system from an industry studio mix

product to a worldwide consumer product. He began his career as a technical director working for National Public Radio in Washington with the program "All Things Considered." Snoddy has degrees in journalism and electronics from the University of South Carolina.

Computer Animation/ Visual Effects

Maurice Benayoun (F)
born in 1957, founded Z. A. Production in 1987, which emphasizes special effects and is particularly

concerned with the potential of the digital image and interactivity. He has taught at the Université 1 (Panthéon Sorbonne) since 1984. Since 1996 he is Artiste Invité at the École Nationale Supérieure des Beaux Arts, Paris. Since 1994 he has been particularly interested in the development of VR installations and interactive Internet applications.

Ines Hardtke (CDN)
is Head of Digital Imaging in the ACI east and Animation/Jeunesse Studios at the National Film Board of Canada in Montreal. She ob-

tained a M.Math (Computer Science—Computer Graphics Lab) from the University of Waterloo in Waterloo, Ontario. She has been Computer Animation Festival Chair at SIGGRAPH 98.

Robert Legato (USA)
graduated from Brooks Institute of Photography with a Bachelor of Arts Degree in Cinematography. After freelance supervising and directing for various commercial companies, he turned to television production, serving as alternating Visual Effects Supervisor for the TV

series *The Twilight Zone*. He earned two Emmy Awards for Visual Effects for his work on Paramount's *Star Trek: The Next Generation* and *Deep Space Nine* in the varying roles of Visual Effects Supervisor/Producer. In 1993 Rob joined Digital Domain, where he has worked as Visual Effects Supervisor/Second Unit Director for Neil Jordan's *Interview With the Vampire* and as Visual Effects Supervisor on *Apollo 13* and James Cameron's *Titanic*. He was nominated for the Academy Award in Visual Effects for *Apollo 13* and won the Visual Effects Academy Award for his work on *Titanic*. He also received the British Academy Award (BAFTA) for *Apollo 13* and was nominated for the same award for his efforts on *Titanic*. Rob is currently Creative Director and Senior Visual Effects Supervisor at Digital Domain

Barbara Robertson (USA)
has been the West Coast Senior Editor for Computer Graphics World since 1985 and in that capacity has written many awardwinning articles on computer ani-

mation, visual effects, and graphics technology as she watched the evolution of computer graphics art and technology. Prior to this work, she was the Editor and Researcher for the *Whole Earth Software Catalog*, West Coast Bureau Chief for Popular Computing, and West Coast Editor for *Byte Magazine*.

Digital Musics

Kodwo Eshun (GB)

At 17, Kodwo Eshun won an Open Scholarship to read Law at University College, Oxford. After 8 days he switched to Literary Theory,

magazine journalism and running clubs. He is not a cultural critic or cultural commentator so much as a concept engineer, an imaginist at the millennium's end writing on electronic music, science fiction, technoculture, architecture, design, post war movies and post war art for *I-D, The Wire, The Face, Arena, Süddeutsche Zeitung, Die Zeit, Melody Maker, The Times* and *The Guardian*. He has published in *The Celluloid Jukebox*, the British Film Institute's critical anthology on the soundtrack and is the youngest writer in Jon Savage and Hanif Kureishi's *The Faber Book of Pop*.

Naut Humon (USA)

conducts, curates and performs his and outside works for Sound Traffic Control, an omniphonic orchestral "dub dashboard" network which remorphs sonic spatial objects from live instrumentalists, audio sculptures, and multiple DJ/VJ configurations for the RECOMBINANT diffusion jockey summits. He also operates as producer and creative director of the Asphodel/Sombient labels from San Francisco to New York.

Jim O'Rourke (USA)

is out of Chicago and involved in many areas simultaneously. As a producer he has worked with Stereolab, Faust, Smog, John Fahey, the High Llamas, and Tony Conrad. He has made remixes for Tortoise,

Autechre, Oval, The Sea and Cake, and the Jesus Lizard, as an improviser has played and recorded with Henry Kaiser, Derek Bailey, Mats Gustafsson, Gunter Muller, Eddie Prevost, and Evan Parker, run 3 record labels (distemper, dexter's cigar, and moikai) which have issued recordings by Arnold Dreyblatt, Folke Rabe, Merzbow, Derek Bailey, Phill Niblock, and Rafael Toral. He has collaborated with mego, sonic youth, and also is a musician for the Merce Cunningham Dance Company. His own records have ranged from electronic/musique concret to americana. He is currently producing and occasionally performing with his powerbook.

Robin Rimbaud (GB)

With his work as Scanner, Robin Rimbaud implicates himself in

processes of surveillance, engendering access to both technology and language and the power games of voyeurism. Dubbed a "telephone terrorist", Rimbaud is a techno-data pirate whose scavenging of the electronic communications highways provides the raw materials for his aural collages of electronic music and 'found' conversations. Musician, writer, media critic, cultural engineer, and host of the monthly digital club the Electronic Lounge at the ICA since 1994, he is currently at work on a variety of projects.
Scanner—A fearless exponent of ambient electronic soundscapes, Scanner is widely recognised as one of the most exciting artist-producers working in instrumental music. His compositions are absorbing, multi-layered soundscapes that twist state-of-the-art technology in gloriously unconventional ways.
He has collaborated and spoken at conferences with Brian Laswell, Brian Eno, Peter Gabriel, Bjork, Derek Jarman and Neville Brot.

Laetitia Sonami (F)

born 1957. She studied with Joel Chadabe at the Electronic Music

Studio in Albany, NY, and with Robert Ashley and David Behrman at the Center for Contemporary Music, Mills College, CA, where she received her MFA in composition in 1980. She has since been developing her own electronic musical instruments for live performance. She lives in Oakland, California.

U19/Cybergeneration

Sirikit M. Amann (A)

studied political science, theater arts and economics in Austria, Germany and the USA. Since 1987 she has worked for the ÖKS—Austrian Culture Service—where she is responsible

for the concept development and implementation of multimedia projects in schools. Austrian Culture Service school projects: 1994 "Computer and Games" and 1995 "Speed" (both at the Ars Electronica Festival).

AGENT etoy.ZAI

is one of the founding members of etoy and has been regarded as the general manager of the etoy. CORPORATION (www.etoy.com) since 1996.

Between 1994 and 1999, operating under the codename AGENT etoy.MATT AKA e07, he was head of a number of etoy.PRODUCTIONS and ɜtoy.MEDIA-HACKS, such as the ‹idnapping of over 1.5 million Internet users in 1996 under the code-ıame "The Digital Hijack" (Golden Nica Prix Ars Electronica 1996) or :he spectacular promotion stunt in ı998, "Protected By etoy", with which the etoy.CORPORATION ›fficially took over the security of :he Museum of Modern Art in San ·rancisco and created unbounded :onfusion. etoy.ZAI is also respon-ıible for the etoy.CORPORATE DENTITY and the operation "leav-ng reality behind." The private lata for AGENT e07 from 1975 to 992 will be held in confidence ıntil 2035 by the etoy. :ORPORATION!

Jorman Filz (A)

has worked for six years for Austria's biggest youth and music magazine, the RENNBAHN EXPRESS, as a film journalist and is also head of the counseling section for young eople there. In addition, Filz works s a musician and freelance writer; :s most recent publication was a ook of advice about love for ɔung people.

Markus Riebe (A)

born 1955, studied at the University for Artistic and Industrial Design in Linz. Art productions from the series "digital/analog", "D/A-Wandler" and "territorien" have been shown at Siggraph ArtShow/Chicago 91, TISEA/Sidney, ComputerArt /BRD and in individual exhibitions.

He has written on museum pedagogy for the Kunsthistorisches Museum, Vienna, Künstlerhaus Vienna, the Upper Austrian Landesgalerie and others.
In the school supervisory council of Upper Austria he is responsible for the art education program for the province of Upper Austria.

Stefan Sagmeister (A)

graduated from the College of Applied Art in Vienna and then studied at Pratt Institute in New York with a Fulbright scholarship.

He worked as Creative Director for Leo Burnett in Hong Kong and M&Co. in New York, after which he opened his own studio Sagmeister Inc. in New York.
He has created CD packaging and graphics for the Rolling Stones, David Byrne, Lou Reed, Aerosmith and Pat Metheny.

PARTICIPANTS

ıie Abrahams
quare Du Collet
ɔo Le Bar Sur Loup, F
ahams@ipmc.cnrs.fr

lyn Addison
Bluff Str.
erside, RI 2915, USA
lyn@home.com

ɔerto Aguirrezabala
Nikolás Ormaetxea,
– 6ºc
ɔ10 Sestao, E
uirre@jet.es

rk Allan
Vectis Av.
ingston, JA
rkallan@nvimedia.com

na Mercedes Alonso
nrichstraße 19
ɔ03 Bremen, D
nso@webmen.de

rk Amerika
. Box 241
ılder, CO 80306-024,
erika@spot.colorado.

Amit
naja 5
ɔ24 Jaffa, IL
eat@inter.net.il

haela Amort
vengasse 53/14
o Wien, A
haela@amort.net

stutis Andrasiunas
sanaviciutes 48–49
o Vilnius, Lithuania
an@o-o.lt

h Andrews
3 Candela Str.
ıta Fe, NM 87505,
A
handrews@worldnet.
net

ı Arenzon
ususo 931
6 Buenos Aires, RA
ı_arenzon@ciudad.
n.ar

on Asher
ɔo Westley Road
stbury, NY 11590, USA
a@jasonasher.com

nniyas Andrej
ıuratova Velikanov
titskaya
berezhnaya, 7-64
ɔ088 Moscow, RUS
ikanov@altavista.net

. Cult. Undo.net
Paolo Sarpi 1
54 Milano, I
ff@undo.net

fan Bachleitner
guaiplatz 12
o Wien, A
chenberger@shortcut.at

lf Harun
chschneider
ertlstr. 11
803 München, D
b@eggs.de

chard Barbeau
35, Rue De Bordeaux
H 1Z6 Montréal, CDN
rsu@dsuper.net

Don Barnett
23502 171 Av. S.e.
Monroe, WA 98272, USA
nekton@cris.com

Chris Bassett
427 S Park St
Kalamazoo, MI 49007,
USA
x96bassett@wmich.edu

Dominik Bauer
Wertachbrucker-
Tor-Str. 3 A
86152 Augsburg, D
dbauer@rz.fh-augsburg.de

Scott Becker
P.O. Box 578956
Chicago, IL 60657-8956,
USA
artscb@interaccess.com

John Beezer
17525 Ne 40th Str.,
Apt. B205
Redmond, WA 98052,
USA
beezer@nwlink.com

Tracey Benson
P.O. Box 5854,
West End
Brisbane 4101, AUS
traceyb@thehub.com.au

Joanna Berzowska
8 Michael Way
Cambridge, MA 02141,
USA
joey@media.mit.edu

Andy Best
Tallberginkatu 1 Box 45
180 Helsinki, SF
best@meetfactory.com

David Bickerstaff
58 Kenway Road
London SW7 4RP, UK
david@atomictv.com

Larisa Blazic
Ive Andrica 23/4
21000 Novi Sad, YU
lab@eunet.yu

Hank Blumenthal
240 Mercer St. #304
New York, NY 10012, NY
cjz1@is.nyu.edu

Goran Boardy
Elfsborgsgatan 33
SE 414 72 Goteborg, S
goran.boardy@valand.
gu.se

George Bond
2231 Cascades
Blvd. #108
Kissimmee, FL 34741,
USA
UKond@kua.net

Joakim Borgström
Avda. Principe De
Asturias 3, 4º
8012 Barcelona, E
joakim@borgstrom.com

Thomas Born
Warschauer Platz 6–8
10245 Berlin, D
tborn@fhtw-berlin.de

Audrey Bradshaw
44 Rochester Court
Stockton on Tees,
TS170FS, UK
audreyanims@geocities.
com

Paul Brown
PO. Box 3603
South Brisbane, QLD
4101, AUS
editor@fineartforum.org

Eva Brunner-Szabo
Währinger Gürtel 51/9
1180 Wien, A
e.b.szabo@to.or.at

Koen Bruynseels
H. Consciencestr. 13
3000 Leuven, BE
koen.bruynseels@med.
kuleuven.ac.be

Andrea Cals
Rua Porto Uniao, 39
04568-020 Sao Paulo, BR
dedeia@dm9.com.br

Carol Caroling Geary
1031 Crestview Dr. #318
Mountain View, CA
94040-3445, USA
caroling@earthlink.net

Rondey Chang
2119 N.king St.,
Suite 206
Honolulu, HI 96819, USA
pygoya@pixi.com

Team Chman
20 Rue Des Vicaires
59800 Lille, F
dja9@chman.com

Mika Cimolini
Hubadova 3
1000 Ljubljana, SLO
mika.cimolini@guest.
arnes.si

Mireille Clavien
35, Rue De Zurich
1201 Genève, CH
mirouille@hotmail.com

Jean-François Colonna
Cmap/Ecole
Polytechnique
91128 Palaiseau, F
colonna@cmapx.
polytechnique.fr

Kieron Convery
6 College Str.
Sydney 2000, AUS
kieron@webboy.net

Shane Cooper
Lorenzstr. 19
76135 Karlsruhe, D
shanecooper@shane
cooper.com

Jim Costanzo
350 Bleecker Str. #4p
New York, NY 10014, USA
costanzo@thing.net

David Crawford
749 Driggs Av #5
Brooklyn, NY 11211, USA
crawford@lightofspeed.
com

Nick Crowe
56 Clarendon Rd.
Manchester M16 8LD, UK
nick@index.u-net.com

Mark Daggett
3927 C Miramar St
La Jolla, CA 92037, USA
mark@flavoredthunder.
com

Diana Danelli
Via Magenta,34
26900 Lodi (LO), I
ddanelli@ns.pmp.it

Gary Danner
Rothschildallee 18
60389 Frankfurt, D
gunafa@well.com

Steve Davis
4047 36th Ave Nw
Olympia, WA 98502, USA
daviss@evergreen.edu

Brendan Dawes
28 Cypress Road
Southport PR8 6HE, UK
bren@subnet.co.uk

Clay Debevoise
10 Heron Str.
San Francisco, CA 94103,
USA
clay@clayd.com

Ryoichiro Debuchi
Court Setagaya 101, 1-15-
11 Misyuku, Setagaya-ku
150-0005 Tokyo, J
debuchi@atom.co.jp

Véronique Decoster
38, Eugène Demolder Av.
1030 Brussels, B
veronique.decoster@keep
sake.be

Johnny Dekam
15 2nd Str. (rear)
Troy, NY 12180, USA
johnny@node.net

Thomas Delmundo
318 E. 15th St. #11b
New York, NY 10003,
USA
tomdelmundo@hotmail.
com

Pascal Derycke
15 Place De La Mairie
55210 Herbeuville, F
hal@halspirit.com

Dimiter Dimitrov
78, Samokov Blvd. Block
305, Ap.61
1113 Sofia, BG
megaart@otel.net

Roz Dimon
2 Charlton Str., #3l
New York, NY 10014, USA
rozdimon@interport.net

Claudio Diolio
Simonstr. 2
3012 Bern, CH
diolio@pop.agri.ch

Rick Doble
PO. Box 117,195 Old
Nassau Rd., Williston
Smyrna, NC 28579, USA
savvynews@mail.clis.com

Hélène Doyon
2533, Rue Fullum
Montréal H2K 3P5, CDN
doydem@cam.org

Reynald Drouhin
31 Rue De Paris
94190 Villeneuve
St. Georges, F
reynald@incident.net

William Duckworth
6109 Boulevard East
West New York, NJ 7093
USA
Wdckwrth@aol.com

Michael Ebbels
31 Turner Str.
Abbotsford,
Victoria 3067, AUS
michaelebbels@hotmail.
com

Santiago Echeverry
Carrera 6 # 57-11,
Apt 1001
Bogotá, CO
santiago@santiago-e.com

Ron Eller
114 Glenbridge Court
Pleasant Hill,
CA 94523, USA
reller@home.com

Ursula Endlicher
224 Metropolitan Av.,
Apt#19
Brooklyn, NY 11211, USA
ursula@thing.net

Aviv Eyal
763 Belmont Place E
#208
Seattle, WA 98102, USA
aviv@dromology.com

Harald Falkenhagen
Industriestrasse 21
27751 Delmenhorst, D
falkenhagen@webmen.de

Jeff Fallen
221 Fallen Road
Ennis, TX 75119,
lampmuz@hpnc.com

Jean Luc Faubert
En Faruselle
31290 Mauremont, F
jlf@noname.fr

Susan Finley
36 West 20th Str.,
2nd Floor
New York, NY 10011, USA
finley@echonyc.com

William Fisher
2205 Pontiac Drive
Tallahassee, FL 32301,
USA
wfisher@mailer.fsu.edu

Zdena Flaskova
Zamek C.p. 57 – Solnice
381 01 Cesky Krumlov, CZ
ois@ck.ipex.cz

Fred Forest
7 Rue Jean Arp
75013 Paris, F
forester@worldnet.fr

Bernward Frank
Adalbertsteinweg 119
52070 Aachen, D
kinetik@popmail.oche.de

Antonie Frank
Skarpnäcksalle 18
SE-128 35 Skarpnäck, S
anfra.picture@swipnet.se

Alvar Freude
Neckarstraße 246
70190 Stuttgart, D
alvar.freude@merz-
akademie.de

Rebecca Frydman
448 Bryant Str.
San Francisco, CA 94107, USA
rivka@construct.net

Didier Gaboulaud
121 Rue De Bordeaux
16000 Angoulême, F
din@cnbdi.fr

Alex Galloway
312 N. Buchanan #406
Durham, NC 27701, USA
arg2@duke.edu

Gerald Ganglbauer
P.O. Box 522
Strawberry Hills, NSW
2102, AUS
gerald@gangan.com

Andrew Garton
55 Smith Str.
Fitzroy 3065, AUS
agarton@toysatellite.com.au

Cem Gencer
Bostanici Sok. No 5 Nebi Bey Apt D 2 – Bostanci
81110 Istanbul, TR
cgencer@turk.net

Peter Gerstmann
133 East Lane Ave, Apt. 2e
Columbus, OH 43201, USA
gerstmann.1@osu.edu

Carol Gigliotti
1552 Wyandotte
Grandview Heights, OH 43212, USA
carol@cgrg.ohio-state.edu

Madge Gleeson
Western Washington University
Bellingham, WA 98225, USA
mgleeson@cc.wwu.edu

Ken Goldberg
4135 Etcheverry Hall
Berkeley, CA 94720, USA
ken@goldberg.net

Jacqueline Goss
230 Amory Str.
Jamaica Plain, MA 02130, USA
jgoss@massart.edu

Fabio Gramazio
Hönggerberg
8093 Zürich, CH
phasex@arch.ethz.ch

Fritz Grohs
Birkenstr. 56 Vh
10559 Berlin, D
fgrohs@to.or.at

Genco Gulan
426 West 46th Str. Apt.
New York, NY 10036 USA,
gencogulan@rocketmail.com

Juliane Hadem
Moselstr. 33
60329 Frankfurt, D
julie@thermofish.com

Marikki Hakola
Magnusborg Studios
6100 Porvoo, SF
marikki@magnusborg.fi

Georg Hartung
Enkingweg 36
48147 Münster, D
hartung@webmen.de

Auriea Harvey
114 East 1st St #20
New York, NY 10009, USA
two@entropy8zuper.org

Graham Harwood
Mongrel
16 A Flodden Road
London SE5 9LH
UK

Lynn Hershman
1201 California St. # 803
San Francisco, CA 94108, USA
lynn2@well.com

Paul Higham
141 Mariulli Arena Operations,
1901 4th St.se
Minneapolis, MN 55414, USA
highaoo1@tc.umn.edu

Michael Hirst
40 Gordon Str.
Allston, MA 02134, USA
mhirst@stumpworld.com

Paul Holcomb
114 Bonaire Blvd
Destin, FL 541, USA
paul@3dstudios.com

Curtis Holloway
507 Bellmar
Friendswood, TX 77546, USA
copzilla@hotmail.com

Peter W. Horton Iii
4220-2 Hutchinson River Parkway East #2c
Bronx, NY 104444475, USA
cyberbrain@pol.com

Andreas Huber
287 Oakwood Ave
Winnipeg R3L 1E8, CDN
hubera@rpi.edu

Arnulf Huck
Ludwig Erhard Straße 16
61440 Oberursel, D
huck@teleaction.com

Leslie Huppert
Adalbertstr.22
10997 Berlin, D
leslie@internett.de

Lisa Hutton
4606 Castelar Str.
San Diego, CA 92107-1412, USA
lhutton@ucsd.edu

Idd Internet Design
Dorfschenke
Am Damm 10
47229 Duisburg, D
info@id.dorfschenke.de

Lena Ivanova
Pushkinskaja 10
191040 St. Petersburg, RUS
tac@spb.cityline.ru

Daniel Jenett
Wrangelstr. 113
20253 Hamburg, D
daniel@jenett.com

Fransje Jepkes
Egelantiensstraat 172 Iii
1015 ND Amsterdam, NL
fransjej@xs4all.nl

Tiia Johannson
Mahtra 21-48
13811 Tallinn, Estonia
xtiiax@hotmail.com

Steve Jones
93 Av. B
New York, NY 10009, USA
gargoyle@echonyc.com

Jérôme Joy
B.p.74
6372 Mouans Sartoux Cedex, F
joy@thing.net

Brian Judy
10428 Kardwright Ct
Gaithersburg, MD 20886, USA
bjudypae@boogaholler.com

Lilian Jüchtern
Oldenburger Str. 11
10551 Berlin, D
p5@digitalworks.org

Daniel Julia Lundgren
Rambla 31
8002 Barcelona, E
dani@iua.upf.es

Dudesek Karel
Gluesingerstr. 40c
21217 Seevetal, D
kdudesek@compuserve.com

Patrik Karolak
4551 Glencoe Av., Suite 160
Marina del Rey, CA 90292, USA
lia@jamisongold.com

Patrick Keller
R. De Langallerie
1003 Lausanne, CH
patrick@fabric.ch

Raivo Kelomees
Tartu Str. 1
10145 Tallinn, Estonia
offline@online.ee

Andruid Kerne
519 W. 26th St., Suite 5000
New York, NY 10001, USA
andruid@mrl.nyu.edu

Albert Kiefer
1e Lambertusstraat 210
5921 JR Venlo, NL
sectora@euronet.nl

Peter King
21 Station Str.
Guildford 6055, AUS
zeug@earthling.net

Olga Kisseleva
30 Rue De L'Echiquier
75010 Paris, F
kisselev@cnam.fr

Fevzi Konuk
Hilschbacherstr.31
66292 Riegelsberg, D
admin@hyper-eden.com

Nicklas Koski
Mellanvägen 11
8700 Virkby, SF
nicklas@nicklaskoski.com

Mary Krafft
P. O. Box 14872
San Francisco, CA 94114, USA
mary@htmlsweatlodge.com

Berislav Krzic
Cesta 9. Avgusta 8d
1410 Zagorje ob Savi, SLO
veselinka.stanisavac@siol.net

Tanja Kühnel
Norbert-Brüll-Str. 28/43
5020 Salzburg, A
tanja.kuehnel@fh-sbg.ac.at

Andreja Kuluncic
Cazmanska 2/16
10 000 Zagreb, HR
andreja.kuluncic@zg.tel.hr

Hartmut Kurz
Immanuelkirchstraße 38
10405 Berlin, D
info@bottledfish.de

Linda Lauro-Lazin
P. O. Box 396
Rifton, NY 12471, USA
llaurola@pratt.edu

Jérôme Lefdup
173 Rue Vercingétorix
75014 Paris, F
jerome@lefdup.com

Marketta Leino
Väliaitankatu 9 E 39
40320 Jyväskylä, SF
marleino@mleino.pp.fi

Ingo Lie
Uelzestrasse 6a
30177 Hannover, D
Lie@rotundblau.com

Jonas Lindkvist
Nytorget 8
116 40 Stockholm, S
jonas@aiia.net

Holger Lippmann
Schöhauser Allee 144
10435 Berlin, D
holger.lippmann@privat.in-berlin.com

Erik Loyer
5430 Bellingham Ave #204
Valley Village, NY 91607, USA
orion17@thegrid.net

Diane Ludin
72 South 8th Str., #4
Brooklyn, NY 11211, USA
duras@thing.net

Gladys Ly-au Young
108 1st Ave. S., 4th Floor
Seattle, WA 98104, USA
gladys@olsonsundberg.com

Stephen K. Mack
108 5th Av., #7b
New York, NY 10011, USA
stephen_mack@gnomist.com

Don Mackinnon
3322-38th Ave. West
Seattle, WA 98199, USA
donjr@hotmail.com

Judy Malloy
5306 Ridgeview #5
El Sobrante, CA 94803, USA
jmalloy@artswire.org

Lev Manovich
1155 Camino Del Mar, #468
Del Mar, CA 92014, USA
manovich@ucsd.edu

Horst W. Martens
Schlangenhacker Str. 16
14197 Berlin, D
outerspace@hotbot.com

Nicole Martin
Oldenburger Str. 11
10551 Berlin, D
p5@digitalworks.org

Fumio Matsumoto
2-11-27-302 Yakumo
Meguro-ku
Tokyo 152-0023, J
mat814@ya2.so-net.ne.j

Louise May
3298 Highway 26
St. Francois-Xavier, Manitoba R4L 1B5, CDN
LouiseMay@mbnet.mb.c

Beth Mcleanknight
4636 S Deyo Ave
Brookfield, IL 60513-2220, USA
gavagi@hotmail.com

Kevin Mcnally
515 Howard St.
Savannah, GA 31401, US
kevin@premierweb.net

Antonio Mendoza
4021 Holly Knoll Drive
Los Angeles, CA 90027, USA
elvision@mayhem.net

Marcello Mercado
Rondeau 548 9 no A
Nueva Córdoba
5000 Córdoba, RA
mmercado@reidel.com.a

Rupert Metnitzer
Untere Teichstraße 34b
8010 Graz, A
office@nextcd.com

Richard Metzger
107 Grand St 3rd Floor
New York, NY 10013, US
metzger@disinfo.com

Liz Miller
811 West Lake Ave.
Baltimore, MD 21210, USA
millee4@rpi.edu

Stephen Miller
P.O. Box 3215
Santa Fe, NM 87501, US
mkzdk@mkzdk.org

Kostja Mitenev
Ul.doblesty 18 Kv.318
198332 St.-Petersburg, RUS
tenev@diUKody.dux.ru

Enrico Mitrovich
Via Della Commenda 18
36100 Vicenza, I
emitrov@goldnet.it

eph Monzo
;o Rubicam Str.
'ladelphia,
19144-1809, USA
nz@juno.com

niel Moreno
Sernambetiba 3300
3 / 302
539-900 Rio de
eiro, BR
nimor@hotmail.com

'ker Moritz
inbergsweg 3
19 Berlin, D
@Restoel.net

'ra Müller
ltgeristraße 50
049 Herford, D
ra.mueller@kunst
mmt.de

lfgang Nagy
enburgerstr. 24
o Wien, A
lfgang@nagy.com

tomichi Nakamura
Ignacio 1001 Y
nzalez Suarez 9no
o / Quito, Ecuador
@juvenilemedia.com

ko Neupert
fourstr. 8
07 Leipzig, D
ko@hUK-leipzig.de

spech Nicolas
e Alexandre Dumas
200 Montélimar, F
monde@cicv.fr

nand Niculescu
d. Victoriei Bl.44b Sc.b
23
00 Sibiu, RO
nand@starnets.ro

omas Noller
Frech
tzstr. 58
77 Berlin, D
ller@typospace.de

sako Odaka
South 6th Str. #213
n Jose, CA 95112 USA,
daka@cadre.sjsu.edu

mohisa Okamoto
-6-b201 Zenpukuji
7-0041 Suginami-ku,
kyo, J
mohisa@oka.urban.ne.

n-Marie Palacios
Av. Maximilien
bespierre
400 Vitry-Sur Seine, F

ncy Paterson
5 West Mall #1513
obicoke M9C 4Z3, CDN
ncy@utcc.utoronto.ca

bin Petterd
Cato Av.
est Hobart 7000, AUS
binp@peg.apc.org

ck Philip
5 Cole St #18
n Francisco, CA 94117,
A
hilip@BEST.COM

Jean-Marc Philippe
65 Bis Boulevard Brune
75014 Paris, F
vquinn@keo.org

Derek Powazek
71 Prosper St.
San Francisco, CA 94114,
USA
prixars@fray.com

Robert Praxmarer
Julius-Raab-Str. 1-3/306
4040 Linz, A
cubic@esh.uni-linz.ac.at

Joanna Priestley
1801 Nw Upshur Str. 630
Portland, OR 97209, USA
joanna@easyStr.com

Various Protozoans
2727 Mariposa Str.,
Studio 100
San Francisco, CA 94110,
USA
carrie@protozoa.com

Melinda Rackham
59 Werri St
Werri Beach, 2534 AUS,
melinda@subtle.net

Rosaria Rainieri
Via San Marco 18
20121 Milano, I
rosy.rainieri@iol.it

Niranjan Rajah
University Malaysia
Sarawak
94300 Kota Samarahan,
Sarawak, MAL
niranjan@faca.unimas.my

Guillem Ramos-Poquí
37 Croxley Road
London W9 3HH, UK
g.ramos-poqui@virgin.net

Donna Randall
1130 N Verdugo Road
#14
Glendale, CA 91206, USA
kalazar@earthlink.net

Sonya Rapoport
6 Hillcrest Court
Berkeley, CA 94705, USA
rapop@socrates.berkeley.
edu

Erika Raser
4457 Temecula #101
San Diego, CA 92107,
USA
elitistknicknak@hotmail.
com

Eric Raymond
2310 Holt
Montreal H2G 1Y4, CDN
raymond.eric@uqam.ca

Andrew Reitemeyer
Stader Postweg 32
27721 Ritterhude, D
kiwano@t-online.de

Stephan Reiter
Libellenweg 4
4030 Linz, A
st_reiter@yahoo.de

Wir Restoel
Weinbergsweg 3
10119 Berlin, D
wir@restoel.net

Klaus Richter
Buchfeldgasse 14/8-9
1080 Wien, A
k.richter@magnet.at

Jay Rogers
1475 Mecaslin St. Nw
#7215
Atlanta, GA 30309, USA
jay.rogers@turner.com

Avi Rosen
22, Hashoshanim
Nesher, IL 36842,
avi@sayfan.technion.ac.il

Scott Rosenberg
138 W. 109th St. 4w
New York, NY 10025,
USA
srosenberg@wesleyan.
edu

Duncan Rowland
409 Comm Arts
E. Lansing, MI 48824,
USA
rowlan18@pilot.msu.edu

Andi Rusu
2246 Nw 61st St
Seattle, WA 98107, USA
andi@redoctober.com

Rw51 Rw51
Po Box 17981
Baton Rouge, LA 70893,
USA
rw51@yahoo.com

Yositaka Saito
1-4-21-302 Sakaigawa
Nishiku
550-0024 Osaka, J
awito@os.xaxon.ne.jp

Debbie Salemink
Jacob V. Lennepstr.302,2
10 53 KE Amsterdam, NL
salemink@salty.org

Michael Samyn
N. Annicqstraat 51
9600 Ronse, B
samyn@zuper.com

Umberto Sartori
Dorsoduro 604
30123 Venezia, I
venetian@tin.it

Inga Schnekenburger
Villingerstr.14
78166 Donaueschingen, D
inga@schnekenburger.de

Dirk Schroeder
Muntpratstr. 7
78462 Konstanz, D
dirk@keine.lake.de

Michael Schwarz
Kleverstücke 21
21339 Lüneburg, D
mschwarz@bigfoot.de

Pierre Schwob
200 Sheridan Av.,
Suite 402
Palo Alto, CA 94306, USA
prs@prs.com

Nikolai Selivanov
Bolotnikovskaja /38/1/58
113209 Moscow, RUS
energy@rsuh.ru

Ajanta Sen Poovaiah
C/csre, 139, Hillside,
Indian Institute Of
Technolgy, Powai,
400 076 Mumbai, India
solaris@idc.iitb.ernet.in

Michal Sersen
Drienova 3
82102 Bratislava, SK
mse@gratex.sk

Tomoo Shimomura
Sun Royal Nagara710 1-5-
19 Nagaranishi Kitaku
531-0061 Osaka, J
tomoo@osk.3web.ne.jp

Img Src Shioirikouji#101
5-2 Shinsen
150-0045
Shibuya-ku Tokyo,
itok@imgsrc.co.jp

Shirley Shor
763 Belmont Place E
#208
Seattle, WA 98102, USA
shirley@dromology.com

Miller Short
4304 Holmes
Kansas City, MO 64110,
USA
groundo@swbell.net

Ralf Skrabs
Hochstr. 46
41836 Hückelhoven, D
ralf@entertainer-club.de

Andrew Skwish
2436 Bush St. #2
San Francisco, CA 94115,
USA
andrew@skwish.com

Nina Sobell
190 Eldridge Str.,
#3 South
New York, NY 10002,
USA
parkbench@cat.nyu.edu

Christa Sommerer
2-2 Hikaridai, Seika-cho,
Soraku-gun
61902 Kyoto, J
christa@mic.atr.co.jp

Teo Spiller
Prazakova 14
1000 Ljubljana, SLO
teo@teo-spiller.org

Joan Stark
P. O. Box 450652
Westlake, OH 44145, USA
spunk1111@juno.com

Nicole Stenger
220 Bay Str. #a
Santa Monica, CA 90405,
USA
Nicole.Stenger@gte.net

Reiner Strasser
Marcobrunnerstr. 3
65197 Wiesbaden, D
r.strasser@xterna-net.de

Kim Stringfellow
651 N. Hoyne Av.
Chicago, IL 60612, USA
mail@kimstringfellow.com

Igor Stromajer
Tabor 7
1000 Ljubljana, SLO
igor.stromajer@guest.
arnes.si

Ferenc Studinger
Hunyadi U 40
7625 Pècs, H
studing@freemail.c3.hu

Mike Swope
1487 East Martin Lane
Mulvane, KS 67110, USA
mike@swopedesign.com

Jorge Tarazona
Jaime Roig, 26 Pta 14
46010 Valencia, E
tarazona@geocities.com

[rooms] Team
ETH Hönggerberg
8093 Zürich, CH
engeli@arch.ethz.ch

Eugene Thacker
81 S. 6th St. #2
Brooklyn, NY 11211, USA
maldoror@eden.rutgers.
edu

South To The Future
2309 Bryant Str.
San Francisco, CA 94110,
USA
holler@sttf.org

The Panoplie Team
38 , Rue De La
Méditerranée
34000 Montpellier, F
info@panoplie.org

C5 Theory As Product
260 N. 4th St.
San Jose, CA 95112, USA.
c5@cadre.sjsu.edu

Paul Thomas
29 Elizabeth St. North
Perth
Perth 6006, AUS
pthomas@odyssey.apana.
org.au

Ansgard Thomson
Box 8
Fort-Assiniboine
TOG 1AO, CDN
athomson@lands.ab.ca

Henning Timcke
Stadtturmstraße 5
5400 Baden, CH
henning.timcke@kunst.ch

Lucas Tirigall Caste
Av Ricardo Balbin 2432
6c
1428 Buenos Aires, RA
lucas2k@yahoo.com

Andrej Tisma
Modene 1
21000 Novi Sad, YU
aart@eunet.yu

Richard Tolenaar
East 84th Str.
New York, NY 10028,
USA
me_richard@geocities.
com

Maria Tomaselli
Av. Oscar Pereira, 5322
91712-320 Porto Alegre,
BR
to@net1.com.br

Graziella Tomasi
Vanoldenbarneveltstraat
127b
3012 GT Rotterdam, NL
graziella@luna.nl

John Tonkin
PO Box 1476 Potts Point
Sydney, NSW 2011, AUS
john.tonkin@bigpond.
com

Timothy Trompeter
28 East 10th St. Apt9b
New York, NY 10003,
USA
tt@artseensoho.com

Pascale Trudel
3555 Berri App.1213
Montreal H2L 4G4, CDN
sdragon@cam.org

Convex Tv.
Straßburger Str.24
10405 Berlin, D
conrads@zedat.fu-
berlin.de

Anna Ursyn
Department Of Visual
Arts
Greeley, CO 80639 USA
azuvsyn@bentley.unco.
edu

Kristi Van Riet
Honthorststraat 2
1071 DD Amsterdam, NL
desk@vanriet.com

Marian Varga
Konventna 8
811 03 Bratislava, SK
festival@artfilm.sk

Roman Verostko
5535 Clinton Av. South
Minneapolis, MN 55419,
USA
roman@verostko.com

Michelângelo Viana
Rua José De Alencar,
1405 Ap. 304 – Menino
Deus
90880-481 Porto Alegre –
RS, BR
michelangelo@innocent.
com

Clea T. Waite
Körner Str. 106
50823 Köln, D
clea@khm.de

Lars Wallin
Grönstensvägen 36
75241 Uppsala, S
lawa@algonet.se

Noah Wardrip-fruin
719 Broadway, 12th Floor
New York, NY 10014, USA
noah@mrl.nyu.edu

Robert Warnke
Schönhauser Allee 73
10437 Berlin, D
info@foerderband.de

David Washington
1326 Lakeview Blvd E
Seattle, WA 98102, USA
david@carbonflux.net

Timothy Weaver
P.O. Box 7048, Crescent
Branch
Golden
CO 80403-0100, USA
tim_weaver@spatial.com

Annette Weintraub
138th Str. & Convent Ave
New York, NY 10031, USA
anwcc@cunyvm.cuny.edu

Alan White
#501-155 Wellesley Str.
East
Toronto M4Y 1J4, CDN
awhite@westlake.com

Markus Winkler
Hauptstr. 116/1
4232 Hagenberg, A
markus.winkler@fhs-
hagenberg.ac.at

Christof Wöstemeyer
Ottweilerstr. 27
40476 Düsseldorf, D
chris-w@weirdweb.de

Virgil Wong
50 Av. A #4d
New York, NY 10009,
USA
virgil@paperveins.org

Michael Wooster
2133 W. 16th Way
Eugene, OR 97402, USA
wooster@fortisgraphix.
com

Judson Wright
220 W 14, Apartment
New York, NY 10011 USA,
judson@interport.net

Stephan Wuethrich
Parkstr. 31
4102 Binningen, CH
falki@fine-art.com

Herb Wurtzel
3515a Monair Dr.
San Diego, CA 92117,
USA
grameo@aol.com

Alex Zavatone
3736 Fillmore
San Francisco, CA 94123,
USA
zav@sirius.com

Gary Zebington
Flat 1, 389 Crown Str.
Surry Hills, NSW 2010,
AUS
garu@eye.usyd.edu.au

Jody Zellen
843 Bay Str. #11
Santa Monica, CA 90405,
USA
jodyzel@aol.com

Ga Zhang
29 King St.#1e
New York, NY 10014, USA
zhang@escape.com

Therese Zoekende
Elandsstraat 96-c
1016 SH Amsterdam, NL
tzoekende@yahoo.com

Neil Zusman
235 E. 26 St. 2b
New York, 10010, USA
zusman@earthlink.net

Electrus Aka Babis Vekris
353 West 56th St.
New York, NY 10019, USA
electrusvekris@yahoo.
com

Jesús Alido
Gran Via 40 , 7º 5
28013 Madrid, E
alido@art2000.net

Rebecca Allen
1200 Dickson Art Center
Los Angeles, CA 90095,
USA
rallen@arts.ucla.edu

Thilo Alt
Schnellhaus 46
51503 Rösrath, D
info@a3w.de

Anna Anders
Corneliusstr. 2
50678 Köln, D
anna@khm.de

Josephine Anstey
851 S. Morgan Rm 1120
Seo
Chicago, IL 60607, USA
anstey@evl.uic.edu

Brooks Anthony
Scheppegrelsgade 8b
8000 C Aarhus, DK
tonyb@post1.tele.dk

Institute For Applied
Autonomy
5216 Fifth Ave, Apt 1
Pittsburgh, PA 15232,
USA
rp3h@andrew.cmu.edu

Adnan Ashraf
628 East 11 St. #4c
New York, NY 10009,
USA
adnan@walrus.com

Sam Auinger
Kantstraße 124
10625 Berlin, D
lowres@berlin.Ssnafu.de

Wolf Harun
Bachschneider
Unertlstr. 11
80803 München, D
whb@eggs.de

Gav Baily
Block H, Flat 8 Rodney
Rd. Peabody Estate
London SE17 1BN, UK
gavinb@hotmail.com

Lucas Bambozzi
Cel Melo De Oliveira, 358
05011-040 Sao Paulo, BR
lbambozzi@comum.com

Stephen Barrass
Schloß Birlinghoven
53754 Sankt Augustin, D
stephen.barrass@gmd.de

Stephan Barron
235 Ave Du Puech De
Massane
34 080 Montpellier, F
sbarron@Fmel.com

Scott Becker
P.O. Box 578956
Chicago, IL 60657-8956,
USA
artscb@interaccess.com

Thomas Bell
2518 Wellington Pl.
Murfreesboro, AR 3712
USA
TRBELL@HOME.COM

Torsten Belschner /
Bernd Lintermann
Lorenzstr. 19
76135 Karlsruhe, D
tb@zkm.de

Jon Berge
753 Oak St.
Columbus, OH 43205,
ohiopartnersms@aol.co

Hisham Bizri
851 S. Morgan St.,
Room 1120 Seo
Chicago, IL 60607-705
USA
bizri@evl.uic.edu

Matt Black
Winchester Wharf,
Clink St.
London SE1 9DG, UK
mattb@ninjatune.net

Joachim Blank
Schönleinstr. 4
10967 Berlin, D
sero@sero.org

Bruce Blumberg
20 Ames St.
Cambridge, MA 2139,
USA
bruce@media.mit.edu

Roberto Bocci
Via Certosa 122
53100 Siena, I
bocci@unisi.it

Marc Boehlen
School Of Art, Cfa 300
Pittsburgh, PA 15213,
USA
bohlen@cs.cmu.edu

Markus Bogensberger
Heinrichstr. 112a
8010 Graz, A
marki@sbox.tu-graz.ac.

Andreas Bohn
Boxhagenstr.18
10245 Berlin, D
contact@twosuns.com

Jakob Brandt-Pedersen
Aksvej 8, Nyord
4780 Stege, DK
jbrandtp@get2net.dk

Emily Brigham
4 Symonds St
3123 East Hawthorn,
Melbourne 3123, AUS
ebrigham@ninenet.
com.au

Benjamin Britton
3404 Middleton St.
A144 #10
Cincinnati, OH 54220,
USA
benb@cerhas.uc.edu

Mark Bromawich
Queensgate
Huddersfield HD1 3DH,
UK
m.a.bRomawich@hud.ac
UK

Timothy Brooke
3 Elm Gardens
London N2 0TF, UK
t.brooke@rca.ac.UK

ıard Brown
sington Gore
don SW7 2EU UK,
own@rca.ac.UK

ldon Brown
o Gilman Drive
olla, CA 92093, USA
rown@ucsd.edu

hael Buckley
Gold St.
ingwood 3066, AUS
ıckley@co31.aone.net.

ey Burns
sauer Str. 25
05 Berlin, D
@berlin.snafu.de

id Kacher-Krupka
zeg. 2
63 Sindelfingen, D
rg@ibm.net

Calin
scu 1
o Arad, RO
ier@kinema-
.sorostm.ro

in Cebul
seg. 41/4/30
o Wien, A
rin@xpoint.at

Chabanaud
Rue Du Faubourg
nt Denis
10 Paris, F
en.sefton.green@wana
.fr

ana Chepelyk
Davydova 6, Apt.24
154 Kiev, UKR
ep@eea.kiev.ua

id C. L. Cheung
Michael Drive
onto, Ontario M2H
, CDN
aamw@yahoo.com

id Clark
3 Duk+A67e St.
fax B3J 3J6, CDN
rk@nscad.ns.ca

Coffin
o Offutt Dr.
s Church, VA 22046,

in@art.net

+ Com
ststr.23
87 Berlin, D
artcom.de

Courchesne
4 Rue Laval
ntreal, QC H2X 3C8,

rchel@ere.umontreal.

gory Cowley
Hoff St.
Francisco, CA 94110,

gory@testsite.org

anie Crean
W. 16th St. #6d
v York,
10011, USA
anie@echonyc.com

O[rphan] D[rift>]
46 Wilton Way
London E8 1BG, UK
103267.2077@compuserve.com

Ursula Damm
Engelbertstr. 20
40233 Düsseldorf, D
ursula@khm.de

Cida De Aragão – Lehmann
Kantstr. 151
10623 Berlin, D
cida@slab-berlin.de

Peter De Lorenzo
26 Caalong St.
Robertson 2577, AUS
pdls@ozemail.com.au

Paul De Marinis
49 Broderich St. Apt. 15
San Francisco, CA 94117, USA
demarini@well.com

Louis-Philippe Demers
2025 Parthenais,
Unit 325
Montreal, QC H2K 3T2, CDN
lpd@cam.org

Ivor Diosi
Túrova 62 /Sturova/
96212 Detva, SK
aeternaz@zv.psg.sk

Steve Dixon
26 Chester Rd.
Halifax HX3 6LS, UK
steve@wallah.demon.co.UK

Kelly Dobson
265 Massachusetts Ave
N51 315b, MIT Visual Studies Program
Cambridge, MA 02139, USA
kdobson@mit.edu

Margaret Dolinsky
851 S. Morgan St. Seo
Rm 1120 M/c 154
Chicago, IL 60607, USA
dolinsky@evl.uic.edu

Sreco Dragan
Prijate Ljeva 20
1000 Ljubljana, SLO
sreco.dragan@uni-lj.si

Scott Draves
3435 Cesar Chavez St, Studio 203
San Francisco, CA 94110, USA
spot@transmeta.com

Erwin / Maria Driessens / Verstappen
Eikenweg 9 D-e
1092 BW Amsterdam, NL
notnot@xs4all.nl

Susan Duby
510 Brighton Ave
Reading, PA 19606, USA
art@artelevision.com

Loop Dundee
Mittenwalder St. 61
10961 Berlin, D
krenzien@arco.met.fu-berlin.de

Alan Dunning
601 25th Ave NW
Calgary T2M 2B1, CDN
einsteins-brain-project@home.com

Christoph Ebener
Mendelssohnstr. 13
22761 Hamburg, D
ebener@c-ebener.de

Masako Eto
#101 2-43-14 Kitasenzoku
Ohta-ku, Tokyo 145-0062, J
m@masako.org

Kouichirou Eto
Dk Bldg.5f,7-18-23
Roppongi,minato-ku
106-0032 Tokyo, J
yshikata@crpg.canon.co.jp

Helen Evans
161 A Herne Hill
London SE24 9LR, UK
h.hansen@rca.ac.UK

Valie Export
Kettenbrückeng. 21
1050 Wien, A
export@khm.de

F.a.b.ri.cators
Via Fratelli Bronzetti. N.6
20129 Milano, I
fabricat@galactica.it

Robert Farkash
Beogradski Kej 27
21 000 Novi Sad, YU
dmita@eunet.yu

Franz Fischnaller
Via Fratelli Bronzetti N. 6
20129 Milano, I
fabricat@galactica.it

Monika Fleischmann
Schloss Birlinghoven
53754 Sankt Augustin, D
fleischmann@gmd.de

Peter G. Franck
59 Letter S Rd.
Ghent, NY 12075, USA
architecture@taconic.net

Paul Friedlander
43 Narcissus Rd.
London NW6 1TL, UK
praskovi@clara.net

Gisle Frøysland
Nyhavnsv. 9
5035 Bergen, N
gif@bgnett.no

Fabrizio Funto
V. Aurelia 58
165 Roma, I
f.funto@acsys.it

Takaumi Furuhashi
Reinhold-Frank-Str. 12
76133 Karlsruhe, D
taka@okay.net

Beate Garmer
Rotenbergstr.24
66111 Saarbrücken, D
B.Garmer@hbks.uni-sb.de

Darryl Georgiou
221 Custard Factory, Gibb St.
Birmingham B9 4AA, UK
georgiou@orangenet.co.UK

Piero Gilardi
Corso Casale 121
10132 Torino, I
piero.gilardi@torino.alpcom.it

Joann Gillerman
950 61st St.
Oakland, CA, USA
viper@metron.com

Ana Giron
164 Ludlow St. Apt 14
New York, NY 10002
USA, ana@belle.sva.edu

Gunther Glöckner
Hoffingerg. 47
1120 Wien, A
office@das-archive.at

Jeff Gompertz
90 North 11th St.
Brooklyn, NY 11211,
New York
floating@thing.net

Margarita Goranova
DondUKoff 57-a
1000 Sofia, BG
margi@inet.bg

Ebere Groenouwe
Bergselaan 157 A
3037 BJ Rotterdam, NL
ebereg@hotmail.com

Alexander Györfi
Alarichstr.18
70469 Stuttgart, D
gyoerfi@aol.com

Marikki Hakola
Magnusborg Studios
6100 Porvoo, SF
marikki@magnusborg.fi

Mongrel Harwood
16a Flodden Rd.
London SE5 9LH, UK
info@mongrel.org.UK

Magnus Helander
Grevgatan 20
114 53 Stockholm, S
mhelander@swipnet.se

Wolf Helzle
Helfferichstr. 11
70192 Stuttgart, D
WOLFHELZLE@n-log.de

Lynn Hershman
1201 California St. # 803
San Francisco, CA 94108, USA
lynn2@well.com

Deanna Herst
Oudzijds Voorburgwal 72
1012 GE Amsterdam, NL
axis@axisvm.nl

Christian Hinreiner
Praterinsel 3-4
80538 München, D
hinreiner@studionine.de

Collaboration Ho
4647 Via Huerto
Santa Barbara, CA 93110, USA
jp@mi-fu.solo.com

Perry Hoberman
167 North 9th St.
Brooklyn, NY 11211, USA
hoberman@bway.net

Perrry Hoberman
Rambles, 31
8002 Barcelona, E
npares@iua.upf.es

Maximilian Hoffs
Parkstr. 1
40477 Düsseldorf, D
x-maxx@2000m.com

Kurt Hofstetter
Langeg. 42/8c
1080 Wien, A
hofstetter@sunpendulum.at

Tiffany Holmes
2000 Bonisteel Blvd.
Ann Arbor, MI 48109-2069, USA
tgholmes@umich.edu

Chiho Hoshino
Luisenstr.85
76137 Karlsruhe, D
chiho.hoshino@inka.de

Markus Huemer
Gereonswall 23b
50668 Köln, D
huemer@khm.de

Mamoru Ichikawa
Takinogowa I-63-6, # 906
Kitaku
114 0023 Tokyo, J
j-vision@momo.so-net.ne.jp

Takahito Iimura
4-50-4 Yamato-cho, Nakano-ku
165-0034 Tokyo, J
iimura@gol.com

Anna Ikramova
Hustadtring 75
44801 Bochum, D
ikramova@folkwang.uni-essen.de

Troy Innocent
Po Box 2070
St Kilda West 3182, AUS
troy@iconica.org

Hiroo Iwata
Institute Of Engineering Mechanics And Systems
305-8573 Tsukuba, J
iwata@kz.tsukuba.ac.jp

Jake Jake
230 Rue Saint Charles
75015 Paris, F
jake@imaginet.fr

Nigel Johnson
Flat 1/3, 83 Magdalen Yard Rd.
Dundee DD2 1BA, UK
nmjohnso@dux.dundee.ac.UK

Peter Jorgensen
30, Strandlodsvej
900 Copenhagen, DK
vizart@centrum.dk

Franklin Joyce
53 Etruria St. #a
Seattle, WA 98109, USA
franklin@electricbaby.com

Lilian Jüchtern
Oldenburger St. 11
10551 Berlin, D
p5@digitalworks.org

Hans-Joachim Jung
Köpenicker Str. 1 a
10997 Berlin, D
atlantis@sfx.de

Eduardo Kac
1167 S. Clarence Ave
Oak Park, IL 60304, USA
ekac@artic.edu

Aarre Kärkkäinen
Aallonhuippu 5 B 33
2320 Espoo, SF
aarre@karkka.pp.fi

Brigitte Kaltenbacher
76-78 Montpelier Rd.,
Flat 3
London SE15 2HE, UK
brigittek@sagnet.co.UK

Karrie Karahalios
20 Ames St. E15-430
Cambridge, MA 2139,
USA
kkarahal@media.mit.edu

Zina Kaye
P.O. Box 950
Darlinghurst, NSW 1300,
AUS
zina@observatine.net

Bill Keays
E15-447, 20 Ames St.
Cambridge, MA 02139,
USA
keays@media.mit.edu

André Keller
Hinter Dem Holze 30
30539 Hannover, D
andre@ponton.de

Raivo Kelomees
Tartu St. 1
10145 Tallinn, Estonia
offline@online.ee

Laszlo Kerekes
Stuttgarter St. 49
12059 Berlin, D
nlipps@t.online.de

Andruid Kerne
519 W. 26th St.,
Suite 5000
New York, NY 10001, USA
andruid@mrl.nyu.edu

Ronaldo Kiel
661 Metropolitan Ave,
Apt #3l
Brooklyn, NY 11211, USA
rkiel@ziplink.net

Mariana Kirby
117 E 11 St
New York, NY 10003,
USA
marianakirby@yahoo.com

Karl Kliem
Weserstr. 7
60329 Frankfurt, D
kliem@meso.net

Peter Kogler
Bechardg. 16
A-1030 Wien, A
pascal@fl.aec.at

Jeffrey Krieger
15 Mckee St.
Manchester, CT 6040,
USA
acdcvc@aol.com

Szabolcs Kspál
Damjanich 26/b Vi.2.
1071 Budapest, H
kspal@intermedia.c3.hu

Volker Kuchelmeister
Lorenzstr. 19
76137 Karlsruhe, D
kuchel@zkm.de

Manuel Labor
2309 Bryant St.
San Francisco, CA 94110,
USA
holler@sttf.org

Christin Lahr
Ackerstr. 18
10115 Berlin, D
lahr@khm.de

Cati Laporte
47 East First St.
New York,NY 10003, USA
cati@panix.com

Sophie Lavaud
7 Rue Jean Arp
75013 Paris, F
sophie.lavaud@worldnet.
fr

Julia Lazarus
Almstadtstr. 24
10119 Berlin, D
julia_lazarus@gmx.de

Russet Lederman
161 West 75th St.
New York, NY 10023,
USA
spud@interport.net

Christine Liu
R.américo Alves Pereira
Filho 565 # 222
05688 000 São Paulo,
BR
cliu@caps.com.br

Marita Liulia
Uudenmaankatu 2 K
120 Helsinki, SF
liulia@medeia.com

Loeil Loeil
Emile Tavan
13 100 Aix en Provence,
F
loeil@ecole-art-aix.fr

Jarryd Lowder
41 E. 28th St. #3a
New York, NY 10016, USA
jarryd@sva.edu

Kieran Lyons
College Crescent
Newport NP6 1YG, UK
k.lyons@newport.ac.uk

Tim Macdonald
418 Wellington St
3068 Clifton Hill, 3068,
AUS
tim_macdonald69@hotma
il.com

John Maeda
20 Ames St.
Cambridge, MA 02139,
USA
maeda@media.mit.edu

Taku Maeda
Takinogandi - 63-6, #906
Kitaku
114 0023 Tokyo, J
j-vision@momo.so-
net.ne.jp

Yesi Maharaj Singh
V. Fratelli Bronzetti 6
20120 Milano, I
fabricat@galactica.it

Eric Maillet
11 Bis, Cité De Trévise
75009 Paris, F
e.mail@nettaxi.com

Sylvie Marchand
7 Rue De La Gare
16240 Villefagnan, F
silva@interpc.fr

Jenny Marketou
189 Franklin St. # 391
New York, NY 10013, USA
jmarketo@thing.net

Robert Martin
613 West Lincoln Ave
Royal Oak, MI 48067,
USA
aa3177@wayne.edu

Michael Mateas
5000 Forbes Ave
Pittsburgh, PA 15213,
USA
michaelm@cs.cmu.edu

Yasushi Matoba
146 Bonsai Oomiya-city
330 Saitama-ken, J
matomato@highway.ne.jp

Matthias Meinharter
Geusaug. 4/3
1030 Wien, A
meinharter@yahoo.com

Bertrand Merlier
Grises
26740 Savasse, F
Bertrand.Merlier@univ-
lyon2.fr

Kathryn Mew
P. O. Box 820 f
Melbourne 3001, AUS
kathryn.mew@ninemsn.
com.au

Steven Middleton
21 Hull St.
Richmond 3121, AUS
stevem@vicnet.net.au

Andreas Miketa
Hinterfeldg. 3
6900 Bregenz, A

John Mills-Cockell
210 Hembrough
Bowser, BC VoR 1Go,
CDN
jmc@musicplanet.com

Achim Mohné
C/o Kopp, Grosse
Telegrafenstr. 27
50676 Köln, D
achim@autopsi.de

Jean-Noël Montagné
11 Av Ste Marguerite
6200 Nice, F
jnm@Roma.fr

Sergio Perez Moretto
Dorfplatz
8911 Rifferswil, CH
ehrensperger.steiner@
bluewin.ch

Vladimir Muzhesky
601 West 26th
New York, NY 10001, USA
basicray@thing.net

Yoichi Nagashima
10-12-301, Sumiyoshi – 5
430-0906 Hamamatsu,
Shizuoka, J
nagasm@computer.org

Dafna Naphtali
224 Sullivan St. #e21
New York, NY 10012, USA
dafna@escape.com

Gordana Navakovic
6 Ashurst Gardens Tulse
Hill
London Sw2 3UH, UK
gordana.novakovic@
virgin.net

Norie Neumark
2/15 Baden St., Coogee
Sydney 2034, AUS
n.neumark@uts.edu.au

Patrick Nijman
Jan Ligthartstraat 1
1817 MR Alkmaar, NL
nijman@nmtrix.com

Alexander Nischelwitzer
Wastiang. 6
8010 Graz, A
alexander.nischelwitzer@
joanneum.ac.at

Bino Nord
Mössebergsvagen 14, 2tr
BRomama
Stockholm, S
gizavrn@hotmail.com

Birgitta Nord
Mössebergsvägen 14
16743 BRomama, S
bino_cyberstar@hotmail.
com

Robert Novak
Na Petrinach 20/219
162 00 Prague, CZ
robmig21@yahoo.com

Catherine Nyeki
61 Rue Olivier Metra
75020 Paris, F
cnyeki@lemel.fr

Tomohisa Okamoto
1-5-6-b201 ZenpUKuji
167-0041 Suginami-ku,
Tokyo, J
tomohisa@oka.urban.ne.
jp

Zaki Omar
Seelingstr. 14
14059 Berlin, D
haza@dm.fh-hannover.de

David Opp
448 W 16th, 2nd Floor
New York, NY 10013, NY
night@day-dream.com

Vito Orazem
Max-reger-str.17-19
45128 Essen, D
design_D@compuserve.
com

Isaias Ortega
Churubusco Y Tlalpan S/n
Col. Country Club
4220 Mexico D.F., MEX
isaiaso@correo.cnart.mx

Garth Paine
30 Moodie St.
Carnegie, Victoria 3163,
AUS
garth@creativeaccess.com
.au

Zoran Pantelic
Milana Rakica 15
21000 Novi Sad, YU
apsolutn@rocketmail.com

Alexandru Patatics
Diaconul Coresi 28a
1900 Timisoara, RO
ap@ambient.dnttm.ro

Eric Paulos
1079 Tennessee St.
San Francisco, CA 941
USA
paulos@cs.berkeley.ed

Alan Peacock
College Lane
Hatfield Herts AL1O 9T
UK
a.d.peacock@herts.ac.

Annika Pehrson
Ringvagen 125
116 61 Stockholm, S
annika@pehrson.com

Sylvia Pengilly
1372 Tourney Hill Lane
Nipomo, CA 93444, US
spengilly@earthlink.net

Simon Penny
College Of Fine Art 30
5000 Forbes Ave
Pittsburgh, PA 15213,
USA
penny+@cmu.edu

Bogdan Perzynski
4305 Shoalwood Ave
Austin, TX 78756, USA
ifzecer@mail.utexas.ed

Arno Peters
Tesselschadestraat 6 B
3521 XV Utrecht, NL
tapetv@knoware.nl

Liz Phillips
39-39 45th St.
Sunnyside, NY 11104-
2103, USA
sculpsound@unidial.co

Thomas Porett
673 Aubrey Ave
Ardmore, OK 19003, U
tporett@op.net

Waldek Pranckiewicz
Kazimierza Wlk. 29 A
50- 061 Wroclaw, PL
12@magic.ic.com.pl

Alan Price
1000 Hilltop Rd
Baltimore, MD 21250,
USA
alan@irc.umbc.edu

Jane Prophet
43 Stapleton Hall Rd.
London N4 3QF, UK
jane@cairn.demon.co.

Sabrina Raaf
1821 W. Hubbard St.
Chicago, IL 60622, US
sraaf@artic.edu

Miroslaw Rajkowski
Ul.dubois 21/17
50-207 Wroclaw, PL
raju@sun20.wcss.wroc.

Alexandra Reill
Walfischg. 10
1010 Wien, A
kanonmedia@yahoo.co

Brandon Rickman
1529 Armacost #9
Los Angeles, CA 90025
CA
ashes@zennet.com

M. Rigoletti
Heslacher Wand 33
70199 Stuttgart, D
ulti_edia@rocketmail.com

Don Ritter
204 15 St.
Brooklyn, NY 11215, USA
ritter@interport.net

Simon Robertshaw
Peru St.
Salford M3 6EQ, UK
sirob@cybase.co.uk

Seth Roe
222a East Park
Savannah, GA 31401, USA
vanroe@excite.com

Miroslaw Rogala
329 W. 18th St.
Chicago, IL 60616, USA
rogala@mcs.com

Franco Rolle
Via S. Antonio Da
Padova 10
10121 Torino, I
nomades@ipsnet.it

Avi Rosen
22, Hashoshanim
36842 Nesher, IL
avi@sayfan.technion.ac.il

Gilles Rouffineau
10 Rue Mathieu De La
Drôme
26000 Valence, F
rouffineau@wanadoo.fr

Duncan Rowland
109 Comm Arts
E. Lansing, MI 48824,
USA
rowlan18@pilot.msu.edu

Daniel Rozin
721 Broadway
New York, NY 10003,
USA
danny.rozin@nyu.edu

Takatsu Ryohei
Seika-cho Soraku-gun
619-0288 Kyoto, J
takatsu,tosa@mic.atr.co.
jp

Egill Sæbjörnsson
Schwedterstr. 250
10119 Berlin, D
egillegill@yahoo.com

Werner Sandhacker
Zeugebäudeplatz 5/1
3100 St. Pölten, A
t@via.at

Daniel Sandin
851 S Morgan St. Rm
120 Seo
Chicago, IL 60607-7053,
USA
dan@uic.edu

Ermine Sangiovanni
Rua Francisco Tapajos,
3 Ap. 11
04153-001 Sao Paulo –
SP, BR
ygo@zaz.com.br

Stefan Schemat
Fleedingsmarkt 14
20459 Hamburg, D
stefan_schemat@media-
com

Thecla Schiphorst
1128 Rose St.
Vancouver, BC V5L 4KB,
CDN
schiphorst@tu.bc.ca

Anne-Marie Schleiner
Se 735 South St.
Pullman, WA 99163, USA
amschle@cadre.sjsu.edu

Jan Schoenfelder
Silberfundstr. 33
31141 Hildesheim, D
jschoenf@rz.uni-
hildesheim.de

Joachim Schütz
Immenhoferstr.13
70180 Stuttgart, D
ekoennem@filmakademie.
de

Remaclus Schuurbiers
Herderstraat 8
2512 CV The Hague, NL
tappo.kontakt@hotbot.
com

Olga Sdoviova
Vul. Skovorody 2
254070 Kiev, UKR
c-chep@cca.kiev.ua

Jean-Robert Sedano
423 Rue Du Paradis
34400 Saint Series, F
ludicart@aol.com

Gebhard Sengmüller
Margaretenstr. 106/17
1050 Wien, A
gebseng@thing.at

Vergil Sharkya
63 Renshaw St.
Liverpool L1 2SJ, UK
vergilreality@merseymail.
com

Hasoon Shin
Allmandring 10d/22
70569 Stuttgart, D
shsfs@hotmail.com

Shirley Shor
763 Belmont Place E
#208
Seattle, WA 98102, USA
shirley@dRomaology.com

George Shortess
3505 Hecktown Rd.
Bethlehem, PA 18020,
USA
george.shortess@lehigh.
edu

Silver
silver@avu.cz

Joel Slayton
One Washington Square
San Jose, CA 95128-0089,
USA
C5@cadre.sjsu.edu

Ernst Slutzky
Nesselbuschstr. 1
60439 Frankfurt/Main, D

Jacqueline Smith-autard
19 Edge Rd., Thornhill
Dewsbury, West
Yorkshire, WF12 0QA, UK
100624.500@compuserve.
com

Laurentina Soares
Rua Rodrigues Gusmão, 21
3000 – 345 Coimbra, P
lsoares@ccg.uc.pt

Andrea Sodomka
Zieglerg. 31/911
1070 Wien, A
sodomka.breindl@thing.at

Christa Sommerer
2-2 Hikaridai, Seika-cho,
Soraku-gun
61902 Kyoto, J
christa@mic.atr.co.jp

Karin Sondergaard
Bjornsonsvej 85
2500 Valky, DK
kjell.yngue@teliamail.dk

Mari Soppela
Stuurmankade 62
1019 KR Amsterdam, NL
ano@xs4all.nl

Kalman Spelletich
1043 Marin St.
San Francisco, CA 94124,
USA
kal@seemen.org

Luc Steels
Pleinlaan 2
1050 Brussels, B
steels@arti.vub.ac.be

Nobuya SuzUKi
3-95 RyoUKe
503-0014 Ogaki, Gifu, J
zuckey@iamas.ac.jp

Peter Svedberg
Bergsrådsvägen 100
12842 Stockholm, S
peter.svedberg@mailbox.
swipnet.se

Bozidar Svetek
Splitska 6
1000 Ljubljana, SLO
interakt@si21.com

Sara Tack
138 Town Garage Rd.
East Nassau, NY 12062,
USA
tacks@rpi.edu

Sam Taylor
2309 Bryant St.
San Francisco, CA 94110,
USA
holler@sttf.org

Aristarkh Tchernishev
Verkhnaya Pervomaiskaya
105264 Moscow, RUS
arist@cityline.ru

Teco/studio21
Lippo Memmi 7
53100 Siena, I
sabbione@tecosistemi.
com

Simon Tegala
Kirkman House, 12/14
Whitfield St.
London W1P 5RD, UK
stegala@iniva.org

Nell Tenhaaf
106 Helena Ave
Toronto M6G 2H2, CDN
tenhaaf@yorku.ca

Paul Thomas
29 Elizabeth St.
North Perth 6006, AUS
pthomas@odyssey.apana.
org.au

Seth Thompson
31-50 35th St., #3b
Astoria, NY 11106, USA
tstudio@seththompson.
com

Stefanie Toth
Schloß Birlinghoven
53754 Sankt Augustin, D
toth@gmd.de

Luis Trevino
P.O. Box 66795
1061-A Caracas, YV
luis_trevino@hotmail.com

Ryan Ulyate
415 S. Topanga Cyn Blvd
#210
Topanga, CA 90290, USA
ryan@synesthesia-
LLC.com

Åsa Unander-scharin
Värtavägen 21
115 53 Stockholm, S
asa.unander-
scharin@telia.com

Olaf Val
Johannesstr. 7
34121 Kassel, D
vahl@studenten.uni-
kassel.de

Ceu San Pablo Valencia
Edificio Seminario S/n
46113 Valencia
(Moncada), E
dprada@ceu.upv.es

Tjebbe Van Tijen
Nieuwe Amstelstraat 70
1011 PM Amsterdam, NL
t.tijen@cable.a2000.nl

Paul Vanouse
5000 Forbes Ave
Pittsburgh, PA 15213-
3890, US
pv28@andrew.cmu.edu

Steina Vasulka
Route 6, Box 100
Santa Fe, NM 87501, USA
woodyv@santafe.edu

Jan Verbeek
Kaiserstr. 105
53113 Bonn, D

Yvon Villarceaux
26-1000 Silver St.
Ottawa, Ontario K1Z 6H6,
yetb@artengine.ca

Kamil Vondrasek
V. Klementa 1
293 60 Mlada Boleslav,
CZ
kamil.vondrasek@skoda-
auto.cz

Fabian Wagmister
1201 California # 302
San Francisco, CA 94108
USA, lynn2@well.com

Emily Weil
721 Broadway 4th Floor
New York, NY 10013, USA
eqw4358@is8.nyu.edu

Teresa Wennberg
Valhallavagen 79
100 44 Stockholm, S
teresa@pdc.kth.se

Stephen Wilson
Art – 1600 Holloway
San Francisco, CA 94132,
USA
swilson@sfsu.edu

Stefan Wölwer
20 Cresent Rd. – Flat 9
London N8 8AX, UK
stefan@esfore-
entropy.com

Jerzy Wozniak
1628-19th Ave N+A208W
Calgary T2M 1B1, CDN
artrecon@artrecon.com

Eunmi Yang
350 7th St. Apt. # B6
Brooklyn, NY 11215, USA
eyang@pratt.edu

Pamela Z
540 Alabama St. Studio
213
San Francisco, CA 94110,
USA
pamelaz@sirius.com

Julia Zdarsky
Alliiertenstr. 16/17
1020 Wien, A
starsky@sil.at

Georg Zeitblom
Dieffenbachstr. 35
10967 Berlin, D
zeitblom@berlin.snafu.de

Eric Zimmerman
49 Mcguinness Blvd
Brooklyn, NY 11222, USA
eric@flat.com

Mubimedia Zush
Mallorca, 275 1º 2ª
8008 Barcelona, E
mubimedia@mubimedia.
com

Christiaan Zwanikken
Convento Sao Francisco
7750 Mertola, P
artfarc@xs4all.nl

Seth Abramovitch
79 Barrow St. #1c
New York, NY 10014, USA
BulletNYC@aol.com

Michael Aerni
Schulstr. 184
8413 Neftenbach, CH
nestor@active.ch

Gorka Aguado
Nueva Fuera, 28
1001 Vitoria-Gasteiz, E
grk@ctv.es

Antonio Alonso
Com.castilla.leon 80 1-4
28230 Las Rozas, Madrid, E
AAlonso@cplus.es

Joao Amorim
2869 22nd St.
San Francisco, CA 94110, USA
amorimjoao@hotmail.com

Masakatsu Aoki
1-1, Hikarinooka
239-0847 Yokosuka-shi, J
aokimas@nttcvg.hil.ntt.co.jp

Luis Araho
Ctra. Valldemossa Rm 7'5
7071 Palma de Mallorca, E
info@studio1.vib.es

Masatsugu Arakawa
Minami-cho 3-4-5 Ing
Studio 301
185-0021 Kokubunji-city, Tokyo, J

Jun Asakawa
Ariake Frontier Building
Tower „a" 17f
135-0064 3-1-25 Ariake, Koto-ku, Tokyo, J
masae@ppi.co.jp

Juhasz Attila
Meszaros 48-52
1016 Budapest, H
haliho99@freemail.c3.hu

Cecilia Avanovich
Ctra. Valldemossa Rm 7`5
7071 Palma de Mallorca, E
info@studio1.vib.es

Dario Bajurin
2. Pracanska 6b
10000 Zagreb, HR
bajurin@usa.net

John S. Banks
562 W. Arlington Place
Suite 4
Chicago, IL 60614, USA
JSBANKS@INTERACCESS.COM

Patricia Barbazan
121 Rue De Bordeaux
16000 Angoulême, F
din@cnbdi.fr

Laura Barbera
1738 East 17th St.
Brooklyn, NY 11229-2102, USA
lbarbera@pratt.edu

Marie-Claire Bazart
Le Fort, Av. De
Normandie, Bp 113
59370 Mons en Baroeul, F
exquise@nordnet.fr

Thomas Berdel
Schießstätte 6
6800 Feldkirch, A
ttl@cyberdude.com

Havard Berstad
Pilestredet 63a
350 Oslo, N
havabers@khio.no

Dirk Bialluch
Rotdornstr. 14 a
23715 Bosau, D
DirkBi@Software2000.de

Nicolas Billiotel
121 Rue De Bordeaux
16000 Angoulême, F
din@cnbdi.fr

Jon Bjarnason
Hverfisgata 39
101 Reykjavik, ISL
nonnib@hi.is

Camilla Blapierre
Le Fort, Av. De
Normandie, Bp 113
59370 Mons en Baroeul, F
exquise@nordnet.fr

Jorge Boada
Ctra. Valldemossa Rm 7'5
7071 Palma de Mallorca, E
info@studio1.vib.es

Igor Borovikov
77 Geary St., Suite 300
San Francisco, CA 94108, USA
elena@animatekusa.com

Anne Bourdais
Le Fort, Av. De
Normandie, Bp 113
59370 Mons en Baroeul, F
exquise@nordnet.fr

Douglas Bowman
525 Biosciences Building,
2500 University Drive Nw
T2N 1N4 Calgary T2N 1N4, CDN
bowman@ucalgary.ca

Michael Buchwald
19 Heisesgade
2100 Copenhagen, DK
michbuch@centrum.de

Brian Burks
2700 N. Tamiami Tr.
Sarasota, FL 34234, USA
strovas@rsad.edu

Adam Byrne
2700 N. Tamiami Trail
Sarasota, FL 34234, USA
strovas@rsad.edu

Joan Cabot
Ctra. Valldemossa Rm 7'5
7071 Palma de Mallorca, E
info@studio1.vib.es

Peter Callas
P.O. Box 599
Avalon Beach, NSW 2107, AUS
Norakuro@hydra.com.au

Toni Camps
Ctra. Valldemossa Rm 7'5
7071 Palma de Mallorca, E
info@studio1.vib.es

Leos Carax
22, Rue Hegesippe Moreau
75018 Paris, F
sophie@exmach.fr

Wooksang Chang
1224 Kinnear Rd.
Columbus,
OH 43212-1154, USA
chang.350@osu.edu

Yu-mei Chang
8505 Waters Av. #14
Savannah, GA 31406, USA

Erwin Charrier
Le Fort, Av. De
Normandie, Bp 113
59370 Mons en Baroeul, F
exquise@nordnet.fr

Sam Chen
950 High School Way #3328
Mountain View, CA 94041, USA
sambochen@yahoo.com

Hiroshi Chida
Ariake Frontier Building
Tower „a" 17f
135-0064 3-1-25 Ariake, Koto-ku, Tokyo, J
masae@ppi.co.jp

Chen Chih-min
506 Riddle Rd. #49
Cincinnati, OH 45220, USA
chencm@email.uc.edu

Se-lien Chuang
Grabenstr. 17
8010 Graz, A
cse-lien@sime.com

Franck Clarenc
Le Fort, Av. De
Normandie, Bp 113
59370 Mons en Baroeul, F
exquise@nordnet.fr

John Clisset
15811 Sanctuary Drive
Tampa, FL 33647, USA
jclisset@Ringling.EDU

Dylan Crooke
P.O. Box 357
3068 Clifton Hill, AUS
agar@melbpc.org.au

Claire Cuinier
Le Fort, Av. De
Normandie, Bp 113
59370 Mons en Baroeul, F
exquise@nordnet.fr

Cassidy Curtis
Box 352350
Seattle, WA 98195-2350, USA
cassidy@cs.washington.edu

Paul Debevec
387 Soda Hall #1776
Berkeley, CA 94720-1776, USA
debevec@cs.berkeley.edu

Bernd Dehne
Roettelbachweg 25
75385 Bad Teinach, D
webmaster@dehne-ehninger.de

Diane Delavallee
12, Rue Vavin
75006 Paris, F
storkcom@club-internet.fr

Julien Delmotte
Le Fort, Av. De
Normandie, Bp 113
59370 Mons en Baroeul, F
exquise@nordnet.fr

Frederic Dervaux
Le Fort, Av. De
Normandie, Bp 113
59370 Mons en Baroeul, F
exquise@nordnet.fr

Sarah Donahue
277 Canterbury Rd.
Rochester, NY 14607, USA
sld3513@rit.edu

Jason Donati
232 East Squire Drive #3
Rochester, NY 14623, USA
jad2782@rit.edu

Zbiqniew Dowgiatto
Ul. Glogera 2m. 30
02 051 Warszawa, PL
dowdow@medianet.

Everett Downing
3000 W. Palmer #2
Chicago, IL 60647, USA
edowning@bigidea.com

Sheldon Drake
93 Av. B
New York, NY 10009, USA
schnoidl@bway.net

Staceyjoy Elkin
127 Berkeley Place #2
Brooklyn, NY 11217, USA
stacey@tiac.net

Mariano Equizzi
Viale Regione Siciliana 7800
90146 Palermo, I
ignazioe@tin.it

George Evelyn
2800 Third St.
San Francisco, CA 94107, USA
jo-carol@colossal.com

Ken Feinstein
614 Madison St.
Hoboken7030, NJ, USA
ktb@brickandcat.com

John Fischer
75 Warren Gt
New York, NY 10007, USA
jfischer@musicarts.org

Derek Flood
Goethestr. 54
80336 München, D
derek@das-werk.de

David Francois
Le Fort, Av. De
Normandie, Bp 113
59370 Mons en Baroeul, F
exquise@nordnet.fr

Tom Frisch
8611 W 29th St.
Minneapolis, MN 55426, USA
tomk@evl.uic.edu

Johannes Fritz
Langstr. 46 A
61276 Weilrod , D
Johannes_Fritz@t-online.de

Miles Murray Sorrell Fue
33 Fournier St.
London E1 6QE, UK
fuel@fuel-design.com

Fuesslin, Beyer, Fiedler, Luedemann, Kurth
Nollendorfstr.1
30163 Hannover, D
michaelf@dm.fh-hannover.de

Isabella Gadbled
Le Fort, Av. De
Normandie, Bp 113
59370 Mons en Baroeu
F
exquise@nordnet.fr

Harry Gamsjager
1151 W. Sepulveda St#
San Pedro, CA 90731, USA
dragonfire@prodigy.net

Gert Garmund
Åløkkevænget 15
5000 Odense, DK
gega@tv2.dk

Andrea Geiger
Bavariafilmplatz 7
82031 Geiselgasteig, D
munich@scanline.de

Andrea Ghalfi
Ctra. Valldemossa Rm 7
7071 Palma de Mallorca
E
info@studio1.vib.es

Beppe Giacobbe
Via Vittadini, 23
20136 Milano, I
giacobbe@micronet.it

James Gibson
3126 Bell Drive
Boulder, CO 80301 USA,

Harvey Goldman
42 Fisher Rd.
Westport, MA 2790, US
hgoldman@umassd.edu

Erwin Gomez Viñales
Ernesto Pinto Lagarrigu
156 B
Recoleta, Santiago, RCH
egomezv@ctcreuna.cl

Stephen Gressak
305 Washington Av. B-2
Brooklyn, NY 11205, US
sgressak@pratt.edu

José Grisius
45 Rue Du Chapeau
1070 Bruxelles, B
drtoon@ping.be

Geoffrey Guiot
Le Fort, Av. De
Normandie, Bp 113
59370 Mons en Baroeu
F
exquise@nordnet.fr

Genco Gulan
426 West 46th St.
New York, NY 10036, USA
gencogulan@rocketmail.
com

Stefan Halter
Hohlstr. 46
8004 Zürich, CH
stefanhalter@datacomm.
ch

Heath Hanlin
102 Shaffer Art
Syracuse, NY 13244, USA
ahanlin@syr.edu

Gerhard Hanzl
Diefenbachg. 35
150 Wien, A
erhard.hanzl@orf.at

Wolfgang Hartl
ahnhofstr. 8
640 Gloggnitz, A
ork@artgraphic.at

avid Haxton
036 Sharon Rd.
Vinter Park, FL 32789,
SA
axton@aol.com

ary Hazlewood
02 Gallup Rd.
pencerport, NY 14559,
SA
fh4618@rit.edu

artin Heigan
O. Box 7708
35 Westgate, ZA
artinh@videolab.co.za

ernan Holland
74 Walnut St.
s Alamos, NM 87544,
A
olland@unm.edu

hee Oh Holmen
upstadringen 49b
78 Saupstad, N
e@emsh.calarts.edu

rs Holmgren
Queens Av., Avalon
07
dney, NSW 2107, AUS
nkenskippy@hotmail.
m

ko Hoshizawa Sedlak
Leonie Hill Rd. #07-04
9196 Singapore, SGP
kos@pacific.net.sg

nedicte Hostache
Fort, Av. De
mandie, Bp 113
370 Mons en Baroeul,

uise@nordnet.fr

nald House
Tauber #1
40 College Station,

hmidt@cs.tamu.edu

Chi Hsu
Box 1559, Shatin
tral Post Office
gkong, HK
su@acm.org

laume Ivernel
Rue Damremont
18 Paris, F
haene@toutenkartoon
n

Orjan Jensen
Odinsgt. 2
265 Oslo, N
barberskum@hotmail.com

Alejandra Jimenez Lopez
20 Heywood House
Tulse Hill
London SW2 2EU, UK
dgcircus@dircon.co.uk

Marcel Cornelius
Hubertus Kaars
Kempstraat 116
2572 GK Den Haag, NL
sram@casema.net

Paul Kaiser
306 West 38th St. #402
New York, NY 10018, NY
paul@riverbed.com

Istvan Kantor
372 Richmond St. W.
#210
Toronto, ONT M5V 1X6,
CDN
amen@interlog.com

Monika Kanz
Annag. 6
1010 Wien, A
kanzmo@mediaartcomp.
telecom.at

Wolfgang Karl
Altes Dorf 23
24855 Jübek, D
heidelore.karl@mark-
tiwo.de

Yoshihiro Katayama
Naritaminami-mati 1-6
572-0003 Neyagawa-si,
Osaka, J
yosikata@mail.goo.ne.jp

Andrew Katumba
Kleinstr. 16
8008 Zürich, CH
info@crambi.com

Yoichiro Kawaguchi
Komaba, 4-6-1,
Meguro-ku
153-8904 Tokyo, J
yoichiro@race.u-
tokyo.ac.jp

Jun Kinoshita
731-13shiromeguri
247-0074 Kamakura-shi,
Kanagawa-ken
ee2s-knst@asahi-net.or.jp

Jeff Kleiser
87 Marshall St., Bldg. 1
N. Adams, MA 1247, USA
amanda@kwcc.com

Eva Könnemann
Immenhoferstr.13
70180 Stuttgart, D
ekoennem@filmakademie.
de

Wobbe Koning
323 1/2 West Hubbard
Ave
Columbus,
OH 43215-1345, USA
wkoning@cgrg.ohio-
state.edu

Patrick Koster
Elandsstraat 96-c
1016 SH Amsterdam, NL
patrickkoster@yahoo.com

Gerald Laimgruber
Mittersteig 2b/15
1050 Wien, A
none@adis.at

Christopher Landreth
210 King St. East
Toronto, ONT M5C 1P1,
CDN
landreth@aw.sgi.com

John Lasseter
1001 W. Cutting Bld.
Richmond, CA 44804,
USA
kass@pixar.com

Sebastian Laudenbach
Le Fort, Av. De
Normandie, Bp 113
59370 Mons en Baroeul,
F
exquise@nordnet.fr

William Le Henanff
121 Rue De Bordeaux
16000 Angoulême, F
din@cnbdi.fr

Anne-Sarah Le Meur
257, Rue Du Faubourg
Saint Martin
75010 Paris, F
aslemeur@hotmail.com

Myeongjae Lee
9400 Abercorn Zxt.
Apt.530
Savannah, GA 31406, USA

Guillaume Lenel
Le Fort, Av. De
Normandie, Bp 113
59370 Mons en Baroeul,
F
exquise@nordnet.fr

Jeff Lew
87 Marshall St., Bldg. 1
N. Adams, MA 1247, USA
amanda@kwcc.com

Aaron Lim
828 Franklin #501
San Francisco, CA 94102,
USA
ahron_68@yahoo.com

Arno Löwecke
Kirchbundtenstr. 34
4107 Ettingen, CH
cmvconnection@bluewin.
ch

Mario Jo Long
Le Fort, Av. De
Normandie, Bp 113
59370 Mons en Baroeul,
F
exquise@nordnet.fr

Sandrine Mabilat
Le Fort, Av. De
Normandie, Bp 113
59370 Mons en Baroeul,
F
exquise@nordnet.fr

Audrey Mahaut
Le Fort, Av. De
Normandie, Bp 113
59370 Mons en Baroeul,
F
exquise@nordnet.fr

Charlotte Manning
Fasanenstr. 81
10623 Berlin, D
office@mental.com

Raul Marroquin
Da Costakade T/o 91a
1053 xk Amsterdam, NL
hksteen@desk.nl

Rachel Mayeri
201 Eldridge Av.
Mill Valley, CA 94941,
USA
rmayeri@ucsd.edu

Cameron Mcnall
12034 Navy St.
Los Angeles, CA 90066,
USA
cmcnall@ucla.edu

Andre Metello
Rua Antonio Parreiras 80
24210-320 Boa Viagem –
Niteroi, BR
metello@microlink.com.br

Michel Metenier
Le Fort, Av. De
Normandie, Bp 113
59370 Mons en Baroeul,
F
exquise@nordnet.fr

Kent Mikalsen
87 Marshall St., Bldg. 1
N. Adams, MA 1247, USA
amanda@kwcc.com

Markus Miklautsch
Papiermühlg. 67
9020 Klagenfurt, A
markus.m@edvART.com

Milla Moilanen
Magnusborg Studios
6100 Porvoo, SF
milla@magnusborg.fi

Daniel Moreno
Av. Sernambetiba 3300
Bl. 3 / 302
22639-900 Rio de
Janeiro, BR
danimor@hotmail.com

Stephen Moros
2107 West Str+A62.
Berkeley, CA 94702, USA
smoros@pixar.com

Brandon Morse
3031 Neil Ave Apt C
Columbus , OH 43202,
USA
emorse@cgrg.ohio-
state.edu

Patrice Mugnier
Le Fort, Av. De
Normandie, Bp 113
59370 Mons en Baroeul,
F
exquise@nordnet.fr

Rodrigo Munoz Kuri
Le Fort, Av. De
Normandie, Bp 113
59370 Mons en Baroeul,
F
exquise@nordnet.fr

Sean Murphy
94 E Casey Drive
Richmond Hill, SD 31324,
USA
Murph1138@aol.com

Takehiko Nagakura
77 Massachusetts Av.
10-472
Cambridge, MA 2139,
USA
takehiko@mit.edu

Monique Nahas
24 Rue Theodore Honoré
94130 Nogent sur Marne,
F
nahas@ccr.jussiev.fr

Ulrich Niemeyer
2300 South Court
Santa Fe, NM 87505, USA
uniemeyer@trail.com

Carlos Nogueira
Rua Rosa Pavone, 30
03638-080 São Paulo, BR
educar@usp.br

Deirdre O'malley
135 Mississippi St,
3rd Floor
San Francisco, CA 94107,
USA
mail@mondomed.com

Tor Oera
Oestgaardsgate 5, #36
474 Oslo, N
oera@online.no

Dietmar Offenhuber
Leonfeldnerstr. 27/8
4040 Linz, A
didi@fl.aec.at

Minoru Okamoto
Ariake Frontier Building
Tower „a" 17f
135-0064 3-1-25 Ariake,
Koto-ku, Tokyo, J
masae@ppi.co.jp

Marko Ormik
Laudong. 39-2-12
1080 Wien, A
reinhard@ris-med.ac.at

Unknown Pechou
Le Fort, Av. De
Normandie, Bp 113
59370 Mons en Baroeul,
F
exquise@nordnet.fr

Lincoln Peirce
11 Weehawken St.
New York, NY 10014, USA
stacy@glc.com

Toby Penrose
Station Rd.
Beaconsfield HP9 1LG UK
jonpersey@bigfoot.com

Martin Pietler
Parcusstr. 6
55116 Mainz, D
mpietler@img.fh-mainz.de

Anna Paola Pizzocaro
Le Fort, Av. De
Normandie, Bp 113
59370 Mons en Baroeul,
F
exquise@nordnet.fr

Christian Pokorny
Bavariafilmplatz 7
82031 Geiselgasteig, D
munich@scanline.de

Andreas Procopiou
2700 N. Tamiami Trail
Sarasota, FL 34234, USA
strovas@rsad.edu

Bruce Pukema
Ronin Animation
2429 Nicollet Ave.
Mpls. MN 55404, USA
roninInc@intxxnet.com

Matthias Pusch
Seelingstr. 28
14059 Berlin, D
toshi@is.in-berlin.de

Magali Quinard
121 Rue De Bordeaux
16000 Angoulême, F
din@cnbdi.fr

Radek
P.O. Box 581, 2200
Mission College Blvd.
Santa Clara,
CA 95052-8119, USA
USA

Paul Rademacher
Cb#3175, Sitterson Hall
Chapel Hill,
NC 27599-3175, USA
rademach@cs.unc.edu

Nathalie Rafiy
267 Promenade
Des Anglais
6200 Nice, F
midi@midiline.com

Rita Inez Reichlhuber
Dr. Rasper Str. 17a
4802 Ebensee, A
rita_inez@hotmail.com

Mathieu Reynes
121 Rue De Bordeaux
16000 Angoulême, F
din@cnbdi.fr

Ricardo Ribenboim
69, François Clovet St.
05451-140 Sao Paulo, BR
ribenboim@uol.com.br

Ryan Rivera
Henry St.
V3H 2K3 Port Moody,
CDN
rrivera19@hotmail.com

Daniel Robichaud
300 Rose Av.
Venice, CA 90291, USA
bhoffman@d2.com

Isabel Roca
Ctra. Valldemossa Rm 7'5
7071 Palma de Mallorca,
E
info@studio1.vib.es

Pablo Rodriguez
Ctra. Valldemossa Rm 7'5
7071 Palma de Mallorca,
E
info@studio1.vib.es

Juan Carlos Rodulfo
Ctra. Valldemossa Rm 7'5
7071 Palma de Mallorca,
E
info@studio1.vib.es

Marion Roger
Le Fort, Av. De
Normandie, Bp 113
59370 Mons en Baroeul,
F
exquise@nordnet.fr

Dani Rosen
2700 N. Tamiami Trail
Sarasota, FL 34234, USA
drosen@ringling.edu

Aaron F. Ross
643 Divisadero St. #102
San Francisco,
CA 94117-1513, USA
aaron@dr-yo.com

Martin Russ
71 Farriers Close,
Martlesham Heath
Ipswich, Suffolk IP5 3SN
UK
martin@betsubetsu.com

Bob Sabiston
4204 Ave H
Austin, TX 78751, USA
d9@eden.com

Richard Sandoval
1732 N. Kingsley Dr. #2
Los Angeles, CA 90027,
USA
rsandova@usc.edu

Kim Sang
Gaya-dong, Pusanjin-gu
614-714 Pusan, ROK
megisaem@hanmail.net

Minoru Sasaki
6-8-8, Akasaka,
Matsubara Bld2f
107-0052 Minato-ku,
Tokyo, J
sasaki-m@technonet.co.jp

Christian Sawade-meyer
Jagdweg 7
32469 Petershagen, D
sawade-meyer@
t-online.de

Dobbie Schiff
5724 West Third St.,
Suite 400
Los Angeles, CA 90036,
USA
dobbie@metrolight.com

Reinhard Schleining
Laudong. 39-2-12
1080 Wien, A
reinhard@ris-med.ac.at

Heidemarie Seblatnig
Florag. 7
1040 Wien, A
sebl@osiris.iemar.tuwien.
ac.at

Miran Shim
1263 Taft Ave
11566 Merrick, USA
miran@interport.net

Tomokazu Shimokawa
Shimoigusa1-7-2-305
167-0022 Suginami, J
shimon@ct-net.co.jp

Seiji Shiota
Ariake Frontier Building
Tower „a“ 17f
135-0064 3-1-25 Ariake,
Koto-ku, Tokyo, J
masae@ppi.co.jp

Jason Shulman
2700 N. Tamiami Trail
Sarasota, FL 34234, USA
strovas@rsad.edu

Mark Simon
8137 Lake Crowell Circle
Orlando, FL 32836, USA
mark@storyboards-
east.com

Dylan Sisson
956 10th Av. East #106
Seattle, WA 98102, USA
dylan@blarg.net

Robert Slawinski
145 N 8th St., Apt 1
Brooklyn NY 11211, USA
ru4d2@interport.net

Hank Smiet
Javastraat 2c
2585 AM Den Haag, NL
office@dpi.nl

Wilson W. Smith
2700 N. Tamiami Trail
Sarasota, FL 34234, USA
strovas@rsad.edu

Kevin Souls
438 1/2 N. Curson Ave,
Los Angeles, CA 90036,
USA
souls1@mindsprin6.com

Peter Spans
Mühlenkamp 59
22303 Hamburg, D
kathrin.j@spans.de

Stefanie Stalf
Bavariafilmplatz 7
82031 Geiselgasteig, D
munich@scanline.de

Leslie Streit
33 Jennings Ct
San Francisco, CA 94124,
USA
robinm@new-
performance.org

Gerd Struwe
Heinrichstr. 45
50676 Köln, D
Struwe@compuserve.com

Yoshinori Sugano
14 Niban-cho
102-8004 Chiyoda-ku,
Tokyo, J
sug@ntv.co.jp

Makoto Sugawara
Minami-cho 3-4-5 Ing
Studio 301
185-0021 Kokubunji-city,
Tokyo, J

Violet Suk
12 West 27th St.
New York, NY 10001, USA
sukkoch@concentric.net

Dennis Summers
3927 Parkview Dr.
Royal Oak, MI 48073,
USA
denniss@ic.net

Nobuo Takahashi
1-1-32 Shin-urashima-cho,
Kanagawa-ku
221-0031 Yokohama, J
nobuo@vs.namco.co.jp

Atsushi Takeuchi
Minami-cho 3-4-5 Ing
Studio 301
185-0021 Kokubunji-city,
Tokyo, J

Andrew Tamandl
Balaclava & Epping Rd.s
North Ryde NSW 2113,
AUS
ruths@aftrs.edu.au

Pablo Rodrigez Tavrega
Ctra. Valldemossa Rm 7`5
7071 Palma de Mallorca,
E
info@studio1.vib.es

Lucas Tirigall Caste
Av Ricardo Balbin 2432
6c
1428 Buenos Aires, RA
lucas2k@yahoo.com

Jon Tojek
3178 16th St. Apt #3
San Francisco, CA 94103,
USA
jtojek@aw.sgi.com

Gianni Toti
1908, Panet, #400, Mtl
Montreal H2L 3A2, CDN
prim@cam.org

Anatoly Trjensimeh
Katunina 3/68
246002 Gomel, BY
tomtrj@usa.net

Stephan Trojansky
Bavariafilmplatz 7
82031 Geiselgasteig, D
munich@scanline.de

Laurence Trouve
121 Rue De Bordeaux
16000 Angoulême, F
din@cnbdi.fr

Penelope Vandecave
Le Fort, Av. De
Normandie, Bp 113
59370 Mons en Baroeul,
F
exquise@nordnet.fr

Lenno Verhoog
Spanjaardstraat 105a
3025 TL Rotterdam, NL
willigeezer@yahoo.com

Romain Villemaine
121 Rue De Bordeaux
16000 Angoulême, F
din@cnbdi.fr

Michael Visser
Jan Ligthartstraat 1
1817 MR Alkmaar, NL
nijman@nmtrix.com

Christian Volckman
6, Boulevard De
Strasbourg
75010 Paris, F
method@cybercable.fr

Frank Wagenknecht
Am Krenzelsberg 83
66115 Saarbrücken, D
fw@factory3.de

Diana Walczak
87 Marshall St., Bldg. 1
N. Adams, MA 1247, USA
amanda@kwcc.com

Enda Walshe
21 Zion Rd.
Dublin 6, IRL
walshee@ncad.ie

Christine Weber
Seminarstr. 11
76133 Karlsruhe, D
cweber@hfg-karlsruhe.de

Claudia Weber
Ostendstr. 27
60314 Frankfurt, D
clweber@gmx.net

Chris Wedge
One South Rd.
Harrison, NY 10528, USA
brooks@blueskystudios.
com

Dina Williams
520 Engleman Av.
Scotia, NY 12302-1611,
USA
willid3@rpi.edu

Sheri Wills
299 Wickenden St.
Providence, RI 2903, US
s.wills@altavista.net

Emily Wilson
66 Rivington St. #19
New York, NY 10002, US
emilyw@sva.edu

Kouichi Yamagishi
Ariake Frontier Building
Tower „a“ 17f
135-0064 3-1-25 Ariake,
Koto-ku, Tokyo, J
masae@ppi.co.jp

Emre Yilmaz
2727 Mariposa St.,
Studio 100
San Francisco, CA 9411o
USA
carrie@protozoa.com

Miguel Ernesto Yusl
Ctra. Valldemossa Rm 7
7071 Palma de Mallorca
E
info@studio1.vib.es

Edward Zajec
516 Kensington Rd.
Syracuse, NY 13210, US
ezajec@syr.edu

Georg Zey
Lindowerstr.18
13347 Berlin, D
georgzey@compuserve.
com

Therese Zoekende
Elandsstraat 96-c
1016 SH Amsterdam, N
tzoekende@yahoo.com

Laurent Benegui
9 Rue De Clignancourt
75018 Paris, F
magouric@aol.com

Niki Bern
Balaclava & Epping Roads
North Ryde NSW 2113, AUS
ruths@aftrs.edu.au

Se-lien Chuang
Grabenstr. 17
8010 Graz, A
cse-lien@sime.com

Pierre Coffin
22, Rue Hégésippe Moreau
75018 Paris, F
sophie@exmach.fr

Alain Escalle
26, Rue Fessart
75019 Paris, F
aescalle@club-internet.fr

Michaela French
Balaclava & Epping Roads
North Ryde NSW 2113, AUS
ruths@aftrs.edu.au

Akemi Fujita
59 Charlesfield St.
Apt 3/5
2906 Providence, USA
p_o_e_s_i_a@hotmail.com

Karin Gemperle
Bahnhofstr. 102
5000 Aarau, CH
karopic@hotmail.com

Celestino Gianotti
Via Crevacuore 70
10146 Torino, I
cele@blisscorporation.com

Ray Giarratana
300 Rose Avenue
90291 Venice, CA 90291, USA
bhoffman@d2.com

Ruth Greenberg
19—23 Wells St.
London W1P 3FP, UK
ruth@cfc.co.uk

Wolfgang Hartl
Bahnhofstr. 8
2640 Gloggnitz, A
work@artgraphic.at

Craig Hayes
2741 10th St.
Berkeley, CA 94710, USA
lisa@tippett.com

Hector Hazard
405 Panther House 38 Mt. Pleasant
London WC1X OAP, UK
HECHazard@aol.com

Lynn Hershman
1201 California St. # 803
San Francisco, CA 94108, USA
lynn2@well.com

Coldcut Hex Static
Winchester Wharf,
Clink St.
London SE1 9DG, UK
mattb@ninjatune.net

Manu Horrillo
c/o Javier Ferrero,12
28002 Madrid, E
Ebox@redestb.es

Niki Laber
Wienerbergstr. 9
1100 Wien, A
nik@neo.at

David Larcher
Château Peugeot
25310 Hérimoncourt, F
francois@cicv.fr

Mark Limburg
Jan Luykenstraat 39
2026AC Haarlem, NL
mlimburg@yahoo.com

Carron Little
1433 N. Oakley Blvd.
Chicago, IL 60622, USA
alittleirrad@yahoo.com

Peter Litwinowicz
18 Vicksburg St.
San Francisco, CA 94114, USA
pete@revisionfx.com

Daniel Moreno
Av. Sernambetiba 3300
Bl. 3 / 302
22639-900 Rio de Janeiro, BR
danimor@hotmail.com

The Poool Nancy Meli Walker, Benton Bainbridge, Angie Eng
335 Court St. #40
Brooklyn, NY 11231, USA
nmw@panix.com

Christoph Nasfeter
Kramg. 4
89073 Ulm, D

Baerbel Neubauer
Lindwurmstr.207
80337 München, D
baerbelneubauer@csi.com

Javier Nuñez
Pza. Santa Barbara, 10
28004 Madrid, E
javiern@infografica.com

Mark9 Oconnell
2318 Second Ave., #313-a
Seattle, WA 98121, USA
oconnell@oz.net

Tor Oera
Oestgaardsgate 5, #36
474 Oslo, N
oera@online.no

Kai Patzold
Medienallee 7
85774 Unterföhring, D
gert.zimmermann@szm.de

Bert & Joachim Praxenthaler
Epfenhausen,
Bahnhofstr. 12
86929 Penzing, D
praxenthaler@t-online.de

Peter Spans
Mühlenkamp 59
22303 Hamburg, D
kathrin.j@spans.de

Dani Sperling
Takustr.45
50825 Köln, D
dani@khm.de

Antoinette Starkiewicz
Balaclava & Epping Roads
North Ryde NSW 2113, AUS
ruths@aftrs.edu.au

Douglas Struble
15455 Court Village Lane, Building #4.
Taylor, MI 48180, USA
dugstruble@ili.net

Phil Tippett
2741 10th St.
Berkeley, CA 94710, USA
lisa@tippett.com

Jon Tojek
3178 16th St. Apt #3
San Francisco, CA 94103, USA
jtojek@aw.sgi.com

Juan Tomicic
C/ Javier Ferrero,12
28002 Madrid, E
Ebox@redestb.es

Koji Tomita
1-15,yamanoue 5 Cho-me
573-0047 Hirakata-shi, Osaka, J
RXV12202@nifty.ne.jp

Peter Wandmose
Mikkel Bryggers Gade 11, 3.tv
1460 K Copenhagen K, DK
danwan@teliamail.dk

Norihiro Yamamoto
Meguro Simomeguro 2-7-10 Kurerumoridou-i 102
153-0064 Tokyo, J
pica4000@cyborg.ne.jp

Ando Yoshiko
5-3-1-209 Sunagawa-cho, Tachikawa-shi
190-0031 Tokyo, J
yoshiko@kcm-sd.ac.jp

Gert Zimmermann
Medienallee 7
85774 Unterföhring, D
gert.zimmermann@szm.de

A.f.r.i. Studios
Mauenheimer St.11
50733 Köln, D
miki@khm.de

Mathew Adkins
9/11 Old Rd.
Holmfirth HD7 1NU , UK
m.adkins@hud.ac.uk

Masayuki Akamatsu
3-95,ryouke-chou
503-0014 Ogaki, Gifu, J
aka@iamas.ac.jp

Olivier Alary
203 Bowes Rd.
London N11 2NH, UK
oa137@mdx.ac.uk

Florence Alix
10 Rue Des Jasmins
74960 Meythet, F
floa@caramail.com

Kristi Allik
788 Cedarwood
Kingston K7P 1M7, CDN
allikk@post.queensu.ca

Birgitte Alsted
Bagerstrμde 3, 4.tv
1617 V Copenhagen, DK
danwan@teliamail.dk

Ernie Althoff
30 Alice St.
3144 Malvern, AUS

Bill Alves
1286 Reims St.
Claremont, CA 91711, USA
alves@hmc.edu

Charles Amirkhanian
7722 Lynn Av.
El Cerrito, CA 94530-
4133, USA
charles@artsplural.com

Randy Anagnostis
210 Crouch Rd.
06231-1611 Amston,
Connecticut, USA
randy@anagnostis.com

Anastasia Anastasia
Leninova 29/3/6
91000 Skopje, MAK
thirdear@mpt.com.mk

Beth Anderson
3213 West Wheeler St.
#196
Seattle, WA 98199, USA
anderson@arkitek.com

Cera Andrea
Largo Trieste 2
36034 Malo (VI), I
andywax@schio.nettuno.it

Minni Ang
3, Jalan Desa Serdang 15
43300 Seri Kembangan,
Selangor, MAL
minni@music.upm.edu.my

Ted Apel
819a Second St.
Encinitas CA, 92024,
tapel@vud.org

Iain G. Armstrong
24 Leeson Walk,
Harborne
Birmingham B17 OLU UK,
ARMSTRIG@hhs.bham.ac.
uk

Georgi Arnaoudov
1, Asparuh
1463 Sofia, BG
garnaoudov@hotmail.com

Hugo Arsenault
579 Cure Labelle
J7C 2H7 Blainville, CDN
brigo@sympatico.ca

Patrick Ascione
14140 Lisores, F

Daniel Asia
5230 North Apache Hills
Trail
Tucson, AZ 85750, USA
asia@u.arizona.edu

Cary August
P.O. Box 150871
San Rafael,
CA 94915-0871, USA
capp@wco.com

Rochus Aust
Thürmchenswall 25
50668 Köln, D

Robert Austin
132 Spring Farm Rd.
Huntsville, 35811, USA
raaustin@aol.com

Larry Austin
2109 Woodbrook Dr.
Denton, TX 76205, USA
austin@sndart.cemi.unt.
edu

Ron Ave.rill
1921 Rainier Av.
Everett, WA 98201, USA
ronkari@gte.net

David Bach
P.O. Box 24529
Baltimore, MD 21214,
USA
bach@charm.net

Wolf Harun
Bachschneider
Unertlstr. 11
80803 München, D
whb@eggs.de

Curtis Bahn
298 New Boston Rd.
Sturbridge, MA 01566,
USA
crb@rpi.edu

John Bain
2733 4th. Av. S.
Seattle, WA 98134-1912,
USA
simlux@hotmail.com

Christian Banasik
Querstr. 16
40227 Düsseldorf, D
c.banasik@t-online.de

Ros Bandt
14 Collings St.
Brunswick West, Victoria
3105, AUS
ralsop@klang.latrobe.edu.
au oder
rossart@uaxc.cc.monash.e
du.au

Alberto Bario
V. Emilia Ponente 211
40133 Bologna, I
albertik@altavista.net

Natasha Barrett
P.O. Box 1137, Blindern
317 Oslo, N
natashab@notam.uio.no

Alain Basso
636, les Devants De
Promery
74370 Pringy, F

Trevor Batten
Kanaalstraat 15
1054 WX Amsterdam, NL
aki@xs4all.nl

Gustav Bauer
Arnsdorf 5
5112 Lamprechtshausen,
A
lehrer@bakip-
bhofen.salzburg.at

Felix Baumgartner
Goethestr. 15
79822 T.-Neustadt, D
NETZdirect@aol.com

Wiliam Beck
25 Linden Ave. #12
Somerville, MA 02143,
USA
aeroea@bu.edu

Neil Benezra
25 9th Ave. 2fl
New York, NY 10014, USA
benezra@concentric.net

Douglas Benford
63 Windmill Rd.
Brentford TW8 0QQ, UK
douglas@benfo.demon.co
.uk

James Bentley
57 Newlands Rd.,
Stirchley
Birmingham B30 25A, UK
jxb505@bham.ac.uk

Gary Berger
Elisabethenstr. 3
8004 Zürich, CH
gberger@access.ch

Georg Bernhard
Friedmanng. 18/13
1160 Wien, A
Gogo@trust-me.com

Stefan Betke
Zehdenickerstr. 14
10119 Berlin, D
pole.@t-online.de

Bruno Beusch
51, Rue Piat
75020 Paris, F
info@tnc.net

Birgit Bingenheimer
Gartenstr. 34
61206 Oberwöllstadt, D
electric_Ariane@csi.com

Ed Bland
5203 Knowlton St. Apt. D
Los Angeles, CA 90045-
2021, USA
osmundmus@aol.com

Larisa Blazic
Ive Andrica 23/4
21000 Novi Sad, YU
lab@eunet.yu

Markus Bless
Ledererg. 9
4861 Schörfling, A
bless@ufg.ac.at

Duke Bojadziev
Naum Naumovski 82
91000 Skopje, MAK
duke@unet.com.mk

Richard Bone
P.O. Box 229
Greenville, RI 2828, USA
Quirkwork@aol.com

Alexei Borisov
Verkhnaya Pervomaiskaya
105264 Moscow, RUS
arist@cityline.ru

Francesco Boschetto
Södermälarstr. 61
11825 Stockholm, S
boschetto@hotmail.com

Jakob Brandt-pedersen
Aksvej 8, Nyord
4780 Stege, DK
jbrandtp@get2net.dk

Kitty Brazelton
172 East 7th St. Apt. 1c
New York, NY 10009, USA
KitBraz@aol.com

Chris Brown
6542 Whitney St.
Oakland, CA 94607, USA
cbmus@mills.edu

Brigid Bruke
P.O. Box 315 Eisternwick
Victoria 3185, AUS
brigidburke@arts.monash.
edu.au

Leif Brush
10 Univ. Circle
Duluth, 55812 USA,
lbrush@d.umn.edu

Susanne Buder
Kirchstetternstr. 47/7
1160 Wien, A
tanga@to.or.at

Somna M. Bulist
P.O. Box 15
Forbes Rd., PA 15633,
USA
somna@angelfire.com

Kristine Burns
School Of Music, Univ Pk
33199 Miami, FL 33199,
USA
burnsk@fiu.edu

Warren Burt
P.O. Box 2154
3182 St. Kilda West, Vic.,
AUS
waburt@melbourne.dialix.
com.au

Matthew Burtner
Mcfarland 6g, Escondido
Village
Standford, CA 94305,
USA
mburtner@ccrma.standfor
d.edu

Christian Calon
Hans-Rosenthal-Platz
10825 Berlin, D
goetz.naleppa@dradio.de

Lelio Camilleri
Conservatory Of Music
G.b. Martini,
Piazza Rossini 2
40126 Bologna, I
l.camilleri@iol.it

Lloyd Canfil
3682 Mississippi St.
San Diego,
CA 92104-4031 USA,
lloyd@canfil.com

Gorazd Capovski
6353 Sunset Boulevard
Hollywood, CA 90028,
USA
tko@tonecasualties.com

Richard Carrick
411 Sloane Av.
San Diego, CA 92103,
USA
rcarrick@ucsd.edu

Roy Carroll
8 Lisburn St.
D7 Dublin, IRL
adarby@indigo.ie

Sebastian Castagna
Flat B, 87 Erlanger Rd.
London SE145TQ, UK
s.castagna@ndirect.co.uk

Damian Castaldi
16/200 Forbes St.
Darlinghurst, NSW 2010,
AUS
D.Castaldi@sca.usyd.edu.
au

Jean François Cavro
44 Rue Raulin
69007 Lyon, F
jfc@ubaye.cnsm-lyon.fr

Victor Cerullo
Via Caneve, 77
30173 Mestre (Venice), I
victor.cerullo@industrysol
utions.it

Ching-wen Chao
Apt. 70 D,
Escondido Village
Stanford, CA 94305, USA
ching@ccrma.stanford.ed

David Chapman
Flat B, 141 Hertford Rd.
Dalston N1 4LR, UK
d.m.chapman@uel.ac.uk

Eric Chasalow
351 Crafts St.
Newtonville,
MA 02460-1116, USA
echasalow@mediaone.ne

Alain Chaudron
Jules Parent
92500 Rueil-Malmaison,
alchau@club-internet.fr

Chin-chin Chen
1107 W. Green St. #633
Urbana, IL 61801-3041,
USA
c-chen8@uiuc.edu

Corey Cheng
Beal Av.
Ann Arbor, MI 48109, US
coreyc@eecs.umich.edu

Unsuk Chin
Danckelmannstr. 20
14059 Berlin, D
seelig@gigant.kgw.tu-
berlin.de

Jef Chippewa
64, Rue Fairmount, Oue
App. 4
Montreal, Quebec H2T
2M2 , CDN
jefchip@cam.org

Martin Christel
Saarbrückenstr. 36
24114 Kiel, D
mchristel@t-online.de

Fabio Cifariello Ciardi
Via Umberto Boccioni 36
67 Morlupo (Roma), I
f.cifariellociardi@agora.stm.it

Philip Clemo
49a Vanbrugh Park
London SE3 7JQ UK,
inspire@globalnet.co.uk

Paul Clouvel
10 Rue De Brives
18000 Bourges, F

Manfred Clynes
19181 Mesquite Court
Sonoma, CA 95476, USA
mclynes1@aol.com

Michaël Cohen
6 Petite Rue D'Austerlitz
67000 Strasbourg, F
mikacohen@hotmail.com

Fred Cole
15 Anstey St.
Lismore NSW 2480, AUS
amused@amused.net

Nicholas Collins
Cea, Middlesex University,
Cat Hill, Barnet
ondon EN4 8HT, UK
.collins@mdx.ac.uk

icolas Collins
eichsstr. 31
4052 Berlin, D
allmancollins@compuserve.com

onny Conrad
ofweg 6
0374 Stuttgart, D
01.79022@Dnet.de

ric Cordier
3 Rue Custine
5018 Paris, F

hristopher Cortez
14 Napoleon Av.
idell, LA 70460, USA
etroc@bellsouth.net

livier Coupille
Rue Du Roule
5001 Paris, F

rant Covell
Smith Av.
merville,
S 02143-4309, USA
ovell@c-bridge.com

egory Cowley
a Hoff St.
n Francisco, CA 94110,
SA
egory@testsite.org

odoro Pedro Cromberg
mbaré 1082 – Dpto
35 Buenos Aires, RA
omberg@sudnet.com.ar

exander Crook
. Box 110342
218 Darmstadt, D
lock_un5179@yahoo.
m

O[rphan] D[rift>]
46 Wilton Way
London E8 1BG, UK
103267.2077@compuserve.com

Patricia Dallio
11 Rue De La Liberté
52000 Chaumont, F

Jack Dangers
C/o Fbm 1321 6th Av.
San Francisco, CA 94122,
USA
spydog@well.com

Drew Daniel
800 Hampshire St.
San Francisco, CA 94110,
USA
mcess@mail.slip.net

Riccardo Dapelo
Via Valente 40
16015 Casella, I
dapelo@infomus.dist.umige.it

Christopher Davidson
295 Oakes Blvd.
San Leandro, 94577, USA
antimatter@earthlink.net

Robin Davies
4209 Drolet
Montreal, Quebec
H2W 2L7, CDN
robin@music.mcgill.ca

Margot Day
Gateway Drive,
P.O. Box 47
Craftsbury, 5826, USA
margot@together.net

Alberto De Campo
Bergstr. 59/33
8042 Graz, A
alberto@create.ucsb.edu

Giovanni De Don
Bologna, I
pollution6@hotmail.com

Roderik De Man
1e Tuindwarsstraat 3
1015 RT Amsterdam, NL
ademan@eva.ahk.nl

Paul De Marinis
49 Broderich St. Apt. 15
San Francisco,
CA 94117-1513, USA
demarini@well.com

Franco Degrassi
Via G. Cozzoli 2
70125 Bari, I
degrassi@tin.it

Brad Derrick
230 Court Square
Charlottesville, VA 22902
USA, bradd@kesmai.com

F. Di Giovanni
Via Nizza 243
10100 Torino, I
pe.a@ipsnet.it

Agostino Di Scipio
Via Salaria Antica Est
33/a
67100 L'Aquila, I
discipio@tin.it

Federico Diaz
Humpolecka 8
140 00 Praha 4, CZ
federico@email.cz

Jorrit Dijkstra
Blankenstraat 270
1018 SJ Amsterdam, NL
101641.1572@compuserve.com

Christopher Dobrian
292 Music, Building 714,
Uci
Irvine, CA 92697-2775,
USA
dobrian@uci.edu

Rose Dodd
9-11 Old Rd., Holmbridge
West Yorkshire HD7 1NU,
UK
m.adkins@hud.ac.uk

Douglas Doherty
41 Tweed St., Hebburn
Tyne and Wear
NE10 0HW, UK
mjumbo@globalnet.co.uk

Periklis Douvitsas
Linzerg. 47
5020 Salzburg, A
periklis.douvitsas@netway.at

Roger Doyle
Rynville Mews,
Killarney Rd.,
Bray, County Wicklow.,
IRL
info@composersink.ie

Ingrid Drese
133, Ave. Du Val D'or
1200 Bruxelles, B

Jon Drummond
14 Point St.
Lilyfield NSW 2040, AUS
jond@mpce.mq.edu.au

Roger Luke Dubois
632 W.125th St.,
Room 318
New York, NY 10027, USA
luke@music.columbia.edu

Curd Duca
Blechturmg. 13/4/17
1050 Wien, A
cduca@to.or.at

John Duncan
Scrutto 48
33040 San Leonardo
(UD), I
jduncan@xs4all.nl

Sasa Dundovic
B.stipcic 41
51000 Rijeka, HR
dundovic@usa.net

Stephan Dunkelman
Loutrier 42
1170 Brussels, B
101612.570@comfuserve.com

Werner Durand
Klausener Platz 11
14059 Berlin, D
cun-dur@berlin.snafu.de

Frank Ekeberg
51 Dunbar Rd.
London E7 9NH, UK
frankh@notam.uio.no

Fredrik Ekman
Ruddammsbacken 41
11423 Stockholm, S

Marc Ellis
Oil & Gas Bldg. #407
1100 Tulane Av
New Orleans, LA 32751
USA,
pmirabeau@nternet.com

Kouichirou Eto
Dk Bldg.5f, 7-18-23
Roppongi, Minato-ku
106-0032 Tokyo, J
yshikata@crpg.canon.co.jp

Maureen Evans-Hansen
456 Dela Vina Av. K4
Monterey, CA 93940, USA
maureen@ultramarineblue.com

John Everall
24 Worcester Rd.
Nottingham NG5 4HY, UK
john.sentrax@ndirect.co.uk

Aviv Eyal
763 Belmont Place E
#208
Seattle, WA 98102, USA
aviv@dromology.com

Michael Fakesch
Leipziger St. 54
10117 Berlin, D
office@studio-k7.de

Jeff Fallen
221 Fallen Rd.
Ennis, TX 75119, USA
lampmuz@hpnc.com

John Farrier
6877 Bejay Drive
Tipp City, OH 45371, USA
farrieje@erinet.com

Jonathan Febland
19 Manor Pk Crescent
Edgware, Middlesex, HA8
7NH, UK
jonfeb@befnojj.freeserve.co.uk

Christian Fennesz
Wimbergerg. 24/8
1070 Wien, A
fennesz@rhiz.org

Antonio Ferreira
Ap. Corte Real, Av.
Gaspar Corte Real N18 4e
2750 Cascais, P
nop35624@mail.telepac.pt

Julian Feyerabend
Rüdigerstr. 10/5
1050 Wien, A
lik@vienna.at

Giuseppe Finotto
Via Ferrara 13
10043 Orbassano (TO), I
igorsc@tin.it

Rajmil Fischman
Music Department
Keele – Staffordshire ST5
5BG, UK
r.a.fischman@mus.keele.ac.uk

Peter Fjeldberg
Harsdorfsvej 1a 1tv
1874 Frederiksberg, DK
peterf@get2net.dk

Kris Force
2440 16th St. #121
San Francisco, CA 94103,
USA
force@sirius.com

Carlo Forlivesi
Via Fratelli Bandiera, 9
40026 Imola (BO), I
carlo_forlivesi@hotmail.com

Robert Frank
P.O. Box 750356
Dallas, TX 75275-0356,
USA
robfrank@aol.com

Martin Franklin
12 Keswick Court,
Stoke Rd.
Slough SL2 5AN, UK
mfranklin@cix.co.uk

Rikhardur H. Fridriksson
Hofteigur 10
105 Reykjavik, ISL
rhf@ismennt.is

Lawrence Fritts
1006 Vmb, School Of
Music
Iowa City, IA 52242, USA
lawrence-fritts@uiowa.edu

Martin Fumarola
Casilla de Correo 1145
5000 Cordoba, RA
maralefo@hotmail.com

Kiyoshi Furukawa
Kobunma 5000
302-0001 Toride, Ibaragi,
J
masaki@sfc.keio.ac.jp

Bulat Galeyev
K.marks,10
420111 Kazan, RUS
galeyev@prometey.kcn.ru

Elena Gantchikova
Einsteinufer 17
10587 Berlin, D
elena@demon.kgw.tu-berlin.de

Eleazar Garzon
Manuel Carles 3280 –
Poeta Fugones
5008 Cordoba, RA
egarzon@mayo.com.ar

Alain Gauthier
2051, De Chambly St.
Montreal, Ontario H1W
3J3, CDN
imp@cam.org

Todd Gautreau
4067 Midrose Trail
Dallas, TX 75287, USA
simulacra1@aol.com

Thomas Gerwin
Seboldstr. 1
76227 Karlsruhe, D
thomas@gerwin.de

Steve Gibson
Multimedia Design
651 88 Karlstad, S
steve.gibson@kau.se

John Gibson
1509 Chesapeake St.
Charlottesville, VA 22902,
USA
jgg9c@virginia.edu

Bruce Gilbert
Unit 49, Bbh, 71,
Henriques St.
London E1 1lZ, UK
stengsmith@aol.com

Mario Giovanoli
Nelkenweg 15
7000 Chur, CH
mcjoe@spin.ch

Kurt Gluck
10006 Wedge Way
Montgomery Village, MD
20886, USA
truthdrug@hotmail.com

Gilles Gobeil
1217 Bernard #30
Outremont, QC H2V 1V7,
CDN
gobeil@cam.org

Rob Godman
4 Mill Close, Wotton-under-Edge
Gloucestershire GL12 7LP,
UK
rob.godman@évirgin.net

Stephen Goldman
140 Candace Drive
Maitland, FL 32751 , USA
goldman@dpt.com

Elizabeth Gonzalez
117 Holleman Dr. W
#1204
College Station,
TX 77840, USA
liz2000@unix.tamu.edu

Annie Gosfield
301 East 12 St. #3d
New York, NY 10003, USA
agosfield@aol.com

Suguru Goto
82, Rue Charles Nodier
93500 Pantin, F
sgoto@ircam.fr

Paul Gough
34 Camellia St.
Greystanes NSW 2145,
AUS
pimmon@bRd.cast.net

Carlos Grätzer
20, Av. Secrétan
75019 Paris Paris, F
cgratzer@club-internet.fr

Richard Graf
Bahnhofstr. 8
2640 Gloggnitz, A
work@artgraphic.at

Justin Greenleaf
Via Tortona 28
20144 Milano, I
niceart@micronet.it

Bruce Gremo
185 Lafayette St.
New York, NY 10013, USA
suddensite@aol.com

Scot Gresham-Lancaster
3148 Sylvan Av.
Oakland, CA 94602, USA
sgresham@csuahyward.edu

Tobias Kazumichi Grime
35 London St., Enmore,
NSW
Sydney 2042 AUS,
toby@ebom.org

Fritz Grohs
Birkenstr. 56
10559 Berlin, D
fgrohs@to.or.at

Alexander Guelfenburg
Aspettenstr. 34/28/7
2380 Perchtoldsdorf, A
virtual-music@aon.at

Bernhard Günter
Firmungsstr. 27
56068 Koblenz, D
bguenter@rz-online.de

Jean Luc Guionnet
23 Rue Custine
75018 Paris, F

Alexander Györfi
Alarichstr.18
70469 Stuttgart, D
gyoerfi@aol.com

Tal Hadad
21 Rue Daval
75011 Paris, F
tal@chez.com

Graham Hadfield
14 B Essex Grove
London SE19 3SX, UK
g.p.hadfield@city.ac.uk

Dion Hämmerle
Harder Straße 14
6972 Fussach, A
godot.wema@vol.at

Simon Hall
University Of Birmingham
Birmingham B15 2TT, UK
S.T.HALL@bham.ac.uk

Jeffrey John Hall
16113 Indus Drive
Woodbridge, VA 22191,
USA
jjhall@erols.com

Aekyung Han
Catherine House,
University of York,
Heslington
York YO10 5DD, UK
ah138@york.ac.uk

Udo Hanten
Moltkestr. 22
47799 Krefeld, D
u.do@visiblesouls.de

Anne Scarlett Harris
13-156 Hillcrest Drive
Whitehorse 41A 4N4, CDN
artsluts@yknet.yk.ca

Jonty Harrison
Edgbaston
Birmingham B15 2TT, UK
d.j.t.harrison@bham.ac.uk

Hanna Hartman
Ahornsgade 18, 1tr.v
2200 Copenhagen N, DK
hanna.hartman@post.tele.dk

Richard Hawtin
731 Walker Rd.
Windsor, ONT N8Y 2N2,
CDN
x@m-nus.com

Andrew Hayleck
4002 Roland Av.
Baltimore, MD 21211, USA
quine@erols.com

Jens Hedman
Södermälarstrand 61
11825 Stockholm, S
jens.hedman@composer.ems.srk.se

Carsten Hennig
Gerberbruch 30
18055 Rostock, D
Hennig@jakota.de

Demilecamps Henri
5 Rue De La Mairie
11220 Villetritouls, F
h2000@club-internet.fr

Gloribel Cecilia
Hernández
Kempstraat 116
2572 GK Den Haag, NL
sram@casema.net

John Herron
P.O. Box 70067
West Valley, UT 84170-0067, USA

Maximilian Hoffs
Parkstr. 1
40477 Düsseldorf, D
x-maxx@2000m.com

Klaus Hollinetz
Steinhumergutstr. 1
4050 Traun, A
klaus.hollinetz@servus.at

Risto Holopainen
Waldemar Thranesgate 34
171 Oslo, N
risto.holopainen@notam.uio.no

Rupert Huber
Laaerbergstr. 2/21
1100 Wien, A
fa.huber@suafu.de

Axel Hufeland
Lerchenkamp 38
22459 Hamburg, D
Axel_Hufeland@compuserve.com

Doug Huff
3213 West Wheeler St.,
Pmb 196
Seattle, WA 98199, USA
drh@arkitek.com

Shintaro Imai
5-5-1 Kashiwa-cho,
Tachikawa-shi
Tokyo 190-8520, J
swinta@kcm-sd.ac.jp

Tetsu Inoue
700 Olima
Sausalito, CA 94965, USA
scooper@best.com

Akemi Ishijima
Flat A 323 Grays Inn Rd.
London WC1X 8PX UK,
akemi@city.ac.uk

Ivan Iusco
Via Giustino Fortunato
70125 Bari, I
i.iusco@AGORA.STM.IT

Phil Jackson
3725 Gorman
Waco, TX 76710, USA
pjfjacks@swbell.net

Veldhuis Ter Jacob
Drift 40
3941 DC Doorn, NL
jtv1@xs4all.nl.

Richard James
210-218 West St.
Sheffield S1 4EU, UK
rachel@warprecords.com

Res Rocket Jammers
Winchester Wharf, Clink St.
London SE1 9DG, UK
mattb@ninjatune.net

Simon Jarosch
Hainbuchenweg 10
72076 Tübingen, D
vivid@gmx.de

Werner Jauk
Ludwig-Benedek-Gasse19
8054 Graz, A
werner.jauk@kfunigraz.ac.at

Tom Jenkinson
210/218 West St.
Sheffield S1 4EU , UK
emma@warprecords.com

Wilfried Jentzsch
Wettiner Platz 13
1067 Dresden, D
jentzsch@hfmdd.de

Kevin Jerome
15445 Beachview Drive
Montclair, VA 22026, USA
MrcuryBlut@hotmail.com

Tim Song Jones
1044a Royal Oaks Drive
Monrovia, CA 91016, USA
fodrjonz@ni.net

Sergi Jordó
Viló I Viló, 101, 1-2
8004 Barcelona, E
sergij@mx3.redestb.es

Jérôme Joy
B.p.74
6372 Mouans Sartoux
Cedex, F
joy@thing.net

Myk Jung
100 South Sunrise Way
#219
Palm Springs, CA 92262,
USA
vrichter@netcom.com

Frederic Kahn
36, Grande Rue De Vaise
69009 Lyon, F

Ti Kai-moy
4th Flr Nldc 129 Jln
Bangsar
59200 K.L. Kuala Lumpur,
MAL
tikaimoy@tnb.com.my

Betty Kainz
Stumperg. 50/24
1060 Wien, A
midimani@site88.ping.at

Jeff Kaiser
P.O. Box 1653
Ventura, CA 93002, USA
pfmentum@jetlink.net

Ioannis Kalantzis
3 Quai Chauveau
69266 Lyon, F
ioannis@ubaye.cnsm-lyon.fr

Inge Kamps
Rolshover St. 97
51105 Köln, D
kampsin@netcologne.de

Bonnie Kane
45 First Av. #5-0
New York, NY 10003, USA
bonnie@bonniekane.com

Bernard Karawatzki
Classensgade 17 B, St.tv.
2100 Copenhagen, DK
bernard@vip.cybercity.dk

Ines Kargel
Mannheimstr. 7
4040 Linz, A
ines.kargel@jk.uni-linz.ac.at

Zbigniew Karkowski
49-1-301 Denenchotu
Honcho, Otha-ku
145-0072 Tokyo, J
zbigniew@sensorband.com

Klaus Karlbauer
Gymnasiumstr. 71/3
1190 Wien, A
karlbauer@moop.or.at

Erik Michael Karlsson
Nybrogade 8
1203 Copenhagen K, DK
emk@teliamail.dk

Paras Kaul
Art Dept, Freeman Hall,
102 Barr Ave.
MS 39762 , USA
paras@ra.msstate.edu

I V O Keers
P.o.box 6002
8902 H A Leeuwarden, NL
pnwmusic@freemail.nl

Alex Keller
6718 12th Av. NW
Seattle, WA 98117, USA
alex_keller@iname.com

Damian Keller
School For The
Contemporary Arts
Burnaby VSA 156, CDN
dkeller@sfu.ca

Cyril Kestellikian
11, Ave. des Coccinelles
13012 Marseille, F
CKestell@aol.com

Mari Kimura
145 West 79th St. Apt. 5
New York, NY 10024, USA
mari.kimura@nyu.edu

Mark Kirschenmann
3244 N. Whipple
Chicago, Il 60618, USA
sonikman@umich.edu

Kazuyuki Kishino
3-690-47 Hibarigaoka
228-0003 Zama,
Kanagawa, J
kknull@fsinet.or.jp

Judy Klein
130 West 17th St. #7 – S
New York, NY 10011, USA
jak@maestro.com

Axel Klepsch
Luisenstr. 25
40215 Düsseldorf, D
A1klepsch@aol.com

Petra Klusmeyer
2458 N.seminary,
Garden Apt.
Chicago, IL 60614, USA
petravonk@aol.com

zysztof Knittel
lcza 51/63
-679 Warszawa, PL

roline Koebel
7 East End Av., Apt. 1
ttsburgh, PA 15221-
31, USA
ebelc@clpgh.org

kashi Koike
2-1-22 Tchisuka,
nan – Cho
5-0002
namikawachi-gun, J
085391660.o@email.
y.kep.ne.jp

trick Kosk
rikagatan 1a/8
o Helsingfors, SF
kosk@clarinet.fi

hannes Kretz
ohllebeng. 11/10
40 Wien, A
hkretz@ping.at

rij Kreuh
lebitska 24
oo Ljubljana, SLO
rij.kreuh@lily.fri.uni-lj.si

ja Kreysing
mbertistr. 40
155 Münster, D
eysing@muenster.de

avid Kristian
25, Sussex #1
3H 2A2 Montreal, CDN
dk@colba.net

anfred Kroboth
ademieplein 1
11 KM Maastricht, NL
neyck@xs4all.nl

rut Krzisnik
ca Bratov Ucakar 46
oo Ljubljana, SLO
rut.krzisnik@guest.
nes.si

om Kubli
ühler St. 42
968 Köln, D
ki@khm.de

kel Kuehn
o West Merry Av.
owling Green, OH
403, USA
kuehn@bgnet.bgsu.edu

c La Casa
Rue Euryale Dehaynin
019 Paris, F
cendre@wanadoo.fr

thy Lane
, Glenarm Rd.
ndon E5 oLY, UK
532@city.ac.uk

cides Lanza
5 Sherbrooke West
ontreal H3A IE3, CDN
cides@music.mcgill.ca

via Lanzalone
a Delle Susine, 48
2 Roma, I
d4716@mclink.it

c Larmor
, Quai Ille Et Rance
000 Rennes, F
c.larmor@wanadoo.fr

Valentin Lazarov
12 Postoyanstvo St.
Bl. 253
1111 Sofia, BG
vlazarov@hotmail.com

Iury Lech
Nou 15
17111 Vulpellac – Girona,
E
insolit@redestb.es

Ye-sung Lee
1 E. Mount Vernon Place
Computer Music
Department
Baltimore, MD 21202,
USA
yslee@peabody.jhu.edu

Martha Lee
Jabatan Muzik
43400 Serdang, Selangor,
MAL
martha@music.upm.edu.
my

Colby Leider
Department Of Music
Princeton, NJ 8544, USA
colby@music.princeton.
edu

Helmut Lenk
Breslauer Str. 8
36151 Burghaun, D
Helmut.Lenk@t-online.de

John Levack Drever
5 Park Rd.
Eskbank Dalkeith EH22
3DF, UK
j.drever@dartington.ac.uk

Drew Lesso
201 S. Santa Fe Av. #300
Los Angeles, CA 90012,
USA
drewlesso@aol.com

Lukas Ligeti
224 East 13th St. #13
New York, NY 10003, USA

Elainie Lillios
2233 Alamo Place
Denton, TX 76201, USA
elillios@unt.edu

Mei-fang Lin
1009 West Stoughton,
Apt. 4
Urbana, IL 61801, USA
mlin1@uiuc.edu

David Clark Little
C. Springerstr. 14 – 2
1073 LJ Amsterdam, NL
d.little@cva.ahk.nl

David Lloyd-Howells
24, Kensington Rd.
Chichester, UK
100622.3205@
compuserve.com

Yeeon Lo
615 Laurel Av.
Menlo Park, CA 94025,
USA
acoustic@netcom.com

Jacques Lochet
9, Rue De Dalhunden
67410 Drusenheim, F

Fernando Lopez-lezcano
4137 Park Blvd.
Palo Alto, CA 94306, USA
nando@ccrma.stanford.
edu

Jarryd Lowder
41 E. 28th St. #3a
New York, NY 10016, USA
jarryd@sva.edu

Ceccarelli Luigi
Via Tevere, 15
198 Rome, I
l.ceccarelli@agora.stm.it

Rasmus Bruuse Lunding
Stationsstien 15
8541 Skoedstrup, DK
ras.blund@get2net.dk

Eric Lyon
Electroacoustic Music
6187 Hopkins Center
Hanover, NH 03755-3599,
USA
Eric.Lyon@Dartmouth.EDU

Robert Mackay
239 Earlsfield Rd.
London SW18 3DE, UK
mupo10@bangor.ac.uk

Thomas Madden
1250 W, Cornelia #3n
Chicago, IL 60657, USA
lichen@heardiagonally.
com

Heinrich Mader
Buchfeldg. 13
1080 Wien, A
a8508701@unet.univie.ac.
at

Manuel João Magalhães
Av. D. Nun'álvares
Pereira, 26 R/c Dto
2700 Amadora, P
rigra@esoterica.pt

Massimo Magrini
Via Laucci, 402
55050 Massa
Pisana/Lucca, I
m.magrini@guest.cnuce.
cnr.it

Franck Mahmoudian
25 Blvd. de Lyon
67000 Strasbourg, F
dariushkader@hotmail.
com

Don Malone
430 S Michigan Av.
Chicago, IL 60605, USA
dmalone@roosevelt.edu

Frederick Malouf
379 Palo Alto Av.
Mountain View, CA 94041,
USA
prixars@chromatonal.com

Love Mangs
Mossvägen 20
745 42 Enköping, S
love.mangs@mail.bip.net

Antonio Martorella
V. Torre Noverana 39
3013 Ferentino, I
a.mart@flashnet.it

Elio Martusciello
Via Montiano, 8b
127 Roma, I
emartus@tin.it

Wade Marynowsky
2/111 Campbell St.
2010 Surry Hills, Sydney
w.marynowsky@student.
unsw.edu.au

Massimo Mascheroni
Via Alla Boschina 13
24039 Sotto il Monte
(BG), I
onderozze@hotmail.com

Dugal Mc Kinnon
7 Pershore Av.
Birmingham B29 7NP, UK
d.c.mckinnon@bham.ac.
uk

Rachel McInturff
1211 W. 8th #102
Austin, TX 78703, USA
mcinturff@mail.utexas.
edu

Elyzabeth Meade
993 East 20th Av.
Eugene, OR 97405, USA
emeade@darkwing.
uoregon.edu

Joaquin Medina
Urb. Loma Linda Fase 7
Num.3
18151 Ogijares, E
quino@goliat.ugr.es

Gebhard Meilinger
Finkengang 51
4048 Puchenau, A
g.meilinger@aon.at

J. Mendes
Pca Padrg Souza 9
20.930-070 Rio de
Janeiro, BR
Jmend@nutecnet.com.br.

Flo Menezes
Al. Dos Guainumbis, 1435
04067-003 São Paulo –
SP, BR
flomenez@uol.com.br

Jacky Merit
La Besserie
86140 Scorbe-Clairvaux, F

Doug Michael
P.O. Box 3166
Antioch, CA 94531-3166,
USA
dmic27@ncal.verio.com

Alain Michon
127 bis, Rue De La
Roquette
75011 Paris, F
michon@ensba.fr

Valeriano Migliorati
Via Piane 21
64013 Corropoli (TE), I
valeriano@itol.it

Alexander Mihalic
8 Residence Des Aigles
93440 Dugny, F
mihalic@club-internet.fr

Piotr Mikotajczak
W. Baleya 4m80
2758 Warschau, PL

Mladen Milicevic
7900 Loyola Bd.
Los Angeles, CA 90045,
USA
mmilicev@lmumail.lmu.
edu

Radovan Milinkovic
Na Hroude 43
100 00 Praha 10, CZ

Raul Minsburg
Bravard 1172 Dto 4
1414 Buenos Aires, RA
Minsburg@pinos.com

Eduardo Reck Miranda
83 Bvld. St Marcel
75013 Paris, F
miranda@csl.sony.fr

Herbert A. Mitschke
Am Klausenberg 44
51109 Köln, D
hermit@netcologne.de

Masahiro Miwa
Ryoke-cho 3-95
503-0014 Ogaki-city, Gifu,
J
mmiwa@iamas.ac.jp

Rene Mogensen
299 Baltic St.
Brooklyn, NY 11201, USA
RQM2132@hotmail.com

Gordon Monahan
R. R. #2
Meaford N4L 1W6, CDN
funnyfarmcity@compuserv
e.com

Erick Montgomery
Suite#363,
208 East 51 St.
New York, NY 10022, USA
erick@cyberhum.demon.
co.uk

Scott Moore
240 Jane St.
Toronto M6S 3Z1, CDN
scott@dreamstate.to

Yura Moorush
Moscow, RUS
moorush@mu.ru

Roberto Morales
Paseo De La Presa # 152
36000 Guanajuato, MEX
roberto@quijote.ugto.mx

Lisa Moren
2107 N Charles St.
Baltimore, MD 21218,
USA
lmoren@umbc.edu

Ikue Mori
124 East 4th St. #22
New York, NY 10003, USA
ikuem@interport.net

Ethan Moseley
74 Marietta St.
Uxbridge, Ontario L9P
1J5, CDN
david@daymen.com

Michael Mscharding
13 Osward Rd.
London SW17 7SS, UK
ashrip@touch.demon.
co.uk

Boris Mueller
Kensington Gore
London SW7 2EU, UK
b.mueller@rca.ac.uk

Sami Santeri Muurimäki
Kauppapuistikko 30 As.6
65100 Vaasa, SF
sane666@hotmail.com

Hagan Myers
1207 Muscatine Av.
Iowa City, IA 52240, USA
hmyers@blue.weeg.uiowa
.edu

Jun-ichi Nagahara
6-7-35
141-0001 Shinagawa-ku,
Tokyo, J
jun@dc.sony.co.jp

Yoichi Nagashima
10-12-301, Sumiyoshi – 5
430-0906 Hamamatsu,
Shizuoka, J
nagasm@computer.org

Shigenobu Nakamura
12-1 Takatsuki-cho
569-0803 Takatsuki-shi,
Osaka-fu, J
nakmra50@mbox.kyoto-inet.or.jp

Ben Neill
53 Mercer St.
New York, NY 10013, USA
bneill@interport.net

Jon Christopher Nelson
P.O. Box 311367
Denton, TX 76203-1367,
USA
jnelson@music.cmm.unt.edu

Mario Neugebauer
Ruckerg. 10/21–22
1120 Wien, A
whybusiness@hotmail.com

Andrew Neumann
300 Summer St. #55
Boston, MA 02210, USA
neumann58@aol.com

Norie Neumark
2/15 Baden St., Coogee
Sydney 2034, AUS
n.neumark@uts.edu.au

Katharine Norman
84 Ainslie Wood Rd.
London E4 9BY, UK
k.norman@gold.ac.uk

Robert Normandeau
7070, Fabre
Montreal H2E 2B2, CDN
normanr@cam.org

Sergey Nosenko
19 University Drive
New York, NY 11733, USA
snosenko@grad.physics.sunysb.edu

Adolfo Nuez
Aniceto Marinas 2, 4f
28008 Madrid, E
adolfo.nunez@cdmc.inaem.es

Juhani Nuorvala
Fredrikinkatu 77 A 18
100 Helsinki, SF
juhani.nuorvala@siba.fi

Vidna Obmana
P.O. Box 54
2600 Berchem 2, B
info@vidnaobmana.org

Akihisa Ohashi
68-11 Yatayama-cho
Yamato-kohriyama
639-1055 Nara, J
a-ohashi@mx1.nisig.net

Fumitake Ohnaka
Shimotsuchidana 1053-205
252-0807 Fujisawa,
Kanagawa, J
fmtk@sfc.keio.ac.jp

Kent Olofsson
Malenas V.19
245 63 Hjärup, S
kent.olofsson@mhm.lu.se

Mouse On Mars
242 Athens St.
San Francisco, CA 94112,
USA
naut@sirius.com

David Oppenheim
400 W 25th St. #3a
New York, NY 10001, USA
darkmildew@yahoo.com

Antti Ortamo
Susitie 8, C 34
800 Helsinki, SF

Ed Osborn
P.O. Box 9121
Oakland, CA 94613, CA
edo@curve.to

Bob Ostertag
735 Capp St.
San Francisco, CA 94110,
USA
bostertag@aol.com

John Oswald
242 Athens St.
San Francisco, CA 94112,
USA
naut@sirius.com

Hitoshi Oyamada
Room 401, Maita
Sanhaimu, Shukumachi,
Minamiku
Yokohama 232-0017, J
topy@yk.rim.or.jp

Claude Pailliot
175, Rue Colbert
59800 Lille, F
tone_rec@nordnet.fr

Garth Paine
30 Moodie St.
Carnegie, Victoria 3163,
AUS
garth@creativeaccess.com.au

John Palmer
70 Western Way
EN5 2BT Barnet, UK
J.Palmer@herts.ac.uk

Vicky Paniale
60 Siege House,
Sidney St.
London E1 2HQ, UK
immedia@hotmail.com

Aquiles Pantaleao
46 Nansen Village, 21
London N12 8RW, UK
a.pantaleao@city.ac.uk

Nye Parry
37c Aubert Park
London N5 1TR UK,
nye@city.ac.uk

Michel Pascal
Rue Sainte Croix
13480 Cabriès, F
cirm_studio@compuserve.com

Samuel Pellman
198 College Hill Rd.
Clinton, NY 13323, USA
spellman@hamilton.edu

Tim Perkis
1050 Santa Fe Ave.
Albany, CA 94706, USA
perkis@artifact.com

Bostjan Perovsek
Dole Pri Krascah 34
1251 Moravce, SLO
bostjan.perovsek@guest.arnes.si

Edward Perraud
23 Rue Custine
75018 Paris, F

Pedro Pestana
R.das Flores, N_5, 4_esq
2800 Almada, P
Rune@esoterica.pt

Cathy Peters
1 Dam Rd.
Wombarra 2515 , AUS
argus@illawarra.hotkey.net.au

Debra Petrovitch
76 Wentworth Park Rd.
Glebe N.S.W. 2037, AUS
petrovitch_d@hotmail.com

Paul Peverelly
116, Rue Des PyrenÉes
75020 Paris, F
kajibi@wanadoo.fr

Hannes Peyer
Krausg. 22
2380 Perchtoldsdorf, A

Jean Piche
4524 Patricia
Montreal, Quebec, H4B
1Z1, CDN
Jean.Piche@umontreal.ca

Jan Pienkowski
6225 Place Northcrest
Montreal H3S 2T5, CDN
jmpien@colba.net

Derek Pierce
Newton St. Loe
Bath BA2 9BN UK,
d.pierce@bathspa.ac.uk

Gyula Pinter
Szinyei Merse U. 16. Ii/1.
1063 Budapest, H
miroy@elender.hu

Jörg Piringer
Pouthong. 2/34
1150 Wien, A
e9225678@stud1.tuwien.ac.at

Pascal Plantinga
P.O. Box 1965
1200 BZ Hilversum, NL

James Plotkin
94 Beucler Place
Bergenfield, NJ 07621,
USA
jimbalaya9@earthlink.net

Andrea Polli
600 S. Michigan
Chicago, IL 60605, USA
apolli@interaccess.com

Johannes Polterauer
Hofmark 183
4792 Münzkirchen, A

Franz Pomassl
Zieglerg. 31/2/12
1070 Wien, A

John Potts
82/103 Victoria St.
2011 Sydney, AUS
jpotts@scmp.mq.edu.au

Pendle Poucher
Carleton Rd.
London N7 OEX, UK
pendlep@aol.com

Bert Praxenthaler
Epfenhausen,
Bahnhofstr. 12
86929 Penzing, D
praxenthaler@t-online.de

David Prior
62 Graham Mansions,
Sylvester Rd.
London E8 1EU, UK
d.j.prior@bham.ac.uk

Rostislav Prochovnik
Zednicka 953
708 00 Ostrava-Poruba,
CZ

Hervé Provini
Rue Du Midi 8
1201 Genève, CH
hprovini@hotmail.com

Daping Qin
Köökarinkuja 7i 70
840 Helsinki, SF
daping76@hotmail.com

Tim Rabjohns Aka
Suite 6,
1 Cranbourn Alley
London WC2H 7AN UK,
tim@zoobee.prestel.co.uk

Waldek Ranckiewicz
Kazimierza Wlk. 29 A
50-061 Wroclaw, PL
12@magic.ic.com.pl

Pedro Rebelo
Alison House,
12 Nicolson Square
Edinburgh EH8 9DF, UK
P.Rebelo@et.ac.uk

Michel Redolfi
735, Ave. De La
Condamine
6230 Villefranche-sur-Mer,
F
MichelRedolfi@compuserve.com

Peter Rehberg
Ruckerg. 10/21–22
1120 Wien, A
pita@mego.co.at

Juan Reyes
Calle 71 # 12-44
DC Bogota, CO
jreyes@uniandes.edu.co

Casey Rice
1141 North Damen Av.
Chicago, IL 60622, USA
lebarn@earthlink.net

Alistair Riddell
12 Napier St.
Fitzroy, Victoria 3065,
AUS
amr@alphalink.com.au

Thanassis Rikakis
790 Riverside Drive,
Apt. 11s
New York, NY 10032, USA
than@music.columbia.edu

Dean Roberts
P.O. Box. 46251 Auckland
1002 NZ,
forma@iconz.co.nz

Hans-Joachim Roedelius
Schimmerg. 35a
2500 Baden, A
roedelius@mycity.at

Laura Romberg
11180 S. Hunter Hill Lane
76226 Argyle, Texas, USA
mpingo@aol.com

Volker Rommel
Neureutherstr. 23
80799 München, D
r.weis@zikg.lrz-muenchen.de

Nicolas Roope
29-35 Lexington St.
London W1R 3HQ, UK
nik@antirom.com

Michael Rosas Cobian
72 Redcliffe Gardens
London SW10 9NE, UK
mrc@gatomesic.dem.co.uk

Aaron Ross
643 Divisadero St. #102
San Francisco,
CA 94117-1513, USA
aaron@dr-yo.com

Stepan Rostomyan
37 Israelyan St., Apt. 24
375 015 Yerevan, ARM
steprost@acc.am

Jean Routhier
358 Powell
Vancouver V6A 1G4, CDN
lab@conspiracy.com

Anna Rubin
77 W. College St.
Oberlin, OH 44074-1588,
USA
anna.rubin@oberlin.edu

André Ruschkowski
Straustr. 3
83457 Bayerisch Gmain,
D
Andre.Ruschkowski@bestnetz.de

Rudolf Ruzicka
Serikova 32
63700 Brno, CZ
ruzicka@ffa.vutbr.cz

Sergei Rychkov
Mushtari, 8/22
420012 Kazan, RUS
galeyev@prometey.kcn.ru

Edson S. Zampronha
Rua Sebastiao Paes, 389
Ap. 91
04625-061 Sao Paulo, BR
zampra@mandic.com.br

Antti Saario
Univ. Of Birmingham,
Music Dept. Eogbaston
Birmingham B15 2TT, UK
a.s.saavio@isdugp.bham.ac.uk

Yukio Saegusa
1-5-9-33 Osone,
Kohoku-ku
222-0003 Yokohama, J
sa-egusa@ba2.so-net.ne.jp

Diane Samuels
330 Sampsonia Way
Pittsburgh, PA 15212, US
samuels@andrew.cmu.ed

'cola Sani
asurenallee 8 - 14
,057 Berlin,
eutschland
sani@tin.it

ccardo Santoboni
a E. Giulioli 3
9 Roma, Italy
santoboni@mclink.it

efan Saskov
nden 79/10
000 Skopje, MAK
igu@soros.org.mk

orut Savski
esta 27. Aprila 31
00 Ljubljana, SLO
orut.savski@kiss.uni-lj.si

efano Scarani
a Bergognone 45
0144 Milano, I
ngatamanu@planet.it

nek Schaefer
4 Crewdson Rd.
ondon SW9 oLJ, UK

ouis Schebeck
O. Box 1259 Strawberry
lls
012 Sydney, AUS
mint@smartchat.net.au

lia Scher
4 West 27th St. #6e
ew York, NY 10001, USA
cher@mit.edu

hristof Schläger
isestr. 3
4628 Herne, D

we Schmidt
edro Lira 1473-a
antiago, RCH
elhaze@netup.cl

rich Schnauss
ornstr. 13
163 Berlin, D

arter Scholz
565 Virginia St.
erkeley, CA 94709, USA
z@well.com

an Schuman
6-1/2 Otis St.
anta Cruz, CA 95060,
SA
lfie@cruzio.com

enz Schuster
anghoferstr. 82
373 München, D

or Sciavolino
a San Martino 11
098 Rivoli (TO), I
orsc@tin.it

roaki Shigetomi
1-9-6 Haramati
32-0025 Kawguti-si,
aitama-ken, J
oods2@ibm.net

ichael Shireman
38 Meadow Drive
orseheads, NY 14845,
SA
vp@servtech.com

ayne Siegel
usikhuset
000 Aarhus C, DK
siegel@daimi.au.dk

Rodrigo Sigal
72 C, Shoot Up Hill
London NW2 3XJ, UK
Sigal@city.ac.uk

Elzbieta Sikora
10 Square Des Cardeurs
,apt. 155
75020 Paris, F

Daniel Silveira
37279oth St., #3d
New York, NY 11372 USA,
kau@etnopop.com

Mary Simoni
1100 Baits Drive
Ann Arbor, MI 48109-
2085, USA
msimoni@umich.edu

Eva Sjuve
Järavallsgatan 31a
216 11 Malmö, S
esjuve@hotmail.com

Daniel Skantze
Stallgatan 9
582 54 Linköping, S
daniel.skantze@ebox.tnin
et.se

John Snell
619 Sarawood
St. Louis, MS 63141, USA
JP_SNELL@MSN.COM

Wouter Snoei
J.h. V. Heekpad 3
1024 BD Amsterdam, NL
wsnoei@koncon.nl

Alexandre Soares
Caixa Postal 100153
24001-970 Niterói - RJ,
BR
heyss@yahoo.com

Lukasz Sobczak
Koscierska 7
80-953 Gdansk, PL
lucas@ibwpan.gda.pl

Andrea Sodomka
Zieglerg. 31/911
1070 Wien, A
sodomka.breindl@thing.at

Dave Solursh
115 First St. Suite #347
Collingwood, Ontario,
L9Y 4W3, CDN
dsolursh@georgian.net

Johannes Strobl
Rodenbergstr. 37
10439 Berlin, D

Arthur Stammet
29, Rue Léon Metz
4238 Esch-sur-Alzette, L
arthur.stammet@ci.educ.
lu

Ipke Starke
Schönhauser Allee 70 A
10437 Berlin, D
IpkeStarke@aol.com

Jennifer Steinkamp
4907 Avoca St.
Los Angeles, CA 90041,
USA
jennifer@artcenter.edu

Gianni Stiletto
Franz Marlin St. 6a/5
5020 Salzburg, A
gianni.stiletto@fh-
sbg.ac.at

Carl Stone
4104 24th St., #410
San Francisco,
CA 94114-3615, USA
cstone@sukothai.com

Peter Strickland
P.O. Box 4749, Earley
Reading, UK
peter@peripheral-
uk.demon.co.uk

Hans Peter Stubbe
Teglbjærg
Gammeltorp, Fyrvej 59
7730 Hanstholm, DK
stubbe@vip.cybercity.dk

Andreas Stürmer
Zoechstr. 16
4203 Altenberg, A
nmp@gmx.net

Andreas H. H. Suberg
Schwarzwaldstr.30
79102 Freiburg, D

Tadeusz Sudnik
Ul. Dzika 19/23 M. 30
00-172 Warszawa, PL

Sean Sullivan
29 Loddon Ave. Reservoir
Melbourne, Victoria 3073
AUS
djspeedloader@hotmail.
com

Frederick Szymanski
110 St. Mark's Place #21
New York, NY 10009, USA
fredsz@cerfnet.com

Mika Taanila
Stenbäckinkatu 1 A 5
250 Helsinki, SF
mtaanila@kuva.fi

Yasuhiro Takenaka
4 - 9 - 8 Ichiban-cho
190 Tachikawa-shi, Tokyo,
J
vyu00430@nifty.ne.jp

Jack Tamul
P.O. Box 10854
Jacksonville, FL 32247-
0854, USA
jacktamul@aol.com

Dante Tanzi
Via Comelico 39/41
20135 Milano, I
tanzi@dsi.unimi.it

Luca Tanzini
Via Dei Termini 6
53100 Siena, I
tanzini@media.unisi.it

Richard Teitelbaum
250 Cold Brook Rd.
Bearsville, NY 12409, USA
teitelba@bard.edu

Terre Thaemlitz
1097-b 54th St.
Oakland, CA 94608-3018,
USA
terre@comatonse.com

Alain Thibault
1309, Bernard St. West
#3
Outremont, QC H2V 1W1,
CDN
thibaul@cam.org

Benjamin Thigpen
191 Rue Du Fg. St. Martin
75010 Paris, F
thigpen@ircam.fr

Joanne Thomas
Northampton Square
London, UK
j.m.thomas@city.ac.uk

Diane Thome
Box 353450
Seattle, WA 98195-3450,
USA
dthome@u.washington.
edu

Robert Scott Thompson
1045 Cresta Ct.
Roswell, GA 30075, USA
musrst@panther.gsu.edu

Wolfgang Thums
Erdenicher Str. 299
53121 Bonn, D

Kalev Tiits
Box 86
251 Helsinki, SF
kalev.tiits@siba.fi

Lucas Tirigall Caste
Av Ricardo Balbin 2432
6c
1428 Buenos Aires, RA
lucas2k@yahoo.com

Todor Todoroff
Rue Du Progrès 273
1030 Brussels, B
TODOR.TODOROFF@SKYN
ET.BE

Yasunao Tone
307 West Broadway
New York, NY 10013, USA
yasunaot@worldnet.att.
net

Barry Truax
School Of Communication
Burnaby, BC V5C 1H4,
CDN
truax@sfu.ca

Yu-chung Tseng
#98 5f-2 Lih Chih St.
Fengshang, Kaohsiung,
ROC
yct60@mail.nsysu.edu.tw

Chloé Dyn Tsoe
66 Upper Richmond Rd.
West
London SW14 8DA, UK
c.d.tsoe@roehampton.ac.
uk

Keiko Uenishi
412 15th St., Apt. 2
11215 Brooklyn, NY 11215,
USA.
oblaat@ibm.net

[the User]
3425, Av. De Vendome
Montreal H4 A3M6, CDN
pear@cam.org

Diego Vainer
Lavalle 3957
1190 Buenos Aires, RA
fantasia@cvtci.com.ar

Mika Vainio
Unit 49, Bbh, 71,
Henriques St.
London E1 1LZ, UK
stengsmith@aol.com

Alexander Valoczki
9201 Lane Av.
Detroit, MI 48209, USA
valoczki@pilot.msu.edu

Jeroen Van Garling
Rozenstraat 148 B
1016 NZ Amsterdam, NL
synchro@xs4all.nl

Annette Vande
Place De Ransbeck 3
1380 Ohain, B
musiques.recherches@sky
net.be

Klemen Veber
Ladja 36
1215 Medvode, SLO
subsonic@cryogen.com

Mario Verandi
59 Cruden House,
Brandon Estate
London SE173PQ, UK
meu533@istugp.bham.uc.
uk

Janco Verduin
Stuiverstraat 42
5611 TC Eindhoven, NL
cobeer@hotmail.com

Marc Verhoeven
Meermanstraat 138
3031 XP Rotterdam, NL
marcv@mediaport.org

Simon Vincent
8 Milton Av.
London N6 5QE, UK
simon.vincent@v-o-
s.dircon.co.uk

Robert Vincs
234 Stkilda Rd.
Melbourne 3004, AUS
r.vincs@vca.unimelb.edu.
au

Norbert Vossiek
Herner Str. 357
44807 Bochum, D
boffin@ruhrnetz.de

Robert Wacha
Gartenstadtstr. 18
4048 Linz, A
robert_wacha@hotmail.
com

Agnieszka Walig_rska
Kajavankuta 4b46
4230 Kerava, SF
agaps@nettilinja.fi

Antone Walloch
6039 Peach Blossom
Lane
Las Vegas, NV 89122,
USA
kybrdgig@ix.netcom.com

Rob & Michael Walsh &
Worthington
2480 Clunes, AUS
stridulation@hotmail.com

Alicyn Warren
1509 Chesapeake St.
Charlottesville, VA 22902,
USA
alicyn@virginia.edu

Thomas Weber
Klauprechtstr. 23
76137 Karlsruhe, D
kflimmer@aol.com

Ralf Wehowsky
Elsa Brändström Str. 33
55124 Mainz, D
conradi.wehowsky@main-
rheiner.de

Georg Weidinger
Getreideweg 6a
2301 Wittau, A

Anne Wellmer
Stille Veerkade 16
2512 BG Den Haag, NL
anne@koncon.nl

Thomas Wells
1866 College Rd.
Columbus, OH 43210,
USA
wells.7@osu.edu

Mike Weltz
2143 Newport Place Nw
Apt. B
Washington, D.C. 20037,
USA
kafka_f@hotmail.com

Lennart Westman
Söder Mälarstrand 61
11825 Stockholm, S
lennart.westman@telia.
com

Fs White
105 Linden Ave.
Princeton, NJ 08540-
8535, U.S.A.
jfwp@earthlink.net

James Whitehead
13 Wells Rd.
Walsingham NR22 6DL,
UK
james@jliat.demon.co.uk

Scott Wilson
Music Department
Middletown, CT 6459,
USA
sdwilson@wesleyan.edu

Amnon Wolman
711 Elgin Rd.
Evanston, IL 60208-1200,
USA
amnon@nwu.edu

Robert Worby
30a Spencer Place
Leeds LS7 4BR, UK
worby@sontec.demon.co.
uk

Daniel Worley
320 E. Cross St.
Ypsilanti, 48198, USA
dworley@artsitedesign.
com

Rob Wright
89 Granville St.
Peterborough PEI 2QL,
UK
R.E.WRIGHT@HERTS.
AC.UK

Anthony Asher Wright
1/141 Griffiths St.
Balgowlah
Sydney 2093 AUS,
ashera@ashera.com

Azlan Yahaya
19, Sri Semantan Satu,
Damansara Heights
50490 Kuala Lumpur,
MAL
dalfina@tm.net.my

Michiaki Yamaguchi
982-4 Kosugi
Toyama, J
peho0200@po.incl.ne.jp

John Young
P.O. Box 600
Wellington, NZ
john.young@vuw.ac.nz

Miki Yui
Neubrückstr. 8
40213 Düsseldorf, D
miki@khm.de

Jeremy Yuille
4/30 Albert
Brisbane 4000, AUS
overt@overlobe.com

Christian Zanèsi
4, Rue Des Trois
Entrepreneurs
93400 Saint-Ouen, F
czanesi@ina.fr

Julia Zdarsky
Alliiertenstr. 16/17
1020 Wien, A
starsky@sil.at

Kristoffer Zegers
Populierstraat 5
4814 HN Breda, NL
kzegers@casema.net

Andy Zufferey
Plantzette 40
3960 Sierre, CH
hostage@multimania.com

*Spz Freistadt/
Unterweissenbach
Markt 91
4273 Unterweissenbach
spzfreistadt@asn.
netway.at*

*HS Hard Mittelweiherburg
Flurstr. 12
6971 Hard
lehr.mwbg@schulen.vol.at*

*BG/BRG Mössingerstr. 25
Mössingerstr. 25
9020 Klagenfurt
rieder.florian@mail.bgmoe
ss-klu.ac.at*

*Gregor Agrinz
c/o Resi Gmbh.
Grottenhofstr. 3
8010 Graz*

*Simon Alber
Feuerwehrstr. 10
2333 Leopoldsdorf
albernerecords@aon.at*

*Martin Allhoff
Gallstr. 32
2500 Baden
martin.allhoff@ycom.at*

*Clemens Appl
Promenade 2
3400 Klosterneuburg
c.appl-sea@aon.at*

*Philipp Auer
Eisenhandstr. 10
4020 Linz*

*Markus Auzinger
Lokalbahnweg 18
4060 Leonding*

*David Bär
Feld 502
6866 Andelsbuch*

*Mario Bauer
c/o Powerplay Software-
Edv
Grazer Str. 18
8600 Bruck/Mur*

*Martin Baumgartner
Schumpeterstr. 20
4040 Linz*

*Lukas Bayer
Norikumstr. 9c
4481 Asten*

*Markus Bell
c/o AEC
Hauptstr. 2
4040 Linz*

*Daniel Bell
Billrothstr. 32
4050 Traun*

*Hans-Peter Benedek
Markt-Allhau 11
7411 Markt-Allhau*

*Franz Berger
Anetsham 1
4906 Eberschwang
berger_franz@yahoo.com*

*Richard Bergmair
Keplerstr. 3
4061 Pasching
richard.bergmair@schuele
r.asn-linz.ac.at*

*Nicole Bernegger
Prutzendorf 13
2048 Prutzendorf*

*Berufsschule Mattersbur
Bahnstr. 41
7210 Mattersburg
sekretariat@bsma.at*

*Hu Bin
Sperrg. 13/2
1150 Wien*

*Kerstin Binder
Grubberg 3
4170 Haslach
texhas@ping.at*

*Robert Binna
Austr. 44
6063 Neu Rum
robert_binna@hotmail.
com*

*Günther Birchbauer
c/o Computerhaus Gmbh
Erzherzog-Johann-Str.
8700 Leoben*

*Mario Bitzner
Thomas-Mann-Str. 5
4060 Leonding*

*Alexander Blaschek
c/o C & M
Direktmarketing-Edv
Kärntnerstr.
8055 Seiersberg*

*Daniel Blecher
2154 Altenmarkt 47
mousetrap@magnet.at*

*Jakob Böhm
Hauptstr. 218
3001 Mauerbach
schoeffel-hs@xpoint.at*

*Thomas Brandfellner
Darwing. 12/2/5/14
1020 Wien*

*Silvia Brandl
Grubberg 3
4170 Haslach
texhas@ping.at*

*Mario Brandtner
Neufeld 4a
3361 Aschach
texhas@ping.at*

*Thomas Brandtner
Mitteregg 5
4421 Aschach/Steyr*

*Nikolaus Brennig
Prof.-Dobrovsky-Str.
14/b/3
3013 Tullnerbach
virtualnik@aol.at*

*Michael Bretterbauer
Tienenweg 361
8911 Admont
mike@schurke.at*

*Peter Bubestinger
Wiener Str. 74/12
2604 Theresienfeld
pbubest@ycom.at*

*Sebastian Buha
Mösingerweg 6
4400 Steyr*

*Philipp Cachée
Wörthg. 26a/4/9
2500 Baden
devil@mycity.at*

ianca Danninger
allnhauserhofstr. 4
400 Hallein
ckh@asn-sbg.ac.at

atthias Derntl
ukasweg 44
060 Leonding

ndreas Dini
ettingsdorferstr. 63
053 Haid
ni@brg-traun.ac.at

rgen Dobetsberger
nnitzstr. 10
600 Wels

aniel Dobler
ennerstr. 7
910 Ried I. Innkreis

smin Doblhofer
nionstr. 31
020 Linz

hilipp Dominik
arrfeldstr. 384
582 St. Michael

ichael Duller
eldweg 3
971 Hard
ichael.duller.bgb-
@schulen.vol.at

a Eberstaller
eutlmayrweg 9
020 Linz

annes Ebner
auptstr. 32
373 Kemmelbach
e@netway.at

hilipp Ebner
plstr. 62
670 Krieglach

exander Ecker
ruberstr. 31
020 Linz

atrick Eder
delsdorf 77
643 Allerheiligen

ebastian Endt
allackstr. 12
600 Wels
endt@datapool.at

ivia Engelmann
ockg. 31
020 Linz

hristiane Essl
arkt 311/9
431 Kuchl
ckh@asn-sbg.ac.at

artin Fahrenberger
eichweg 10
541 Schwanberg
artin.fahrenberger@usa.
et

tefan Fahrngruber
laaerstr. 10
230 Wien
efan.fahrngruber@bigfo
.com

homas Felberbauer
iedengürtel 488
225 Pöllau
y_redaktion@yahoo.de

Georg Fennesz
Johannesg. 5
7312 Horitschon
fenpe@netway.at

Markus Ferringer
Unterm Wald 4
4810 Gmunden
ferrymax@hotmail.com

Lukas Fichtinger
Neuhaus 35
4943 Geinberg

Stefan Fiegl
Függn 160
6263 Függn

Eva Fischer-Ankern
Hsnr. 1
3932 Kirchberg am Walde
eva.fischerankern@wvnet.
at

Alexander Fischl
Voltag. 45/3/4
1210 Wien

Thomas Fitzka
Mühlhofstr. 4
3503 Krems-rehberg
thfitzka@yahoo.com

Wolfgang Flossmann
Dorfplatz 93
6263 Fügen
bubuschule@asn.netway.
at

Gerald Friesenecker
Im Steinach 22
6923 Lauterach

Bernhard Fröhler
Hochpointstr. 13a
4600 Wels

Tanja Frühwirth
c/o Grubberg 3
4170 Haslach
texhas@ping.at

Jürgen Furthmayr
c/o Grubberg 3
4170 Haslach
texhas@ping.at

Nina Gaisbauer
Weierfing 29
4971 Aurolzmünster
lee_1917@hotmail.com

Ludwig Ganter
Am Stritzelberg 11
3564 Plank

Simon Gaßner
Siezenheimerstr. 74
5020 Salzburg
gassner.simon@gmx.at

Alexander Gattringer
c/o Grubberg 3
4170 Haslach
texhas@ping.at

Thomas Glanz
Höflach 17
8350 Fehring
thomas.glanz@gmx.net

Christian Görgl
Kinkstrasse 1
9020 Klagenfurt
c.goergl@netway.at

Eva Gossenreiter
c/o Grubberg 3
4170 Haslach
texhas@ping.at

Gerstorfer Gregor
Miller V. Aichholzstr. 34b
4810 Gmunden

Rudolf Gresak
Gruberstr. 49
4020 Linz
rudolf.gresak@hyperbox.
org

Alexander Gröber
Waldrain 47
9710 Feistritz
207171@asn.netway.at

Maja Grosinic
Grundsteing. 18/1/3
1160 Wien

Daniel Großhaupt
Hausleitnerweg 61
4020 Linz

Karin Grünauer
Rosenstr. 23
4623 Gunskirchen
karin.gue@kabelnet.at

Daniel Grurl
Honauerstr. 31
4020 Linz

Elvira Gschwantner
Werkganer Str. 9
4432 Ernsthofen

Arnold Gutsche
Ettendorf 72
9472 Ettendorf
gutarn@yahoo.com

Informatikgruppe, 7.Kl
Gymn. Perchtholdsdorf
Roseggerg. 2–4
2380 Perchtholdsdorf
s317036@as.netway.at

Erich Habian
Zohmanng. 11/12
1100 Wien
habian@compuserve.com

Stefan Hackl
Unteramt 119
3264 Gresten
stefanhackl@hotmail.com

Robert Hafner
Radau 100
5351 Aigen-Voglhub
reinhold.hafner@schule.at

Stephanie Hagmüller
Kopernikusstr. 43
4020 Linz
k.hagmueller@mail.asn-
linz.ac.at

Dieter Hahn
Mühlenstr. 5
8074 Raaba
manuel@grazforyou.at

Franz Haider
Schwindg. 9/4
1040 Wien
franzhai@yahoo.com

Philipp E. Haindl
Rembrandtstr. 29
4060 Leonding
office@leonardo.or.at

Hansjörg Haller
Unterpinswang 74
6600 Reutte
h_hansi@yahoo.com

Rene Haller
Petersbaumgarten 49
2840 Grimmenstein
challer@grasc.co.at

Nikolaus Hammerschmid
Reisenbichler Str. 2
4810 Gmunden
eh@aon.at

Jörg Hanke
Lohbachweg C 46
6020 Innsbruck
klaus.hanke@uibk.ac.at

Markus Haslinger
c/o Grubberg 3
4170 Haslach a. d. Mühl
texhas@ping.at

Christina Haslinger
Julius-Raab-Str. 17
4040 Linz

Stefan Hauser
Griffen 142
9112 Griffen

Yvonne Havranek
Sperberweg 5
4063 Hörsching

Gerald Heilmann
Mitterweg 8
4222 St. Georgen
geraldheilmann@yahoo.
com

Armin Heindl
Lärbaumweg 16b
2393 Sittendorf
armin_heindl@iname.com

Christian Herzog
Grubweg 16
8580 Köflach
noeffred@gmx.net

Martin Hieslmair
Waidachg. 183
4580 Windischgarsten
martin@him.at

Thomas Hirtenfelder
Stremayrg. 6/46
8010 Graz
thegrafx@usa.net

Michael Hobitsch
Franzbergstr. 4
2161 Poysbrunn
pentium@nanet.at

Thomas Hochwallner
Penz 3
4441 Behamberg
alien_o in
www.cycosmos.com

Constanze Hodina
Naumanng. 11a
5020 Salzburg

Bernhard Hoisl
Sh. Milesstr. 10
9100 Völkermarkt
w.hoisl@carinthia.com

Christoph Holas
Am Aigen 12
8046 Graz
christoph.holas@carneri.
asn-graz.ac.at

Andreas Hold
Blumeng. 6
8600 Bruck/Mur

David Horn
Haagberg 40
3364 Neuhofen/Ybbs
d.horn@pgv.at

Jakob Hörtner
Mitterstr. 40
8055 Graz

HS Hard
Flurstr.12
6971 Hard
lehr.mwbg@schulen.vol.at

Bernhard Huber
Hohe-Wand-G. 18
2700 Wr. Neustadt
berni@bgzehnwn.ac.at

Martin Huber
Lederer G. 7
4716 Hofkirchen
g.huber@mail.asn-
linz.ac.at

Martin Huber
Ledererg. 7
4716 Hofkirchen
g.huber@mail.asn-
linz.ac.at

Claudia Hubmann
Birkenweg 9
8740 Zeltweg
coolgirl@austro.net

Christoph Illnar
Bäreng. 2
2560 Berndorf
christoph.illnar@ycom.at

Ibrahim Imam
Otto-Probst-Str. 3/11/8
1100 Wien

HS Hard/Internet-Team
Flurstr.12
6971 Hard
lehr.mwbg@schulen.vol.at

Emanuel Jauk
Ludwig Benedek G. 19
8054 Graz
grelle.musik@kfunigraz.ac
.at

Simone Kaiser
c/o Grubberg 3
4170 Haslach
texhas@ping.at

Thomas Kaltofen
Griesstr. 23
4502 St. Marien
thomas.kaltofen@trust-
me.com

Lukas Kammerlander
Dorf 251
6441 Umhausen

Anna Kantner
c/o Grubberg 3
4170 Haslach
texhas@ping.at

Martin Karastojanoff
Wiener Neustädter Str. 14
7202 Bad Sauerbrunn
d94010@htlwrn.ac.at

Magdalena Kasperek
Audorferstr. 39
4052 Ansfelden

Manuel Katzenschläger
Sommerhausstr. 1
4311 Schwertberg

Simone Keclik
Langfeldstr. 1c
4040 Linz

Sandra Keimel
c/o Mayer Peter-Edv
Grazer Str. 126
8082 Kirchbach

Andreas Ketter
c/o Grubberg 3
4170 Haslach
texhas@ping.at

4a Klasse
HS Poysdorf 1
Hindenburgstr. 34
2170 Poysdorf
316102@asn.netway.at

Europagymnasium
Baumgartenberg
Klasse 3a/3b
Baumgartenberg 1
4342 Baumgartenberg
k.bachler@asn-linz.ac.at

Werner Klockner
Weidachstr. 41
6900 Bregenz

Manfred Knabl
Römerstr. 14
6500 Landeck
m.knabl@brg-
landeck.asn-ibk.ac.at

Thomas Köckerbauer
Tarsdorf 110
5121 Tarsdorf

Birgit Kohlbacher
Hausleitnerweg 22
4040 Linz

Christian Kohout
Stronsdorf 268
2153 Stronsdorf

Christina König
Jungmairstr. 4a
4020 Linz

Christoph Konrad
c/o Nippon Computer-Edv
Gleichenbergerstr. 5
8330 Feldbach

Daniel Krebs
Weideng. 14
2542 Kottingbrunn
daniel.krebs@magnet.at

Rene Krenn
Mössingerstr. 25
9020 Klagenfurt
decoda@aon.at

Michael Krenn
c/o Tscherne Computer-
Edv
Karlauer Gürtel 1
8010 Graz

Armin Philipp Krenn
Nelkeng. 13
4050 Traun

Elisabeth Kronschläger
Deutlweg 4
4020 Linz

Daniel Krug
Am Sonnenhang 41
8511 St. Stefan ob Stainz
klug_d@hotmail.com

Daniel Kuales
Schlierbach 349
4553 Schlierbach
r.kuales@asn-linz.ac.at

Bernhard Kunnert
Unterhumstr. 121
5412 Puch

Alexander Kvasnicka
Halbg. 24/3
1070 Wien
quasmaster@yahoo.com

Robert Lamprecht
Dirnberg 9
4550 Kremsmünster

Benjamin Lang
Michael-Hainisch-Str. 15
4040 Linz

Heide Marie Langegger
Alte Bundesstr. 10
5600 St. Johann
hickh@asn-sbg.ac.at

Daniel Längle
Kirchstr. 14
6972 Fussach
lehr.mwbg@schulen.vol.at

Viktoria Lanzersdorfer
Harterfeldstr. 16
4060 Leonding

Paul Lanzerstorfer
Hochgärten 24
4170 Haslach
pol@mail.schueler.asn-
linz.ac.at

Letitia Lehner
Gernlandweg 63
4060 Leoning

Peter Leib
Ortmayrstr. 43
4460 Losenstein

Oliver Leibetseder
Hasnerstr. 10
4020 Linz

Christoph Leiter
Humpenhof 4
6671 Weissenbach

Roman Leitner
Schörgenhubstr. 18
4020 Linz

Sarah Lengauer
Karl-Steiger-Str.
4030 Linz

Emanuel Liedl
Hörschingergutstr. 30
4040 Linz

Stefanie Mader
Wachtelweg 6
4063 Hörsching

Jacqueline Mader
Wachtelweg 6
4063 Hörsching

Melanie Mair
Innstr.50/xiii/333
6063 Rum

Simon Martin
Irnharting 29
4623 Gunskirchen
samuelsimon@hotmail.
com

Anton Mauer
Schloßg. 24/7
1050 Wien
mauer@grg5.asn-
wien.ac.at

Gunther Mauerkirchner
Hongarstr. 21
4600 Wels
e.hiesmayr@mail.asn-
linz.ac.at

Mario Meir-Huber
Spreitzenberg 4
5222 Muderfing

Gerold Meisinger
Margeritenstr. 26
4481 Asten
geri_meisi@yahoo.com

Adnan Mekic
Sandg. 40
8010 Graz
ameki@wiku.asn-
graz.ac.at

Rupert Metnitzer
Untere Teichstr. 34b
8010 Graz
office@nextcd.com

Dominik Millinger
Filsen 102 A
6391 St. Jakob

Christoph Mitasch
Lärchenstr. 25
4210 Gallneukirchen

Stefanie Mitter
Robert-Stolz-Str. 8
4020 Linz

Sandra Mitterschiffthaler
Schefersteinweg
4460 Losenstein

Maoi
Modern Art On Internet
Thalsdorf 7
9314 Launsdorf
reichhold.m@gmx.net

Peter Mohr
St. Peter Hauptstr. 33c
8042 Graz
pietro122@hotmail.com

Julia Mollnhuber
Harbacherstr. 2
4040 Linz

Astrid Mollnhuber
Harbacherstr. 2
4040 Linz

Martin Moravec
Gabesstr. 26
4030 Linz

Roman Moser
Erichfriedweg 18
4030 Linz

Herwig Moser
Sippachzeller Str. 7
4609 Thalheim
herwigmoser@earthling.
net

Melanie Moser
Haydnstr. 5
4050 Traun

Marina Nather
Am Mühlbach 24
8501 Lieboch

Robert Neuner
Mistelbach 6
4613 Mistelbach
karlseitz@reicom.at

Thomas Niefergall
Obere Siedlungsstr. 3
2421 Wolfsthal

Takuya Nimmerrichter
Scherzerg. 1
1020 Wien
nimmerrichter@vienna.at

Christian Nimmervoll
Birkenstrasse 2
4191 Vorderweissenbach
fona@altavista.net

Sarah Nimmervoll
c/o Grubberg 3
4170 Haslach
texhas@ping.at

Verena Nutz
Birkeng. 169
2640 Enzenreith
vnutz@ycom.at

Simon Oberhammer
Bubing 95
4780 Schärding
nostalgiker@yahoo.com

Thomas Oberhauser
Mitteldorf 30
6886 Schoppernau
t_018@hotmail.com

Sabine Obermaier
Josef-Ressl-Str. 7
5020 Salzburg

Jürgen Oman
Grillparzerstr. 15
4614 Marchtrenk

Gernot Ottowitz
Doppler G. 2
9020 Klagenfurt

Robert Ötzinger
Bluderstr. 9
4540 Bad Hall
robert.oetzinger@schueler
.dsn-linz.ac.at

Uros Pancur
Dr.-Josko-Tischler-Park 1
9020 Klagenfurt

Isabella Pangerl
c/o Grubberg 3
4170 Haslach
texhas@ping.at

Pia Paukner
Lokalbahnweg 11
4060 Leonding
k.hagmueller@mail.asn-
linz.ac.at

Catharina Paukner
Am Buchberg 18
4060 Leonding

Richard Pentz
Weigunystr. 4b
4020 Linz

Astrid Pentz
Weigunystr. 4b
4040 Linz

Christoph Peterseil
Wüstenrotstr. 13
4020 Linz

Andreas Petrovic
Rudolf Listg. 27
8010 Graz
apetro@wiku.asn-
graz.ac.at

Carina Pfandl
Fisching 9
8741 Weißkirchen

Rene Pichler
Flugplatzweg 33
8772 Timmersdorf

Elisabeth Pichler
c/o Network Data
Computer-Edv
Fichtestr. 66 - 68
8010 Graz

Christoffer Piereder
Stelzhamer Str. 11
5280 Braunau

Lukas Pilat
Wilbrandtg. 23
1180 Wien
lukas@workmail.com

Elmar Pitzer
c/o Grubberg 3
4170 Haslach
texhas@ping.at

Gerhard Planitzer
Haus 120
8982 Tauplitz
planitzer@gmx.at

Stefan Poiss
Ferd. Marklstr. 3
4040 Linz

Anna Maria Poll
Hauserstr. 13a
4040 Linz

Kerstin Popodi
Gartenweg 6
5162 Obertrum a. See
popodi@net4you.co.at

Roland Poppenreiter
Picassostr. 31
4053 Pucking
poppenreiter@mauimail.
com

Patrick Pöschl
Bucheng. 2
2384 Breitenfurt/wien
patrick@mauimail.com

Thomas Prammer
Kalkgruberweg 24
4020 Linz

Florian Pressler
Josef Haydng. 8
2603 Felixdorf
florianp@hotmail.com

Andrea Prieschl
Ringelwiese 11
4224 Wartberg/Aist

Stefanie Priewasser
Pfongau 28
5202 Neumarkt
nieli@salzburg.co.at

Thomas Prötsch
Gartenstr. 10
4910 Ried Im Innkreis
tproetsc@htl-
braunau.asn-linz.ac.at

Stefan Prohaszka
Lizumstr. 16a
6094 Axams
row@riot.org

Margit Pucher
St. Peter Pfarrweg 34
8042 Graz
mpucher@wiku.asn-graz.ac.at

Stefan Pühringer
Columbusstr. 7
4600 Wels
pstefan@gmx.at

Horst Reiterer
Galvanistr. 8
4020 Linz
reitere@rocketmail.com

Alexander Reitinger
Schloßparkg. 7
4050 Traun

Sabine Riegler
Haidershofen 43
4431 Haidershofen

ike Rochowanski
indeng. 25/12
070 Wien
iketigerente@gmx.de

David Roithner
Kramerpromenade 22
990 Bad Aussee
david.rothner@telecom.at

hristoph Rosenlechner
lonsbergerg. 16
010 Graz
aller@borg-graz.ac.at

mar Rückert
ahnhofstr. 48
301 Laßnitzhöhe

mmanuel Ruez
allusstr. 5
900 Bregenz

ebastian Ruf
orellig. 4–6/9/2/7
10 Wien

ichael Rupprechter
us 61
52 Breitenbach

inhard Rzepa
rg 3
71 Böheimkirchen
pa@gmx.at

rtin Samal
nengang 7
40 Puchenau
samal@asn-linz.ac.at

chael Santek
nz-Fischer-Str. 17a
20 Innsbruck
chsantek@aon.at

rian Sarec
e 83
72 Fußach
ian.sarec@vol.at

o Schachner
heng. 1
4 Guntramsdorf

mas Schadenbauer
Nippon Computer-Edv
chenbergerstr. 5
o Feldbach

Christian Schafleitner
Forsthubstr. 15
4400 Steyr
christian.schafleitner@gmx.at

Benedikt Schalk
Gladbeckstr. 1/12b/2
2320 Schwechat
bschalk@gmx.net

Emanuel Schamp
Germerg. 57
2500 Baden
d94015@htlwrn.ac.at

Wolfgang Schedl
Maroltingerg. 9a
1160 Wien
wolfgang.schedl@blackbox.net

Peter Scheffknecht
Sonnenbergstr.2a
6700 Bludenz
pe.sche@vlbg.at

Bernhard Schenkenfelder
Hagauerstr. 17
4190 Bad Leonfelden
adminleon@asn-linz.ac.at

Sabine Scherer
c/o Pablitos Gmbh
Eggersdorf
8063 Eggersdorf/G.

Margarita Maria Schilcher
Hausleitnerweg 36b
4020 Linz
k.hagmueller@mail.asn-linz.ac.at

Markus Schimautz
Heimweg 1
8430 Kaindorf
markus.schimautz@styria.com

Nina Schindlauer
Ringweg 23a
5400 Hallein
hickh@asn-sbg.ac.at

Daniela Schlechmair
Kühbschweg Nr. 3
5230 Mattighofen
hickh@asn-sbg.ac.at

Christoph Schnauder
Leonfeldner Str. 280
4040 Linz
quarxmurx@yahoo.com

Matthias Schobesberger
Sonnenweg 4
4202 Kirchschlag

Stefan Schobesberger
Sonnenweg 4
4202 Kirchschlag

Elisabeth Scholz
Babenbergerring 10
A-2700 Wiener Neustadt
comenius@bg-bab.ac.at

Birgit Scholz
Rupertistr. 23
8075 Hart
bscholz@wiku.asn-graz.ac.at

Roland Schönhart
Obdachegg 71
8742 Obdach

Martin Schöpf
Pirchhof 166
6432 Sautens

Andreas Schuller
Lerchenstr. 30
4702 Wallern

Raimund Schumacher
Kircheng. 17
4061 Pasching
sr@cso.at

Jacob Schumann
Hauptstr. 46
7361 Lutzmannsburg
jacob.schumann@borg-op.asn-bgld.ac.at

Tina Schwaiger
Bader-Moserstr. 16
4563 Kirchdorf
tina_sch@rocketmail.com

Thomas Schwarz
c/o Dad+t-Edv
Gewerbepark 16
4052 Ansfelden

Philipp Schweiger
Nr. 255
8380 Neumarkt/Raab
ph_schweiger@hotmail.com

Carina Schweighofer
Schönweg 17
2500 Sooß
vssooss@asn.netway.at

Wolfgang Schwetz
Rodlstr. 7
4100 Ottensheim

Gerhard Schwoiger
Hernstorfer
Str. 22–32/23/2
1140 Wien
schwoiger@usa.net

Sandra Seidl
Zibermayer Str. 93
4020 Linz

Johannes Seifert
Prinz-Eugen-Str. 3b
4061 Pasching

Philipp Seifried
St. Peter Hauptstr. 29e
8042 Graz
philipp.seifried@styria.com

Kurt Seinitzer
c/o Saturn Electro
Gmbh-Edv
Bahnhofstr. 85
8010 Graz

Cornelia Siedl
Liebermayer Str. 93
4020 Linz

Evelyn Spindler
Leitersdorf 129
8330 Feldbach

Wolfgang Spreicer
Wiesbergstr. 3
5400 Hallein
fuffl@yahoo.com

Thomas Springer
c/o Richter Gmbh
Starhembergstr. 7
4070 Eferding

Benjamin Stangl
Adlerg. 10
4020 Linz
benjamin.f.s.stangl@usa.net

Jakob Stangl
R.-H.-Bartsch Str.11
8042 Graz
jstangl@yahoo.com

Franziska Stecher
Oerlachweg 12
6433 Oetz

Rene Steger
Franz-Schmidt-G. 5
8230 Hartberg

Paul Steiner
Katzelsdorfer Str. 185
2821 Lanzenkirchen

Nikolaus Steiner
Leoplold-Werndl-Str. 5
4400 Steyr

Bianca Steiner
Harterfeldstr. 16/1/7
4060 Leonding

Mario Stieger
S. Freudstr. 5
4050 Traun

Florian Stöger
Vogelweiderstr. 150
4600 Wels

Claudia Stögerer
Margarethenstr. 105 1/3
1050 Wien

Alexander Stolar
Freyungplatz 2
4850 Timelkam
alex.stolar@netway.at

Markus Strahlhofer
Josef-Postl-G. 25
2332 Hennersdorf
paradise@inode.at

Daniel Strigl
Ebene 23
6433 Ötz
jb_dani@hotmail.com

Tanja Stroißnigg
c/o Pablitos Gmbh
Eggersdorf
8063 Eggersdorf

Julia Stundner
Babenbergerring 10
2700 Wr. Neustadt
gschoedl@ycom.at

Markus Stütz
Christkindlweg 38
4400 Steyr

Lydia Tannhäuser
Panholzerweg 24
4020 Linz

Gernot Teuermann
Oberzeiring
8762 Katzling 30
gernot.th@aon.at

Wolfgang Thaller
Schillerplatz 9
8010 Graz
wolfgang.thaller@gmx.net

Patrick Toifl
Treustr. 40/1/6
1200 Wien
p_toifl@hotmail.com

Mario Topf
Birkenweg 32
4816 Gschwandt Bei Gmunden
mario_3_16@yahoo.com

Martin Topf
Brahmsstr. 9
4810 Gmunden
mtopf@hotmail.com

Raffael Traxler
Blindendorf 64
4312 Ried i.d. Riedmark

Stefan Trischler
Wiener G. 6/1/1
1210 Wien
exxon@bigfoot.com

Günther Tschabuschnig
Sonnwiesen 1/44
9702 Ferndorf
tschabuschnig@gmx.net

Michael Tumfart
c/o Grubberg 3
4170 Haslach
texhas@ping.at

Florian Türk
Ressnig 40
9170 Ferlach
florian_tuerk@deltacom.Edv.net

Rainer Unterassinger
Lieserrain 7a
9800 Spittal/drau

4.d Klasse
VS Seiersberg
Berta-von-Suttner-Str. 10
8054 Seiersberg
seiersberg@email.com

Daniel Wagner
Gradau 4
4591 Molln
ej_resonance@technologist.com

Paul Wagner
Schottenfeldg. 78
1070 Wien

Benjamin Wagner
Mistlberger
Freistätter Str. 309
4040 Linz

Rainer Watzenböck
Im Bachfeld 28
4020 Linz

Gerulf Weber
Josefinumstr. 12
9020 Klagenfurt
ge.weber@magnet.at

Kerstin Weberberger
Kleinwört 8
4030 Linz

Martin Weiglhofer
Zeil-Pöllau 98
8225 Pöllau

Sarah Weiguny
c/o Grubberg 3
4170 Haslach
texhas@ping.at

Armin Weihbold
Vormarktstr. 17
4310 Mauthausen
auwe@gmx.net

Florian Wesp
Leoplold-Werndl-Str. 5
4400 Steyr

Nikolaus Wienerroither
Bergg. 8
4040 Linz

Katharina Wienerroither
Bergg. 8
4040 Linz

Christoph Wiesenhofer
c/o Kriegsauer Gmbh
Wiener Str. 5
8230 Hartberg

Andreas Wieser
Loiblstr. 55
9170 Ferlach
jwieser@netway.at

Uwe Wiesinger
Beethoveng. 64
7400 Oberwart

Peter Wild
O.-v.-Lilienthalstr. 19
5020 Salzburg
peter.wild@sbg.ac.at

Barbara Wimmer
Kircheng. 52
7052 Müllendorf
bebs_w@hotmail.com

Christian Witamwas
Sparbersbachg. 21
8010 Graz

Andreas Wolf
Waldsiedlung 124
2823 Pitten
dj_ndee@gmx.at

Thomas Wolf
Lackenweg 20
9020 Klagenfurt
seawolf@net4you.co.at

Kristoffer Wolfinger
Prennlehner Weg 30
4060 Leonding
kristofferw@,mail.fadi.asn
-linz.ac.at

Manuela Worm
c/o Grubberg 3
4170 Haslach
texhas@ping.at

Ernst Wuger
Wangerweg 10
5301 Eugendorf

Leopold Wurstbauer-
Heiss
c/o HLUW Ysper
Ysper 34
3603 Ysper
leo_wurstbauer@gmx.at

Stefanie Wuschitz
Nordbergstr. 6/17
1090 Wien
stefaniewusch@gmx.de

Mario Zeller
St. Paulg. 6
3500 Krems

Stefan Zipko
Bachweg 6
4614 Marchtrenk
szipko@hotmail.com

David Zoderstorfer
Windhaag 23
4322 Windhaag

Roswitha Zopf
Straubinger Str. 24/1/4
4600 Wels